The Fighting Times
of Abe Attell

ALSO BY MARK ALLEN BAKER

Battling Nelson, the Durable Dane:
World Lightweight Champion, 1882–1954
(McFarland, 2017)

The Fighting Times of Abe Attell

MARK ALLEN BAKER

McFarland & Company, Inc., Publishers
Jefferson, North Carolina

ISBN (print) 978-1-4766-6432-3 ∞
ISBN (ebook) 978-1-4766-2899-8

LIBRARY OF CONGRESS CATALOGUING DATA ARE AVAILABLE

BRITISH LIBRARY CATALOGUING DATA ARE AVAILABLE

Front cover photograph: Abe Attell, 1900 (Library of Congress)

Printed in the United States of America

McFarland & Company, Inc., Publishers
Box 611, Jefferson, North Carolina 28640
www.mcfarlandpub.com

To Dana Beck and Brian Brinkman,
my heartfelt appreciation for your thoughts,
prayers and support,
offered when I needed them most

Table of Contents

Acknowledgments   x

Preface   1

Introduction   3

ONE. Rising to the Occasion, 1900–1901   5

TWO. A Champion's Ascent, 1902–1903   23

THREE. The Triad to Legitimacy, 1904   38

FOUR. Not So Fast, 1905   49

FIVE. As World Champion, 1906   58

SIX. Preserve and Defend, 1907   72

SEVEN. Minister of Defense, 1908   81

EIGHT. Two Champions, Two Divisions and One Family, 1909   101

NINE. A Champion's Pace, 1910   114

TEN. From the Comfort of Home, 1911   128

ELEVEN. Losing the Title, 1912   144

TWELVE. The Thrill Is Gone, 1913–1919   163

THIRTEEN. The Black Sox Scandal of 1919, 1919–1921   183

FOURTEEN. Misdeeds and Mishaps in the Roaring Twenties   207

FIFTEEN. The Great Depression and Beyond   220

SIXTEEN. Clever Beyond Words   232

Appendix: Abe Attell Official Record   235

Chapter Notes   243

Bibliography   261

Index   265

Acknowledgments

Conversations with those who had met Abe Attell inspired me to write a biography of the controversial boxer, who was perhaps the cleverest fighter ever to enter the ring.

Abraham Washington "Abe" Attell's six consecutive years as World Featherweight Champion, from 1906 to 1912, not only guaranteed his immortality but made his name synonymous with the division. And what a division it has become, thanks to boxers such as Johnny Kilbane, Tony Canzoneri, Bat Battalino, Henry Armstrong, Willie Pep, Sandy Saddler, and later Sugar Ramos, Vicente Saldivar, Eder Jofre, Ruben Olivares, Alexis Argüello, Eusebio Pedroza, Barry McGuigan, Danny Lopez, Salvador Sanchez, Wilfredo Gomez, Azumah Nelson, Jeff Fenech, and so many others.

It is shameful that so little has been written about Abe Attell's brilliant boxing career. Some historians find it difficult to imagine the sport without Attell's contributions, while others seem content to write him off as an anomaly of the sport.

I had many seconds in my corner.

I am very proud of my association with the International Boxing Hall of Fame in Canastota, New York. My service—as an author, biographer, historian, chairperson, sponsor and volunteer—has been particularly rewarding because of the following individuals: Edward Brophy, Jeffrey S. Brophy, Chris Bowers, Rachel Shaw, Mike Delaney, Angelo Testani, Anthony Testani, Eric Warren, Ruth Tabor, Craig Bailey, Grace Rapasadi, Melody Smith, Mike Burch, John Hunt, Jean Palmer, Alexia Conrad, Carol Burch, Pat Prettyman, Dr. Juan Kassab, Charlene Barres, Pat Orr, Chuck Sgroi, Ada Sgroi, Doug Gustin, Joyce Gustin, Deb Gustin, Nanci Knox, Mike Brophy, Holly Lynch, Diana Colon, Scott Rapasadi, T.J. Tornatore, Kim Myers, Geoff Burch, Joey Fiato, Don Ackerman, Walt Stokes, Randy Smithers, Henry Brown, Scott Flaherty, Mike Rouse, Matt Enigk, Tito Colon, Rich Brophy, Ross Stagnitti, Marie Sgroi, Jim Clark, Jennifer Warner, Tammie Alter, Kyle Cashel and Linda Pease, Mike Milmoe, Donald Hamilton, Bob Davidson, Jimmy Prettyman, Billy Backus, and Tony Graziano. I would like to single out in particular the efforts of Jeffrey S. Brophy for his outstanding research and ongoing friendship.

Over the years I have had the opportunity to share many a word, both spoken and written, with some incredible athletes and coaches on the topic of Abe Attell and the 1919 Chicago White Sox. They included, from the world of baseball, A. Barlett Giamatti, Walter Alston, Luke Appling, Earl Averill, Joe Cronin, Bill Dickey, Charley Gehringer, Hank Greenberg, Burleigh Grimes, Waite Hoyt, Carl Hubbell, Bob Lemon, Al Lopez, Ted Lyons, Edd Roush, Red Ruffing, Joe Sewell, and Bill Terry. From boxing, they included Carmen Basilio, Gene Fullmer, Kid Gavilan, Archie Moore, Bobo Olson, Willie Pep, Max Schmeling, and Ike Williams. Many other individuals were also gracious with their time, including Vikki LaMotta, Eugene J. McCarthy, Strom Thurmond, and numerous state governors. To the resourceful National Baseball Hall of Fame and Museum, where I proudly hold a Lifetime Donor Membership, I offer my sincere appreciation.

This book would not have been possible without the assistance of the Library of Congress and their Digital Collections and Services staff. The George Grantham Bain photographs came to the Library of Congress with very little description but tremendous potential. I am proud to display many of those images in this work. Chronicling America, a website providing access to information about historical newspapers and to digitized newspaper pages, was also a useful tool. Produced by the National Digital Newspaper Program, which is a partnership between the National Endowment for the Humanities and the Library of Congress, the project is a long-term effort to develop an Internet-based, searchable database of U.S. newspapers. Also a word of thanks to the University of Sussex and Heritage Auctions fort their support.

Living in the historic state of Connecticut, I am fortunate to have a great support system. My gratitude to all of the independent bookstores, especially Bank Square Books in Mystic, and Byrd's Books in Bethel. Also, my appreciation to Larry Dasilva (Nutmeg TV), Larry Rifkin (WATR), Ray Bendici (*CONNECTICUT* Magazine), Nathan Grube (The Travelers), and Geeta Schrayter (Rivereast News Bulletin) for their contributions. I would also like to acknowledge our state's historical sites and institutions, especially Nathan Hale Schoolhouse in New London, Fairfield Museum, Jonathan Trumbull House, the Litchfield Historical Society, and the Norwich Historical Society. Also, thanks to my friends Dana Beck and Brian Brinkman, Kelly and Dennis DiGiovanni, Ann and Mark Lepkowski, Paul Mancuso, Mark and Michelle Brett, and Jim Risley.

I would also like to express gratitude for some others who played a role in the preparation of this work, including the staff at the Marlborough Medical Center, Hartford Hospital, David A. Kvam, M.D., Danny Mancini, PA-C, and Lindsey E. Lien, PA-C.

To my family, Marilyn Allen Baker, Aaron, Sharon and Elliott Baker, Elizabeth Baker and Mark Taylor, Brad, Rebecca and Elijah Lane, and Cyndie Long, thank you for your love and support. I wish to extend a special note of appreciation to my wonderful father-in-law, Richard Long, who continues to inspire me to do more.

To the loving memory of Ford William Baker, James Buford Bird, Flavil Q. Van Dyke III, Deborah Jean Long and David Arthur Mumper.

In the words of Mr. Tennyson, "If I had a flower for every time I thought of you…. I could walk through my garden forever." My wife Alison has been my flower and I could not be more thankful.

Preface

The sport of fighting with the fists, especially with padded gloves in a roped square ring according to prescribed rules, has always been, even in its most primitive form, a reflection of society. So powerful is it, that even reduced to a single event, or a three-minute round, the diversion can speak volumes about our culture. No other sport—not baseball, basketball, football or hockey, not even soccer—say so much in so little time. Without a rival, boxing contends only with itself. That is the reason why so many, including me, are seduced by the sweet science.

I'm the grandson of a boxer and the son of a professional baseball player, so most people aren't surprised to learn of my fascination with, and love for, both sports. By the time I was seven years old, I thought everyone had bedtime stories that took place in Madison Square Garden or Yankee Stadium. Sure, I played stickball, listened to sports on the radio, sat in dugouts while others watched from the stands—my father played ball with Louis Marchegiano (that's Rocky Marciano's brother) and his pitching coach was Carl Hubbell—and I collected trading cards, but I also put pen to paper and corresponded with my heroes. When Gene Tunney and Jack Dempsey wrote back, I dug deeper.

While I had written to Abraham Attell before his death in 1970, I never met him. Thankfully, however, I have met many who did meet this remarkable fighter. I, like others, marveled at the stories of Attell's ring dominance I read in *The Ring*. As you read the history of his accomplishments, it is hard enough to imagine fighting a legend like George Dixon once, yet alone a trilogy. Then you add names like Battling Nelson, Owen Moran, Freddie Welsh, Ad Wolgast, Jem Driscoll, and Johnny Kilbane, and you start asking yourself: just who was this man? In 1908, he fought twelve times, with five of those battles against future members of the International Boxing Hall of Fame. The ring tales about Attell made him sound almost superhuman.

When I searched library shelves for a book, or any resource about Attell, I found nothing to satisfy my thirst. Sure, there were tidbits, stories like Joe Williams's piece "Abe Attell Takes the Stand," in the wonderful compilation *The Fireside Book of Boxing*, edited by W.C. Heinz, but they served only to whet my appetite for more. Yet the more I dug, the less substance I found, or so it seemed.

Then there were the stories of Attell's indiscretions, one in particular. Here was a man, a gifted professional athlete and easily one of the finest boxers of his generation, who lived well into his eighties, or 31,396 days, to be exact, and he's to be defined by one event that totaled 91 days? I think not.

Having been involved with the International Boxing Hall of Fame—an association that allowed me to work with some of the finest ring historians, including Hank Kaplan—

1

I believed it was time to revisit the life of "The Little Champ." Time to blow a few decades', if not a century's, worth of dust from accounts of this extraordinary man, and re-examine the life of Abraham Washington Attell. Just who was this mythological figure who dominated the featherweight division? And how was it conceivable that a single family could produce not one world champion, but two?

As you examine the history of the feathers, you will find that Attell was essentially the bridge between the old-school fighters like George Dixon and Terry McGovern, and the more modern and dominant fighters like Johnny Kilbane, and later Willie Pep—and, yes, you can throw Johnny Dundee and Tony Canzoneri into that mix as well. Attell, well aware of the fistic prowess of these pugilists, would have agreed with the analogy.

This work, built primarily from contemporaneous sources, allows a very private Abe Attell to speak for himself whenever and wherever possible—which was rare in comparison to others like Battling Nelson, who wore his heart on his sleeve. It adds insights at every angle—from referees and opponents, to family members and even former world champions—by using hundreds of eyewitness accounts. The approach was selective but maintains a traditional commitment to chronology. The goal was to capture Attell at notable moments in his life, to concentrate on his thoughts and actions, his values and convictions, all while providing the reader with sufficient background on what happened between sightings along his eighty-five-year lifeline.

There were times I rode the Attell emotional roller coaster, as I had done with my previous biography on Battling Nelson. The anti–Semitism nauseated me, as did the "rush to judgment" made by many with regard to the "Black Sox Scandal." Time and testimony have served to contaminate the latter to such an extent that many have forgotten precisely how the event unfolded. While there is a chapter dedicated to the conspiracy, this is not a book to debate Attell's participation in the event. That task has been left to other dedicated works.

There has always been a delicate balance between a biographer and a subject, involving lines that should or shouldn't be crossed. Abraham Washington Attell was a complex man, and very private despite occasional bouts with compulsive behavior. Keeping his relationships confidential—with both his wives, not to mention other family members— was how Abe would have wanted it, and thus how it is presented.

An extraordinary story, filled with intrigue around every corner, now rests in your hands. It includes: drama, such as a white contender battling a legendary black former champion; family, a story of two brothers who not only found each other through the sport, but who both became world championships along the way; hope, whereby a Jewish fighter, raised by a resolute mother, defies the odds and not only captures a world title, but defends it for years; nostalgia, as the featherweight division has existed since the 1890s; survival, despite numerous adverse scenarios, Attell manages to pick himself up, dust himself off and begin again. Most of all, it gives a great boxer a forum to once again be heard.

Arthur Mercante, Sr., the great boxing referee whom I was proud to call a friend, once told me that what separates a good referee from a great one is anonymity. Arthur also felt that to some extent the comparison holds true for a writer. Every boxing fan recalls the details of the first Muhammad Ali–Joe Frazier fight on March 8, 1971, but few recall the referee. That's because he, Arthur, did his job and did it well. I feel much the same about my role: if you leave these pages with more than just the basic facts—like education, work, relationships, and death—but also with a portrait of Attell's experience of these life events, then perhaps I have done my job. I must add, however, that because of my empathy for Attell, I am more of a second in the fighter's corner than an arbiter.

Introduction

Without question, the cleverest and most scientific professional boxer ever to enter a ring was Abraham Washington Attell. This assertion is no better substantiated than by his inclusion as part of the premier induction class of the International Boxing Hall of Fame in 1990. There he will forever be linked to names such as Muhammad Ali, Henry Armstrong, Jack Dempsey, Harry Greb, Jack Johnson, Benny Leonard, Joe Louis, Willie Pep, and Sugar Ray Robinson. Attell was so talented, most boxing historians rank him among boxing's greatest fighters—Bert Randolph Sugar ranked him ahead of George Dixon, Maxi Rosenbloom, Pernell Whitaker, Battling Nelson, and John L. Sullivan.[1] Since Abe Attell has been deceased for nearly a half a century, and has not fought for nearly a full one, such an acknowledgment attests to his extraordinary talent.

Born into a large Jewish family, Abraham and his siblings were raised by a resolute mother, at a time when anti–Semitism was widespread. Countering opposition with fistic prowess, the gifted Attell brothers, Abraham, Monte and Caesar, assisted in transforming San Francisco into a Mecca for fans of the sweet science while placing the name Attell into the pantheon of boxing's elite families. To do so not only took guts, but a level of fraternal performance beyond what many thought achievable: two concurrent world champion boxers in two separate weight divisions.

From the moment Abe set foot in the ring, he appeared unconquerable, especially during a short-distance encounter. Initially gaining fame as a knockout artist, Albie, as many would also call Abe, quickly matured into a commanding featherweight. While still a teenager, "The Little Hebrew" fought the great George Dixon, whose defensive dexterity was unmatched. His ring ascendancy was rapid and fueled by self-confidence. Valid title claim began in 1906 for Abraham and didn't end until 1912. Double-digit title defenses rank him among the most successful featherweight champions ever. Never had a fighter understood the parameters of the ring, in terms of risk versus reward, better than Abe Attell. Battling the elite of pugilism, Attell entered the ring not only against Dixon, but also Battling Nelson, Owen Moran, Freddie Welsh, Ad Wolgast, Jem Driscoll, and Johnny Kilbane. In 1908, he fought twelve times, with five of those battles against future members of the International Boxing Hall of Fame.

It wasn't the boundaries inside a ring that bothered Attell; it was those on the outside. Unlike other fighters, he tried to keep his personal life private, but wasn't always success-ful. In the eyes of some, his love for a wager often overshadowed his devotion to the ring. Nevertheless, that was not the view of boxing scholars, who saw him for what he was: a ring craftsman. As a world featherweight champion—and entertainer, bodyguard, entre-preneur, and lady's man—he could be as mysterious or fascinating as he was charismatic.

The captivating underpinnings of his career include a meteoric rise as a knockout artist; a transformation into one of the greatest defensive fighters ever; an intense trilogy against nonpareil boxer George Dixon, or a black Canadian versus a white Jew; holding division championships alongside his brother; a six-month suspension for faking a fight; and winning and losing a championship on his birthday. Fighting in an era when his occupation was considered uncivilized and corrupt, Attell lived in the fast lane, occasionally associating himself with some unpalatable characters, including Arnold Rothstein.

In the years since his death in 1970, there has been little disagreement over the significance of his life. He was a bona fide ring champion, who reigned supremely over the featherweight division from 1906 until 1912, and who, along with his brothers, helped transform San Francisco into a boxing epicenter, while solidifying the name of Attell as one of the sport's most prestigious families. Attell is still remembered today as another genuine ring hero whose tabloid exploits out of the ring, in particular his association with the Black Sox Scandal, a 1919 Major League Baseball gambling impropriety, did much to taint a spectacular featherweight career.

It has been over a century since Abe Attell first stepped into a boxing ring, captured his first featherweight division crown, and lost the title during a record-breaking defense. During this same period, and too often overlooked, Attell was inducted into The Ring Boxing Hall of Fame (1955), the World Boxing Hall of Fame (1981), the National Jewish Sports Hall of Fame (1982), the International Jewish Sports Hall of Fame (1983), the San Francisco Boxing Hall of Fame (1985), and the premier class of the International Boxing Hall of Fame (1990). The name Attell—and aliases like Abe Attell, Young Attell, and Young Abe Attell—struck so much fear in opponents, and commanded so much respect, that it was used as a moniker for dozens of fighters.

Abraham Attell lived an extraordinary life, beyond the imagination of the finest Hollywood screenwriters, and beyond the reach of the thousands of pugilists who have been trying to emulate his accomplishments ever since. It was a story of courage and resilience, of opportunity and reward. To quote a line from W.C. Fields, "It ain't what they call you, it's what you answer to." Abe Attell answered to "The Little Champ."

CHAPTER ONE

Rising to the Occasion, 1900–1901

"Hard hitting alone cannot win a fight. Neither can defensive properties alone be depended upon. When a man is only clever in one of these lines, even though his cleverness is such that he can hold his own with the best in that respect, his downfall is only a question of time."[1]*—Abe Attell*

Majestic in its presence, the San Francisco Bay, a shallow estuary, seems to magically attract life to its waters. As the Sacramento and San Joaquin rivers flow into Suisun Bay, they combined with the mystical waters from the Sierra Nevada Mountains, then flow through the Carquinez Strait, where they join with the Napa River at the entrance to San Pablo Bay. It was here that the waters collect at the south to form the eye-catching San Francisco Bay. The adjacent region, which hugs the waters and includes the cities of San Francisco, Oakland and San Jose, continues to be referred to as "the Bay Area." The Golden Gate, or waterway entrance to San Francisco Bay from the Pacific Ocean, would not see the opening of a bridge until May 27, 1937, when man and nature were finally disposed to meet. As you enjoy the view from a point anywhere along its rim, it will take you only seconds to realize why man was so drawn to its vista.

San Francisco, which encompasses a land area of nearly 50 square miles, occupies the northern end of a peninsula. Although the city was not incorporated until 1850, its roots can be traced back to the founding of a mission in 1776, when colonists from Spain established Presidio of San Francisco at the Golden Gate, and Mission San Francisco de Asís (named for St. Francis of Assisi) just a few miles away. San Francisco's rapid growth, attributed to the Gold Rush of 1849, quickly transformed it into the largest city on the West Coast—a fact that couldn't be ignored by its neighbors, who turned the California Republic into a state the following year. Now having to defend its borders, the United States military built Fort Point at the Golden Gate and a fort on Alcatraz Island to secure the San Francisco Bay.

By 1849, the population of San Francisco had risen to 25,000, as prospectors and everyone associated with the mining industry sought their fate in the neighboring rolling hills. As fortunes were found in those grounds, so too were they obtained in the streets, in the form of robbery, prostitution and gambling. The widespread lawlessness was no better exemplified than the red-light district of San Francisco's Barbary Coast during the second half of the 19th and early 20th centuries. Along a three-block stretch of Pacific

Street, now Pacific Avenue, between Montgomery and Stockton Streets, entertainment, in every form possible, was at a prospector's fingertips.

This growing population led to transportation needs, specifically a cost-effective route between San Francisco and what is now Marin County. Ferries were the answer, starting in 1820, but they didn't offer regular service until the 1840s. The Golden Gate Ferry Company, originally the Sausalito Land and Ferry Company, slowly became the largest ferry operation in the world and a key element of the local economy.

Entrepreneurs, in every form imaginable, flocked to the new state to capitalize on its riches. Banks thrived, such as the Bank of California and Wells Fargo, as did transportation systems like cable cars and the Pacific Railroad, which gave visitors access to the rail systems of the eastern United States. Levi Strauss saw riches in the form of dry goods, while Domingo Ghirardelli turned to the epicurean delight of chocolate. Many of these new businesses thrived thanks to "cheap labor," much of it from the growing Asian population. When the laborers weren't working along the rails, they were building a sea of Victorian houses that soon dotted the hillsides.

Recreation also flourished, be it inside athletic clubs, such as the lavish San Francisco Olympic Club (established on May 6, 1860, making it the oldest in the United States), or outside in neighborhood parks. Sport often meant the art of manly defense, or practice of fighting with fists, be it with or without padded gloves, a roped square ring, or pre-scribed rules. Disagreements, typically solved by disenfranchised youth on street corners, took on an entirely different meaning inside a club or venue. Why fight for free, many thought, when you can punch for profit? If you were a talented fighter, there seemed no limit to what you could attain.

Abraham Washington Attell

Abraham Washington Attell was born in San Francisco on February 22, 1884, which makes his middle name self-explanatory. His father Max, born in 1846, was from Krakow, Malopolskie, Poland, while his mother Anna (Annie) Rothlotz, born in 1849, was from Poznan, Poland. Married in Europe, or so it was believed, the couple migrated to the United States in the early 1870s. Some accounts have them settling first in Syracuse, New York, where the patriarch of the family owned and operated a jewelry business. After a few years in central New York, the family headed west to San Francisco. Abraham, the third youngest, was part of a family of twelve children: seven boys—Coleman, Joseph, Jacob, Meyer, Caesar, then Abraham and Monte; and five girls—Yetta, Sarah, Rose, Rachel (Rae) and Florence (Flora). Abraham was a scrappy kid—fighting on the streets was nothing, so he thought, compared with battling his brothers—with little interest in school, or responsibility for that matter. When he was five his father left the household on Third Street, or "died," according to what Abe later told the press, leaving his extraordinary mother to raise the family. Often overwhelmed with responsibility, when she could no longer control the tenacious boy, she shipped Abraham off to his uncle in Los Angeles.

There he soon learned that only good behavior could earn him a return trip home. So behavior modification, never before an option, became one. Abraham didn't like it, but if that could buy him a ticket north to Frisco, the option became a consideration. His uncle soon took notice, and the youngster's new outlook prompted many things, including a music education. Reluctantly, Abraham complied and was soon playing, of

The view from the Nucleus Hotel, corner Market and Third Streets in San Francisco, looking west in the year 1866 (Library of Congress).

all things, the cornet. After Abe had spent fifteen months in southern California, his uncle returned the polished youth home, back to the old neighborhood. Abraham learned that while he was banging out notes, his former adversaries were flinging punches as part of the local fight game. One amateur in particular, Kid Lennett—whom Abraham used to whip good—had even won ten consecutive fights. It was now time, he believed, to replace one type of mouthpiece (musical) for another (boxing).

Peer pressure, or so he said, pushed Abraham toward the San Francisco Athletic Club, run by Alex (or Alec) Greggains. Promoting four-round bouts in his venue known as "The Bear Garden," Greggains was a local impresario. As fighters applied to him, a participation prerequisite, Greggains had his own litmus test: when nobody was looking he would toss a stiff cuff at the youth, and if he countered, he accepted them. Noting Attell's desire, and his assertive parrying, Greggains quickly matched the young man with Lennett; all he needed now was his mother's permission. As the story was printed in *Pearson's Magazine*:

Abe rushed home to tell his mother. It was the middle of the week. As a matter of fact, the family had not had any meat for four days, and not one of them was sufficiently nourished. None of the boys had any shoes and only the oldest girl, who had just been able to get a job as a cash girl in a department store, had enough clothes to keep her warm. The Attell family was at the point where poverty was separated from beggary only by the conscience of a proud spirit.[2]

As Abe told his mother of his newly found opportunity, she wept pitifully. Despite the circumstances, she did not want her son, or the family, disgraced in a boxing ring. The answer was a firm "no."

Disconsolate Abraham then had to pass the word back to Greggains, but it was too late: the bout card had already been printed and distributed. It was the first time Abe had seen his name in print: "KID LENNETT VS. ABE ATTELL, Four Rounds." With card in hand and nothing but persuasion on his mind, Abraham returned home for round two. "The boys are calling me a quitter. Please let me fight," Abraham was said to have begged his mother, or so *Pearson's Magazine* noted. Finally, she capitulated.

Lennett, already a bit of a local celebrity, then faced a "slim, aquiline-nosed little Jew who advanced from his corner with a McCoy-like sneer."[3] In order to create rivalries, and for a bit of convenience, fighters were often defined by their looks, ethnicity, class and neighborhood, to name only a few characteristics. Lennett went right after his nemesis. Attell let him lead, then after about a minute, let loose with a flurry of punches. When the gong sounded, Lennett was nearly out on his feet. A minute of rest allowed the "Kid" ample time to gain his senses, at least enough to answer the bell. But a swift Attell uppercut soon sent his schoolyard antagonist to the canvas. After only two rounds, Lennett was out, and Abe was in, not to mention $15 richer.

In August 1900, Abraham's purse went a long way to feed a large family in need. While no mother likes to see her child being beaten upon, she also doesn't enjoy watching him starve. Ten days later, on August 29, Abraham sent Kid Dodson a finishing blow to collect another $15 purse. It was about this time that Abraham finally landed his dream job as a messenger boy, which also secured his first moniker, "The Fighting Messenger Boy."

Abe quickly found a home at Alex Greggains's old club, the San Francisco Athletic Club, "south of the slot"; locations, at that time, were defined by the cable lines that ran up Market Street or Howard Street.[4] Greggains was a gladiator from the past, having fought eighty rounds against Buffalo Costello at Coney Island; he loved telling all the young boxers how the spectators were asleep in their chairs when the fight finally finished. Later, Alex would use his power of persuasion to enter politics; his fists could also be influential at the ballot box, especially in doubtful districts. Greggains was convinced there was only one way to do things: his.

In front of "The Bear Garden," or the venue that held the twenty-foot boxing ring, rested Greggains's saloon, situated at the street corner. The entrance to the club was a short distance down the road, through a dark, narrow doorway. A tiny dressing room was located between the saloon and the fighting arena; on one side the door opened to the arena, while on the other into the rear of the tavern. Greggains used to kid how he "got them coming and going." Word was, if a fighter didn't run a bar tab, he wouldn't be invited back.

The stench of stale beer, sweat and vomit, which never seemed to matter much to Greggains's young gladiators, could be as overpowering as a wintry breeze coming off the bay. Wagers were sounded and taken at will, with any necessary arbitration handled by the owner himself.

The Attell family had a store front for their jewelry business on Third Street, and the family is said to have lived in the rear of the store. This is a view of 555 Third Street from Market Street in San Francisco (Library of Congress).

Almost any time of day or night you could step in there and see a three-carat diamond screwed into a dickey under a celluloid collar. Except when Jim Corbett made his semiannual visit, spats were not allowable, but chokers were. Jimmy Britt's three-inch collar was the delight of the place, and it could be seen there only on very rare occasions, for Jimmy was no low-brow, no cheap sport who made a business of hanging out in such a dump as that.[5]

Let's just say the San Francisco Athletic Club, where a ten-dollar bill would have covered the cost of the equipment, was in sharp contrast to the aristocratic home of the Olympic Club, only a mile away.

As master and commander, Greggains was both the announcer and the referee. If you didn't "dog it" in the ring, he liked you and brought you back, but if not, it was out the back door with a boot in the ass. It was this filtering system that kept his competitive bouts fresh: if he put on an eight- or ten-bout card for the evening, you could bet—and bet they did—that each would be a veritable fight. Entrance to the Garden, as Greggains saw it, was a bargain: a dollar to enter, two dollars to sit at ringside.

It was in this tiny, dimly lit arena that spectators parked their backsides on cramped plank bleacher seats to watch the evening's festivities; they weren't only blue-collar boxing fans, either, but politicians and businessmen.[6] The combination of the cigar smoke and arc lights created a heavy bluish haze that hung over the arena, like a morning mist over a local pier. It was beastly hot, the imperfect ventilation only provided by the aforementioned doorway. It was in this chamber that the celebrated ring reporter Robert Edgren first saw Abe Attell, describing him as "a black-haired, quick-eyed, muscular, wiry, dark-skinned boy ... with a fixed and menacing stare."[7] The reporter watched in disbelief as Attell dropped his opponent with a single punch. Attell's punch hit his opponent's jaw, "and he went down so hard that it sounded as if someone had tossed a sack of sand into the ring from the gallery."[8]

Attell was not just a mercenary, but a survivor—sometimes just living became an act of courage. Albie, as many would call him, was a picture of confidence: standing tall, thin and muscular, he was not lanky; when he stood he did not look awkward, not like you could just walk up and push him down, but balanced. His long, stiff countenance painted a picture of conviction and was highlighted by a thick brow and distinctive muzzle. If his broad shoulders weren't impressive enough, they connected to a set of massive, muscular arms—his tricep development alone was soon to be extraordinary for his weight class. An imposing figure, Attell knew how to look and act.

Early Rounds

People forget how quickly he finished. Attell didn't just punch a clock and ride; just look at the adversaries he faced in his first year. He picked off each opponent with clean knockouts; only one went five rounds, and that was Eddie Hanlon, one of the better lightweight contenders of his day. In his first year as a professional, six of his sixteen adversaries had the common moniker "Kid" (a common sobriquet given by Greggains); all but one, Hanlon, were part of two impressive knockout streaks, the longest of which was ten; and none of his victims asked for a rematch.

Many of Attell's early ring battles were billed as boxing exhibitions by amateurs, some part of the Bay City Athletic Club's monthly fistic showcase. However, since the boxers were paid, it certainly stretched the definition of "amateur." As Greggains saw it, these were just young kids trying to pick up a few bucks banging heads in the ring instead of engaging in street vendettas; he believed he was even doing the community a favor. For most, their skills were limited and a career in boxing nothing more than a pipe dream. But on rare occasions a talented fighter, such as Abraham, might emerge from a club, creating a road to prosperity for a pugilist and a meal ticket for a club owner.

While the story of Attell's fight with Lennett, which took place on August 19, 1900, was true, often left out was that one "A. A[t]tell [was given] a chance to 'rattle the slats' of William Schoenbeim as part of a nine glove affair conducted by the San Francisco Athletic Club at the clubrooms on Sixth and Shipley streets on August 15, 1900."[9] The result, so the *San Francisco Call* continued, was that Schoenbeim "found Attell's punches unstomachable, so he quit" in the second round. So perhaps Greggains told Attell he would try him out first before matching him against Lennett, or substituted him for another fighter; it's just too hard to say. Attell, as we will learn, will become a favorite raconteur to many an interviewer for a reason.

Regardless of the yarn, and a common lack of fight accounting, Attell's career was off to a swift and impressive start. In August 1900, he picked up at least four victories and began his first streak of five straight knockouts: Schoenbeim, W [win] 2 [round], on August 15; Lennett, KO [knockout] 2 [round], on August 19; Kid Dodson, KO2, on August 29; and Joe O'Leary, KO4, on August 31.

On September 18, in one of his early battles, Abraham fought Benny Dwyer inside Washington Square Hall. "Dwyer fought three hard rounds, but in the fourth Dwyer got winded and to save a knockout threw up the sponge."[10]

After picking up a fourth round knockout against Joe Hill on October 4, Attell then faced a talented Eddie Hanlon on October 10. This fight too was a part of the boxing exhibition sponsored by the Golden Gate Athletic Club and held at Washington Square Hall.[11] Although he picked up an impressive five-round victory, it ended Attell's streak of five straight knockouts. On October 18, Abraham embarked another kayo streak— three first-rounders in a row—with Dick Collins KO1, followed by Lew White KO1 and finally Jim Barry, KO1, on November 2.[12] Having garnered some local press, Abe Attell, or "The Fighting Messenger Boy," was starting to make a name for himself.

On November 8, Attell met Frank Dell at Palo Alto Hall, over at 320 O'Farrell Street. The event, part of another monthly fistic exhibition, took place in front of a large and enthusiastic crowd. Both fighters weighed in at 107 pounds. As reported in the *Call*:

Dell, a chunky, cross-eyed young Italian, when the gong sounded, crouched so low and swung about so wildly that he seemed to be giving an imitation of a first attempt at swimming. For two rounds his work consisted of long distance swings. Attell caught him a couple of stiff ones in the third round and after a mix-up in his corner he took the advice of his seconds and went to sleep.[13]

Attell would finish the month of November with two knockouts: Kid O'Neil, KO1, on the 18th, and George Brown, KO2, on the 24th. He continued his knockout streak into the following month: Kid Jones, KO1, on December 4; Pete Carroll, KO2, on December 8; and Kid Dulley, KO1 on December 15.[14] He likely (again, records from this era were often incomplete) also fought Kid Powers to a knockout, a victory in a battle that took place prior to his next fight.

What better way to finish the year than with his professional debut, which took place in San Francisco on December 20, 1900? According to the *San Francisco Call*:

Abe Attell's first professional fight was a victory. After ten rounds of hard fighting Attell was proclaimed the victor over Jockey Bozeman. While the fight was close enough for the crowd to hang upon the referee's decision for a clue, the great majority of the spectators were of the opinion that Referee Jack Welch knew his business when he pointed to Attell as the winner. The leading was primarily the work of Attell, who offset the superior strength of Bozeman by an exercise of a mild sort of cleverness.[15]

The fight was on the undercard of the Otto Cribb versus Frank McConnell welterweight clash, a battle won by Cribb, who knocked out McConnell in the fourth round. Also on the ticket was a no-contest between Doc Flynn and Spider Kelly.

The sport of boxing had six weight classes and five world champions in 1900. James J. Jeffries was the Heavyweight Champion; Tommy Ryan was the Middleweight Champion;

William "Matty" Matthews was the Welterweight Champion; Frank Erne was the Lightweight Champion; "Terrible" Terry McGovern was the Featherweight Champion and claimed the Bantamweight title. As a featherweight, Attell marveled at the year McGovern had. First, in New York on January 9, less than four months after winning the bantam title, McGovern picked himself up from the canvas in the fourth round to floor George Dixon eight times in the final round, winning the feather crown. Then, on July 16 in New York, McGovern, in a bout held at the 128-pound limit, stopped lightweight champ Erne in the third round of a non-title battle. If this, as Attell thought, was the caliber of fighter he may encounter, then preparation was the key. Instruction and dedication became paramount.

Of the other notable battles, to assist in framing the fight game of 1900: Joe Walcott punished veteran heavy Joe Choynski on the way to a seven-round victory in New York

on February 23; James J. Jeffries dropped Jack Finnegan twice in just fifty-five seconds during his first-round victory in Detroit on April 6. Just over a month later, Jeffries rallied from behind to defeat James J. Corbett in the twenty-third round of their May 11 clash at Coney Island, New York. Finally, Bob Fitzsimmons defeated Tom Sharkey in the second round of their August 24 encounter at Coney Island, New York.

Regardless of how you interpret the fighting prowess of Abraham Attell, he was undefeated in a year that would witness his professional debut. As a sixteen-year-old fighter, he showed enormous potential, with some believing his younger brother Monte was not far behind.

Monte Attell, born on July 28, 1885, in San Francisco, would attain the same height as Abe, five feet and four inches tall, but have a slight reach advantage—one inch, to be exact—at sixty-seven inches. The year for Monte was marked by a Fourth of July accident that saw him badly burned on the face and hands as a result of

Born in Johnstown, Pennsylvania, John Terrence McGovern held the world bantamweight (1899) and featherweight championships (1900) (Library of Congress).

playing games with a toy cannon. He was firing the toy "on Clara Street, near Ritch, when a spark evidently got into the can in which he carried his stock of powder, exploding it. He was treated at the Receiving Hospital."[16] Also with an interest in boxing, bantamweight Monte hoped to follow in his older brother's footsteps; in fact, he followed closely behind, as he would begin in his fistic journey at the end of the following year.

It was Abraham and his success that planted the seed of pugilism firmly in the Attell family. It became an option when few appeared on the horizon, and a lucrative one at that. Older brother Caesar (1880–1979) boxed professionally from about 1902 until 1910, as did Abraham's nephew, welterweight Gilbert (1906–1970), from about 1920 until 1934.

Following a few notable losses, Caesar Attell hung up the gloves, his decision to leave the sweet science a wise one. Worth noting is that featherweights Caesar and Monte did share a card or two. For example, both were part of a March 19, 1902, amateur boxing exhibition sponsored by the Hayes Valley Club at the Pavilion Annex.[17]

Gilbert Attell, Abe's nephew, became a prolific fighter who struggled for years (1920–34) to get by some of the more experienced boxers he faced, and eventually held victories over Herman Auerbach, Jack Silver, and Charlie Hernandez. He was a determined pugilist who did not duck competition; his losses were against some outstanding fighters, including Fred Apostoli, Battling Dozier, and Freddie Steele.

The Attell clan, who resided at 255 Third Street, at times resembled an athletic club, with fighters constantly coming and going. The brothers were not the only siblings to grace the ring with their presence; there were many others. Notable immediately, at least to the Attell brothers, would be the fighting McGovern brothers, "Terrible" Terry, Hughey and Phil.[18] The McGovern family had moved from Pennsylvania to Brooklyn, where the boys soon made a name for themselves. Of the three, Terry would take the decision as a better fighter.

Jim Jeffries's brother Jack fought, but was not as skilled as his brother. Tom Sharkey had a brother of the same name, who didn't accomplish much in the ring. Joe Walcott's brother was fighting at the same time as his brother, but with limited success. The same was also true of Kid McCoy's brother Homer Selby.

Also, Joe Handler had a brother Jimmy; Billy Gardner, George's brother, was considered above average; Billy Murphy had two brothers, Jimmy and Tom, who were in the fight game; Spike Sullivan's brother Dave showed some brief brilliance; Harry and Clarence Forbes also fought, the former exhibiting greater ability; Denver Ed Smith and his brother Paddy collected a paycheck or two, as did Johnny and Clarence Ritchie. There were also Dan, John and Charlie Daily fighting out of St. Louis, and the four Bezenah boys, of which Andy and Gus were the better of the crew. Should brotherly love ever have bounds, let it be a ring with four corners.

1901

The year 1901 was filled with memorable local events. In San Francisco, the previous year's report of bubonic plague prompted a bacteriologist with the U.S. Public Health and Marine Hospital Service to visit the city in January. In February, the steamer *City of Rio de Janeiro* struck the rocks at Fort Point at the bay entrance of San Francisco, and only 82 of some 210 people on board were rescued. United States President William McKinley visited the city on May 12. On November 30, the ferryboat *San Rafael* sank in a collision off Alcatraz. Author and boxing columnist Jack London, who was born near Third and Brannan Streets, used the setting for the first chapter in *The Sea Wolf*. Boxing promoter James W. Coffroth staged the city's first heavyweight boxing championship, James J. Jeffries versus Gus Ruhlin, and bandleader turned politician Eugene Schmitz was elected mayor. "The City by the Bay" had taken on a charm as unique as its ostentatious mansions on Nob Hill.

In his first fight of the calendar year, a restless Abe Atell, now clashing professionally, dropped tomato can Mike Smith in the second round of his January 26 battle in San Francisco. But the victory did little to calm his recent frustrations: a concern that he would not get the matches he needed to move his career at a satisfactory pace, nor the money he felt he deserved. Attell began looking for answers. A conversation with featherweight Eddie Toy persuaded him to head east, borrowing car-fare from his mother. Both fighters found themselves in Denver, a hotbed for boxing, two days later.

Denver, the Queen City of the Plains, was undergoing a dynamic and very impressive transformation from a struggling town of tents and mud-roofed cabins, many lining the west bank of Cherry Creek, to a booming metropolis. Denver, without the natural resources that contributed to other great cities, had found a recipe for success. With an estimated population of about 134,000 in 1901, the city was less than a fifth the size of San Francisco and growing at a rate of just over 25 percent. When the Denver Pacific completed the link to the transcontinental railroad, it truly ushered in a new age of prosperity for Denver. A term used by Denver locals, historians and preservationists, to refer to the period between the 1880s and 1930s when the floriculture (flower farming) industry developed and thrived in Colorado, was "The Carnation Gold Rush." Denver had a growing population of German, Italian, and Chinese laborers, soon followed by African Americans and Spanish-surname workers. And as the laborers found their way west, so too did fight fans.

Eager to do battle, both fighters turned up on a February 15 fight card: Atell to meet Kid Buck, the "Newsboy's Pride," while Eddie Toy met Denver's Danny Coogan. The fight, conducted by the Colorado Athletic Association, was headlined by a bout between Buddy King and Kid Parker. The newspaper reports the following morning spelled it out: "Abe Attell had young Buck nearly out and was given the decision at the end of a five-round go."[19] The fight not only earned Attell his first out-of-state victory, but a large purse as well—sixty dollars. Toy was not so lucky. He struck Danny Coogan while he was "on his knees, the blow knocking him out. Because of the foul the referee decided against him."[20] As for King, he picked up the decision over Parker. A week later, in a rematch, Attell picked up a victory in a much closer decision.[21]

With a renewed sense of confidence, Abe Attell set out to establish himself in the local fight scene. It began with his first professional knockout streak. He dropped three "no-names": Kid Delaney collapsed in the fourth round of their March 1 fight; Kid Pieser, equally unknown, hit the canvas one round sooner on March 24; and Scotty Williams beat them both to the canvas by hitting it in the second round on April 12. The money, which Attell sent home to his family, continued to incentivize the youth even if the competition did not.

On April 26, Attell faced Young Cassidy of Colorado Springs in the main event of a Friday evening show at the Colorado Athletic Club in Denver. Adorning the bill also were two undercards, Billy Stift versus Jack Johnson, and Spider Kelly versus Sam Bolan. The carrot dangling in front of Attell was this: should he whip the undefeated and very popular Cassidy, he could be slated to meet Danny Dougherty, Terry McGovern's sparring partner.

Attell, cognizant of the significance of the fight, put on a brilliant display. Cassidy, who had been down twice and endured a terrific beating, was staggering around the ring nearly out on his feet in the second round when Referee George English stopped the bout. Even the partisan Denver fight fans cheered at Attell's performance over the favored Young Cassidy. For Attell, it was all in a day's work, and he was giving fans their money's worth.

Jockey Bozeman was the familiar face greeting Attell on June 26 in Denver; as Abe had worked in the Corbett camp as a sparring partner, the pair's second match was a preliminary bout or showcase for the main event: a battle between Young Corbett and Oscar Gardner.

In that event, Gardner was knocked out by standout Corbett in the sixth round, the latter feather having already compiled over thirty victories. "Gardner went down in the sixth from a right hand swing on the jaw. This blow was struck when Gardner's arms hung at his sides, he apparently having grown tired."[22] The crowd was mesmerized at Gardner's determination: while enduring a brutal beating, he struggled to his feet numerous times from the canvas. The police finally put a stop to the fight in the sixth round.

As noted by the *Butte Inter Mountain*:

Abe Attell and Jockey Bozeman, both of San Francisco, fought three fast rounds, when Bozeman's seconds announced that he had broken his hand in the second round and could not continue the bout. Bozeman receiving terrific punishment in the third, and though he fought gamely, he could not have stood up further against Attell's fierce fighting.[23]

Following the Bozeman victory, Attell may have squeezed in one, if not two, additional bouts—a July Fourth victory over Kid Buck in Denver has been reported by some sources—as he was aggressively trying to be matched.[24] The following month it was off to Pueblo, Colorado, about 115 miles south of Denver.

On August 1, Attell knocked out Kid Decker, an unversed fighter, in the third round of their Pueblo confrontation. True to style, it was a short but sweet victory. Attell, who was slated for his first twenty-round battle in less than two weeks, needed target practice and got it, albeit briefly.

"Colorado" Jack Dempsey, who had fought an impressive trilogy against Denver's Young Corbett II, was Attell's next adversary on August 12. A noisy, not to mention demanding, crowd at Pueblo's Rovers Club saw a skillful night of sparring, but not much more. Dempsey, a Pueblo resident, who shed some gore, managed to garner the slim decision. The crowd, however, immediately objected to the referee's call and began throwing everything they could find at the arbiter. Fearing for his life, the referee had little choice but to reverse his call.

The capitulation seemed to ignite promoter interest, as some big names were now being tossed around with regard to meeting Attell. But the fighter, who was now under the management of "Bad Jack" McKenna of Denver, was not looking for just any match, but the right match. And it didn't take him long to find it.

George Dixon

Born in Halifax, Nova Scotia, Canada, in 1870, George Dixon entered the pro ring at the age of sixteen; he had grown interested in the art of self-defense by assisting a photographer who was taking posed images of fighters. Like most youths of his day, he had scrapped in the streets, and while boxing was looked at as far from an admirable calling, he decided to take his chances. Billing himself as "George Dixon, Little Chocolate," the eighty-seven pound youth—who just happened to be another former messenger boy—began honing his skills.

Soon Dixon caught the eye of pugilist and boxing instructor Tom O'Rourke, who molded him into a compact and skilled fighter. Leaving Halifax for Boston, he fought the club circuit—the Athenian, Pelican, Cribb's and other athletic clubs and gymnasiums. It was inside these ropes that he quickly created quite a name for himself with a plethora of solid victories and even impressive draws. Dixon's first big break occurred on February 7, 1890, when he was matched with Cal McCarthy for the American Featherweight Title. After a vicious and exhausting seventy-round conflict using two-ounce gloves, the bout was declared a draw. The arduous yet impressive event, a four-hour and forty-minute affair, led Dixon to claim the title. The assertion actually led to a match against the bantamweight champion of England, Nunc Wallace. On June 27, 1890, Dixon delivered a brutal beating to Wallace in London, forcing his opponent to "give in." With the capitulation came the English bantam crown, bringing Dixon now one step closer to becoming the undisputed bantamweight champion. On March 31, 1891, in Troy, New York, Dixon soundly defeated Cal McCarthy; a knockout in the twenty-second round gave him the American bantamweight title. He would later add a world featherweight title to his name and defend it on numerous occasions during an era when the distinction between title and non-title fights was not clear.

Possessing a champion's swagger, Dixon became the talk of every town he visited. Savoring the attention, he also dressed the part of a real bon vivant, wearing tailored suits and his trademark brown derby, with that slight "Dixon tilt" to the right. Like many from his era, he battled with his demons, but always managed to defend his championship. Until, as it seems is always the case, they finally got the best of him. On January 9, 1900, Terry McGovern implacably pounded Dixon to the canvas, effectively ending his calling. O'Rourke threw up the sponge when he had seen enough.

Devastated by the defeat, Dixon had reached the pinnacle of his career. Nevertheless, even his fight management knew that a shadow of George Dixon was better than most rivals. And they were right. The question was, for how long? It was this George Dixon who would face Abe Attell. Yes, the name Dixon still sent fear through the hearts of most featherweights, and it did with Abraham. However, this was the first elite-level boxer Attell had an opportunity to meet, and he was exhilarated at the chance.

At this moment, fighting ten rounds to a draw with George Dixon was not the fight Abe Attell had envisioned. Nevertheless, that was the result of the confrontation that took place at Coliseum Hall in Denver on August 24.[25] Like anyone in his shoes, Attell wanted a clean victory, or at the worst, a decisive loss.

As the *Butte Inter Mountain* reported: "Up to the last round the fight was practically a sparring contest. Only once or twice did the men undertake to mix it up, and when they did neither had the advantage. In the tenth, however, they went at each other with a vengeance and in this round Dixon appeared to land two blows to Attell's one."[26] The only notable moment came about a minute into the first round when Attell, staggered by a few shots to the jaw, dropped to the canvas—the result of a straight right by Dixon that scored a bullseye. Later, Attell's camp was quick to note that the latter occurrence had less to do with the force of the blow, than the sudden moment it was delivered.

The newspapers had a field day following the fight, the primary claim being that George Dixon, the former featherweight champion of the world, had allowed Abe Attell to stay the ten rounds to a draw, simply to increase interest in a proposed battle against Young Corbett II. Having defeated Dixon the previous week in Denver, Corbett was not only at the battle, but he was in Dixon's corner. The irony of the entire situation was actually jeered by a few people at the club. "When the hissing subsided he [Corbett] went to the center of the ring and said: 'I am in this man's corner because he has treated me right. That,' he said while pointing to Attell, 'has not treated me right.'"[27] The entire play, with its choreographed moves, was regarded with suspicion. Corbett even childishly claimed that not only had Attell taken some of his garments, but was not interested in befriending him. Ringside attendees greeted the hyperbole with the same level of skepticism as Dixon's performance.

While the dust was settling on the Dixon affair, Attell promptly disposed of two more knockout victims: Scotty Williams, whom he dropped in the first round during their August 28 meeting; and Johnny Kid Lewis, kayoed in the third of their battle the following night. Both fights took place in Denver.[28]

Resting at an elevation of nearly ten thousand feet, the town of Cripple Creek, Colorado, had already experienced its fair share of torrid times by 1901. A prospecting hoax, or fake mini-gold rush—the Mount Pisgah hoax, caused by salting or adding gold to worthless rock—brought many to the town early in its history. Then, as fate might have it, the legitimate strike of 1890 started the last great Colorado gold rush. From 1890 until 1893, the town grew from five hundred people to ten thousand. If you just wanted to get rich quick, Cripple Creek seemed to be the place to be.

Three years later, two fires took turns burning the town to the ground. It was later rebuilt, thanks to the mining economy. In particular, the Western Federation of Miners—who, when not striking in a mine, were striking out at nonunion members—kept the economy afloat with their actions.

As for the inevitable Attell-versus-Dixon rematch, the Grand Opera House, built in 1897, seemed the perfect venue for the Olympic Athletic Club to host a rematch. And that they did, on October 20, as two extraordinary boxers skated to a twenty-round draw. It was as if the ghosts of the Mount Pisgah hoax had awakened. The fight proved to be nothing more than a routine sparring match. The *Denver Post* stated, "It could not exactly be called a fake." It was also stated that a large percentage of the audience left in disappointment and disgust over the event.

Since neither fighter incurred even the slightest scratch, cries of foul could be heard as far as South Platte River Valley on the western edge of the High Plains, the *Denver Rocky Mountain News* accusing Attell's manager Jack McKenna of adding a bit of salt of his own. Manipulation or not, the fighters had their purses, a foremost consideration in the mind of Dixon.

It was no secret that Dixon was plagued with financial problems. A month later Terry McGovern wasn't shy when commenting about the fighter to the *Topeka State Journal*: "Look at him! A champion for 12 years and a few weeks ago fought for a small purse and then had his end attached by his former manager for debts. He ought to have a quarter of a million and instead he is penniless and all because he was what they call a good fellow."[29]

Although fans scoffed at the thought of another Dixon-Attell battle, most knew there had to be a rubber match in the cards, and there was. But for safety's sake, it was moved to the Midwest. It took Referee George Siler (if it had to be anybody, it had to be someone with a degree of integrity, or so it was believed) to hand down a very unpopular decision at the West End Club in St. Louis that Monday evening, October 28. After fifteen rounds, the decision went to the young Californian. Subtracting the obvious cheers from Attell supporters, and hisses from Dixon fans, it was received with an uneasy silence.

The local newspaper reported, "By far the vast majority of the spectators seemed to believe that Dixon had all the better of the bout at every stage of the game. From start to finish he pushed the fighting, and in the ninth round seemed to have Attell all but out. Had Dixon's blows possessed their former steam, Attell could never have gone the distance."[30]

For Attell, the engagement was a showcase of his defensive skills, as he reported to the *St. Louis Republic*: "He did not back off from Dixon's rushes, except in a few instances, defending himself with blocking and dodging. His work at blocking was particularly good, and he stopped many of Dixon's blows that would have given him serious trouble. In the clinches, which were frequent, he would fight back at close range, but his blows seemed more love taps beside those of the Negro."[31]

Dixon was aggressive throughout the battle, sending blows nearly at will, many hitting their targets with precision. In the ninth round, he appeared to weaken Attell by drawing blood from his nose. Having been on the defensive for three rounds, a fatigued Attell responded only when and where he had to against Dixon. The ropes also belonged to the former champ, who bounced Attell against them repeatedly. Many enjoyed Dixon's protective skills, his ducking and blocking; his trademark cleverness was still there, even if his power was not.

The opening rounds highlighted Dixon's offense, his consistent rushes and skillful combinations to the jaw and stomach. Attell countered with his defending dexterity, blocking and evading, rather than trying to answer each assault. As was often the case, spectators saw the fight as being owned by the more truculent boxer, which was Dixon. Little respect was given Attell for his protective efforts, and certainly not during the ninth round. It was, according to some, Attell's ability to thwart the most dangerous blows that gave him the fight. All the same, when Siler held up the hand of Attell, there was only an eerie silence.

Dixon, who had his eye and mouth cut slightly, otherwise showed no marks. He joked afterward that he should now be matched against a ten-year-old boy so that he would be sure of a decision. Frankly speaking, with the racism and bigotry that surrounded the fight game, Dixon would have been lucky even to achieve that.

Jack McKenna had stated before the fight that his man "is in the best of trim and that a first-class bout can be expected."[32] Attell, who had been billed as having a record of thirty-three straight knockouts, took some heat over the affair, but not as much as his manager.[33] As Attell's reputation grew, so did the repute of McKenna—who, as some saw it, could sell salt water to a sailor. He would later be known by his clients as being one of the roughest and hardest of all managers.

Abraham Attell, the Master of Defense

Even if the Dixon trilogy was controversial, it was, as mentioned, an impressive display of Attell's defensive deftness. It was a skill that exhibited refinement with each passing battle. The fighter was breaking new ground with his art of resistance and it was being recognized.

Speaking again to the *St. Louis Republic*, Attell said:

Too many fighters depend upon someone property to win their fights, some depending upon hard hitting, others upon jabbing with the left and following it up when the opponent is worn out, and others upon their quickness in ducking and dodging. To my mind, a fighter depending upon any one of these properties cannot claim to be in the first rank, as boxing is such a science nowadays that a fighter has to know every branch of the game to reach the top.[34]

Attell went on to state to the *Republic* in November more of his protective philosophy:

Defensive fighting is particularly weak in many otherwise good fighters. How many men do you see in a fight who judge the blows of their opponents and allow them to pass by a narrow margin, coming in at once with their return? For every boxer of this sort in the ring you see ten who jump several feet to evade a lead and then think they have displayed their cleverness.[35]

In Attell's opinion, "The advantage of judging distance cannot be overestimated."[36] Pointing out a flaw in a recent fight between Forbes and Daugherty to the newspaper, Attell used the latter as an example of a boxer who did not accurately judge distance: "Hard hitting alone cannot win a fight. Neither can defensive properties alone be depended upon. When a man is only clever in one of these lines, even though his cleverness is such that he can hold his own with the best in that respect, his downfall is only a question of time."[37]

Attell also advocated the study of defensive tactics, altering movements especially with the head and not being afraid to withdraw a bit from a lead in order to be successful with a counter. An inch, as he couldn't overstate, can make a difference. He reiterated that wildness or irregular movements are of no use. As the *Republic* noted:

Attell's system of defense was something new here, and that is why popular opinion seemed to favor Dixon in their fight. Nearly every body lead of Dixon's was blocked by a slight movement of Attell's arms, while leads for the head were evaded by a slight movement of Attell's head. In every case Abe responded with counters which may have seemed light, but which, nevertheless, punished Dixon considerably. In that fight (October 28) Abe was not trying for a knockout, but merely to get the decision. "In the fight Monday [a fight that would be cancelled] he will go in to win from the start," claimed Attell's Manager Jack McKenna.[38]

With regard to Attell's defensive training, he remarked only that he preferred to spend a half hour each day sparring with his partner Tommy Bramble, followed by work on the heavy bag.

The First Loss

"Harry Forbes Won From Abe Attell, Substituted for His Brother Clarence on Account of Latter's Indisposition," read the bold headlines of the *St. Louis Republic*.[39] Calling it "the fastest and most scientific battle ever witnessed in the city," Forbes, who claimed he had captured the vacant bantam title in April, took a points victory over Abe Attell of San Francisco.[40] Before the West End Club, on November 4, both fighters gave what looked to be every ounce of energy they could summon.

Forbes, a Chicago resident, was not just fast but relentless, battling Attell every step of the way. The first three rounds established both the pace and the style, with swift counters, numerous notable blocks, and superb fighting at close distance. An enthusiastic crowd cheered and seemed to enjoy every moment of the skillful display. From his unbeatable infighting to his impressive artillery, Forbes managed to accomplish what was believed impossible, penetrating Attell's defense. And that was clear by the fourth round.

By the fifth round, Attell was weary—he was being steadily worn down by his antagonist and he knew it. But to the fighter's credit, he was still doing his best to make the fifteen rounds. When he could, he hit angles, but not with the power necessary to inflict damage.

Both fighters entered the ring about 9:30 p.m. Attell was said to have looked bigger than when he tangled with Dixon, yet still smaller than Forbes; both men were under the 116-pound mark.[41] The *St. Louis Republic* noted, "Attell was seconded by his manager (Jack) McKenna, by Billy Saunders and Jack Cento. Forbes had in his corner his brother Clarence and Jack Sims. The men fought hitting in clinches with one hand free. George Siler served as referee."[42]

In the first round Attell landed some solid combinations to the face of Forbes, and even backed him to the ropes. But Forbes's returns found Attell's jaw and stomach, soon making the fighter more cautious and reliant on his defense.

Attell came out strong in the second, but was met by some savage countering by his opposer. Forbes worked the body with proficiency as Attell continued to target the head. The *Republic* noted, "In a hard rally and interchange Forbes went to the floor, and remained down for eight-seconds getting his breath. Rising, he rushed at Attell, and the men fought desperately to the close, the gong ringing among the shouts of the Attell faction, who believed their man was winning."[43]

Shifting strategies in the fourth, Attell backed off the pace and began a play for points. Standing off, he now relied on his left jab. Forbes sensed the shift and continued his aggressive exchanges. Every time Abe seemed to land a hard right, his artillery was answered by twice the amount of return fire. The fighter was now finding it difficult to hide the frustration.

Forbes bored in during the fifth round, opting for the stomach and head, but Attell countered well, even sending Forbes's head back with a robust combination. The next two rounds found Forbes continuing the aggression as Attell stayed with his defense. Rallying in the eighth, Attell finally altered the course of the fight by putting Forbes in a defensive mode. The Midwestern fighter, however, returned the favor in the ninth, staggering Attell with his steady artillery.

In the tenth, it was all Forbes, who delivered powerful blends to the head and body. Attell could not return successfully and at the close was hanging onto the ropes, in what appeared to be a state of desperation. In the eleventh both danced, with Forbes leading. Both combatants conducted a tenacious display in the twelfth, with Forbes landing some distance ordnance. The newspaper continued, "In the thirteenth Forbes got in a wicked right-hand punch under the heart as he stepped in, which sent Attell to his knees with a thump. The Hebrew seemed much distressed as he arose and limped badly for the remainder of the round, evidently being weak."[44]

After recuperating in his corner, Abe tried in torment to land and slow Forbes in the fourteenth, but he could not. He was clearly in pain.

In the final round, Forbes went for the knockout, but Attell would not relent. Sending just enough fire to keep Forbes at a distance, Abe was able to make it to the close—a wise strategy for such a young fighter. A pandemonium of applause greeted both fighters at the gong, just as Siler held up the hand of Forbes.

Who would have guessed that a substitute, and in this case a brother, could have fought so admirably? Yet that was precisely what the prolific boxer Harry Forbes (who had an estimated seventy fights' worth of experience prior to entering the ring against Attell) delivered, a solid performance.

As for Attell:

Manager McKenna, who is looking after Abe Attell, called at *The [St. Louis] Republic* office last night and stated that immediately after the fight Attell was taken to his room, where Doctor H.L. Staudinger of No. 304 South Jefferson Avenue examined him and pronounced him in bad shape. The blow from which Attell suffered was delivered in the thirteenth round, and sent Attell staggering to his knees. Manager McKenna claims that blow was low enough for a foul, and it struck Attel so low in the hypogastric region that it was with difficulty that he could regain his feet."[45]

McKenna went on to claim that Referee Siler believed the blow was low and that neither he himself, nor Attell, wanted to see the fight end that way; the fight, it was their belief, needed to be decided on its merits and to a finish, rather than won on a foul. Attell, whose body was badly swollen, was still in pain, and the doctor recommended several days of rest. This was why Attell appeared so lethargic in the last two rounds, McKenna believed: he was suffering.

"Attell has been fighting for less than two years and this is the first decision that ever went against him. Most of his fights were on the coast. He has fought thirty-eight battles in his career and the majority of them were knock-outs," McKenna pointed out.[46]

McKenna's remarks did not fall on deaf ears. It was reported on November 14 that Siler had lost his position as referee of the West End Athletic Club of St. Louis and was replaced by local Joe Stewart. The removal was a result of several decisions that received complaints, not just the Dixon-Attell and Forbes-Attell fights. McKenna's claim read, "Siler permitted Forbes to use all sorts of foul tactics, which not only lost the chances of victory for Attell, but came near ending his ring career."[47]

Five days later, Chief of Police Kelly put an end to prizefights and boxing contests in St. Louis. It was also stated, "George Dixon and Abe Attell, who were to fight at the West End club Monday night, will not do so."[48] (A quartet for the duo; who would have thought?)

The *Topeka State Journal* reported:

"Some time ago I told the *Post-Dispatch* that the contests that have been given at the West End club and the Olympic club were violations of the law," said Chief Kelly, and so there will be none for the present at least. "Other violations of the law are being tolerated. For instance, there is a law against saloons being open on Sunday. Public sentiment, however, has made a sentiment that it would be difficult to overcome. But prizefighting has become too much of a business in St. Louis. At first we permitted clubs to hold boxing contests, but now the West End club pulls off a fight every week; so does the Olympic. These are not clubs in fact."[49]

With this bold and accurate statement, Chief Kelly spoke for many men in similar positions who were afraid to do so.

As for the dynamic world of boxing: James J. Jeffries (heavyweight), Tommy Ryan (middleweight) and Frank Erne (lightweight) stayed atop their respective divisions, while Barbados Joe Walcott captured the welterweight crown; Young Corbett II, the featherweight championship; and Harry Harris, or perhaps Harry Forbes, ended up with the bantamweight title. After years of frustration, Walcott, perhaps the greatest welterweight ever, pushed aside the hopes of William "Matty" Matthews and James "Rube" Ferns to take the crown on December 18 at Fort Erie, Ontario. In the upset of the year, Young Corbett II bad-mouthed Terry McGovern before sending the distraught one hundred and twenty-six–pound puncher to the canvas in the second round of their clash in Hartford, Connecticut, on November 28. The bantam division saw Harry Harris fail to defend his title, so it was awarded to Harry Forbes following his quick knockout of Danny Dougherty.

Of the other notable battles of 1901: Tommy Ryan took seventeen bloody rounds to dispose of Tommy West on March 4 in Louisville, Kentucky; on May 29, in San Francisco, Terry McGovern, nearly out on his feet from a right to the jaw in the fourth round, managed to send the hard-hitting Auerelio Herrera to the canvas in the fifth round; and in San Francisco, to the delight of many on November 15, James J. Jeffries put away Gus Ruhlin in the fifth round of their heavyweight encounter.

In a year of firsts—his first win outside San Francisco, his first trilogy against an elite opponent, and his first loss—featherweight Abraham Attell exhibited remarkable growth as a fighter. Establishing himself in the Denver market proved a wise decision—it landed him far better matches and purses. Credit too belongs to Jack McKenna, who was in a position to place his fighter in a fraternity that included both Forbes and Corbett.[50] The controversy over the Dixon battles wasn't fun, yet Attell matured, and handled himself well. Speaking of firsts, brother Monte "laced 'em up" on behalf of the San Francisco Athletic Club at the end of the year and would be fighting at the one hundred and ten–pound mark.

In McKenna's view, if you have to cut deals to move a fighter along, then you do it. That's the fight game and you work it, or it works you out of the picture. As a capable manager, he wanted his fighter in the featherweight mix and was hell-bent on getting him there.[51] It was reported in New York on December 28:

> Jack McKenna of Denver, Colorado, deposited a forfeit of $1,000 today to bind a match between Abe Attell and Terry McGovern for the featherweight championship of the world. McKenna stipulates that the boys shall meet at 122 pounds, the featherweight limit, the bout to take place regardless of the outcome of the coming bout between McGovern and Dave Sullivan. Sam Harris, McGovern's manager, is out of the city but will be back tomorrow, when he will consider the proposition.[52]

The offer, despite McKenna's tenacity, was rejected, and the two fighters never met.

CHAPTER TWO

A Champion's Ascent, 1902–1903

"The fact remains that McKenna brought little Attell to the front and that Abe would not now occupy the position he holds in ring affairs were it not for his former manager."—St. Louis Republic[1]

Hosting a heavyweight boxing championship—in this case, that of James J. Jeffries versus Robert Fitzsimmons—seemed to overshadow just about everything else that happened in the City of San Francisco in 1902. Dwarfed was the news of the sinking of the steamship *Walla Walla*, construction of Dutch windmills to pump water to a reservoir on Strawberry Hill in Golden Gate Park, and even the city's banning the sale of cemetery lots.[2] As for the latter, a small incorporated town called Colma, in San Mateo County near the northern end of the San Francisco Peninsula, would be founded as a necropolis in 1924, and as fate might have it, would play a role in the sport of boxing. And frankly, after the battle between Jeff and "Ruby Robert," both fighters felt themselves one step closer to Colma. In the eighth round, barely able to even see his adversary, let alone hit him, Jeffries miraculously fired a left hook to Fitzsimmons's liver, followed by a right to the jaw, to retain his title.

City residents were optimistic about the future, and dressed the part. Men in their single- or double-breasted sack suits, cutaway frock suits, and Prince Alberts in a variety of worsteds, sewed throughout with silk, could be seen walking the streets downtown. A quality suit could cost a fellow $11.25, an overcoat doubling the price. Clothes, after all, made the man.

As for the ladies, they could be seen in the best styles of the season in colored all-wool tailored dresses, in the best shades of gray, brown and navy. A quality dress had a price range of from $10.00 to $25.00, taste dependent.

It wasn't unusual to see a boxer "dressed to the nines," as they used to say. Abraham Attell always admired the way in which "Gentleman Jim" Corbett, the former heavyweight champion and San Francisco native, dressed and carried himself. If you were going to be a champion, Attell believed, then why not look like one?

1902

For Abe Attell, his first battle of the year wouldn't come until March 20. The Forbes loss was still playing out in his head and casting a bit of uncertainty as to which direction

Golden Gate Park, located in San Francisco, was a popular attraction for many on a Sunday afternoon (1902) (Library of Congress).

to take his career. In St. Louis, Attell drew Kid Broad of Cleveland in fifteen very fast rounds before the West End Athletic club. Broad, or William M. Thomas, was born in the United Kingdom. Having begun his career in the Midwest about 1897, Broad had over forty battles under his belt by the time he fought Attell, including George Dixon, Tommy White, Oscar Gardner, Terry McGovern and Young Corbett II.

As the *Arizona Republican* saw it: "Broad was the aggressor throughout, but his bull-dog style availed him nothing against the extreme cleverness of the Californian. Broad strove with might and main to land a knockout blow in every round, but his efforts were futile. Attell either blocking his leads or getting inside of them, and at times fighting Broad viciously in Broad's own style."[3] Attell was razor-sharp with his left jab and stayed in command as long as he didn't venture inside. In the clinches, Broad got the better of the situations.

If there was ever an adjective to describe Abraham Attell, it was *clever*. Used over and over by everyone to describe the fighter, the word means "quick to understand, learn, and devise or apply ideas, and intelligent," and Abraham was certainly all that. Able to quickly assess a situation allowed him to respond with the appropriate action. As he matured, his reactions became instinctive. While this sounds simple, even fundamental, it is not. Many fighters just weren't programmed that way. Take elite boxers such as Ad Wolgast or Battling Nelson: both possessed a ceaseless offense, minimal defense, and little regard for any strategy implemented by an opponent. Attell had the innate ability

The right-handed Abe Attell stood 5'4" tall with a 66" reach and was most comfortable fighting as a 122-pound featherweight (Library of Congress).

to instantly survey a situation and chart a strategic course to success. And it was improving with age and experience.

Familiarity has traditionally been a two-edged sword in boxing, because the tranquility that accompanies it can often breed complacency. Fortunately, such had not been the case with Attell, who seemed to fare better in his repeat performances—just look at his battles with Kid Buck and George Dixon. It was almost as if Attell's confidence was bolstered by a rematch.

On April 10, before the West End Athletic Club in St. Louis, Abe Attell picked up a twenty-round points victory in a rematch with Kid Broad. According to the *San Francisco Call*, "Broad forced the fight from start to finish, but, as in his previous battle here with the clever Californian, his tenacious style availed him nothing. Attell flitted in and out and away like a shadow, all the time playing a tantalizing tattoo of light left jabs on Broad's physiognomy, interspersing them with rights to the head and body."[4]

An inch taller than his opponent, the harder-hitting Broad centered his body attack on Attell's kidneys, which clearly exhibited damage by the end of the fight. Nevertheless, his strategy proved to be too little, and too late. Attell, having tried to mix it up in the seventh round, quickly backed off when it became clear that he would get the worst of Broad's tactics. In a sign of maturity, it was his switch back to a defensive style that would secure his victory.

In another observation by the *Call*:

In the concluding round Broad tried vainly to stem the tide of defeat. He rushed Attell to the ropes as the round opened and belabored him with right and left swings. Cornering Attell a moment later he again administered heavy punishment, the round ending with Broad chasing Attell around the ring. Broad showed to better advantage in this round than any other.[5]

While Attell picked up the win, it was Broad who was matched against Young Corbett II in a world featherweight title bout; that event would be held in Denver the following month. None too happy, Attell just shook his head in disbelief when he heard the news. Maybe he had scared Corbett away with his style. Attell just didn't know. Such was the fight game, and a fighter has to just let it go or it will eat at him. In what would prove to be Broad's last title shot, he would lose the ten-round decision to Corbett.[6]

For Attell, it was on to meet "The Tipton Slasher," or Benny Yanger, at the West End Club in St. Louis on April 24. A seasoned, compact and undefeated fighter, Yanger already held victories over Harry Forbes, Young Corbett II, and Kid Herrick. Born in New York City, but fighting out of Chicago, he was a dangerous fighter with a swift knockout punch.[7]

With both men fighting at 122 pounds, the featherweight limit, much was expected and much was indeed delivered. The opening fifteen rounds would be fought with the stipulation—written into the articles—that an additional five rounds would be left to the discretion of the referee. In this case that decision fell to George Siler. With a five-round option in play, what course does a fighter take? Attell decided on a strategy of running up the score early in hopes of a points victory over Yanger, then the five additional rounds, he believed, would likely be inconsequential.

Since it was billed as a battle for the featherweight championship, which it was only in Yanger's mind, the last thing spectators anticipated was their own cries for intervention.[8] Wisely, Sergeant Lavin jumped into the ring during the nineteenth round and ordered Referee George Siler to send both combatants to their corners. Everyone had witnessed enough. Attell, who had been dropped five times in the preceding round, was "simply staggering blindly around the ring and quivering under the most terrible punishment."[9] He found himself in dire need of assistance.

As the *Jennings Daily Record* observed:

> Yanger's victory was thus fairly earned, but only after the fiercest sort of fighting, and after an exhibition of pluck and endurance on the part of his opponent that was fairly wonderful. How any man could take the drubbing that Attell suffered and remain on his feet was almost beyond comprehension, and at that, he was still game and with bulldog tenacity was willing to hang on until some merciful blow knocked him into oblivion.[10]

To little surprise, it was Attell's fight for the first seven rounds. Using his left jab to perfection, Attell was mounting significant punishment to the face of Yanger. Angered by the perpetual facial pounding, not to mention his own inability to land any offense, Yanger gradually lost his self-control. Wild assaults then became an option. Yanger began firing randomly and with such a force that several times he sent himself to the canvas. Perplexed, Attell did his best to stay out of range, but the avoidance added to his fatigue.

Attell had gashed Yanger's face in the fourth, sent him to the canvas in the thirteenth with a left to the jaw, and bloodied his face again in the fifteenth. The assault only served to ignite the anger in the Chicagoan. As Attell slowed, by the eighth round, he was not able to slip the assault. Yanger saw this and began going to the body, pounding Attell's stomach as he bounced him about the ring.

The *Jennings Daily Record* also noted: "In the eighteenth round he put Attell to the floor for the count five times and the bell found Attell on his knees and almost done for.

In the nineteenth Yanger rushed Attell to the ropes in a neutral corner and uppercut him with right and left swings. Attell seemed on the point of going to dreamland, when to the surprise of the excited spectators, he suddenly regained his lost vitality."[11] Attell suddenly had his bearings, rushed Yanger and delivered a shower of blows before the police intervened. Proving as fruitless as it was tardy, the assault was abandoned. In spite of the decision, Yanger seemed to endure the greater punishment, his features nearly unrecognizable after the fight. It was Attell's second loss, his first ever by knockout (KO).

As another newspaper reported, "That Yanger wants no more of Attell's game was evident by the flat refusal of John Hertz (his manager) to allow his man to meet the San Francisco boxer again under the same conditions. Yanger admitted that the fight was the hardest of his career and both he and his manager are unwilling to risk a second encounter with Attell."[12] Pushed as to whether any conditions would have him reconsider, Hertz stated that only if the fight was in Chicago, at 126 pounds or catch weights, and limited to six rounds. Naturally, Hertz would also expect a Chicago referee.

Looking back at a very memorable battle, many agreed that had the fight "stopped at the end of the thirteenth round or even at the end of the fifteenth, Attell probably would have garnered the decision."[13]

This was how many sources saw it, including the *St. Louis Republic*:

Yanger upset all calculations, however, by his speed and aggressiveness. Rushing in regardless of Attell's blows he sent right and left punches to the latter as fast as he could work his arms, wrestling hard in the clinches and fighting himself loose when Attell attempted to cling to him. This treatment wore down Attell's strength and his guard was beaten down by Yanger's shower of blows. Abe tired rapidly in the seventeenth and the end was apparent early in the eighteenth.[14]

Meanwhile, Jack McKenna was busy plotting the course for not only Attell, but for a growing list of fighters in his stable. The *St. Louis Republic* noted, "He keeps several boxers of the preliminary class to work out with Attell and entertains them all at his hotel. His running expenses, accordingly, are extremely high."[15]

On May 26, articles were signed for a fight between Abe Attell and Young Corbett II to take place in Denver on June 6. According to the *Butte Inter Mountain*, "The weight to be 126 pounds at 3 o'clock in the afternoon and the purse will be divided 75 percent to the winner and 25 percent to the loser." The newspaper continued, "Attell is a 'comer.' The best has not been brought out of the game little fellow and it would be no surprise to see him get a decision over Corbett, if such a thing is possible in Denver (Corbett's hometown)." But, as can be the case, the articles didn't hold, so another set was signed on June 6. They called for a ten-round fight on June 27, before the Coliseum Athletic club, the men to weigh 127 pounds at 3 o'clock. This agreement could also be tentative, as a recent order forbidding prizefights had been put in place.[16] As it turned out, the two fighters would never meet.

All the eyes of the boxing world turned to San Francisco on July 25 for the heavyweight fight between James J. Jeffries and Robert Fitzsimmons. It was a rematch of their June 9, 1899, battle held at Coney Island, New York, in which Jeffries shocked everyone by not only flooring Fitz in the second round, but also knocking him out to win the heavyweight title.

As the *San Francisco Call* noted:

After the fighters entered the ring there were a number of details to be disposed of. Sam Thall, stakeholder for the fight, returned $2500 in gold to Fitzsimmons, a $2500 check to Jeffries and a $5000 check to the promoting club. These were the forfeits guaranteeing the presence of the fighters and the ability of the club to bring the affair to a successful issue.[17]

The stakes alone captured the attention of most, and a punch had yet to be thrown.

The two gladiators promised an impressive showing and delivered precisely that. For the first seven rounds, Fitzsimmons was getting the best of Jeff, cutting him badly over both eyes and slashing his face. When the gong sounded for round eight, Jeffries could barely see. Then, partway into the round, the press noted:

> Jeffries forced the fighting at this stage, crouching low and carrying his right high and left far back. They came together and clinched. As Fitzsimmons stepped back, he smiled and spoke to Jeffries. Before he could get out of reach, Jeffries quickly hooked his left on the body and sent a right to the jaw, and Fitzsimmons went down, clutching feebly at the lower rope, and shook his head in a signal of defeat. He came up slowly, but before he could get up on both feet the referee counted ten, and the fight was over.[18]

Jeffries, who might have shown more emotion if he were capable, was then assisted to his dressing room. Taking a look at some of the details: the contest was conducted under straight Marquess of Queensberry rules; Edward M. Graney was the referee; each contestant furnished his own gloves, which were to be five ounces each; and the ring was regulation size of twenty-four feet inside.

As had often been done in boxing, although this too was evolving, the bigger the men, the larger the take. The gate receipts totaled $31,800, the fighters to split seventy percent of the gross receipts. Of that seventy percent, the winner would receive sixty percent, to the loser forty percent. With regard to film, or "moving pictures," those receipts were to be divided as follows: eighty percent to the winning contestant and twenty percent to the San Francisco Athletic Club.

Answering the question why anyone would want to be a fighter: the average wage in the United States was 22 cents an hour, with the average worker taking home about $300 per year. A good dentist, who by the way could fix the damage carried out by a boxer, might take home $2,500 a year. So, dangerous sport or not, it was an alternative.

Once the fight between Abe Attell and Young Corbett II fell through, it was time to reshuffle the deck and deal again. On August 22, it was reported that the Acme Club of Oakland had paired Benny Yanger with Abe Attell in a rematch—to be billed as a featherweight championship fight—scheduled for October 7 in San Francisco. Unexpected based on the Yanger team's earlier comments, the news brought a degree of excitement to the Attell camp as they prepared for their next two battles, both against Chicago fighter Barney "Kid" Abel.

Attell had first met Abel at the American Athletic Club in Chicago for a short six-round affair on Monday, August 25. The fight allowed Attell an opportunity to evaluate the skills of his adversary before "taking him," or agreeing to box, at a greater distance. As it was, Abel supporters complained that "six rounds was too short to afford Abel a single opportunity to land a telling blow."[19] Limited telegraph accounts of the fight confirmed: "Attell simply played with him," and "modeled his campaign accordingly."[20] In the end, it was Attell in a six-round points victory.

Having danced with Kid Abel for eighteen minutes, Attell felt comfortable taking the rematch at a longer distance. His now former manager, Jack McKenna, had reminded him that despite Abel's poor record, he was a hard-hitting boxer, the type Attell didn't want to slug it out with. McKenna had also recalled for his fighter how veteran Tommy Sullivan, who after fourteen rounds of sparring with the bleeding fighter had victory in his hands, was suddenly caught with a single Abel punch that ended the fight. This sound advice was heeded by Attell. As for the falling-out between boxer and manager, Attell commented only that the gentlemen now handling his affairs hailed from Chicago.

With twenty rounds, Attell implemented his points strategy accordingly. It was an action that frustrated Abel, who understood that if he could not reach his antagonist, he couldn't win a round. "Abel was the aggressor through the greater part of the contest and forced the fighting until he was nearly blinded."[21] Attell just sliced and diced with the jab, leaving Abel's eyes nearly closed during the final rounds. Referee Harry Sharpe kept it clean, and when it was over Attell had a points victory. The fight was held on Thursday evening, September 11, at the West End Club.

The truth eventually surfaces in boxing, if, of course, you live long enough. In this case, it came during negotiations for a possible Attell versus Johnny Reagan clash. Apparently a decisive beating administered to Attell by Johnny Reagan—both fighters under McKenna's management—while the two were working together was the true reason for Abe's departure. It happened while Reagan was preparing for his fight with Goodman, according to McKenna. A quarrel broke out and the result was Abe's breaking ties with the manager and establishing a new base in Chicago. According to the *St. Louis Republic*: "Jealousy always existed between them," McKenna validated, "and I think, it would be a good fight (Attell v. Reagan). Reagan will give Attell the weight and will whip him. He has always been able to do this, and Attell knows it; and that is why there was feeling between them."[22]

Now under the care of Jack Cohan, Attell was doing his best to get over his former Denver manager. Observed again by the *St. Louis Republic*:

Attell's case is a typical example of the precariousness of handling a pugilist, as slight success serves to swell a fighter's head to such an extent as to make him believe he is a world-beater. Attell is certainly a wonder in his class, but it remains to be seen whether he will do as well under other hands as he did in McKenna's. The fact remains that McKenna brought little Attell to the front and that Abe would not now occupy the position he holds in ring affairs were it not for his former manager. Abe was fighting preliminaries in San Francisco when McKenna first saw the possibilities in his style and assumed control of him. Within four months from that time Attell gained a national reputation by his meetings with George Dixon, the matches being secured by McKenna.[23]

These are sound points with little room for argument. But to the contrary, the same source noted:

Of course, there are two sides to each question and McKenna has something to bear in the way of blame for the episode. He is said not to be the most patient man in the world and there are rumors of frequent disagreements in his camp. He was probably as much to blame as Attell for this trouble, but it looks as though Attell should not have deserted his manager in this manner.[24]

Saying that a good left hand would end Abe Attell's winning career, Harry Lombard, an unknown pugilist from Elgin, Illinois, wanted the opportunity to prove it. In an attempt to secure a match with Attell, Lombard was doing his best to draw attention to himself. Noting that he had "knocked out 16 opponents, drawn with four, and suffered defeat but twice," the youngster believed Attell should step up and take notice.[25] Challenges like this, often ridiculous in nature, become more common as a fighter ascends the division ladder. Attell understood this and the danger of accepting such provocations. Time, not to mention performance, would determine if Mr. Lombard could work his way through the proper channels for a match with any contender, yet alone Attell.

Attell was firmly offered a match with his former sparring partner Johnny Reagan, but declined and departed for Chicago. It came from Charles Haughton of the West End

Club, who needed a filler bout on September 22. While Haughton felt it might work, he wasn't overly optimistic. Attell claimed the reason for not meeting was that he and Reagan were *great* friends and that he had to prepare for the Yanger clash. Obviously the former wasn't true, and soon neither was the latter.

On September 21, John Hertz, Benny Yanger's manager, called off the October 4 scheduled fight between his boxer and Abe Attell. The cancellation was attributed to a ruptured vein in Yanger's thigh that may require a slight operation. Disappointed, Attell's camp had little time to dwell on the situation, as they had their own set of challenges to face, beginning with Californian Aurelio Herrera.[26]

It was fifteen rounds of clever boxing at the Acme Club in Oakland on October 15, as Abe Attell won a decision over Bakersfield fighter Aurelio Herrera. Although Attell took what proved to be a relatively easy decision, he did not have the power to put away the Bakersfield boxer—a characteristic he shared with many a Herrera opponent. As the *Call* noted: "Attell's ducking, dodging, jabbing and marvelous ability in escaping from dangerous positions were a revelation to the big crowd that witnessed the fight. They won applause for him in every round."[27]

Attell was simply too fast for the slow, yet aggressive Herrera, which was a good thing for Abe, as his opponent packed devastating punching power. The first two rounds, both fighters moved and measured with light shots, but in the third Attell landed four machine-gun lefts to Herrera's face, then scampered away before his opponent knew what hit him. Abe continued working the left jab effectively in the fourth. In the fifth round, Attell slipped to the canvas during a rush by his adversary and it cost him. Cornered by Herrera, he endured several brutal stomach shots.

Both boxers danced and rested in the sixth. In the seventh round, a powerful Herrara left found Attell's jaw and appeared to lift the fighter off the ground. Regaining his composure, Attell drew blood from Herrera shortly after. The eighth belonged to Attell, who managed to connect with a solid left that angered his rival. Despite his combatant's rage and rallies, Abe managed, and wisely so, to stay out of range. Attell turned up his game in the ninth, dispatching some sharp lefts to Herrera's neck and face, again careful to maintain a safe distance.

The final rounds were yawners, with little action or damage. Even if Herrera occasionally chased his opponent around the ring, he was firing wildly and coming up empty, or hitting only air—a bit humiliating for a fighter with over forty professional battles. When the end came, Referee Eddie Smith signaled to Attell as the points winner.

Coincidentally, Herrera would leave one Attell for another, Caesar. The Bakersfield fighter would knock out the older Attell in the third round of his next fight on November 2, then kayo him one round sooner on November 21. This is certainly no slight to Caesar, as Herrera kayoed nine of thirteen opponents in 1902.

It was seasoned bantamweight champion Harry Forbes who stared across the ring at Abe Attell in Chicago on November 10. The man who handed Attell his first professional loss was back for a rematch, and Attell couldn't have been happier. Time to vindicate a defeat, even if it wouldn't be easy. The Rockford, Illinois, fighter now had some title defenses under his belt to support his claim. It had been over a year since the pair last met, when Forbes took the decision in St. Louis. Both fighters were a little bit more polished now. Attell's progress we have witnessed, while Forbes was routinely disposing of his adversaries. Foes such as Tommy Feltz (a title defense), Kid Goodman, and Maurice Rauch had all been on the back end of decisions.

Under Illinois law there was a six-round limit—hardly enough time for either combatant to break a sweat, let alone exhibit an arsenal of punches, but it was a match and a good one at that. The American Club hosted the limited-round affair that attracted considerable interest despite not being a title defense. But it was due to go the distance, unless either fighter made a major error. For Attell, that would be getting caught with one of Forbes's dynamite-packed punches; as for the latter, losing his composure and opening himself up to the perfect punch.

The fight went off precisely as expected, ending in a six-round draw. Neither fighter had a scratch after the clash, but both had lined their pockets. An account noted: "Forbes thought he had a shade the best of his bout with the Californian in their six-round contest, while Attell admitted he made a poor showing."[28] Both fighters appeared anxious for a rematch, hopefully at a greater distance, and even willing to fight in St. Louis. According to the same source, "Forbes wants to fight at 118 pounds, but that is where a hitch will likely occur, for Attell is getting heavy and can no longer fight his best at that weight."[29]

Some of the Chicago pugilists had been complaining that the "fighters who mounted to higher positions in the pugilistic work, through reputations built up in St. Louis, are now getting easy money in Chicago."[30] Matchmakers loved the new blood because it generated interest, and the fighters enjoyed the chance to fight once a week or so at six rounds. A novice fighter need only be reminded that it's not the number of matches, but the quality of matches, that brings titles.

In his final engagement of the year, Abe Attell outpointed Buddy Ryan of Chicago in the Windy City. The six-round contest took place on December 8. The *St. Paul Globe* discerned: "Attell made a running fight of it. In the third round, however, Ryan, after a hard chase, cornered Attell and put him down with a left hook to the jaw. Attell took a count of nine and got to his feet without showing any ill effects from the blow."[31] Abe then went on to dominate in the closing rounds using his exceptional left jab. In the end, it was Attell by points.

In Monte's Corner

Early in 1902, amateur boxer Monte Attell was flying beneath the horizon, so to speak, of the Pacific Association of the Amateur Athletic Union in order to avoid questions regarding his fight status. Having taken part in the San Francisco Athletics Club's regular monthly contests, not to mention others including the Hayes Valley Club's amateur boxing exhibitions and events conducted by the Ariel Rowing Club, Monte was breaking even against opponents such as Joe O'Brien, Barney Driscoll, Pete Carroll, William Tardelli, Mike Maher and Al Mejia. But like his brother, Monte had his sights on higher ground. The question was just when to go pro. That answer came in August when the *Call* reported: "At a meeting of the registration committee of the Pacific Association of the Amateur Athletic Union last night Monte Attell was declared a professional. The busy boxer was unable to satisfy the committee as to the nature of his prizes and the disposition he has made of them. Attell has been fighting regularly, sometimes twice a week for a year or more."[32] By July, the sixteen-year-old Attell already held the 100- and 105-pound championships of San Francisco and the Pacific Coast. Unlike his brother Abraham, he was a scrapper who rushed in after an opponent with both hands blazing.

"He is a biff-bang sort of a fighter," claimed Abe to a St. Louis reporter, "and he goes in at his man from the start. I used to fight him myself in training practice on the coast, and I never could make him quit. He was much lighter than me, of course, but he could take anything I gave him."[33]

For Monte, three fights and fourteen rounds would mark his first year as a professional, according to most sources. Just the name Attell would work to his advantage, since Abraham had made a notable climb up the featherweight division, but Monte wanted more. Monte shared the handsome characteristics of his siblings, but at a lighter weight (118 pounds). While he certainly was very proud of his brother, the younger Attell wanted to establish his own ground, and his own reputation. This he hoped to do in the bantamweight division.

In the only change of lineal champions, Joe Gans won the world lightweight championship by knocking out Frank Erne in the very first round on May 12 at Fort Erie, Ontario, Canada. Gans, an African American boxer, born in Baltimore, Maryland, then successfully defended the title five times by the end of the year. James J. Jeffries (heavy), Tommy Ryan (middle), Barbados Joe Walcott (welter), Young Corbett II (feather) and Harry Forbes (bantam), all stayed atop their respective divisions.

Other notable fights of 1902: in a clash between two former featherweight champions, Terry McGovern knocked out Dave Sullivan in the fifteenth round of their February 22 fight in Louisville, Kentucky; Tommy Ryan, in his last middleweight defense, knocked out Kid Carter in the sixteenth round of their September 15 clash, also at Fort Erie; and future lightweight champion Battling Nelson, having himself hit the canvas seven times, floored opponent Christy Williams forty-two times, in a December 26 "knockout extravaganza" in Hot Springs, Arkansas.

In his second consecutive year of battling over one hundred rounds, Abraham Attell brawled eight times, picking up five victories, two draws and his second loss. It was the first year that he did not battle in the City of San Francisco. Attell clashed with two opponents, Broad and Abel, in consecutive bouts, something he had done before and seemed comfortable with. Despite the Yanger loss, it was a solid performance by the fighter and nothing to feel ashamed about. And while numerous concerns remained regarding Abe Attell's future, the biggest question was: could his management steer him to a championship?

1903

Technology, both in communication and transportation, did its best to transform the City of San Francisco in 1903. The first electronic message was sent across the 2,610 mile Pacific Cable from Honolulu to the city; the first electric trolley began running from San Francisco to San Mateo; and the first transcontinental automobile trip, which began in the city, finally arrived in New York City three months later. Possessing talent, brilliance and capability, not to mention being "clever," seemed to be popular assets in a variety of fields.

The first fight of the year for Abe Attell came on January 29, and it was against a familiar face, his old neighbor, Eddie Hanlon. The event also marked his return home; he had not fought in his hometown since January 26, 1901. In San Francisco, as in many cities, a bout needed to be licensed, and the San Francisco Club had secured the permit for a battle at Woodward's Pavilion. In fewer than ten professional fights, the scrappy

Hanlon, who met Attell back in 1900, had created a reputation for himself as a tough competitor. Born Charles Walter in San Francisco, "Cute Eddie" had fought, and won, over the likes of Maurice Rauch, Kid McFadden and Maxie Haugh. The fighters would battle for fifty percent of the receipts at 122 pounds, the scales confirmed at a 3 o'clock afternoon weigh-in at Harry Corbett's, the popular poolroom at Ellis and Powell.[34]

Betting was brisk, as both local boys had a strong fan base. The *Call* previewed the fight, and of course, the odds: "It is expected that the boxers will be at even money before they enter the ring. Ike Bloom of Chicago made one bet of $1,000 to $800, with Attell the favorite. At the track (a place frequented by both participants) some friends of Hanlon made him favorite at 10 to 7 in their eagerness to get their money down."[35]

The pre-fight hype was strong, but was cautious not to disparage either fighter: "In meeting Attell, cute little Eddie Hanlon will be up against the toughest proposition that he has ever tackled: Attell has won from such men as George Dixon, Buddy Ryan, Kid Abel and others, and he gave Benny Yanger the hardest kind of argument. Attell is not what might be termed a knocker-out, still he has a punch that is far from being a love-tap, as a good many imagine."[36]

Comparing Attell to Jim Corbett, by noting that it was the latter's "extreme clever-ness" that him helped win the heavyweight championship, the newspapers declared that much was anticipated from the former. "In Attell, Hanlon will find a worthy opponent, and one that he must expect to give him a decidedly hard run for the money."[37] A quick and decisive win by either man would no doubt put him in line for a match the following month against Young Corbett II.

The *Butte Inter Mountain* witnessed: "The fight was fast from the start and was the most scientific seen here in many months. Hanlon was the aggressor during the early stages of the fight. He played for Attell's stomach and the little Hebrew came back with straight left jabs for the face. Attell didn't seem able to hurt the man and was able to avoid severe punishment through his extreme cleverness."[38] Attell seemed to pick up the pace during the last five rounds and it may have confirmed the draw for him.

In the end, neither fighter showed any sign of damage, and the twenty-round deci-sion was popular. Also noted by the newspaper: "A telegram from Young Corbett chal-lenging the winner was read at the ringside and was met with applause. Attell's manager stated after the fight that he would post $1,000 with Harry Corbett for his man to meet Young Corbett and that he was willing to bet that amount on the side his man would win."[39] An Attell-Corbett match, in the eyes of countless fight fans, would be the perfect draw, as both men were extremely skillful and each possessed a style all his own. The *Republic* went on to prognosticate:

> Corbett can send in slashing swings in a manner calculated to keep Attell on the jump straight through, while any one of these blows, if it lands, will dispose of Attell. The latter will depend on his speed to out-sprint and outpoint the champion. Such a contest should furnish a scientific display at least, no matter how much disapproval it might excite in the breasts of old timers, or those who like to see two men stand up and exchange blow for blow.[40]

But in the end, it was Eddie Hanlon, not Attell, who would be matched against Young Corbett II. At this point, how could one not believe that Corbett was ducking Attell?

Held on February 26, at Mechanic's Pavilion in San Francisco, their twenty-round confrontation did not, however, end up in a decisive win. Fans of the sweet science do indeed prefer binary conclusions to their distance affairs. Instead, the Corbett v. Hanlon bout, a clean and scientific battle, which was billed for the world featherweight title (130 pounds), ended in a draw. As the *St. Paul Globe* saw it, "Young Corbett clearly demonstrated to the immense crowd present that he has not gone back, as some sporting writers would have the public believe. Hanlon also showed that the high opinion in which he has been held by California boxing enthusiasts has been justified."[41]

With such a low frequency of fights, many were wondering, just where was Abraham Attell? Well, you could have found him at the Central Theater over on Market Street, near Eighth. There, he and brother Monte were sparring three rounds in the second act of the show, *Boy Wanted*, during the first week of February. Prices were reasonable at ten to fifty cents for evenings and ten, fifteen and twenty-five cents for matinees. Fighters love an audience, and it sure beats getting pounded around in a ring.

What many believed would happen did: Governor Yates announced that he would no longer permit boxing bouts to be conducted anywhere in Illinois. The fight game was pushing its limits of acceptance, or that fine line between sport and barbarism. The termination of boxing in Chicago, an anticipated decision, had already led to an exodus of the best men in the lighter classes, including Attell. Coming to the forefront of the pugilistic world would be three markets: Fort Erie, St. Louis and San Francisco.

Word came on March 4 that the San Francisco Athletic Club had matched Abe Attell with his friend Eddie Toy in a charity event. The twenty-round confrontation was scheduled for March 12, in Woodward's Pavilion in San Francisco. The fighters would weigh in at 130 pounds ringside, Attell obviously conceding several pounds at the mark. Adding a bit more interest in the event, as the *Call* stated: "For preliminaries Mississippi, Joe Macias' colored wonder, and Monte Attell will box ten rounds."[42] The event, with all its local association, was shaping up to be an extravaganza.

For Abe it was an opportunity to pick up some needed rounds, not having fought since January 29; and for Eddie it was a chance to add a name to his fight record, which up until the previous year was far from impressive. As anticipated, Abe was given the twenty-round decision victory over Eddie Toy. Yes, it was easy money, but more importantly it was for a very good cause: The McConnell Benefit—all proceeds from the proceeding were given to the mother of injured fighter Frank McConnell. As Toy entered the battle overweight, all bets were off. It was further agreed that if Attell remained standing in the end, he would be deemed victorious. Many notables were there on hand to support one of their own, including Terry McGovern, Young Corbett II and Jimmy Britt.

Slow from the start, the battle didn't ignite until the halfway mark. It was then that Toy tried to rough things up a bit with Attell, through the usual shoving and head butting. Immediately, in fact several times, Referee Alex Greggains, another familiar face, warned the fighter about his behavior.[43] In the seventeenth, Attell, having had enough, dropped Toy with a solid combination to the jaw, but he was saved from what appeared to be a sure knockout by the bell.

In the undercard, Monte Attell worked six fast rounds to a draw with Mississippi; it was agreed upon that if both were still standing at the end that the fight would be declared even. Although Attell was forced around the ring by Mississippi, he beat him to the punch in nearly every instance. A newspaper account recalled, "He cut the colored boxer's eyes, nose and mouth, but could not put him out. In the third round Mississippi floored Attell with a swing to the jaw. He stayed down seven seconds."[44] The incident persuaded Monte to keep his distance the rest of the bout. Overall, it was a wonderful evening of boxing and underscored the commitment the San Francisco community had for each other.

When Abe Attell reached St. Louis on Thursday, July 23, he immediately met with Charley Haughton of the West End Club. The result was *the* match—finally, as the process had gone through a confusing on-again, off-again cycle for weeks—a twenty-round battle with Johnny Reagan scheduled for September 3, before the club.[45] The newspapers noted, "Regan [as it too was often misspelled] and his manager, Mal Doyle, were perfectly willing for the fight, and had a standing offer to Attell to go any distance at any weight. When Abe reached the city, therefore, there was no delay. The affair was concluded in a hurry, and Attell departed for the Autenreith Hotel at Clayton to seek training quarters."[46]

The press thought Abe looked good, perhaps a few pounds heavier. The fighter stated that he had taken things easy for the past year, thus allowing him to "keep ahead of the Chicago races.... Incidentally, while conversing at the club, he displayed a roll of bills that made the eyes of the attendants at that institution bulge out in surprise."[47] For Attell, the greatest risk at the track was not taking any. After the battle, if another match could not be made for Attell, he intended to depart for San Francisco. There he expected to witness the Corbett-Jeffries battle and then either train through the winter, or possibly set up a business. Later, he would talk about the period as a six-month vacation.

Johnny Reagan trained at his St. Louis quarters over on South Street. Following his last battle, which was against Clarence Forbes (whom he nearly knocked out; Forbes's seconds threw up the sponge in the seventh round), Reagan was in fine shape and anxious to settle matters with Abe. It was Attell's belief that he secured the championship by forfeit from Terry McGovern, while Reagan also claimed the title, thus the need for resolution.

In a contest billed as the decider for the vacant world's featherweight championship, weight 122 pounds ringside, Abe Attell took the decision over Johnnie Reagan of New York. Clever and fast was the name of the game for both fighters, as Reagan's improved defensive skills—a scenario Attell was unaccustomed to—impressed many early in the bout. According to one observation, "Attell was unable to land an effective blow, while on the other hand Reagan repeatedly sent his left and right to Attell's head and stomach. Attell seemed clearly beaten for the first fifteen rounds, but in the sixteenth Abe sent in a left and right which shook Johnnie up considerably, and the tide then changed to the Californian's favor."[48]

Attell then took the better of the following rounds. In the nineteenth round, Abe pounded Reagan into the ropes, and while the fighter fought back, there simply was no power left in his punches. After the twentieth round, which was even, the decision went to Attell; many felt a draw would have been a more appropriate call.

Early in his career, you could always ascertain when Attell had too much free time by just reading the newspapers. Abe, unlike a fighter such as Battling Nelson, wasn't one to stir up the beat reporters, unless, of course, it was to his advantage. Early in December he made the suggestion that a light featherweight class be formed. His reasoning was that the featherweight limit of one hundred and fifteen pounds had been raised to almost any weight and was not being adhered to. Attell pointed out at that when Dixon had the feather crown he was forced to fight inside 122 pounds, or relinquish the title. Then, along came Terry McGovern, who did nothing but steadily increase the weight to meet his own needs.

Attell then gave his overview of the division, fighter by fighter, to the *Indianapolis Journal*:

Young Corbett is fighting at 128 or 129 pounds and claiming the championship; Benny Yanger is between 128 and 130 pounds; Eddie Hanlon claims he is the featherweight champion at the same weights as Corbett; Terry McGovern is weak at 126 pounds; "Kid" Broad is a big lightweight at 130 pounds; Tommy Mowatt could make 126 pounds, but prefers 128 and a side bet of $500; Tim Callahan is a lightweight and a big mystery; Hughey McFadden is legitimate at 124 pounds; Hugh Murphy is a tough man who can not do better than 128 pounds; Aurelio Herrera is simply a lightweight and Tommy Sullivan can't do better than 126 pounds. These were the artificial featherweights in the eyes of Abe Attell.[49]

Now to the real featherweights, Attell continued:

Abe Attell [mentioning himself in the third person] has fought everybody and anybody within ten pounds of his weight. His record stands alone as the greatest of any of the little fellows, despite his defeats at the hands of bigger men; Frankie Neil has made a wonderful record with everybody he fought. A lot of people have thought they beat him, but he always got away with the decision. He can beat almost anybody; Harry Forbes is a legitimate featherweight. Has fought for years in the bantam class, but now says he cannot make 116 pounds any more; Tommy Feltz is a tough youngster, whose best weight is 122 pounds and is a tough match for any of them. He was beaten the other night by Joe Cherry. Good and strong, he can hold his own with champions; Joe Cherry is a recent discovery, whose defeat of Tommy Feltz boosted him to the top notch.... Johnny Reagan is one of the hardest men in the business.... He is one of the most clever men that ever put on a glove, especially in a long fight; Billy Rotchford is thought by many to be a "dead one" but a pretty tough fellow for any of them; Kid Herman can make 122 pounds and is willing to do it. He is a lively one, and can satisfy anybody at a route of six to twenty rounds. As for Kid Abel, the same applies to him ... and Kid Goodman can make 122 pounds at ringside and be strong, and is one of the real good men of the country at that weight....[50]

So, could Attell sell the idea of a heavy feather or small lightweight division? Or was there simply a need for regulation? Regardless, Abe's assessment—or verbal jab at McGovern—was an interesting glimpse into the division.

The day after Christmas, the McGovern team got an unexpected present when the *Butte Inter Mountain* printed:

Abe Attell stated that Joe Humphries, who is employed by Sam Harris in the management of Terry McGovern, has asked him to lay down to Terry and that he was willing to pay almost any price for the favor. That has caused some speculation as to how many fights the Brooklyn Terror really won on the square, as it is well known that Joe Gans laid down to the little champion.[51]

Nothing like stirring up a bit of controversy to begin the New Year.

In Monte's Corner

Six fights, tallying about 35 rounds, gave Monte Attell some serious exposure. The fighter had found himself on some impressive undercards, even managing to appear on the same card with Abraham. He also worked with some very talented boxers, including Benny Yanger and Young Corbett II, gaining an invaluable ring education. Having yet to experience a loss, Monte was optimistic about his future and getting stronger with each passing day. Assisting his brother with his theater appearance, the young man also learned a valuable lesson: profit without pain was not such a bad idea.

Changes in the lineal champions found Bob Fitzsimmons atop a new division, that of the light heavyweights. Jack Root was the inaugural champion, but lost the title to George Gardiner in July. Then, on November 25 in San Francisco, Gardiner lost the title to ex-middle and heavyweight champion Fitzsimmons after 20 rounds. Frankie Neil defeated Harry Forbes in San Francisco by a second-round knockout to take the world bantamweight championship. Young Corbett, having moved to the lightweight division in December 1902, then appeared to vacate the feather division, leaving many claimants scrambling for clarification. On March 31, in San Francisco, Corbett decisively put away ex-champ Terry McGovern with an eleventh-round knockout. Abe Attell then claimed a portion of the featherweight title.

Other notable fights of 1903: A James J. Jeffries tenth-round knockout of James J. Corbett in San Francisco on August 14 sent the latter into retirement; and, in a non-title bout, lightweight champion Joe Gans lost to a stronger Sam Langford in fifteen rounds at Boston.

Sixty rounds and only three fights left Abe Attell with two victories and a draw. In retrospect, it proved to be one of the most unproductive years in the fighter's career. And it came at a time when he should have been one of the most active fighters in the division instead of a procrastinating pug. If he was charting a path toward the title, this wasn't it. It was time to manage Attell to the next level, or risk the chance that he would be matched out of the mix.

CHAPTER THREE

The Triad to Legitimacy, 1904

"Since the night that I won over Dixon I have never knocked a man out, but I have defeated many on decisions through my cleverness."[1]—Abe Attell

For a record twenty-three days it rained in the month of March 1904, poured as if it were washing away the sins of every San Francisco resident, and then, in what many considered a sign of the apocalypse, the city recorded the hottest day in its history. It was on September 8, when the mercury reached a sizzling 100.2 degrees. Despite the conditions, construction seemed to be reaching a pinnacle, as the Grant Building, Atlas Building, and Pershing Hall were only a few of the new buildings dotting the landscape. For Abe Attell, who spent much of his time in the Midwest, it was one of the rare times he was happy to be away from home.

Known for his defensive stratagems, Attell felt a need to curtail some of the critical opprobrium regarding his knockout skills. To achieve this he sat down with the press before his first fight of the year. Recognized as one of the best fighters on the West Coast for several years before venturing east to improve his opportunities, not to mention his finances, he had a reputation of disposing of his opponents early. One to four rounds were all it typically took to conclude a contest—a systematic, short-order approach. But now, he had turned his back away from the strategy.

"It was then my style to jump from my corner and rush at my opponent with the intention of putting him out of business as quickly as possible," Attell claimed to an Indianapolis reporter, describing his early days in the ring. "I was a pretty good fighter in those days, but I was not clever like I am now."[2]

Fighting in preliminaries, it was time for a change, which is part of why the fighter headed to Denver. Attell continued:

> I had not acquired the ability to side-step and block blows that is one of the chief requirements of a clever boxer. I was at ringside in Denver the night [August 16, 1901] that Young Corbett gained the decision over George Dixon in a ten-round bout. I watched the two fellows very closely, as at that time Dixon was probably the cleverest blocker in the world. Young Corbett was also very clever, and I was desirous of learning something from that fight. I noticed how Dixon blocked blows with his elbows and arms, always keeping his face and body protected, and I also noticed that Young Corbett did not try to wade in and make a finish of it in a round or two. I got to thinking about the matter, and decided that I would become a clever boxer instead of a fighter who depended upon the knockout punch to win fights.[3]

When learning of the opportunity to fight Dixon, Attell was exhilarated. He trained hard and worked on the shielding methods he had witnessed. And while every fighter enters a competition confident, Attell understood who was standing across from him; overconfidence could be a death sentence against a fighter like Dixon. So too could be intimidation, and Attell wanted no part of that; he did not fear injury or harm from any man, not even Dixon. Fighting the Canadian boxer at his own style, Attell hoped for the best, and that proved to be two draws and a victory. The fighter continued to reflect:

> Since the night that I won over Dixon I have never knocked a man out, but I have defeated many on decisions through my cleverness. I defeated Kid Abel twice and won from Aurelio Herrera, the only man that ever knocked out Kid Broad, in fifteen rounds. I fought two draws with Harry Forbes, the man I am to box in Indianapolis, and won over Buddy Ryan. I defeated Hanlon in four rounds, and later fought a twenty-round draw with him. I have also defeated several other boxers without knocking them out.[4]

Two 122-pound men acknowledged for being the most scientific boxers in their class, Abe Attell and Harry Forbes, were the feature bout at the first boxing carnival of the season hosted by the Indianapolis Athletic Club on January 4. The ten-round clash was held at the Auditorium polo rink on Virginia Avenue, and according to the club: "It will not be a championship battle, a prize fight, or slugging match. The club has never promoted a prize fight and its contracts with the boxers stipulate that the referee shall stop the contest should it become in the least brutal, or should one man have a decided advantage."[5] This fine line, not easy to sustain, needed to be drawn to avoid intervention by the authorities, and the club wisely accomplished this through advanced newspaper coverage.

Thanks to the media tactics, as noted by the *Call*, the contest took place without interruption:

> Harry Forbes and Abe Attell sparred ten rounds to a draw here (Indianapolis) tonight. The men fought fiercely in the last five rounds, but the seven-ounce gloves used prevented much damage. Forbes was the instigator in the first few rounds, and after the sixth added strength and punching power to his skill at defense. He made such a vigorous showing against Attell in the tenth round that many thought Forbes should have the decision.[6]

Although neither fighter scored a knockdown, the crowd of 3,000 spectators seemed to enjoy every minute. The fight completed a trilogy for the two, but not in the way either would have hoped—they wanted a finish fight to determine the better boxer. Having amassed a local following, Attell was happy to build on the Midwest momentum by staying in Indiana.

On January 25, inside the auditorium polo rink, and in front of the Indianapolis Athletic Club, spectators sat patiently—if there is such a condition at a boxing match—through three preliminaries in anticipation of the main event: Abe Attell of San Francisco versus Maurice Rauch of Chicago. For Attell the fight made sense as it was in Indianapolis, and a sound warm-up for another battle against Forbes, scheduled for St. Louis on February 1; this time the honors included a featherweight title claim. The crowd was comparatively small in light of the talent, but not considering the conditions: a cold spell, combined with a terrific snowstorm and a wreck on the Virginia Avenue line, made streetcar service nearly impossible. Attell's new manager, Ike Bloom, noting that there was little fortune to a house his team had a percentage of, then had to make a difficult decision: does he let his fighter box for such a weak purse, or does he demand more money before the fight? Bloom chose the latter and demanded a figure that the club would not meet. Incensed by the tactic, the organization opted to refund the money to its patrons. The local newspaper concluded:

Attell claimed that he would not take a chance on injuring his hands against Rauch [with the house as it stood], as he is [soon] matched to meet Harry Forbes in St. Louis. It would have been necessary for him to have boxed hard to have won the decision against Rauch and he said he could not take a chance.... He thought more of that than carrying out his part of the agreement.[7]

The debacle was clearly the fault of Attell's management, who structured the deal that forced the cancellation. After all, it was January in Indiana.

Every fight fan was ready for it: Abe Attell tackling Harry Forbes, who was finally putting the 120-pound featherweight title (an ambiguous assertion that both Jimmy Britt of California, and Brooklyn Tommy Sullivan, took issue with) on the line in a distance affair. It was twenty scientific rounds, or so it was believed, before the West End Club in St. Louis.[8] Planned for February 1, the Monday evening event would also celebrate the opening of the West End Club's new coliseum. Excitement filled the air as many considered it one of the most evenly matched affairs in years and the perfect event to draw interest to the venue. Attell's supporters were optimistic, figuring their fighter would simply outpoint Harry. They understood Abe wasn't a mixer, or a heavy hitter for that matter, so speed would be his biggest asset. As for the Forbes delegation, well, they were equally confident that Harry could wear down Abe, then connect with a fight-ending shot.

Setting aside all speculation, or so it appeared, was an Attell punch that landed perfectly on the jaw of Forbes in the fifth round. Spectators arose to their feet dumbfounded—as stunned by the blow as by its apparent devastation. Many watched in disbelief as Harry rolled to the floor after the wallop. Awaiting the resurrection, screaming fans from every corner of the venue demanded an immediate recovery. When it became clear that would not be the case, his fans just gasped. They watched in vain as Forbes struggled against the count, but he could not beat it. Just as the count hit "ten," a towel from his corner came sailing into the ring. It was too late to surrender. Their man was out.

From this point forward, every sportswriter in the country cried, "Foul!" Account after account appeared in dailies claiming that Abe Attell and Harry Forbes had faked their recent fight. Regardless of the fact that many agreed that Abe had a clean record, they also concurred that Forbes did not. Specific incidents came to mind, such as one the previous summer in Salt Lake, when Forbes was said to have agreed to let a local fighter go ten rounds to improve his reputation. The anticipated large gate receipts could then be divided up accordingly. Even though the fight never came off, the story haunted Forbes.

Two days later, the *St. Louis Republic* reported: "The grumblings of discontent found greater force when it was noised about that Danny Lynch, the man who engineered the notorious fight between Tom Sharkey and Bob Fitzsimmons on the Pacific Coast, was in St. Louis, and was betting rather too freely on Attell and offering all sorts of odds when he could get his money on in no other way."[9] Also, the newspaper claimed, "The local betting took a queer trend the night of the fight, and it was pointed out that some of Forbes's friends were betting freely on Attell. This was taken as a suspicious circumstance, despite the fact that Al Lippe, who handled Forbes for this fight, was reported to have bet $1,000 in St. Louis on his man."[10]

In another article, the paper printed a Forbes perspective:

"I knocked myself out. It wasn't Attell that put me away." That was the statement made by Harry Forbes yesterday morning [February 2] when he departed for Chicago. The former bantam champion claims that the blow, which stowed him away in the West End Club ring would not have hurt him had he been facing [looking at] Attell at the time.... "I was dazed and dizzy and simply had no control over myself."[11]

He then went on to stress how he had not positioned himself properly against his opponent.

As for Attell, he gave his observation to the *St. Louis Republic*:

His cleverness at boxing was never so manifesting as when he faced the hard-hitting Forbes Monday. Several of the blows Abe sent in were hard enough to stagger anybody his weight, and there is no question that he can wear down any opponent of his weight with these, if he can land them squarely. Even if he has not yet acquired the ability to land a single knock-out punch, as Forbes does, Abe has shown sufficient punching power to make it seem likely that knock-outs will be more conspicuous on his record hereafter than before.[12]

In a sign of the times, two paragraphs down from these comments we read:

One move agreed upon in Chicago by boxing promoters is in the matter of sending white men against Negroes in bouts. While the black fighters will not be barred, it is understood that they will hereafter be sent only against men of their own color. Adverse sentiment aroused when a Negro punishes a white man badly is said to be the reason for this ordinance.[13]

Such bigotry and injustice prompt the Goethe quote, "There is nothing more frightful than ignorance in action." One can only imagine how far the sport, yet alone society, might have progressed had not such intolerance existed. Some larger cities however, were experiencing change, according to the U.S. Census Bureau. For example, the African American population of Philadelphia—a city Attell would visit for the first time at the end of the month—increased from almost 32,000 to over 210,000 between 1880 and 1930, as part of the Great Migration out of the rural South to northern and Midwestern industrial cities.

On February 18, Abe Attell agreed to substitute for a sick Tommy Mowatt and oppose Kid Herman in Chicago at the Ninth Ward Athletic Club.[14] Herman Landfield, a.k.a. Kid Herman, was a competitive featherweight from Canada, who was making a name for himself in the Midwest. Having already held victories over Tommy Sullivan, Austin Rice, Jack McClelland and Clarence Forbes, Herman was confident, but so was Abe—only a handful of days from his twentieth birthday. A victory, as he knew, would make the perfect birthday gift.

To stay the limit (the fight was only six rounds) against Herman, Attell wasn't shy about letting his opponent do most of the fighting. That Herman could corner Attell repeatedly was not only exemplary of his talent, but also a bit of a concern. The Canadian's problem, however, was his inability to finish his stationary foe. Attell was just too slick, with far more defensive skills. Offensively, Attell attacked with his straight lefts while using his left jab as a rudder. And, while his remaining arsenal proved less effective against Herman, the overall package was sufficient to gather Attell the win.

Meanwhile, back home in San Francisco, an arrogant Young Corbett, who was training for his February 29 skirmish with Dave Sullivan, began spouting off against "The Little Hebrew":

Abe Attell is about the softest thing I know of and I accept his challenge to fight. He can name his own time and the other conditions of the meeting are to be as he stated in his challenge to me. It is laughable that he claims the featherweight championship, says the correct weight for it is 122 pounds and yet wants to meet me at any weight. Why does he not show some consistency? If he can induce some club here or somewhere else to offer a purse for a meeting, he is on as soon as I hear of it.[15]

The Intercity Boxing Carnival at the National Athletic Club was proud to announce the perfect main event for the City of Philadelphia, Abe Attell against Young Erne. For the match between Attell and a hometown favorite, a large crowd was expected and it did not disappoint on Saturday, February 27. To even greater delight, every bout on the card went the limit, with the best match of the evening, at least to some, being that of Philadelphia's Danny Dougherty versus Tommy Murphy. But that being said, the crowd cheered loudly for "Yi Yi" Erne.

Content to let Abe handle the first three rounds, Erne commenced his assault in the fourth. He began rushing Attell, who had already accumulated a lead. Hoping to land the big blow, Erne kept the pressure on his rival even if it looked at times that he was getting the worst of it. Attell sent a nose-bleeding Erne down on one knee in both the fourth and fifth rounds, and even though the fighter arose immediately, the damage was taking its toll. Upon its conclusion, the fight entered the record books as a six-round "no decision."

Young Erne, or Hugh Frank Clavin, was from Philadelphia and had been fighting there since 1900. By the time he entered the ring with Attell, he had already fought some good fighters including Young Corbett II, Kid Goodman, and Tommy Love. Because he seldom left the city, and always put on a fine show, he became a popular draw for area athletic clubs such as the Broadway, Kensington, Manhattan, National, and Richmond, to name only a few. He and Attell would complete a trilogy this annum.

From his initial visit to Philadelphia, Attell turned his attention to a spa town that was attracting lots of attention. Known for its hot spring water—believed for centuries to possess medicinal properties, or at least that was the legend among several Native American tribes—not to mention horse racing, illegal gambling, gangsters and saloons, Hot Springs, Arkansas, had a distinctive edge to it. Fighting there for the very first time, and astutely avoiding the West Coast showers, Abe Attell was scheduled for a twenty-round affair against Buffalo's Patsy Haley on March 9.[16] The battle, conducted before Andy Mulligan's popular Whittington Athletic Club, saw Attell weighing in at 122 pounds, with Haley a pound heavier. From the opening bell, Attell took charge and fired at will against Haley. The Buffalo fighter, a bit overpowered, lasted until the fifth round before being knocked out.[17]

Still in Hot Springs, Attell was once again matched with Maurice Rauch. It was surmised that this time the circumstances would be different, and they were; not only did Attell make it into the ring, but he knocked out the Chicago fighter in the sixth round. Granted, not much was expected of the six-round affair—Rauch had only fought once in 1904, and it was in a losing effort against tomato can Willie Spracklin—but it would prove to be the last time Hot Springs boxing fans had a chance to witness Attell's defensive mastery in the their city.

Five days later it was back in Chicago, at the American Athletic Club, where the self-anointed "light featherweight champion" easily outpointed Aurelio Herrera in a six-round affair. As one account noted, "Abe had the better of every round but the second, in which Herrera forced him to the ropes repeatedly and had much the better of the several rallies that cropped up."[18] Even Herrera knew Abe was good at math. "Attell showed wonderful cleverness in ducking, slipping, side-stepping and weaving himself inside of Herrera's leads. He peppered the Mexican [Herrera was born in California] with straight lefts, had him bleeding from nose and mouth early in the first round and more than held him even in the exchanges which Aurelio forced him into during the last half of the battle."[19]

If there was a criticism of Attell, and there was, it was his perceived lack of interest in engagement. Choosing not to engage his antagonist within arm's length, Attell believed, was a defensive tactic. But this action, or lack there of, was incorrectly discerned as cowardly. Simply put, the defensive fighter had yet to gain the respect among the casual follower of the sweet science. Indeed, most spectators would have preferred a toe-to-toe battle between Attell and his hard-hitting opponent, but that would have been suicide for the little fighter—had Herrera connected, Abe might not have woken up until the following morning. A mature fighter knows his limits; only a fool is in breach.

In support of his strategy, not to mention the growing appreciation for the art of defense, was this observation by *The Evening World*: "His [Attell] work on the whole, from a scientific standpoint, was the best seen in years, and while those of the crowd that do not appreciate that sort of work hooted him, students of the game applauded him throughout the mill. He won the decision in six rounds by a city block."[20]

On May 14, Attell was back in the ring, albeit briefly, taking on again Young Erne in a six-round affair in Philadelphia—where else? Again, Attell's defensive dexterity dominated the quick encounter. The no-decision bout, or a sparring exhibition, made for an easy paycheck for both fighters, but not much entertainment for the spectators. And that was a matter of concern. The fighters, who had barely enough time to execute a fight strategy, were hissed for not readily disposing of their rival. Spectators, many of whom felt cheated, desired to see action or least a definitive decision. Overexposure in a market such as this could hurt a fighter. Comprehending this, Attell headed west.

Back to St. Louis on June 2, Attell found himself facing Pittsburgh's Jack McClelland for fifteen rounds at the West End Club.[21] A very large and enthusiastic crowd greeted both fighters as they entered the ring at 9:30 p.m. "McClelland was accompanied by James Mason of Pittsburg [*sic*], his backer; Brooklyn Tommy Sullivan and Jimmy Dunn, George Munroe and Eddy Trendal acted as sponsors for the little Californian."[22]

Attell took charge right from the start, and for the first three rounds displayed the cleverness and ring generalship he was known for. Landing a couple stinging uppercuts, he was swift to remind his rival of his intent. Nevertheless, the momentum from that point until the tenth shifted to McClelland, who was also fighting from a bit of a scientific viewpoint of his own, still slashing and striking, but more cautious than usual. Attell, having not fought over ten rounds this year, looked winded early; he was opting to clinch so much that the referee had to repeatedly warn him to break.

The *St. Louis Republic* concluded, "After the tenth round it was evident that McClelland was much the stronger and more rugged fighter. From the tenth to the thirteenth Jack would walk in almost open in his efforts to coax a lead from the Californian."[23] Watching and waiting for the perfect moment, when McClelland found it, to his credit, he was quick to land a couple of good lefts that sent Attell's head back. Then, in the thirteenth round, McClelland rushed from his corner, spotted another opportunity and took it, landing a forceful shot to the stomach that had Attell writhing with pain and to the floor.

The same source noted the arbiter's actions:

Referee Sharpe sent the men to their corner, and, after allowing them to remain there three minutes, ordered them back to the center of the ring to renew hostilities. After the bout Sharpe claimed that this was done by agreement of the parties concerned, but the action has but one precedent in pugilism. After the fight, Doctor Barish said that Attell had been struck low. "Red" Mason, who was back of McClelland, denied that he agreed to any such action. The spectators were dumbfounded, and vociferous cries for a decision in favor of McClelland in the thirteenth round were heard in all parts of the house.[24]

Attell managed to get through the round once the fighting resumed, the time between rounds assisting the fighter in regaining his wind in the fourteenth. Attell judiciously attempted to avoid his opponent from that point forward, but could not; McClelland was able to catch Attell and pummel him about the ropes.

The newspaper confirmed, "The fifteenth round was all McClelland's and the gong interfered just in time to save him [Attell]. McClelland was loudly cheered when [referee] Harry Sharpe upheld his hand in token of victory for the little Pittsburg miller."[25] It was Abraham Attell's third professional loss, or was it?

Looking at the Marquess of Queensberry rules: the fifth clause provides that if a contestant is knocked down, he must arise unassisted within ten seconds or be considered defeated. The seventh and eighth clauses state that if a foul, which the referee deems deliberate or likely to injure the chances of a contestant, is committed, the offender shall be disqualified. However, the ninth clause claims that the referee shall decide questions not provided for in the rules themselves in case of emergency.

Later, it was claimed by Jim Mason, McClelland's handler, that Attell's party were most arrogant before the fight, taking their victory as a foregone conclusion. McClelland's manager, nauseated by the hyperbole, bit his tongue and awaited any fallout from the pairing; Attell's reputation had a tendency to precede him. True to form, it wasn't until the men were in their dressing rooms just before the fight that Team Attell demanded that the purse be split 60 and 40, an alteration of the terms. Mason pretended, or so he stated to the press, to object, then consented with apparent reluctance. This was what he wanted, believing first that he had a better fighter, and secondly that it would make Attell overconfident.

Three weeks later, and still in St. Louis, boxing fans delighted in a rematch between former stablemates, Brooklyn's Johnny Reagan and Abe Attell. While both fighters promised a respectable showing, evident between the two was the animosity created by their history. For the record: Attell was seconded by Jack Root, George Munroe and Tommy Brandle, while Reagan had the familiar faces of Jack McKenna, Joe Lydon and Billy McGivney looking after him.[26] The twenty-round confrontation started out slow, very slow; it wasn't until the sixth round that Reagan tried to force the battle inside, but wasn't successful.

According to the *Republic*, "In the seventh round Regan [sic] fell to the floor partly from a blow by Attell and partly from slipping. While on the floor Abe stumbled over Regan's leg and both went sprawling on the canvas. They were up in a second and resumed fighting."[27]

Reagan had Attell a bit concerned in the twelfth with numerous blows to the stomach, likely a reminder of the McClelland fight. As Attell tried to retaliate, Reagan did a laudable job of ducking and blocking. As the *Republic* saw it, "The thirteenth round was about even, with Attell having the best of the first part. He landed several swings to John's jaw, but near the end of the round Reagan was right back at him, and his fast showing at the time brought the spectators to their feet. Both tried hard for an ending in the fourteenth, with honors about even. The fifteenth round was fast and furious, the hardest blows being landed in this period."[28]

At the end of the fifteenth round, however, Referee Harry Sharpe gave the decision before the West End Club to Abe Attell. Things may have gone differently for Reagan had he not repeatedly held his opponent—he had a way of holding his opponent's arm with his wrists bent up, a matter that sparked multiple exhortations by Attell to the referee.

The greatest action may have occurred after the fight, when Attell's second Tommy Brandle was so happy with the decision that he threw himself in front of Reagan. The latter couldn't resist the opportunity to land a few solid punches on Brandle's jaw. In a flash, the ring filled with police and spectators. According to one newspaper account, "Referee Sharpe ran after Brandle and held him against the ropes. Joe Lydon was right behind Sharpe and tried to land on Brandle. Lieutenant McKenna swung at Sharpe and landed on his face. The police soon subdued the men, and Brandle was thrown out of the ring. Lieutenant McKenna did not hit Sharpe intentionally, thinking that he was one of the fighters instead of a peacemaker."[29]

Since arriving in St. Louis, Attell had appeared a bit distracted, or just not himself. The transition from six to fifteen rounds, or more, was not going as smoothly as imagined. And while it was exciting traveling across the continental United States, and essentially building a fan base, it was also time-consuming and expensive. But if the competition doesn't want to come to you, what's a contender to do?

The headlines in the *St. Louis Republic* read: "SULLIVAN KNOCKS OUT ATTELL IN FIFTH ROUND."[30]

On October 13, in St. Louis at the West End Club, "Brooklyn" Tommy Sullivan fought Abe Attell for the vacant world featherweight title, or alleged "122-pound championship."[31] The decision was given to Sullivan in the fifth round of a scheduled twenty-round contest when a low left uppercut to the stomach of Attell sent the fighter down for the count. The blow "lifted the San Francisco boxer off his feet and sent him writhing and sprawling on the floor."[32] Cries of foul, from both sides, could be heard as far as San Francisco, but few were listening. Sullivan, who saw legitimacy to the blow but not to the title, did not lay claim to the latter.

The first four rounds were a display of proficiency, some of the best sparring the city had witnessed in ages—fast, furious and with little damage. The crowd thrilled at watching the moves of both fighters, with Attell given a slight edge to that point. Both boxers used their jabs magnificently to control the action and to score when and where they could. When the fifth round came, so too did the decisive, or perhaps indecisive, blow. It was later pointed out: "The battle was the third occasion whereon Attell has claimed a foul in the local ring. In each case his claim has been disallowed."[33]

The only thing clear about the encounter was that fighters should be mandated to wear some protection for the groin region. A shield constructed of leather or aluminum had been the suggestion. Attell, for one, flatly refused, saying it would interfere with his speed and footwork; however, other fighters had harnessed themselves in such equipment with little complaint.

Title talk, often cyclical with its appearance in the sport sections, again bounced to the forefront with this battle. There was nothing to prevent the holder of, say, a bantam title, to raise the weight limit to his weight of choice. Fitzsimmons did it when he lifted the middleweight limit to 158 pounds from 154. Additional classes, as previously mentioned, gradually followed suit, the feathers stepping up thanks to Terry McGovern. A new class was being coined, that of the "light heavyweights."

Playing host to not one, but two Attells on Saturday night, November 19, was the West End Club in St. Louis. Abe took on Young Erne of Philadelphia, and Monte tangled with "Dusty" Miller of Chicago. The bout was initially scheduled for November 17, but Billy McCarney, manager of Young Erne, said his fighter would be arriving late by rail and would not be in peak form, so it was held over until Saturday evening. Abe's affair was slated for fifteen rounds at 120 pounds, while Monte prepared for eight at 115 pounds.

Erne, in his first long fight—so proud of the interval he asked the referee to announce the accomplishment—went the distance, but lost the decision to Abe. Attell did all the leading while Erne covered up. The latter did have two opportunities to get the best of "The Little Hebrew": in the eleventh, he put Attell down for the count of six, but he could not put him away—Abe came back strong. And, in the eighteenth, an Erne right to the jaw dazed Attell, but the Philadelphia fighter did not resume his assault. Erne faded in the last three rounds, at a time when a whirlwind finish might have added greatly to his chances.

The *St. Louis Republic* added, "Whenever Erne cut loose they [audience] showed their approval by wild applause. A hard fighting, mixing man is always popular with the followers of the game. When Monte Attell and Dusty Miller stood up and swapped blows, the spectators were aroused to a high pitch of enthusiasm."[34] As expected, Monte's decision over Miller proved the perfect wind-up for the main event.

Former Senator Dave Nelson was the referee for the Attell versus Erne affair. Still relatively new to the trade, he took his role seriously and was not yet known as a humorist. A friend of Nelson's, who sat front row ringside, was said to have leaned forward in the interval between the nineteenth and twentieth round, and asked: "Well, Dave, how things were going? What chance had Erne?"

"No chance," Nelson was said to have curtly responded.

Rather surprised at hearing so decided an opinion handed down when there was still a possible chance for a knockout by Erne, the friend spoke to that effect.

"I don't think Erne has a chance for a knockout," Nelson is then quoted as saying. "You see, he's an Irishman, but he let the seventeenth round go without cutting loose. If an Irishman can't fight in the seventeenth, he's got no chance in the twentieth."[35]

Ethnicity has always been a factor in the fight game, be it as simple as a moniker, or as complex as

Jewish boxer Joseph Youngs, a.k.a. Tommy Ryan, was considered an excellent boxer-puncher, and many consider him one of the all-time greatest middleweight champions (Library of Congress).

prejudice, such as anti–Semitism. As the *Spokane Press* observed, "It is only within the past few years that members of the [Jewish] race have assumed so many prominent places in athletics. Many are pugilists, and the majority of these are hard men to whip. 'Tommy Ryan' is the recognized middleweight champion for the world. His real name is Joseph Youngs, and he is a Jew. Although preferring an Irish name to fight under, Tommy never denies his nationality."[36] Also, Joe Choynski, Kid Abel, and now the Attells had stepped to the forefront of pugilism.

In his final fight of the year, Abe Attell was matched against Savannah heavy-hitter Tommy Feltz on December 8 at the West End Club in St. Louis.[37] The *St. Louis Republic* previewed the match:

> The contest of Thursday will be a battle of the typical hard hitter against the highly scientific boxer. No one who saw Forbes send his punches into Tommy's face, with all the force he could put behind them, will believe that Attell, admittedly a lighter hitter than Harry, can put the Southern fighter away. Feltz can bore in, at pleasure, and can take all the punches Attell can send. Tommy's supporters argue that if Jack McClelland can reach Attell, Feltz certainly can. They predict a victory for Feltz on this ground.[38]

Feltz arrived a couple of days early to train and was quartered at the St. James hotel, while Attell preferred to train in Chicago. The same source noted, "Both boys are well known here and, by a singular coincidence, each made his best record in the local ring. When Abe Attell fought George Dixon here, it was his first step up the pugilistic ladder. When Tommy Feltz fought Harry Forbes in his first local appearance, even though he went down in defeat, it made his record 'solid' locally."[39]

Attell's strategy would be rushing and outpointing Feltz, while the latter hoped to bore in steadily and gradually wear down his opponent.

The pre-fight hype did little to impact the outcome as Attell was granted the decision at the end of the fifteen rounds. Lackluster and extremely slow, Abe's narrow margin of victory was attributed to his doing most of the leading. The highly anticipated forceful blows from Feltz never emerged. A more appropriate contest might have been which audience member could fall asleep first.

In Monte's Corner

It was an impressive year for Monte Attell as Bobby Johnson handed him his only loss. And in his first trilogy, against Johnny Reagan, Monte picked up all three victories, the most impressive his seventeenth-round knockout on December 22.

Monte was now playing his part in moving the surname of Attell another step closer to West Coast immortality, placing them alongside the McGoverns, Sullivans and the Corbetts. The latter was likely the most familiar, as nearly every living member of the tribe was a well-known character in his own particular branch of sport: James J. Corbett, heavyweight champion; Harry Corbett, who has been mentioned and "is admittedly one of the largest bookmakers and holders of stakes on the Coast; Tom Corbett has not developed in any particular line, other than being generally recognized in baseball and turf circles; and Joe Corbett is well known in baseball,"[40] having played for the Orioles, Cardinals and Senators. If immortality was destined for the Attells, then Monte wanted in.

In the only change of lineal champions, a weakened Joe Gans slipped to the canvas more than once before a heavy-handed Jimmy Britt was disqualified for hitting his opponent while he was down in the fifth round. The fight, which took place in San Francisco on October 31, was billed for the world lightweight title, 133 pounds ringside. There was some dispute as to whether Gans ever relinquished his lightweight crown in 1904. Joe Bowker defeated Frankie Neil in a distance battle to claim world bantamweight title at 116 pounds.

Other notable scraps: On April 30, in San Francisco, Dixie Kid defeated Joe Walcott on a twentieth-round invisible foul. On September 5, in Butte, Montana, Battling Nelson tolerated some powerful punching by Aurelio Herrera to capture a twenty-round decision, and on September 30 in San Francisco, having broken his left elbow in the third round and endured a vicious beating, Joe Walcott somehow managed an incredible draw with lightweight champion Joe Gans. Naturally, both Kid and Walcott victories carried significant speculation regarding the decisions. To infer in boxing is jest, as truth only lies in the punch line, or is it betting line?

An active year for Abraham Attell found the boxer scheduled for fourteen fights, yet battling in thirteen, while compiling over one hundred rounds. Controversy, never far from anything having to do with the game, accompanied Attell like thunder follows lightning—the Rauch debacle, for one, accompanied later by the second Forbes fight. Demoralizing as the associations were, so too were Attell's defeats, his third and fourth career losses—to McClelland and Sullivan respectively. Both casualties called into question any claims the fighter made to any title.

CHAPTER FOUR

Not So Fast, 1905

"In these days when the fighting game is being strangled by fakers and sure thing men, an example should be made of boys of the Attell type, and they should not be allowed to appear before reputable clubs. It is a pity, too, for Abe is one of the fastest and cleverest men in the ring, and Monte is also a good man."[1]—Washington Times

In San Francisco, Eugene Schmitz, president of the Musicians Union, was re-elected mayor, the De Forest Wireless and Telegraph Company established its radio station KPH and began broadcasting from the Palace Hotel, and the bubonic plague, after killing 113 people, appeared to be eradicated. Progress on a variety of fronts, political, technological and biological, was being made, or so it was believed, as the city continued to grow at a brisk pace. As for Abe, he would center his geographic efforts primarily in the East, battling in cities like Philadelphia for his short-distance (six rounds) no-decision fights, and Baltimore for longer-distance (fifteen rounds) decision battles.

The news out of St. Louis was not good. The morning headlines, in newspapers such as the *St. Paul Globe*, read: "Attells Are Barred, Fighters on West End Club's Black List Through Scandal." Certainly not the way a fighter, yet alone a fighting family, wants to begin a new year, but there it was, front and center in a few daily sports sections. The *St. Paul Globe* was one daily that carried the news: "At a meeting of the directors of the West End Club, held last night (December 31, 1904), Abe and Monte Attell, of Chicago; Johnny Reagan, of Brooklyn; John Reid, manager of Reagan, of Brooklyn, and Thomas Smith, who acted as referee in the Monte Attell-Reagan bout of December 15, were suspended from the boxing game until further notice."[2] Several club members were also suspended, but their names were conveniently withheld.

In a brief statement released by President Haughton: "When Monte Attell faced Reagan on Dec. 15, Abe Attell, brother of the bantam, endeavored to place a bet of $100 to $50 on Monte with the understanding that if a draw decision would be given, Abe would win."[3] Thus the action adopted by the board of directors.

When President Haughton caught wind of the wager, he took steps, to thwart the effort. Monte, after going the route, did in fact get the decision. The following morning Haughton questioned Reid, who "finally admitted that they all met in Attell's room at the Lindell Hotel in the afternoon and the matter was fixed up."[4] (The event, as it turned out, would become one of the eeriest preludes in the life of Abraham Attell, but more on that later.) Case closed, correct?

Not so fast. Still not convinced he had enough evidence to condemn the men of questionable work, Haughton, of all things, arranged another meeting between the fighters the following Thursday, December 22. One wonders just whose behavior Haughton happened to be observing. The same source continued, "While the men were in the ring he [Haughton] became satisfied that the go was not on the square. [The reason was not given.] In this mill, Monte knocked out Reagan in the seventeenth round. Satisfied that he had a case, President Haughton laid the matter before the board of directors and action was taken as above."[5]

The incident—the *Topeka State Journal* called it a "joke"—cast a dark shadow on the West End club; it didn't take a cryptologist to read between the lines. Abe Attell had written a letter to Haughton admitting the entire affair, but he and Reid still received six-month suspensions. As for Tom Smith, Johnny Reagan and Monte Attell, it was a resolution of censure. The entire embarrassing affair, which Haughton felt worthy of a public condemnation, might have been better handled privately.

The *Washington Times* carried word that "Jules Hurtig, of Hurtig & Seamon, who is a great lover of the prize ring, has hit upon a novel idea to settle the much discussed question as to who is who in the featherweight ranks. There are several claimants for the honor, but none of them thus far has shown that he is really entitled to be recognized as the real head of this class."[6] So why not fight it out among themselves—Abe Attell, Monte Attell, Harry Forbes, Hughey McGovern, Tommy Murphy, Frankie Neil and Johnny Reagan—in a series of twenty-round bouts a month apart? The idea was a terrific example of just how frustrated fight fans had become with the featherweight division and its inability to clarify itself.[7] For his part, Hurtig was willing to contribute a $300 silver cup or trophy to the winner at between 118 and 120 pounds. Hurtig, a theatrical and burlesque producer, was president of Hurtig & Seamon Enterprises. His association with Mr. Harry J. Seamon was responsible for opening the first music hall in Harlem.

Substituting for Hughey McGovern (Terry's younger brother), Abe Attell opened his ring year with a six-round Philadelphia clash against Harlem Tommy Murphy at the National Sporting Club. The fighters, brawling at 122 pounds (or so it was hoped), would split sixty percent of the gross receipts.

Although no decision could be given in the city, according to the law, a large house nevertheless watched Attell completely outclass his adversary on January 28, in spite of a height and reach advantage for the New York fighter. The *Daily Press* observed, "Murphy fought wildly and was unable to avoid the punishment inflicted by his opponent."[8] Murphy would get his rematch with Hughey McGovern in May, and in a hotly contested six-round battle that the newspapers believed he won.

Moving from "no decision" Philadelphia to Baltimore, Attell was next matched for fifteen rounds against Brooklyn's Tommy Feltz; the two had met only 57 days earlier in St. Louis. This fight, however, took place on February 3, before the Eureka Athletic Club at Germania Maennerchor Hall. Having a lead in every round, Attell outfought his familiar rival from start to finish. Landing both combinations to the face and solid shots to the stomach, Abe wore down Feltz. In the fourteenth round, a powerful left closed Feltz's left eye, leaving the scrappy fighter doing everything possible to stay the limit, which he somehow managed to do. The decision, to no surprise, landed in Attell's favor and was not disputed.

Both fighters were aware that a clean decision meant a workable match with Frankie Neil in San Francisco, according to a letter from Yosemite Athletic Club manager Alex

Greggains. Worth noting: Brooklyn Tommy Sullivan, who picked up the vacant world feather crown by defeating Attell the previous October, remained inactive for the entire year. Commenting before the fight, Attell stated to the *Washington Times*:

> Now let it be known right from the very start that little Tommy Feltz is a mighty tough lad, and that I entertain no idea of beating him in one or two rounds. However, I feel sure that when the smoke clears away I will have surely won. You know that I fight in a pretty fast style, and intend to show the Baltimore people a thing or two tonight at quick boxing. The talk of the decision I received over him being a bit shady in St. Louis will be done away with after tonight.[9]

New York lightweight Harlem Tommy Murphy (circa 1934), who began his professional career in 1903, was a contender in three different divisions: bantamweight, featherweight and lightweight classes (Library of Congress).

Attell was correct, but as a fish is never far from water, a pugilist is never devoid of controversy.

A journey up the East Coast was next for Abe Attell. At Chelsea, in the city of Boston, he would confront the New England featherweight champion, Abraham "Kid" Goodman, in a fifteen-round event at the Douglas Athletic Club. A crowd of nearly 2,800 turned out for the event, held on Attell's twenty-first birthday. Both fighters weighed in at 122 pounds four hours before the battle.

Fighting his fight, Attell was quick and elusive. Goodman, on the contrary, who held recent victories over Art Simms, Chester Goodwin and Austin Rice, appeared a bit lethargic. To most it appeared Attell was a shade better than his hometown opponent. Yet the fight ended in a draw. Many of the spectators felt deceived. Referee Jack Sheehan had been implored several times to remove both participants from the ring. While proof would not immediately confirm speculation, it was generally believed that many of the spectators were correct. The Attell team's tactics had certainly been questioned of late, and three days later the truth surfaced. On February 25, the *Washington Times* printed: "Attell claimed that there was a secret agreement between the men that the fight should be a draw if both were on their feet at the end of the fifteen rounds."[10]

The result was predictable: both Attells were reportedly barred from boxing before the Boston clubs. It was not the kind of birthday gift Albie anticipated.

The *Times* reluctantly stated, "In these days when the fighting game is being strangled by fakers and sure thing men, an example should be made of boys of the Attell type, and they should not be allowed to appear before reputable clubs. It is a pity, too, for Abe is one of the fastest and cleverest men in the ring, and Monte is also a good man."[11]

To no surprise, a small Philadelphia audience watched Abe Attell dance circles around Eddie Hanlon for six rounds at the Industrial Hall on February 24. The latter, the heavier of the two fighters, was ineffective in nearly every circumstance but clinches. The *Evening World* reported:

> The few people present laughed and roared as Hanlon belted the air trying to punch to Attell's face, Attell sometimes being several feet away.... Once while trying to get a punch to Attell, Hanlon, who was wild with excitement, almost knocked the referee down.... Attell took a rest [in the last round] by simply holding Hanlon off and try as he would, Hanlon could not do anything against the cleverness of Abe, who simply laughed at the desperate tactics which Hanlon was trying.[12]

For Albie, it was a quick paycheck before some much-needed time off. Attell, who had broken his nose in a battle with George Dixon three years earlier, claimed it hadn't been set properly. Since it was impacting his breathing, he wanted it reset. For Hanlon, it was off to match with, train for, then battle against Young Corbett II—the June 2 fight, which would go the distance, ended in a points victory for Eddie.

The featherweight championship of Eastern Ohio and Western Pennsylvania was placed on the line, or so it was billed, on April 25, as Abe Attell was scheduled to meet Jimmy Dunn in a twelve-round bout before the Nonpareil Athletic Club of Sharon, Pennsylvania. One wonders if either combatant was even aware of what appeared to be an illusory title. But Attell had been sick, or so the newspapers reported, so the fight didn't take place until May 1. Newcastle's Jimmy Dunn, who had never defeated a fighter with over five career wins, did his best to try to catch Attell, but he was simply outclassed from the start. About 1,000 spectators watched as Attell hardly broke a sweat on the way to a twelve-round draw, with many believing it was a pre-arranged stalemate. They may have been correct, as only eight blows were exchanged in the first round. Even if the fight was on the square, Attell was now haunted by speculation.

Just two years earlier, Henry Ford founded the Ford Motor Company, and it quickly established Detroit's status in the early 20th century as the world's automotive capital. Where there were talented industrial workers, there had to be fight fans. Attell, having never fought in the city, wanted to greet them. Only nine days after his fight with Dunn, Harry Forbes and Abe Attell were matched for a ten-round scuffle at the Light Guard Armory in Detroit. Fighting at 122 pounds ringside, the featherweight limit, the winner hoped to dismiss the title claims made by Young Corbett, who did not once fight within six pounds of the limit. This is why some believe Attell—always ready to defend his belt against all comers at that weight—held the feather title. Forbes, who had outgrown the bantam class, took the fight comfortably at the stated weight and was confident that it would be a great battle.

After ten rounds of tame sparring, Attell picked up the decision over his all-too-familiar antagonist. The large crowd, who began expressing their discontent from the first round, became frustrated when the boxers failed to engage. Many spent the entire fight hooting and hissing, and a large contingent actually left before the fight was half over. A dispirited Attell, despite the victory, would never return to the city.

Signing to fight six rounds at 130 pounds before the National Sporting Club of Philadelphia on May 22, Attell looked up for his next opponent. He found him in Battling Nelson.[13] New York's Willie Lewis was originally scheduled to meet "The Battler," but he could not make weight. With so much being written about the latter, the Philly crowd was eager to see Nelson, who had never fought in the city before. Fan interest was met when Attell, recently dissatisfied with the response he was given in his own weight class, took the fight despite being outweighed by ten to twelve pounds. The Dane's pure fighting style was in stark contrast to the defensive ways of Attell, so the fight was seen as a fast scientific boxer against a rushing, rugged fighter. The *Minneapolis Journal* noted:

> Until within a few minutes of the time when the men entered the ring it was not known whom Nelson would fight. Yesterday [May 22, 1905] morning Attell appeared at the Hotel Scott and weighed in with his clothes on, without raising the beam, which was set at 130 pounds. Attell then demanded that Nelson should also weigh in. This Nelson, whose usual fighting weight is 130 pounds, refused to do. Attell then declared the match off and Kid Herman was substituted. While the crowd, which only about two-thirds filled the hall at prices of from $1 to $5, was witnessing the preliminaries, Nelson and Attell and their managers met in the dressing room. Attell was willing to meet Nelson after a great deal of haggling between the mangers. Nelson ended up remarking: "Put Attell or anyone else on; they all look alike to me."[14]

Nelson, over such a short distance, was no match for Attell's ring craftsmanship. In the first four rounds, Abe jabbed at will and controlled the fight.

The *Times Dispatch* saw it this way: "In the fifth round Attell's strength began to wane. In the latter part of the sixth round, however, Attell recovered himself and was hammering Nelson with rights and lefts when the bell sounded."[15] While ringside saw the bout advantage for Attell, it would enter the books as an "ND6."

As for Nelson, only three fights removed from picking up the world white lightweight title from Jimmy Britt, it was a sound diversion. Attell planned to sail for England in just days, where he expected to take on Jem Bowker.[16] With a backer, and plenty of confidence, Abe was sure of whipping the English fighter if (and it was indeed questionable) he could get a match. The *Topeka State Journal* observed Abe's travel plans:

> The fighter's decision to go abroad was made rather suddenly. Even if he is not successful in getting a match with Bowker, he has no doubt of finding plenty to keep him busy on the other side. He still has a go with the winner of the Britt-Nelson fight in mind. Young Corbett is willing to back him in this matter. "I want to bet $4,000 against $5,000," said Young Corbett, "that Abe Attell can whip the winner of the Britt-Nelson fight, and I am specially anxious to bet it if Britt is the winner, as he will be if the fight comes off as scheduled in the state of California."[17]

Later, the *Salt Lake Herald* noted Abe's return comments: "England is a great country, but it is some distance from Broadway and Forty-second Street—too far, in fact—and that is why I am back. I will return to England in about five weeks, and the next time I come back to New York it will be as a world's champion."[18]

Having returned from the United Kingdom, and not having fought since May, Abraham Attell was given a dose of his own medicine on October 4. He was outclassed by the familiar face of Young Erne for six rounds at the National Athletic Club in Philadelphia. Having noticeably dropped speed, Abe was simply unable to catch Erne, and this frustrated the fighter. Beginning to lose his temper, Abe became a bit rough, even prompting numerous warnings from the referee. A source noted, "There were no knock downs and both fighters were fresh at the conclusion of the bout."[19] For Attell the battle, a no-decision, could not end soon enough.

Attell planned on meeting Jem Bowker of England for the international featherweight championship on November 23, but was informed by letter that the conflict would have to wait, possibly until some time after the first of the year. The *Evening Statesman* reported, "Bowker is to be married and his wife-to-be does not wish to spend her honeymoon nursing him back to health. 'Besides,' Bowker naively writes, 'you might trim me, and I want to be a champion all through my honeymoon.'"[20]

As a Chicago feather and lightweight, Tommy Mowatt had been fighting around the Midwest for the past five years. He was a distance scrapper who fought at the level of competition. Certainly not a "topnotcher," Mowatt was strong as a bull and rushed in like a wild animal, thus making him popular with spectators, but not so popular with many opponents. In his Philadelphia debut on November 8, Mowatt, or the "Fighting Conductor," met Attell, who had been substituted for an injured Young Corbett. For six rounds the duo danced to a no-decision, picked up a nice paycheck, and agreed to carry their battle to another city.

The pair then went on to Baltimore eight days later, to fight before the Eureka Athletic Club at Germania Maennerchor Hall. This time, the longer distance favored Attell, who was much quicker and sharper than in their previous battle. Scrambling to avoid desperate swings by Mowatt, Attell continually worked the jab and slowly battered Mowatt's physiognomy. In the eleventh round Mowatt looked groggy and vulnerable, but the gong saved him. Although both men had been floored by decisive blows, at no time were they close to being knocked out.

Attell's ring rust showed, and although he had met Chick Tucker in a New York exhibition the first day of the month, it did little to prepare him for Mowatt.

A week later, and in his final struggle of the year, Abraham Attell met Kid Sullivan of Washington in a fifteen-round affair, also before the Eureka Athletic Club. The Baltimore crowd watched intently as Sullivan, a local fighter (Washington, D.C.) led most of the fight. Sullivan was certainly talented enough to inflict punishment, just not quick enough to land a decisive knockout blow. The *Evening Star* confirmed the outcome:

At the end of the bout the referee called it a draw, to the general satisfaction of the audience which packed the hall. It would have been called a draw at the end of the bout in any event other than a knockout

Kid Sullivan, bantamweight champion of Canada (Library of Congress).

or disqualification, as the men had agreed for the decision to be rendered a draw if both should be on their feet at the end of the journey. This agreement was made at the insistence of Attell, who held out for it in his dressing room before the battle.[21]

Now, could the fight been a no-decision? A no-decision bout, often abbreviated in the record books as "ND," occurred when a fight was conducted at a place where the laws prohibited a decision. Even so, a no-decision could also be prearranged by both boxers. For example, if both combatants were still standing at the bout's conclusion and there was no knockout, the bout could be scored a no-decision. This raises the question: Why would a fighter battle under such conditions? Money and exposure were the answer. A weaker fighter could expand his reputation and improve his skills. For a reigning champion, it was a means to protect a title. A no decision guaranteed a titleholder that he would not lose his crown by a win on points, yet could make a decent buck by taking the fight.

A draw is based on judging. For instance, if all three judges call the fight even, it is a draw. If one judge favors one fighter, a second judge another, and the third calls the fight a draw, it's a draw. If the referee, as a sole arbiter, determines it even, it's a draw.

Now, gamblers have always loved boxers—and in most cases vice versa—but they also like a winner. So when decisions were deemed illegal, they turned ringside, to reporters or people who could give a consensus result. Printed newspaper decisions became an unofficial result, but decent enough for the gamblers. However, reporters were people too, despite what many believe, and could be prone to the vices of the day. Therefore, not all newspaper decisions could be considered accurate, especially in certain markets—Philadelphia, for example.[22]

A frustrated *Spokane Press* was quick to bury Attell:

Abe Attell's poor showing against Kid Sullivan practically marks his passing from ring activities into the class of formerly-weres.[23] Attell's refusal to go on without an agreement that there should be no decision if both men were on their feet at the end of fifteen rounds and his dilatory tactics in the ring demonstrated that he is no longer the aggressive Abe of old. His punch is no longer steamed over but is about as annoying as a blow in the face from a feather pillow.[24]

This view was printed eighty-three days before Abraham Attell picked up a major title, and twelve years before the fighter hung up his gloves. So much for newspaper assessments.

In Monte's Corner

From a January censure and two challenging fights with Jimmy Walsh in March, to a secret fight against Owen Moran in May and an incredible battle with Harry Tenny in September, it was a memorable year for Monte Attell. The latter event, which took place in Goldfield, Nevada, saw Monte down and out a dozen times, but continually rising for more until finally being put away in the twenty-fifth round.

The *Call* noted the historical event:

The fight was pronounced the greatest ever held in Nevada. He [Attell] was knocked down three times in the last round. He was much the cleverer man, but he lacked strength toward the last. Tenny covered his head with his arms and rested while Attell feebly tried to put him out. Tenny's nose was broken in the fifth round. He bled freely, but simply shook his head and went to it again. Both men were covered with blood and fought like wild men.[25]

Born in Copenhagen, Denmark, Battling Nelson brought great prominence to his Chicago neighborhood of Hegewisch, Illinois, as he ascended the lightweight division (Library of Congress).

Clearly in the bantam mix for the championship, Monte Attell need only sustain himself and wait for his shot.

Changes of lineal champions in 1905: Marvin Hart replaced a retired James J. Jeffries atop the heavyweights by defeating Jack Root with a twelfth-round knockout in Reno, Nevada; Bob Fitzsimmons lost his light heavy crown to Philadelphia Jack O'Brien, who will later relinquish it; and Battling Nelson placed himself atop the lights with a defeat of Jimmy Britt via an eighteenth-round kayo in Colma, California (however, nobody asked Joe Gans). Without a loss, Abe Attell stayed amongst the feather claims, unless of course you speak to a fighter like Jimmy Walsh.

Other notable confrontations: Marvin Hart won a twenty-round disputed decision over Jack Johnson on March 28 in San Francisco; and washed-up former ex-bantam and feather champ Terry McGovern revived boxing experts by dropping Harlem Tommy Murphy four times in the first and only round of their October 18 contest in Philadelphia.

Battling over one hundred rounds for the second consecutive year, Abe Attell took eleven fights, and did not lose a contest. Suspended in St. Louis and essentially barred in Boston, Attell found solace in other cities. Just the same, he was running out of boxing real estate and he knew it. For the second straight year, he did not battle in the city of San Francisco, a hometown that he missed. In Battling Nelson, he engaged in another one of the sport's elite participants—another name to be added to his growing list. But it is also another year in which Abe Attell came under criticism for his negotiation tactics, or his dressing-room holdouts, a factor he had to correct if he was to gain the respect of his peers.

CHAPTER FIVE

As World Champion, 1906

"The fires are spreading rapidly, and unless the wind comes up from the West and blows the flames toward the bay nothing can stop the destruction of the city. The whole north end of the city is wrecked, and the flames are spreading in all directions. In the absence of water the fire department has resorted to the use of dynamite, and buildings are being demolished in hope of staying the conflagration."[1]—Evening Star

At 5:12 a.m. on April 18, 1906, the City of San Francisco had its landscape altered forever by a magnitude 8.2 earthquake.[2] Panic broke out as residents, fearing for their lives, had no place to call safe.

The *Daily Telegram* confirmed the horror:

> The shock lasted three minutes and thousands of buildings were damaged and destroyed. The loss of life is reported great. The City Hall, costing seven million dollars, is in ruins. The terror and excitement are indescribable. Buildings swayed and crashed, burying the occupants. A panic ensued in the downtown hotels. The greatest damage to buildings was on South Market Street, where mostly frame buildings and tenement houses were located. There were fires in every block of that district. Fire is eating its way along Market Street....[3]

An estimated 28,000 buildings were destroyed and 498 blocks leveled, as rescue efforts were hindered by the debris and smoke. One quarter of the city was burning and an estimated 700 people killed. Many of the 30,000 people left homeless turned to Golden Gate Park, not realizing that for many their stay would last well over a year.

For Abraham Attell, perhaps the most memorable year of his life begins in Chelsea, Massachusetts, a working-class community that rests a stone's throw from the city of Boston. Chelsea was a major destination for the "great wave" of Russian and Eastern European immigrants, especially Russian Jews, who came to the United States after 1890. There Attell met local boxer Chester Goodwin on January 15.[4] As a seasoned New England fighter, Goodwin held recent victories over Matty Baldwin and Clarence Forbes, and had fought Tommy Feltz to a draw. He was no tomato can and was not afraid to mix it up for fifteen rounds with a fighter like Attell.

But the fight proved to be a very slow encounter, as both men danced to a distance draw before the Douglas Athletic Club. The *Call* reported, "Goodwin seemed to have the better of the contest up to the tenth round, when Attell came up strong and showed particularly clever work until the finish."[5] It was a sluggish beginning, but that was consistent with Abe's past, as he also opened 1902, 1903 and 1904 with draws.

Removing debris at Third, Kearney and Market Streets following the 1906 San Francisco earthquake (1906) (Library of Congress).

Two days later, Attell was back in New York City, at the Olympic Club, participating in a number of three-round exhibitions. The process kept a fighter sharp while lining his pockets. The beauty of "The City" was that if you needed inspiration, or proof of what success can bring, you need simply to stroll down Fifth Avenue along millionaire's row, lined with great Gilded Age mansions. There were times Attell did precisely that, wondering to himself what his own prosperity might someday bring.

Finding himself at the Auditorium in Portland, Maine, on January 22, Attell tackled human sacrifice Billy Maynard in a fight scheduled for fifteen rounds. Maynard, who clearly had connections with deep pockets, had four losses and one draw in his last four fights—a record you don't write home about until you look closer at the names, which included Terry McGovern and two fights with Young Corbett II. Maynard hit the canvas four times in the tenth round before the referee decided to halt the fight.

The brawl took place on the same day it was announced that Attell would travel to England in the spring to finally meet former British bantam Champion Jem Bowker, whom he has been trying for months to make a match with. The *Palestine Daily Herald* stated, "Bowker has agreed to fight him before the National Sporting Club of London next Derby night. The men are to weigh in at 122 pounds at 2 o'clock on the day of the battle for a purse of $2,500, with 75 percent to the winner and 25 percent to the loser. The rounds are to be limited to twenty of three minutes each, and Attell is to receive $360 for expenses."[6]

But no sooner had this been announced than it looked as if an even better opportunity was imminent. When Bowker outgrew the bantams, both Digger Stanley of England and Boston's Jimmy Walsh claimed the title. Walsh had then outpointed Stanley in Chelsea back in October of the previous year to claim the crown. But Walsh was slowly outgrowing his class and looking up.

Title fights are what boxers dream about at night, especially competitors as gifted as Abe Attell. With the table set for February 22 at the Lincoln Athletic Club in Chelsea, Abe Attell would defend his version of the crown against Jimmy Walsh, who some believed to be the best in the division.[7] A fifteen-round contest would see both fighters at or under 122 pounds, the legitimate featherweight limit, and promised to be nothing short of an action-filled night of championship boxing. Without hesitation, each fighter posted his $500 forfeiture as a sign of commitment.

Walsh hailed from New England—Newton, Massachusetts, to be specific. At five feet and two inches, with a 65" reach, he had been boxing professionally since 1902. The previous year, he proved himself a force to contend with in the sport: After being down in the fifth round, he came back strong to pick up a six-round newspaper decision over Monte Attell on March 20, 1905, took out tomato can Joe Wagner in two rounds, then faced Monte once again. In the latter event, a six-round controversial battle, Walsh eventually found himself facing a Philadelphia magistrate in addition to Attell. The *St. Louis Republic* noted:

> [Monte] Attell and Walsh were the stars of the wind-up bout at the National Club Wednesday night [March 29, 1905]. The Boston boy had the better of the contest in every round and was certain winner when, just before the end of the sixth round, Walsh landed a blow that appeared to strike Attell in the region of the stomach [as they used to say]. Attell suddenly uttered a sharp cry of pain and dropped his hands. Before he could stop his blows Walsh sent his left and right, swinging against Attell's jaw, and Monte dropped to the mat.[8]

Clearly distressed, Monte was carried from the ring and ordered to the hospital by the tending physician. Following a thorough examination, doctors failed to find any sign of injury despite claims to the contrary. Attell made no charge against Walsh, who was released following a hearing. Walsh claimed he won because nobody was sure of the low blow, but the referee disqualified him. The event would later enter most record books as a "KO6."

In the nine fights since, Walsh had won seven, including victories over Digger Stanley and Johnny Reagan, lost one and drew one.[9] Honestly, as impressive as it sounded, Abe couldn't have cared less. The title, he knew, spoke for itself and absolved the Attell name.

In the eyes of most, this would be a legitimate battle for the featherweight championship of the world, the first since Terry McGovern knocked out George Dixon in eight rounds at the Broadway Athletic Club back in 1900. Since that time the division had been dominated by Young Corbett II, Jimmy Britt and Brooklyn Tommy Sullivan, all of whom had stirred the featherweight pot, but never put the cover on, so they say.[10] Sullivan, perceived by some as the last titleholder, picked it up in 1904 from Abe Attell, but was inactive in 1905, and lost his recognition in 1906.

The World Featherweight Title—Abraham Attell Versus Jimmy Walsh—February 22, 1906

If for one night the boxing gods could shine the light of majesty on a fighter, then let it be me, Abe thought, let it be me. It wasn't the climatic knockout, nor was it a battle between two bloodied and fatigued scrappers, but it was a masterful display of defensive deftness, mixed with just enough calculated offense, to allow Abe Attell to gain a fifteen-round decision over his antagonist, Jimmy Walsh.

Fifteen hundred spectators inside the Lincoln Athletic Club watched in amazement as Attell worked swiftly, systematically and with a degree of precision few had witnessed. He reached Walsh often, occasionally to his own amazement. As he worked the left jab, it was frequency that worked to Albie's advantage, not power. When he needed a "go to" punch, it was there—a right uppercut to the jaw. In the end, it was Walsh who was badly cut up, not Attell. Neither fighter hit the floor, but the New Englander drove Attell into the ropes in the tenth round, and only Abe's clever blocking saved him from a knockout. The *Barre Daily Times* reported:

> For the first five rounds neither did any leading. In the sixth, however, Attell began to land some telling blows and his clever footwork enabled him to get away from Walsh's returns. The champion rushed the Newton man about the ring and succeeded in bringing blood by a stiff jab on the nose. Walsh rallied in the seventh, however, and landed several good punches, so that the round was practically an even one. Attell, however, went after his man in the eighth, and after an exchange drove a hard right to Walsh's face, which cut his lip. Walsh was bleeding profusely when the gong sounded.[11]

The ninth belonged to Attell, but Walsh rallied in the tenth, chasing, but not catching, his adversary. It was Attell's fight at this point, as he worked combinations to the face, contrasted against swift body blows. Walsh just could not block the assault. The *Times* also noted the damage: "Attell, however, did not appear to have the requisite power to finish his opponent. In the last round, both mixed frequently and Walsh showed that he had plenty of reserve by landing often but without inflicting damage. At the close, both men were strong. Jack Sheehan was the referee, while Miah Nurray and W.A. Pierce acted as judges."[12]

Despite a few faint calls for a draw, nearly every spectator rose to his feet and applauded the decision: Abraham Attell was now the undisputed world featherweight champion. And it was the perfect birthday present.

The new champion couldn't resist the opportunity to stop by a friend's jewelry shop on the last day of February. The *New York Sun* noted:

> Kid McCoy, who has gone into the diamond trade here [New York City], superintended yesterday afternoon the cutting up of what he said was a 150 carat diamond. After treatment by his diamond experts, the rock was destined for [actress] Lillian Russell via [businessman] Jesse Lewisohn. When it arrives it will be in the form of a heart shaped brooch—a 5 carat ruby surrounded by fifty diamonds of one carat each, all of which, besides a few more, are coming out of the big diamond. It is understood that Lillian is going to have a birthday soon.[13]

McCoy, born Norman Selby, was a colorful character both inside and outside a prize ring. He had been married ten times, so if anyone knew anything about diamonds and women, it would most certainly be Selby. Attell enjoyed the display, since his family was familiar with the jewelry trade, primarily in the form of watches. Brother Caesar was a watchmaker who would eventually own his own business in San Francisco; his business cards would feature images of three boys, Monte, Caesar and Abe, in boxing poses.

The exhibition circuit, which Attell quickly returned to, now took on an entirely new meaning: everyone wanted to see the champion in person—and given the rare opportunity, perhaps even take a shot at him in the ring. On March 7, this time at the Consolidated Athletic Club, Attell had quite a scare when a clean blow to the jaw from Tony Belder, also referred to as Bender, sent him to the canvas in the first round. The *Call*

The intimidating battle pose of Abe Attell (Library of Congress).

stated, "He got up slowly. After a few seconds of boxing Belder put over a left hook to Abe's jaw and the champion went down for the second time."[14] Arising a bit groggy, no doubt comforted by the fact it was only a display, Attell was able to get through the round. The champion quickly reestablished his composure and took control of the fight. Exhibitions—though some claim otherwise—were supposedly easy money for the featherweight champion, not work.

At the end of February, there was talk of an exodus of Broadway fighters to the West. *The Hawaiian Star* provided details: "Abe Attell, featherweight champion, Gus Ruhlin, the Akron Giant, and Jimmy Gardner of Lowell will move on San Francisco under the guidance of Harry Pollack, who once had the pugilistic destinies of Young Corbett in his keeping and will work with the 'fight trust' out there in getting matches for these three 'soak' artists."[15]

It was noted that Attell had his eye on the winner of the of the Frankie Neil–Harry Tenny battle, followed by that of Jimmy Britt at 133 pounds. Nonetheless, the former proposition came to an end with the death of Harry Tenny from injuries he suffered in that fight (February 28). The *Evening Statesman* was one of many newspapers that reported the tragedy:

> Harry Tenny, who was severely beaten by Frankie Neil and knocked out in the fourteenth round last night, died at 7:30 o'clock this morning and his body was taken to the morgue. The dead fighter was one of the most promising amateurs in the country and secured 29 knockouts before he turned professional. In his first professional fight, which was with Neil in Colma, the pair went twenty-five rounds, Neil getting the decision. Tenny's second fight was Monte Attell, whom he knocked out in

twenty-five rounds at Goldfield. Neil, as champion bantam of the United States, fought Jem Bowker, English champion, who got the decision.[16]

The event, as was always the case with a ring death, was a reminder of just how dangerous the fight game can be. The physician's statement read: "According to the autopsy of the surgeon, death was due to cerebral hemorrhage. There was [a] laceration of the left wall of the superior longitudinal sinus or the big vein in the left side of the brain. Hemorrhage might have been caused by the fall, the succession of blows or over-exertion of the heart."[17]

Attell then announced he intended to stay in the East indefinitely and perhaps would finally match with relentless challenger, Harry Harris.

On March 19, at the Washington Sporting Club in Philadelphia, the champion fought six rounds to a no-decision against Phil Logan. Having faced some of the better names in the division, including Jimmy Walsh, Harry Forbes and Harlem Tommy Murphy, Logan was a popular hometown fighter. The fight catered to the needs of the new champion: popular draw, short distance, able competition, etc. The *Evening World* reported:

> In the third, Attell began using his right for the first time, and landed often on Logan's wind, but the blows did no damage. In the fourth, he sent home a hard right to the heart and shook Logan badly. Until the fifth Logan had not landed a blow. Then he momentarily forced the fighting and drew blood from Attell's nose with a right swing. This stirred up the champion, and he hammered Logan viciously around the mouth, soon bringing red spots. This caused Logan to break ground, and Attell kept after him, sending in left jabs and crossing his right until the Quaker was in a bad way.[18]

Observations of the fight varied: Round six saw Logan battered unmercifully, according to one account, while the *Times Dispatch* of Richmond stated he had a "good finish." Regardless of the details, the record book saw it as a "ND6."

The *Pacific Commercial Advertiser* reported on April 6 that Abe Attell and Jem Bowker would indeed meet for the featherweight championship of the world at 122 pounds in London, on May 28. The winner would receive $1,500 and the loser $1,000. There was a level of uncertainty however, as Attell, after carefully examining all his options, decided to make the western move with Harry Pollack.

Arriving in Los Angeles at 12:55 the afternoon of April 8, Attell began training for his next battle. As anticipated, it was Frankie Neil. That altercation was planned for April 20. The *Los Angeles Herald* noted Attell's arrival: "Harry Pollack, who is manager of the clever little boxer, will accompany Attell and direct him in his training."[19] Local featherweights were impressed at the assistants and sparring partners used by the fighter during the ten days of work and the camp had its fair share of spectators. It was pointed out: "In six years of fighting Attell has made a remarkable record. He has fought sixty-nine times and lost but three decisions."[20] Meanwhile, Frankie Neil had been training at Croll's Gardens, near Alameda, and would not come to Los Angeles until a day or two before the fight. Following the tragic death of Harry Tenny, one could only imagine what was going through the minds of both fighters.

As the Earth Shook

How does one begin to assess the death and devastation left behind by the San Francisco earthquake? Simply put, it was beyond imagination. Looking at the front of the *Lewiston Evening Teller* on April 18, the headlines paint the picture:

Death and Ruin Follow Earthquake Shock in San Francisco; Palace Hotel Is Burned; 400 Bodies Placed in Morgue—Death List May Reach 1,000; Hundreds Killed, Loss Will be in Millions; Fire Is Burning Up the Dead and Injured; Pacific Squadron Sunk; Berkeley College Is Wrecked; Stanford University Demolished; All South of Market is Gone; Every Building in City Damaged....[21]

The human heart could not exude enough compassion to the souls affected. For those who had looked to the sweet science for solace, many now found their homes, or gymnasiums and athletic clubs, in ruins. Only one facility of any size was left standing, the Hayes Valley Athletic Club. The group leased a large building known as Mowry Hall, at the corner of Hayes and Laguna Streets, and converted it into a well-equipped athletic club. It was furnished with an up-to-date gymnasium, baths, reception rooms and all the amenities an athlete might desire. Since it was one of the few buildings left, city authorities had no choice but to seize it for their use.

The Hayes Valley Club, and its organizer Morris Levy, had been instrumental in pulling off numerous important amateur and professional fights, many held in Woodward's Gardens. Gladiators such as Jim Jeffries, Peter Jackson, Alex Greggains, Young Corbett, Battling Nelson, Jimmy Britt, Joe Walcott, George Gardner, Jack O'Brien, Jack Johnson, Jabez White, George Green, Jimmy Ryan, and Al Neil, all displayed abilities that marked San Francisco as a pugilistic capital. Now the Gardens sat silently in ruin. The only historic battleground to eclipse Woodward's was that of Mechanic's Pavilion, and it too had been turned into rubble.

There was no longer that place, just as you remembered it, that you could take your child to and recall a memory. Holding twice the capacity as Woodward's, Mechanic's Pavilion was notable for the Sharkey–Fitzsimmons confrontation.

That match was considered one of the gigantic fakes of the ring. Referee Wyatt Earp (U.S. Marshal and frontiersman), Danny Lynch and others robbed Robert Fitzsimmons of a hard-earned victory and its fruits. In the words of Fitzsimmons's attorney, "It was a clear and dirty theft."[22] Referee Earp awarded Tom Sharkey an eighth-round decision on a foul, after Fitzsimmons had scored what many believed to have been a clean knock-out.

Nearly 20,000 people occupied every inch of the pavilion to witness one of the most momentous events of pugilism on the Pacific Coast. From their perspective, it was for the championship of the world. Earp remained steadfast in his claim of a foul. Fitzsimmons believed differently: "Earp knows and so does Sharkey, I did not hit the sailor where they say I did. My left landed straight on his stomach, where I had a right to hit him. I am willing to meet both Sharkey and Corbett in the same ring any day. No pugilist can get a square deal from the thieves who handle the fighting in this city."[23]

As the fires burned, the tears flowed.

"Tears, idle tears, I know not what they mean,/Tears from the depths of some divine despair/Rise in the heart, and gather to the eyes,/In looking on the happy Autumn-fields,/And thinking of the days that are no more."—Alfred, Lord Tennyson

McCarey's Carnival: What Could Have Been

A fistic carnival to many meant turning back the clock to 1897, and the figures of Jim Corbett and Robert Fitzsimmons battling it out in Carson City, Nevada. But to the imagination of Pacific Athletic Club manager Tom McCarey, it could mean much more.

He wanted his own memorable match, and in his mind, it began with the heavyweights, matching Tommy Burns against Jack O'Brien for the championship. Nevertheless, as of April, articles still hadn't been signed. His back-up plan would then look to a lighter class, like the feathers, where he would match Abe Attell against Frankie Neil for the championship on April 20; as the first argument on his hallowed card, or carnival if you will, it would be the perfect opening statement. McCarey already had Jimmy Britt going twenty rounds against "Kid" Herman on May 8, backed four days later by Battling Nelson and Aurelio Herrera going the same distance. Never before had a fight promoter been so ambitious, so willing to collect such a trio of important contests.

The talent would be there because McCarey had lined up enormous purses. The Nelson and Herrera contest, for example, had the capital prize of $20,000, of which $9,600 went into the hands of the winner, while the loser put $6,400 in his pocket. Move over, John "Dough" Rockefeller, as you are clearly playing in the wrong ring.

Drawing spectators to the Los Angeles area would not be a concern, as scheduled events—the Fiesta and the Shriners—were to attract 75,000 strangers alone during that time. If anybody could draw additional attention, it was McCarey, who had become a shining star in area promotions. The trio of battles was scheduled for Naud Junction Pavilion, although there was hope that it might be too small.

Training facilities were expected as follows: Nelson in Avalon, Catalina Island, and at Fairview, near Newport; Herrera would be at Baldwin's Ranch at Arcadia and at his training quarters at Forty-ninth Street and Central Avenue; Britt liked the mountains in Santa Monica; Herman used training quarters near Eastlake Park; Frankie Neil would be at Croll's Gardens up in 'Frisco and would head south a few days before the battle; and Abe Attell would train at Lewis's gymnasium on South Spring Street.

Various ring celebrities pledged their support and promised to attend, including James J. Jeffries, Jack O'Brien, Jim Corbett, Bob Fitzsimmons, Terry McGovern, George Siler, and Bat Masterson. Everything looked to be in its place, and then the ground shook. Or, as the *Los Angeles Herald* put it on May 30, "Three great battles gone to rack; two of them because of the power that rules the universe and the last because of the rankest sort of human treachery."[24]

The latter comment is a reference to the Nelson versus Herrera fight, which was finally going to take place on May 25, but was declared off when Herrera would not weigh in. The *Los Angeles Herald* observed:

> Had not the San Francisco earthquake occurred Abe Attell and Frankie Neil would now be discussing their battle scheduled for several weeks ago. If Jimmy Britt's flats were still intact Kid Herman might have been busy explaining how he defeated or lost to the former champion. The elements, however, chose to behave badly, and two of the bouts went glimmering through no fault of the Pacific Athletic Club, which had made every preparation for the battles. The spectacular termination of the last and greatest contest of the three was the straw that blasted McCarey's already frazzled hopes and incidentally caused a wave of disappointment to sweep where lovers of the boxing game were anxiously awaiting the outcome.[25]

On May 24, the day before the Nelson versus Herrera match was to take place, a boxing exhibition was held for the benefit of the San Francisco sufferers. It took place at the Naud Junction Pavilion, the Pacific Athletic Club having donated the use of their facility to the Chamber of Commerce. Aided by the numerous society parties that supported the event, the turnout was large. For the first time in the history of the facility, women witnessed the exhibitions.

The boxing benefit program included also wrestling, fencing and music. Four-round boxing exhibitions saw Jim Jeffries versus Jack Root, Battling Nelson versus Eddie Robinson, Kid Herman versus Abe Attell, Aurelio Herrera versus Mauro Herrera, and Tommy Burns versus George Blake. Wrestlers William Desmond battled Joe Keley for three rounds. And Matt Keefe, the yodeler, sang several songs prior to a fencing exhibition conducted by Harry Maloney and Albert Bartell. Pugilism was determined to provide its fair share of support for quake victims, and it did just that.

Back to Business as Usual

Touted as the greatest ring battle in years, it occurred on Friday, May 11, when Abe Attell met Kid Herman before the Pacific Club in Los Angeles. Since they last met on February 18, 1904, Herman had put together a nice streak of wins, which included Billy Finucane and Dave Sullivan, and was coming off a twenty-round win over Eddie Hanlon and a draw with the hard-hitting Aurelio Herrera. But this time it was a twenty-round brawl with the champion. Held at catch weights, the event, despite the quake or because of it, was conducted in front of a large crowd at the Naud Junction Pavilion.

Be it fate or coincidence, this match occurred due to the sudden cancellation of those previously scheduled: Jimmy Britt called off his bout against Herman because of his sister's death, and a wire to Attell's party confirmed that Frankie Neil had flown to the east, forcing the cancellation their bout. So Herman and Attell wisely decided to make the best of the situation. The local newspapers carried details of the incentives: "Manager Tom McCarey offered the boys a purse of $3500, or fifty percent of the gate receipts. Attell liked the purse proposition while Herman favored the gate. As a result, an agreement was affected whereby Attell will be entitled to the winner's end of the purse, at a division of sixty and forty percent should he win, while Herman will annex half of the gate receipts in the event of a victory."[26]

Both fighters had completed an industrious course of training. What advanced promotion there was managed to gain the respect of legions of fans. It would be a fight, as many saw it, where there was no real loser. Attell would box at 122 pounds, while Herman was expected to weigh in at about 128 to 129 pounds.

Although many had been disappointed when Attell and Neil were unable to meet as scheduled, the alternative looked promising: "[This battle] will culminate one of the most unique matches made within the memory of any living follower of the game, bringing together as it does the most clever ringster of the times in combat with a youngster whose ability to take and give, combined with an advantage of eight or nine pounds, has placed him as an 8–10 favorite."[27]

The questions were obvious, and were noted in the Los Angeles Herald:

Will Attell be able to withstand the rushes of Herman? Is Herman knockout-proof against the rain of thrusts and jabs, which will surely be his portion when he crawls between the ropes with Attell? Herman, because of his weight and admitted cleverness, is judged by the majority as capable of wearing Attell down and at the same time withstanding the hardest blow that Albie can send. Attell will stay with Herman throughout the twenty rounds and win on a decision. Both boys are demanding that a decision, other than a draw, be given by Referee Eyton, should they be on their feet at the end. They have gone the no-decision route before and the termination had no pleasant feature for either of them.[28]

In the end, and despite the fighter's demands, the twenty rounds closed in a draw. The *Herald* noted, "There was no dissenting cry, mingled with the roar of approval, as the little boxers climbed from the ring after as fast a battle as has been witnessed in Los Angeles."[29]

Attell, with his magnificent footwork, had not only stayed the distance against a man eight pounds heavier, but made him appear as an amateur. He was simply far quicker. When his aggressor managed to rush him to the ropes, Herman couldn't keep him there; the bigger fighter was naturally more than happy to mix it up with the little man.

Attell entered the ring first after the preliminaries, followed by Herman. Both men stood in the background during the pre-fight festivities, which included the introduction of both Battling Nelson and Aurelio Herrera, who were promoting their upcoming fisticuffs. Numerous newspapers detailed the confrontation: "There was considerable discussion regarding the bandages on Attell's hands, Herman claiming that too much tape had been bound about the champion's wrist. Referee Eyton was called upon and Herman at last gave in. Before the gong sounded Herman demanded that no hairline decision be given and that the usual order of things prevail in the event of the battle reaching the limit. Attell agreed and the bell rang."[30]

Attell's cleverness was on display right from the start, as he dodged a terrific right from Herman in the first round. In a preview of coming attractions, when Herman rushed the feather champ to the ropes in the second round, he glided away like a ghost, casting an image of only where he once was. The first hard blow didn't come until the fourth, when Herman sent a powerful right to his adversary's neck. Attell wisely clinched, but received a left to the jaw after the breakaway. The *Herald* observed:

> In the fifth a burst of acclaim greeted Attell as he side stepped a bull-like rush of Herman's and drove in a terrific series of rights and lefts. The sixth was another marvelous exhibition by Attell and in this round he made "The Ghetto Boy" appear much to the bad. Laughing, he avoided one of the Kid's wildest rushes, and then coming to a clinch brought across the overhand wallop that made Young Corbett famous, raining repeatedly upon the Kid's head.[31]

Even if Herman's constant rushes dominated the battle, they were met each time with a barrage of combinations from Attell. The *Herald* continued, "An incident occurred in the fifteenth which brought the crowd to its feet. Herman had encountered several lefts, which did not add to his temperament. He threw a bad left to Abe's ribs, which sent the latter against the ropes. Like a rubber ball Attell bounded away from the swinging limits of the circle and, turning completely around in the maneuver, eluded the follow-tactics of the Kid."[32]

The only knockout of the evening happened in the first preliminary when Kid Dalton dropped Joe Kelcy. When the word was given that Terry Davis, who was matched with Mike Bartley in another preliminary, was injured in an afternoon automobile accident, the audience was certain of a cancellation. While everybody's thoughts and prayers were with Davis, many were satisfied when Abe's brother Monte went on with Bartley. Monte, who fought much in the manner of his brother, earned the six-round decision. For a time, albeit brief, pugilism had consoled the souls of so many in need.

Always on the verge of meeting Frankie Neil, but forever encountering something to prevent it, the champion finally entered the ring against him. The former bantamweight champion had made the decision to "step up." On the Fourth of July, at 2:30 p.m., these twenty-three year-old gladiators did battle for twenty rounds before the Pacific Athletic Club.

Born Francis James Neil in San Francisco, Frankie stood 5'4" with a reach of 64½". Debuting in 1900, Neil moved quickly through bantam rankings. After losing to champ Harry Forbes in 1902, Neil knocked him out in the second round of their August 1903 rematch. He defended his title against Johnny Reagan, but lost his fight with Joe Bowker, who held the world 116-pound bantam title. He then regained the American bantam crown by defeating Harry Tenny, at least in his mind. Granted, it's all a bit confusing, but such was the time.

So how would Neil fare against the new feather champion, both fighters battling at one hundred and twenty and a quarter pounds? Simply put: Attell dominated the duel, landing six blows to Neil's one. A damage assessment from the Rock Island Argus noted, "Neil's eye was closed early in the contest and his face was battered black and blue. Neil, however, appeared to be the stronger throughout the fight and his blows, when they landed, had force behind them. Attell's cleverness in covering up and sidestepping his opponent's vicious swings saved him repeatedly."[33]

The last two rounds made the entire battle worthwhile viewing, as both fighters fought head to head, tearing into each other through vicious assaults to the face. And it was said: "Neil landed more blows in these two rounds than he did in nearly all the rest of the fight."[34]

Continuing the damage evaluation, "Attell, although both eyes were slightly discolored, otherwise showed little effect of the terrific mill. On the other hand, the left side of Neil's face was black, his eye closed tightly, and his nose bruised and bleeding from the seemingly countless jabs which Attell landed."[35]

The amphitheater crowd cheered when the decision for Attell was announced.[36] In a sportsmanlike gesture, the winner rushed across the ring and embraced his defeated opponent. In his first title defense, Attell had been successful. The lion's share of the gate receipts were his, as was a $1,000 belt awarded by club manager Tom McCarey to the winner. This was the first belt fight since the Richard K. Fox diamond belt.[37]

On August 4, Abe Attell accepted a battle against Chicago fighter Frank Carsey before Michigan's Grand Rapids Club. The fifteen-round contest was to be held on Wednesday evening, August 15, and conducted under the management of P.J. Carroll. The champion took the fight at 122 pounds at the 3 o'clock weigh-in, with the referee George Siler.

Born Frank Carsello in New Orleans, Frank Carsey made his professional debut in 1903. While working out of the Midwest (Chicago) he picked up a couple of nice wins— the first over Eddie Gardner and the next over Maurice Rauch—on his way through the division. Fighting regularly over the past twelve months, he entered the battle with Attell not having lost in his last five bouts. However, just days prior to their battle, Carsey's trainer, Eldridge Smith, drowned in a swimming accident. The catastrophic loss and its impact quickly became a concern to everyone involved in the event.

They came in droves, from all across the state, to see the feather champion. A crowd of 3,000 watched, some in awe, as Attell performed a fifteen-round scientific display while garnering a decision. However, when it was over, a consensus was difficult to find; the partisan crowd disagreed with the outcome, believing Carsey had at least earned a draw.

As the *Evening Star* reported:

Attell claimed that the reason why he did not finish Carsey early was because Frank would not come to him. He stepped to the press box and made this remark, which the crowd jeered and yelled, "Go get him then; it is your business, not our fight." [Then] Attell reportedly slugged a heckler while returning to his dressing room. Frank Carsey had the reputation of never having been floored, but he came very near being sent to the mat in the thirteenth round when Abe gave him a terrific left swing to the jaw. Neither fighter was marked at the close, although Abe's nose bled profusely for the last three rounds.[38]

The event cried for a champion's vindication, which he agreed to. According to the *Rock Island Argus*:

A contract has been closed for the use of the Burtis opera house in Davenport, Iowa for the championship battle between Abe Attell and Frank Carsey on the evening of Labor Day. The seating capacity of the house is ordinarily 1,357, but additional room will be made for spectators. Five hundred additional seats will be erected on the stage. The men will weigh in at 124 pounds. The match will go 15 rounds, and there will be several good preliminaries. The Tri-City Athletic club, newly reorganized, will give the tournament.[39]

Attell, who rarely shunned a rematch, gave Carsey one, but was damned if he would fight again in Grand Rapids. Also, Abe Pollock would oversee this meeting; George Siler had refereed in Grand Rapids.

As if he had better things to do with his time, Attell worked with haste and exactitude to dispense with his opponent by knockout in the third round. Carsey's seconds, witnessing the ravages of their fighter, threw up the sponge. Outclassed and outmaneuvered, withstanding enormous abuse, the Chicago fighter began losing control and swinging wildly. The fighter's loss squelched any criticism of the champion.

According to the *Evening Star*:

News comes from Chicago that Abe Attell has accepted the offer to meet Jimmy Walsh of Boston, the recognized bantamweight champion, in a finish fight at Manhattan, Nevada. The battle will be one of a series given during a three-day fistic carnival. Attell's offer comes from Harry Center of Boston, who wired that a $10,000 purse would be offered. The contest will take place the first week in November and will be for the featherweight championship.[40]

While Attell may have accepted the offer, he harbored a degree of skepticism—as his own history had proven—regarding such events. The proof was in the details, and they had yet to be negotiated.

Back in Los Angeles, on October 30, "The Little Champ" met Harry Baker—a recent graduate from the amateur ranks, where he reigned supreme—in a twenty round feature event at the Naud Junction Pavilion. Baker, who entered the fight having just taken an impressive twenty-round points victory over Frankie Neil, felt he was ready for the champion, even if some disagreed.

According to the *Rock Island Argus*, "When the bell rang at the end of the 20th round last night it found Abe Attell and Harry Baker fighting like two tigers, and when Referee [Eddie] Robinson hoisted Attell's glove Baker threw his hands up and staggered to his corner crying like a baby."[41] Robinson made the correct call, as both fighters sustained minor damage, and Attell was clearly ahead on points. Baker started out strong, commanding attention with the use of an effective straight left and matching it with a stout defense. But it was only a matter of time before Attell started slicing with the left jab, the damage slowly accumulating.

During the course of the action, Baker complained numerous times to Robinson that Attell was hitting low. Yet it was the referee's opinion that Baker was moving into the punches and that they were not fouls. "After the eleventh round Baker remained on the defensive and landed few telling blows. The claim of foul had its effect on the crowd (of 4,500 spectators) and the decision was not popular, Attell being roundly hissed."[42] Attell taunted Baker throughout the fight, calling him a "cry baby," a term stated loud enough to be heard ringside. Robinson, who clearly made the only decision possible, needed a police escort in order to leave the pavilion.

Deciding to finish the year off on the West Coast, specifically southern California, Team Attell lined up their final two events. Born Earl Lemoine, and residing in Saskatoon, Saskatchewan, Canada, Billy DeCoursey was Attell's next scheduled opponent. The light-weight had been fighting sporadically around San Diego, taking on fighters like Johnny Ritchie and Billy Snailham, so Attell agreed to give him a title shot and keep him there in town.

As the *Herald* observed, "Before a small crowd assembled at the National Athletic club tonight [November 16] Abe Attell, featherweight champion of the world, successfully defended his title by gaining a decision over Canadian Billy DeCoursey at the end of fif-teen rounds, which were marked by miserably slow fighting."[43]

Beyond the obvious poor attendance, suspicion was aroused when it appeared that Attell could have easily knocked out his older opponent. Instead, Attell played with DeCoursey as a cat might play with a mouse—the comparison used by the *Los Angeles Herald*. Attell's actions were not indicative of a champion making a statement. Instead, they were more like a friend returning a favor; going the distance with the incumbent world champion has always been quick to inflate any fighter's price tag, even one at the tail end of his career.

After the fight, Attell headed back to Los Angeles, where he was due in a Bakersfield court on November 22. The champion was the star witness for manager Tom McCarey, who had sued Aurelio Herrera for $2,000 forfeiture money. Attell believed Herrera was 11 pounds overweight for his contracted fight and would testify to that account. Herrera, who stopped payment on the check that McCarey was rightfully due, disagreed with almost everyone.

Understanding the cost of a missed opportunity, Attell was more than generous with his time. The champion agreed to a rematch with Jimmy Walsh. Pacific Club Manager McCarey wired Boston with an offer and the fighter accepted, the Nevada carnival deal having fallen through. The fight was scheduled for twenty rounds at the Naud Junction Pavilion on December 7.

According to a stark synopsis in the *Herald*, "Technically speaking Attell did not score a knockout [in the ninth round], as a towel flew into the ring before Referee Tommy Burns had counted four. Walsh however was completely out and did not come to until several minutes after being carried to his corner."[44] The damage was clear in the eighth round as Walsh was weak and staggering. Seeing his fighter in this condition, Manager McKeever hurled the towel into the ring while both fighters were engaging. Still, the vicious brawling would not cease. Attell's seconds ended up dragging their fighter to his chair while Walsh was waving to his corner that he was not out.

Referee Burns, who was caught up in the mess, could not sort things out in a timely manner. No bell sounded even though another round was due. The ninth round dawned when the two men came together again. Attell, seeing his advantage, delivered a stinging left to the eye that stunned Walsh. According to accounts, "As he backed toward the ropes Abe sent a vicious left to the stomach and Jimmy went down for good. Burns started tolling seconds and as he counted three the towel went in the ring. Walsh was taken to his corner and revived under the efforts of his seconds."[45]

Having gone home to San Francisco after the fight, Attell returned to Los Angeles at the end of December. A rumor had spread that Abe had retired, which he denied. "The Little Champ" did state that he has "made arrangements to open a cigar and refreshment establishment in San Francisco, but will not be averse to entering the ring when something in the way of financial return is shown him."[46]

Former bantam champ Harry Harris continued to hound Attell about a match and stated on December 27 that he would gladly battle the champ in Goldfield, Nevada, for which promoters had offered a $10,000 purse. Attell, who had received any number of challenges from Harris, had always avoided them due to the terms—primarily the weight limits. Although the challenge seemed legitimate, Attell appeared unenthusiastic about the offer.

In Monte's Corner

The highlight of the year for Monte Attell involved a ring of a different sort. On April 1, the twenty-year-old pugilist married Miss Annie Leamer, age nineteen, of San Francisco. Rabbi Levy performed the ceremony. In a year that turned the city of San Francisco into rubble, few minds were on the sport of boxing. Monte assisted his brother often during the year and even appeared on the undercard of the Herman fight. His only ring disappointment was a controversial loss to Freddie Weeks.

Changes of lineal champions in 1906 included: Tommy Burns defeated Marvin Hart, on February 23 in Los Angeles, to pick up the heavy crown; both the light heavyweight and middleweight top spots were vacant; William "Honey" Mellody took the welter top spot and Joe Gans unified the lightweight division by defeating white claimant Battling Nelson by a forty-second round foul in Goldfield, Nevada, on September 3.

Of other notable fights: Jack Johnson defeated Sam Langford in a fifteen-rounder on April 26 in Chelsea, Massachusetts; and Tommy Burns, the shortest heavyweight champion ever (5'7"), surprised everyone by knocking out Fireman Jim Flynn in the fifteenth round of their October 2 clash.

On his birthday, Abraham Attell became the undisputed world featherweight champion. What else could a boxer ask for? Then, in a bold but sportsmanlike manner, he confirmed his status by defeating Jimmy Walsh in a rematch. "The Little Champ" had never fought quicker, wiser or better.

Chapter Six

Preserve and Defend, 1907

"'Ven Abie fights I never vorry one bit, because Abie can take of himself. Ven Monte goes into de ring I'm not quite so certain, yet, because he isn't half so smart as Abie. But I'm vorried every minute ven I know dat Caesar is going to fight for fear dat he vill get killed."[1]—Anna Rothlotz Attell

As San Francisco rebuilt—some 600 new houses were built on the 440-foot-tall Bernal Hill—bubonic plague broke out again while corruption enveloped city politics. San Francisco Mayor Eugene Schmitz was sentenced to five years in San Quentin for graft and bribery, while others were forced out of office for accepting bribes from the telephone company, gas company, trolley company, local skating rinks, and of all things, boxing promoters. Survival, for many, had become a daily consternation.

For the Attell family, they greeted the New Year by being featured in the *Spokane Press* in an article titled "A Whole Family of Fighters." Adorned with boxing images of the three boys, Caesar, Abe, and Monte, the two-column piece features, as it should, comments from the—matriarch of the family. Mrs. Attell candidly declared that Abe "has the stamp of greatness," Monte "is a fair performer," and Caesar "has not yet developed anything that would stamp him even as a comer."[2] Difficult enough to imagine a family with the talent of only one of the boys, yet alone three. Mrs. Attell was portrayed as the loving mother that she truly was.

When asked of her fear of the children getting hurt, she stated (accent included): "'Vell," replied Mrs. Attell, "ven Abie fights I never vorry one bit, because Abie can take of himself. Ven Monte goes into de ring I'm not quite so certain, yet, because he isn't half so smart as Abie. But I'm vorried every minute ven I know dat Caesar is going to fight for fear dat he vill get killed."[3] The family matriarch expressed a valid concern, as thirteen deaths from boxing were recorded in 1906, more than the two previous years.[4]

The article confirmed the frugality of the family by stating that Abe hung on to every cent, Monte had picked up a fair cigar business, and Caesar "is still doing stints in the second-hand store."[5] All three brothers, as Mrs. Attell noted, were involved in the latter enterprise.

It would be Attell's first rematch as reigning champion, which was why Harry Baker was the envy of many feathers; most desired just one crack at "The Little Champ." On January 18, Baker would once again find himself in a Los Angeles boxing ring. Ever since his twenty-round controversial defeat by Attell the previous October, Baker had been hell-bent on a second chance. Yes, he wanted to vindicate his loss, but also, he didn't believe he was treated fairly by the press—a point easily understood by those who read the coverage.

The Friday evening event was scheduled for twenty rounds at Naud Junction, or the Pacific Athletic Club Pavilion. Situated in northern downtown Los Angeles, the area rested at the junction of Main Street and Alameda Street, where Southern Pacific Railroad trains veered off Alameda to tracks along Alhambra Avenue and the Los Angeles River. Thomas McCarey built the pavilion in 1905 to house his promotions. If you were arriving by car, you took Eastlake Park or Downey Avenue, then went north on Spring Street to Naud Junction. Reserved seats were priced at $3 and $5, while general admission was $1.50. Admission included the championship fight and two respectable preliminaries.

Baker entered the ring first, followed by the champion. As the pair hailed from San Francisco, a rival market, both receptions were rather cool, which was a bit of a surprise since it was a title fight. According to the *Herald*, "Abe disputed Baker's right to the southeast corner and a coin was tossed. Baker won. The men stepped to the scales and both were within the featherweight limit. In the meantime, a list of challenges was being read. Harry Harris sent a telegram offering to meet the winner and telling of a $5,000 side bet."[6]

Auto enthusiast Barney Oldfield—the first man to drive a car at 60 miles per hour—was introduced to a warm welcome just before big Jim Jeffries, who would referee the contest, began peeling off his coat. Both fighters looked in superb condition, with Attell sporting a more muscular physique. Approaching center ring slowly, both gladiators touched gloves, and it was fight on. The *Herald* detailed each round: "Following a [short] sparring session Attell sent a light left to the face. Harry rushed but met with a staggering right to the head. Probably he was a bit dazed, as Attell shot a hard right to the jaw, Baker fell on his back, but was up in a second, he came back and boxed."[7] Both fighters remained composed until the round closed, Attell clearly the stronger of the pair.

Baker pulled back a bit in the second, just trying to stay out of range. His trademark move had been a quick sidestep to the right, once he planted himself. Attell, familiar with the maneuver, "caused a laugh by walking in and then turning neatly from Baker's lead."[8] The champion's mockery didn't please Baker, who turned up the intensity for the remainder of the round.

In the third, Attell became frustrated with Baker's "out of range" approach and uncharacteristically decided to charge his opponent. The strategy shift caused both men to stumble over one another. The fourth round was tame, while the fifth saw Attell driving Baker against the ropes. As in previous rounds, Baker suffered only minor damage.

In the sixth, the newspaper reported, "Attell pushed Baker to his back. He offered his hand to aid Harry, but the latter was not inconvenienced. It was hammer and tongs for Attell and he warmed to the fray."[9]

The pair traded blows to open the seventh. Attell targeted the stomach and face, while Baker opted to cover and block. A left to Attell's face was Baker's unimpressive response. Just after punishing Baker against the ropes, Attell prepared for a major assault:

> Attell lands a left swing to the face and Baker goes to the floor with Attell standing over him, but is motioned away by Jeffries. Baker rises at the count of six and starts toward his corner in an attempt to escape Attell, who follows closely. Attell swings again and Baker goes through the ropes but manages to get back into the ring and to his feet at the count of nine. Attell, who is standing directly behind him, hits Baker in the back with his right and Baker again goes to the floor.[10]

Baker looked all but out, yet remained on his knees at the count of eight. Miraculously, at the count of nine, he was saved by the bell.

Naturally, Attell was on Baker like a dog on a bone in round eight. Covering, Baker did his best to counter the assault while staggering about the ring. Yet Attell found an angle and landed a firm left to his target. The result was noted: "Baker goes backward but manages to keep his feet, backing into his own corner. As Baker comes close to the ropes with Attell following behind him waiting for a chance to put him out, a sponge goes into the ring, giving Abe the decision."[11]

In the end there was praise for both fighters, Baker for his determination and Attell for his command performance. Many newspapers summarized the encounter with a line that had become all too familiar to Attell followers: "It was simply an instance of the clever boxer and yet rugged fighter meeting a clever opponent who could not withstand the strength to which he was opposed."[12] Baker's take for the fight was $1,863, or the loser's end. For his twenty-one minutes of work, Jim Jeffries received $750. As for the champion, Attell put $2,794.50 in his pocket, before heading home. He would later board a train for Philadelphia to meet English featherweight Spike Robson.[13] But before the latter, rumors were flying that Attell was in love and planning to get married.

Mr. and Mrs. Abraham Attell

"'This isn't so bad as going twenty rounds,' remarked Abe Attell when Justice of the Peace Ed Smithwick had pronounced the featherweight champion and Miss Elizabeth Egan husband and wife in the county clerk's office at Santa Ana yesterday [March 14]."[14] This was the news reported by many, including the *Herald*.

In typical Attell style, he kept the entire event secret. After the ceremony, his response to the press varied significantly. To some he told the truth and provided a few details, while to others he conveyed a different story, going so far as to deny the event, or even claiming he was married back in Chicago on July 23, 1906, and his wife's name was Evans, not Egan. In detailing the event, the *Herald* penned, "Mrs. Attell, who is of the brunette type, wore a brown traveling suit, while Abe, faultlessly attired as usual, gave Santa Ana an opportunity of viewing the ultra fashions in men's garments. The couple, both age 23, had known each other for some time and returned to Los Angeles on the 5 o'clock train."[15]

A certified copy of the marriage license was sent to the Hotel Sherman in Chicago, Illinois.

Back to Work

Before the National Athletic Club in Philadelphia, it was six rounds of boxing against Englishman Spike Robson. New York fans had grown so interested in the match, a special train had been arranged; on the morning of the clash the locomotive carried a large metropolitan contingent to Philadelphia. Demand quickly exceeded ticket supply, and more than 1,000 fans were unable to get into the venue.

In an *Evening Times* evaluation of the contest, "The general opinion is that the bloody Henglishman will be dill pickles and cold boiled ham for Abraham but there are many willing to back Spike to stick the limit. The men will fight at 124 pounds."[16]

Robson had stunned many with his strong performances over his much heavier rivals—five pounds, to be exact—Tommy Murphy and Young Erne. Quick, but without a knockout punch, the Englishman was expected to give Attell a dose of his own medicine. The *Evening Times* laid out the conditions: "The fight is limited to six rounds with no decision. If both fighters are on their feet and in fair condition at the end of the go the result naturally will be unsatisfactory, so far as deciding the international championship."[17]

To little surprise, the engagement was swift and defensive, ending in the mandatory "ND6." Watching these two fighters from the start, you could have predicted the ending, as not a single blow was strong enough by either fighter to do any damage. "Aside from a bloody nose, which Attell received in the closing round, neither man bore any mark of the encounter."[18]

Ever since Joe Bowker, the English bantam, decisively defeated Spike Robson, market pressure had been on promoters to match the Englishman with Attell. Bowker, who would sail to the States soon, planned to continue negotiations with the champion; they had been talking a Los Angeles venue for a $10,000 purse. Bowker was under the control of the astute Billy Nolan, who had been the rudder for both Jack O'Brien and Battling Nelson. One thing you could be certain of, as a Nolan client, was that Billy would squeeze every dime possible out of a negotiation.

As for Attell, the newlywed headed back to Chicago. Robson delayed his departure on a gamble and stayed in Philadelphia. Knowing that Attell was scheduled to meet Tom O'Toole in the city on April 17, Robson hoped his impressive showing against the champion might entice a western promoter to match himself against Abe in a long bout. However, Attell's poor performance against O'Toole negated prospects, and Robson's hopes quickly vanished.

Tom O'Toole, a hometown boy who had some good fights under his belt, including Jimmy Walsh and Harry Forbes, had been training hard for his battle against Attell. The champion, who had taken a flying trip from Chicago, rested for a day or two rather than training for his next scheduled fight. As a result of the complacency, Attell, one of the most accurate punchers in the ring, was missing his targets and even resorting to wild punches. His fight against O'Toole wasn't pretty, nor was it the reflection of a champion: there weren't any knockdowns, and at the end of the six rounds the only noticeable damage was bleeding from the mouth and nose of O'Toole.

A change of scenery was in order, or so "The Little Champ" believed, so he headed back to Los Angeles, where he was scheduled on May 24 to meet Benny "Kid" Solomon at the Naud Junction Pavilion for twenty rounds. Attell, well aware that he had disappointed both himself and his fans with his recent performance, was erring on the side of redemption. He was taking far too many chances and he knew it—a defeat at the hands of "Kid" Solomon could prove disastrous.

A championship mindset doesn't come with the title. It's a delicate balance of "risk versus reward," and Attell needed to find it, and find it fast. Every decision needed to be calculated, from the length of battle and choice of competition, to where a confrontation was taking place. And he must remember that a champion's behavior is always under a magnifying glass.

McCarey too had been under scrutiny of late for putting on substandard matches. The local newspaper noted, "McCarey has been harassed during the past few weeks that another smash up would probably send him high and dry from the fight game."[19]

As for the odds game, considered a promotion's bellwether, very few bets were forthcoming. The *Herald* even noted, "A round at the cigar stands where wagers may be placed yesterday [May 22] revealed the fact that no large commissions have thus far been received. It was practically impossible to lay $10 against Attell."[20]

In a review that appeared in the *Evening World*:

> Kid Solomon had no show in his fight with Abe Attell for the featherweight championship before the Pacific Athletic Club last night, Attell winning the decision in the twentieth round, though he could have knocked out his man at almost any time. Attell made the crowd sore by delaying the fight forty minutes and trying to remove padding from his left glove. Solomon was weak and his famous left punch did not materialize. Attell was very strong and had his man at his mercy throughout.[21]

Solomon landed scarcely a blow but endured a terrible beating. According to one account, "Solomon's face was cut and pounded into a mass of bruises and covered with gore."[22] As for Attell, there was not a mark on the champion, his superb defensive skills overshadowing the reach advantage of his opponent.

Following the fight, however, manager Tom McCarey couldn't escape the scrutiny. A dispatch from Los Angeles to the *San Francisco Call* read:

> The fact that pugilistic encounters in Los Angeles had been crooked and that the manager of the club which has a monopoly on such affairs had been a party to the fakes, if not directly benefited by them, had a dampening effect upon the fight last night in which Kid Solomon tried to wrest the featherweight championship from Abe Attell. Hours before the fight the tip went out that it was to be a frame-up and that the mill would go the full 20 rounds and that Attell would get the decision. It did go the full 20 rounds and Attell got the decision. It was such a one sided affair that the only suspicion of crooked work lies in the fact that Attell did not put Solomon out. It was Attell's battle throughout to such a degree that it is surprising that he permitted Solomon to stay the limit. It may have been just a guess, but it is a fact that nearly everybody who saw the fight had the tip that the result would be just what it was. It is not likely that there will be any more important fights here in a long time.[23]

This was not the step that Team Attell needed to take, not at this time and certainly not under McCarey's roof.

The champion paid little attention to the opprobrium, opting instead to feed the press his desire to meet lightweight champion Joe Gans. Had Attell been matched with lightweight legend, it likely would have been a calamitous encounter, as "The Little Champ" was not meeting ring expectations and Gans hadn't had a decisive loss in years.

As for Kid Solomon, he was arrested and ordered to pay a fine of $10 on July 11 for killing a bird, an oriole, while he was training for the fight with Attell; the warrant was sworn out by one J. Cunningham, who testified that he saw Solomon shoot the creature. As the *Herald* documented:

> Solomon denied shooting at the Baltimore warbler, saying that he had found the dead bird and carried it to the training quarters, where, he declared, Cunningham was employed as a dishwasher. After the fight he had discharged the kitchen mechanic, and in revenge, Solomon averred, his erstwhile employee had brought the charge. "How could he see me kill anything," protested Kid, "when he was washing pots when I went hunting?"[24]

On August 3, Solomon was taken to a local receiving hospital still suffering from blows, it was said, from his fight with Abe Attell. Doctors would claim that the blows so weakened the fighter that they would have a lasting effect on the man.[25] There have always been times in the sport of boxing when truth seems stranger than fiction.

Taking a break from the fight game, Attell didn't surface until the first week of September. That is when he and Boston bantam Jimmy Walsh chose to complete their trilogy by signing articles with Sylvie Ferretti. The articles called for a ten-round clash on

September 12 before the Indianapolis Athletic Club, and the two agreed on 122 pounds ringside. The *Topeka State Journal* noted, "Ferretti says he will make an effort to have the weighing in at 6 o'clock, inasmuch as Walsh is able to make 116 or 118 easily. He [Attell] will be able to make weight in time, he says. Walsh is now in Boston, where he rose to pugilistic fame."[26]

Indianapolis fans yearned to witness the slashing little kingpin of the feathers tearing up Walsh, then delivering him quicker than the five rounds it took only a few months earlier. But instead they witnessed Attell outpoint Jimmy Walsh in a fast-paced ten-round rumpus. According to the *Rock Island Argus*:

> The boys went at it hammer and tongs all the way, there being few idle moments from the time they entered the ring until the final gong at the end of the tenth round. Attell's cleverness was too much for the Bostonian, who cut out a terrific pace, but failed to land the haymakers he sent to Albie's jaw. Attell covered up beautifully and when he cut loose he fairly jabbed the challenger's head until it rocked. His jabs, however, lacked the necessary punishing power to put Walsh to sleep, and the latter stuck through the 10 rounds, fighting gamely all the way.[27]

A large crowd of several thousand, many having not seen Attell since January of 1904 when he fought Harry Forbes in Indy, cheered both fighters the entire distance. What they saw was truly a champion's performance. Attell was on his game, exhibiting his fabulous footwork, hitting angles, and dropping artillery from his distance of choice. Perhaps, some thought, the rest between fights did him some good.

In Alton, Illinois, about fifteen miles north of St. Louis, Missouri, Team Attell was busy planning their next move. As the *Herald* noted:

> Jack Sullivan and Carl Zork (remember this name), representing "Brooklyn Tommy" Sullivan, and Abe Attell are trying hard to arrange a battle between their charges. Attell has sent on his terms. They are 128 pounds ringside and a division of the receipts on a 60 and 40 percent basis. Sullivan said Saturday 127 pounds was the very best he could do. But when Attell said 126 was as high as he would let him scale—and that's four pounds above the featherweight notch—Tommy swung in line.[28]

Zork wanted a suitable guarantee, so when the money went up it was match on.

For red-topped Brooklyn native Tommy Sullivan, a former factory boy who had now been employed for several years as a boxing instructor at the Missouri Athletic Club in St. Louis, asking for a battle against Attell, whom he knocked out in the fifth round of a 1904 conflict, was a right he deserved. After all, Attell still insisted that the left-hand uppercut to the pit of his stomach was a foul. Sullivan's take of the fifth round was a bit different: Attell tried to confuse Sullivan with his footwork, but it failed. When Attell tried to plant a left jab on Tommy's nose, Sullivan ducked it before countering to the stomach. The pain, written all over Attell's mug, caused the fighter to fall to the canvas and roll over repeatedly. Cries of foul could be heard throughout the venue. Nonetheless, upon the examination by three doctors, no marks could be found below the belt, just a red spot in the pit of Attell's stomach. The decision, as you recall, went to Sullivan.

Now in Alton, a city on the Mississippi River, Abe Attell drew "Brooklyn Tommy" Sullivan after six quick rounds on a Saturday afternoon. Bob Douglas refereed a close bout held at the Physical Cultural farm, maintained by a group of St. Louis businessmen. A split lip suffered in round one by Sullivan and a slight cut under Attell's eye were the only noticeable bits of damage. On the authority of the *Evening World*, "Sullivan made an awful howl when the verdict was rendered, as he claimed he should have received the judgment. The majority of spectators also thought Sullivan had the better of the battle."[29]

Bob Edgren, the noted New York boxing columnist for the *Evening World*, wasted little time slamming both fighters. It was a frame-up in hopes of landing a big purse out west, was his decree. However, Attell was said to be on his way to New York. To that Edgren replied, "Attell will find this climate good for his health. Fakers thrive here."[30]

"The British are coming" was a report that hit many of the dailies on September 27. Sailing from London to New York tomorrow would be Owen Moran, Johnny Summers and Pat O'Keefe. It was Moran's hopes to match with Attell as soon as possible. Even so, whenever a boxing entourage sailed across the pond, the results were seldom predictable. As for Attell, he would mind the time, along with any offers.

As the dust had settled a bit in Los Angeles, Attell settled in New York. "The Little Champ" did, however, agree to meet Freddie Weeks for twenty rounds, before the Pacific Athletic Club on October 29. In the face of all the recent reports, area boxing fans were excited: it was the champion in a title defense. The only drawback appeared to be Weeks, whom few had any knowledge of; Weeks had never fought on the West Coast. The Cripple Creek, Colorado, resident had few fights to his credit, with wins over Grover Hayes and Jimmy Walsh. Abe's brother Monte was also a Weeks knockout victim. A bit of publicity around Weeks, it was believed, would quickly solve the problem.

Suffering from a severe cold, Attell was unable to immediately train for his fight with Weeks—not until the end of the month, anyway. He was generally silent with regard to his personal life, so many were surprised to learn from the *Herald* that the fighter had converted his faith: "Since he was last here [Los Angeles] Attell has changed his faith and is no longer of the Jewish belief, on behest of his wife [Ethel] the champion joined the Catholic Church, and from now on will worship accordingly to the belief of the denomination."[31] Now attending Mass, Abraham was sincere about his conversion and even made his ring contests the subject for prayer. Attell declared to the press, "No more running around town for me. I have changed my faith and, of course, my way of living. The belief of my church does not permit me to act as I formerly did, and I will live strictly according to the creed in which I have faith."[32]

It was what the fans of Los Angeles wanted, what Abraham Attell so much desired, perhaps even prayed for, and what Tom McCarey needed: a decisive fourth-round knockout of Colorado boy Freddie Weeks by the undisputed featherweight champion. Weeks was just no match, as Attell turned up his game to the champion's setting. It turned out to be the perfect event at the perfect time. As stated by the *Call*:

> In the first round before the fight had progressed as much as a minute Attell sent a swift right cross to Weeks' jaw and the Cripple Creek boy staggered back, dazed and tottering. It was evident to every spectator that Attell could have knocked him out then without effort, but he refrained from doing so. He punched his staggering opponent with light jabs and with both hands and Weeks held tightly. The referee [Charles Eyton] separated them several times, Weeks clinging to Attell closely. When the round ended the Cripple Creek boy was weak and groggy.[33]

Two humdrum rounds followed, as Attell toyed with his opponent. Weeks could not land, as he was too slow a match for Abe's footwork. Then came the fourth round. As Attell was walking into his opponent, he delivered a stiff right punch directly to the point of the jaw of Weeks. Dazed, Weeks staggered and fell to the mat. The fight appeared over as Referee Eyton counted, but Weeks slowly gained his footing. He then took another vicious blow by Attell and went down again. Twice more the cycle occurred before the fighter's seconds, seeing Weeks battered on the mat, threw up the sponge.

Word was now hitting the streets of San Francisco that Owen Moran would battle with Abe Attell on New Year's Day. The *Evening Statesman* reported, "Manager McCarey is after the bout and is now negotiating with James Coffroth for the fight. McCarey offers fifty percent of the house which he estimates will equal $10,000."[34] Confirmation, it was hoped, would come in the days ahead.

Finally, on December 13, word came out of 'Frisco that:

> Owen Moran of England and Abe Attell, holder of the American Featherweight Championship title, have signed articles of agreement for a fight to be held on New Year's Day at Coffroth's Mission Street Arena. The men have agreed to weigh 120 pounds three hours before the fight. James J. Jeffries has been selected as referee, his fee of $1,000 to be paid by contestants. Each boxer posted a weight forfeit of $1,500 with W.W. Naughton, sporting editor of *The Examiner*, but it is safe to say that neither forfeit will be claimed.[35]

Ever since Moran defeated the hard-hitting Frankie Neil, this was the fight boxing fans wanted to see. Attell knew it and was driving a hard deal with Coffroth right up until the end. The *Evening Teller* reported: "The champion was insisting on ringside weight and the option of taking 60 percent or a guarantee of $6,000. Coffroth said he would have to take one or the other. Last night Attell chose the percentage and also gave way to the weight question, as Moran flatly refused to make ringside weight and Coffroth at the same time declined to handle any match where the men were to weigh in at the ring."[36] The battle then shifted to the referee question, Attell wanting Jeffries, Coffroth opting for Billy Roche. The issue was Jeff's fee of $1,000, which was finally split between the two fighters ($500) and the club ($500).

In Monte's Corner

It was not a particularly stressful year for Monte Attell, who fought all of his fights on the West Coast, in San Francisco, Los Angeles or Sacramento. Although a tough loss to Jimmy Carroll hurt, it was Attell's only defeat. He finished his short year—he fought only until October—with a solid twenty-round win over Al Emmick, a fighter he had knocked out in the previous month. Not enough can be said, however, for all the assistance—from hints on the opponents they shared to corner support—Monte provided his brother Abraham.

The only changes of lineal champions in 1907: Stanley Ketchel took over the middles and Mike "Twin" Sullivan took over the welters from William "Honey" Mellody.

There were, however, a few other notable fights: Tommy Burns finished off Bill Squires in the first round of their July 4 meeting in Colma, California; Stanley Ketchel came back to kayo Joe Thomas in the thirty-second round of their brawl, also in Colma, on September 2; Joe Gans retained his lightweight crown when Jimmy Britt couldn't answer in the sixth round of their September 9 fracas in San Francisco; and Jack Johnson broke Fireman Jim Flynn's jaw before grabbing an eleventh-round knockout on November 2, the bout also held in San Francisco.

In his first full year as world featherweight champion, Abe Attell took seven fights, battled 60 rounds, and saw no defeat. In successfully defending his title three times, "The Little Champ" had even done so twice against one opponent, Harry Baker. Though the opponents he faced were strong, none would fall into boxing's elite class. Understanding that a champion was often judged by the competition he faced, Attell hoped to change this in the months ahead. Between battles, Abraham managed to get married in a quiet California ceremony that was indicative of the privacy the fighter maintained. Having witnessed the personal lives of many fighters played out in the press, a low profile, he understood, better suited his lifestyle.

CHAPTER SEVEN

Minister of Defense, 1908

"There was no thrill, no excitement, nothing to give intense interest to the battle, though before the men entered the ring everything pointed to a typical championship mill. There was the immense crowd, the lively betting and the perfect weather. The fighters spoiled all this with their indifferent work."[1]—A newspaper review of Attell versus Moran.

The Progressive Era (1890s until 1920s), a period of widespread social activism and political reform across the United States, continued and in some cases found sports a worthy platform. On February 12, 1908, the first around-the-world car race began in New York City. On July 4, Battling Nelson, a white Danish immigrant, defeated the black lightweight boxing champion Joe Gans in a seventeen-round contest in Colma, California, exactly two years before Jack Johnson met James J. Jeffries in Reno, Nevada. On October 14, the Chicago Cubs won the 1908 World Series—for many it would always be their last time—by defeating the Detroit Tigers in Game 5. And U.S. President Theodore Roosevelt continued to inspire with quotations like, "Nothing in the world is worth having or worth doing unless it means effort, pain, difficulty.... I have never in my life envied a human being who led an easy life. I have envied a great many people who led difficult lives and led them well."[2]

For the first time since 1900, Abraham Attell would see his first four fights take place in his hometown. He, like most, continued to marvel at all the new construction—some 14,000 building permits were issued in 1908 alone—from the triangular, 11-story Phelan building to the 14-story Adam Grant Building, as the residents of San Francisco continued to persevere. Attell was amazed at the effect the earthquake had on the lives of so many people. That a single moment could change the course of so many lives was mind-boggling to the fighter. He marveled that so many residents decided to stay and rebuild—they did not want a single event to destroy the human spirit or define them in a negative light. Walking with his wife through the same streets he strolled as a child, Abe remarked on the city's transition while sharing stories of his youth; from selling newspapers to scrapping with his brothers, the champ enjoyed spinning a story as much as his new bride enjoyed listening. For "The Little Champ," this year would be all about the ring and his position atop the feathers, leaving the domestic vicissitudes to the attention of Mrs. Attell.

Abraham Attell Versus Owen Moran—January 1, 1908

On New Year's Day, in a highly publicized twenty-five round confrontation at Cof-froth's Arena in Colma, California, Abe Attell faced Owen Moran.[3] The fight had mes-merized the city for months, almost on a daily basis, and it was now coming to fruition—the first *real* international championship battle between featherweights in some time. Attell, a solid 1 to 2 public choice in the betting, was confident but cautious.

To little surprise, the *Call* reported the details:

Owen Moran and Abe Attell struggled for twenty-five rounds in the prize ring yesterday [New Year's Day] and at the close of their work was so evenly balanced that Referee Jim Jeffries called the cham-pionship match a draw. The big fellow had gauged the struggle accurately, as the experts at the ring-side who had kept a record round by round agreed with him. The referee expressed the sentiment of the big crowd of spectators when he said, "Two champions were fighting and I could not take the title from either of them on a hairline decision."[4]

It was a defensive battle, in which few aggressive blows were landed. Abe wisely allowed Moran, the featherweight champion of England, to assume the lead while he conserved his energy. After all, this was the same skillful Brit who had knocked out Frankie Neil in town the previous month and beat Tommy O'Toole in Philadelphia shortly before that. Both fighters proved indefatigable warriors whose systematic approach to a battle was their recipe for success. But, like any recipe, it's the quality of the ingredients that guarantees satisfaction. Those who thought Moran the shrewder of the two pugilists were quickly reminded that the Brit took the fight at 120 pounds—Attell's acute action serving to diminish, he believed, the power of his antagonist. Newspaper accounts were quick to describe the fight conditions:

The bout was brought off under ideal weather conditions and attracted the largest audience seen at such an affair since the fire. The crowd filled every part of the big arena and presented a remarkable picture when the featherweights stripped for action. The place was covered with a tent as neatly fitted as the sails of one of the yachts intended for the defense of the America's Cup. The canvas was spot-less and shed a soft light over the crowd, which brought it out in stronger relief than would have been the case at either a night fight or one in which the sun beat down upon the crowd.[5]

The atmosphere was electric as people from all walks of life mingled about. If you followed the fight game, you might catch a glimpse of a former star chatting or wading through the sea of spectators. Most arrived by streetcar, but numerous automobiles were also pressed to into action; whatever method it took was employed to watch this inter-national event.

Much of the credit for the fine battle needs also to go to Jeffries, who allowed the feathers to fight their fight, fast and without interruption: if Attell held Moran, or vice versa, Jeff would simply allow them to fight out. The *Call*, for one, detailed each act of the pugilists' performance:

It was a surprise to the spectators to see so much clinching done by Attell, as it was believed that he would be able to outfight Moran in a standup contest. There were many times when, after consider-able feinting between the two boys, Moran beat Attell to the punch, jabbing him and sending back his head. A number of times during the fight one or the other of the boys were half outside the ring, being supported only by the lower ropes. This did not prevent either of them from fighting, however, as they stood up and exchanged blows in this awkward position. This was an unusual spectacle for the crowd and was explained by the size of the fighters. When they crouched their heads were below the level of the upper rope.[6]

Two fighters with abundant patience typically yield little action, if of course you don't view waiting as an action. The fighters did not. Restraint, in generous supply, was the first step in determining the right time to act. It was this strategic assessment both fighters hoped to use to gain momentum. But what if that time never came? It's a risk every fighter takes. In the end, the damage assessment spoke for itself: Moran had only a black eye and a cut around his mouth, while Attell, just a few facial scars around the nose and mouth.

It was 2:38 p.m. when Moran, wearing a hat, overcoat, sweater and underclothing, entered the ring with Professor Jimmie Kelley, Alf Wicks and Tiv Kreling. Attell followed along with Battling Nelson, Kid Farmer, and brothers Monte and Caesar Attell.[7] Moran's bandages, as was often the case in a title fight, were examined by a member of Attell's team—in this case Nelson—before the toss for corners, Moran winning and selecting the southeast of the ring. At that time a hush came over the audience as Billy Jordan went to the center of the ring for the announcements: "Gentlemen, the English crackajack Champion of England, Owen Moran." As the warm reception died down, it was time for the hometown boy made good: "The cleverest boy in the world, and the featherweight champion of America, Abe Attell."[8]

Attell, sporting white trunks with a red, white and blue belt, looked in fine condition, and Moran, wearing black trunks, look equally fit. The challenges, as traditional, were subsequently read. They included those from Spider Garrity of Cleveland, Tommy O'Toole from Philadelphia, Eddie Kelley of Buffalo, Jim Neil on behalf of his brother Frankie, plus an indirect challenge from Mike "Twin" Sullivan to Young Ketchel.

A roar then went up, as Jeff took off his coat to the recognition of everyone ringside. Billy Jordan then stepped forward to continue, "The only undefeated champion of the world, Honest Jim Jeffries."[9] Another clamor arose as Jeff jokingly jabbed Jordan for his proclamation. As Jeff stood alongside the two combatants, the contrast in size proved quite the juxtaposition.

From the opening round, it was obvious you were looking at two crack fighters evenly matched. Both combatants relied heavily on their lefts to guide them through the action. After an opening round of measuring and cautious sparring, Attell staggered Moran with a left to the face near the end of round two. The pair had to be pulled apart by Jeff after the gong.

Moran hurt Attell with a sound left to the stomach in the third, and Moran's lips began to bleed in the fourth. As Moran concentrated on the stomach, Attell was using his short arm jolts effectively, especially his left. Not surprisingly, Attell complained of holding.

The combatants were inseparable in the fifth, even as the bell rang. Attell out-feinted Moran in the sixth, both fighters trading punch for punch—a Moran right to the body countered with a vicious left to the jaw.

The seventh belonged to Moran, even after taking an opening right to the jaw and slipping to his knees. When not in a clinch, the body damage Attell withstood during the seventh round, he gave back in the eighth.

The ninth round was even, while most gave Moran a slight edge in the tenth.

The crowd jeered Attell for using his shoulder on Moran in the eleventh. This came after Attell staggered Moran with a vicious right to the jaw followed by a right cross to the nose. Attell had a shot at an unbalanced Moran in the twelfth, but could not capitalize. Moran's best blow of the fight came in this round as he landed a direct right to the jaw of Attell.

Moran did take a solid right on the mouth in the thirteenth, not to mention an unexpected Attell thumb to the eye. Attell warned Moran against holding, then, perhaps in frustration, delivered some punches after the gong. The crowd jeered Abe for his actions.

Attell, who perpetually complained about holding, landed hard on Moran's left eye in the fifteenth. The sixteenth to most was even, with some giving Moran a slight edge.

A hard overhand swing from Moran hurt Attell in the seventeenth, and such a rally ensued that many thought the end was near. Thrice Referee Jeffries had to split the fighters. Attell regained his composure and delivered some damaging face and body blows in the eighteenth.

Moran landed two left hooks on Attell in the nineteenth before "The Little Champ" could step out of range. Moran continued to put Attell to the ropes, but could not keep him there. The crowd turned to Moran's side by yelling his name—prompted by some wild swings—in the twentieth, but it did little to entice a conclusion.

"While the boys were clinched in the twenty-first round Jeffries separated them and said rebukingly, 'Children!'" as though they were a pair of boys scrapping in a lot.[10] The pace was a little slow in the twenty-second round, but it soon livened up as Moran rushed Attell to the ropes. The Californian balanced himself on the lower rope and kept on fighting. The Mighty Jeffries raised a laugh when he looked reprovingly at Attell after the latter had struck him a chance blow on the chest. The twenty-third was an even round, while a slow twenty-fourth could have been given to either combatant.

As the gong for the final round sounded, there was considerable anticipation. Moran landed a hard left hook as they broke out of a clinch, and it shook Attell. The champion then held, only to encounter rights from Moran. Following another clinch, Attell managed two good lefts that nearly brought Moran down. Angered, Moran retaliated with a sound blow to the head. A hard right to the jaw of Attell near the end looked promising, but it was too late. The bell sounded and Referee Jeffries raised the hands of both gladiators.

In the words of James J. Jeffries:

There was only one decision to render and I think that every student of the game who saw the go will agree with me. Both boys were fighting all the time and both displayed such marvelous cleverness that neither could obtain a commanding lead over the other. It was a case of a champion of our country fighting against a champion of another for the world's title, and under these circumstances there was no chance to give either man the decision unless he had a commanding lead. It was a great battle, one of the best that I have ever witnessed. The science displayed by both men was remarkable and I was bewildered by the way they came back fighting round after round when it seemed as though such little fellows would be exhausted.[11]

In the words of Abe Attell:

I will not complain against the decision, though I really believe that I had a commanding lead. I did all the fighting in the earlier rounds and Moran simply came back in the last five simply to make a dying show. I will take off my hat to him as being the toughest and cleverest man I have met in my long career in the ring. He has everything and he kept me going pretty lively all the time. I will fight him again any time he wants to, but I insist that he do 120 pounds. He was overweight when he weighed in and I think that I was entitled to collect half his forfeit. I have a good line on his style of fighting now and the next time we hook up I will put him away. I was not tired at the finish and his blows did not affect me.[12]

In the words of Owen Moran:

The weight was too much for me. I was weak when I entered the ring and unable to put the steam behind my blows. I was compelled to run on the road for two hours in order to get down to weight, and then I was a bit over the notch. This worried and fatigued me. The decision was all right and the way the crowd treated me touched my heart. I did the best I could to win, but I was too weak to do myself justice. The next time I fight Attell the weight will be 122 pounds or nothing. He is a wonderful man. They have nothing like him in England. The way he blocked my punches and came back at me was marvelous. I was trying all the time, and even though I was weak I believed that I could manage to wing in one that would end the battle.[13]

After the battle, Moran made up his mind to head east and accept a much safer option: a ten-week theater engagement. As for Attell, there was talk of another battle with Frankie Neil, but the latter wanted twenty rounds, while the champ only six.

Obvious to Attell's adversaries and anyone who followed the fight game was "The Little Champ's" astute use of weight as both a psychological and physical advantage, no better exemplified than with this fight. Weight was utilized to distract Moran. His concern over making weight diverted his attention from other elements of his game, including improving his punching power—the more weight a fighter can efficiently shift, likely the more powerful the punch.[14]

When dealing with boxers who have this level of expertise, any factor or issue an opponent can find, then employ to his advantage, should be optimized. Taking a closer look: Moran's camp had a discrepancy between their scales and those used to weigh in, which was a huge mistake on their part. This forced their fighter into an immediate weight loss program before one of the biggest fights of his life. When Moran officially stepped on the scales he was slightly over (estimated at two ounces), so Attell, as might be expected, declared he was overweight and claimed the forfeit of $1,500—a strategic move on the part of the champion to irritate his adversary and hopefully force him into a concession. According to the *Call*, "He [Attell] then asked for 60 percent of the purse, win, lose or draw. Charley Harvey, the representative of Moran, finally agreed to forfeit $250."[15]

Neither, the referee nor the official stakeholder was present, another huge mistake by Moran. If they had been, and Attell knew this, they could have declared the process satisfactory without issue. Quintessential Attell, from start to finish, always the master mediator—the goal was tantamount to upsetting the apple cart, without losing the apples. Evident by the fight—which brought a $15,000 gate, by the way—was that Moran would have been better served at 122 pounds, instead of 120, and the Attell team knew this before the match was ever made.

Although Attell, as a rule, kept his cards close to his vest, occasionally one would slip out, as it did on January 28 when it was pointed out that the fighter was broke. While it was no secret "The Little Champ" enjoyed the ponies, few were conscious of the fortune he squandered on the activity. With regard to the avocation, the *Topeka State Journal* noted:

Some friend tipped Abe that the races were a snap to beat, and he has been following them ever since. When he has no fight on hand the little Hebrew scrapper can be found at Emeryville hopscotching about for inside information. Inside information is for suckers, and Attell gets his share. Before Attell went into the ring for his last battle he was practically broke. His forfeit was posted by a Fillmore Street friend, who has too much brains to dabble with the bookmakers. Abe even had to borrow money to tide him over until after the fight. But for the horses he would now be in comfortable circumstances, for he has earned a big bunch of money.[16]

Having last met Attell in Los Angeles, Frankie Neil now traveled north to meet "The Little Champ" at Dreamland Pavilion in San Francisco on January 31, an action to absolve him from his loss, or so it was hoped. Neil, who had more canards following him than Attell, intended to be in peak shape. However, the prevailing odds were even money that Attell would knock out his opponent before the twentieth round. As for Attell, he had paid little attention to Neil, having just come out of his rigorous training for Moran. Both fighters were rumored to have been working a book (sportsbook, or a venue where a gambler could wager on a variety of competitions) at the local racetracks as a training diversion. The boxers agreed to weigh 122 pounds ringside, with Jack Welsh serving as referee.

As for the money, the *Call* reported, "Fifty-five percent of the gross receipts will go to the fighters, and according to the articles, the winner is to receive 60 percent and the loser 40 percent. But, apparently there was a private agreement between the boxers to split the money 50 percent each."[17] This according to Team Neil, who signed the articles as written, but stated the fight was off if the money wasn't divided equally. "Neil will train at Shannon's, near San Rafael, while Attell will go to Millett's, at 7700 Mission Street in Colma, where he trained for Moran."[18]

Attell, well versed in the skills of his antagonist, gave Neil an unmerciful beating for thirteen rounds until his seconds finally threw up the sponge. It was a pitiful performance by Neil, who scarcely landed a blow in the first six rounds. Only in the seventh and eighth rounds did Neil show signs of life, but by that time his face mimicked a topographical map from Attell's ordnance. Though Neil protested the action of his seconds, it was obviously a wise decision.

Catching Abe or other prominent athletes at the racetrack or other sporting events was common. Wagers were as frequent as building permits in San Francisco, and money changed hands, as the rumors changed the odds. The newspapers not only loved the gossip, they printed it. The longer a champion held the title, the more redundant the rumors; common for an Attell fight was, "the clever boxer will likely stall to get another big purse."

New York State fighter Eddie Kelly, a.k.a. "Buffalo Newsboy" or "Buffalo Whirlwind," had been fighting down in Los Angeles, and caught the eye of horseman Frank Dwyer. When the entrepreneur wired up an offer to back Kelly against the champion, Attell bit. The twenty-round romp, at 122 pounds, was planned for February 29, but the actual date ended up being February 28 in Dreamland Pavilion in San Francisco. Attell was an immediate 1 to 2 favorite over Kelly, who was also a regular sparring partner with Battling Nelson. Neither of the fighters was expected to struggle to meet the beam, the weigh-in to take place at Leap's Billiard Parlor. Even the local papers, thanks to a shrewd Billy Nolan, who could sell hay to a farmer, were hyping Kelly, with columnist R.A. Smyth referring to "Eddie Kelly, who looks to be fully as good a bet as Owen Moran."[19] After the fight, the veteran wordsmith, dining on crow, would equate the fighter's performance to stage fright.

As stated by the *Call*, "Attell will have his brothers and Dick Cullen in his corner while Kelly will be advised by Billy Nolan and Harry Foley. Referee Jack Welsh will have charge of the weighing in, as well as the subsequent proceedings in the ring."[20]

The contest wasn't pretty, nor was it a competitive encounter, as Abe Attell quickly sent Eddie Kelly, the Buffalo newsboy, to fairyland. According to the *Hawaiian Gazette*:

Down three times last night in rapid succession in the seventh round, and only the interference of the police prevented an actual knockout. A stiff right swing to the jaw sent the Easterner down for the count of five. As he rose to his feet, vicious rights and lefts dropped him for a second time on the carpet, and the same lightning punches that he was powerless to block put him down on the third occasion. Eight seconds had been told off when Captain of Police Duke called an end to the one-sided affair.[21]

For Attell, there was too much cash initially floating around not to take the fight, not to mention Kelly had a face like Terry McGovern, so the champ could simply call it target practice.

Attell wanted Joe Gans next, but got Battling Nelson instead. Sam Berger, representing the Washington Athletic Club, put together the fifteen-round fight, set for March 31, at 132 pounds. Worth noting were the articles, as they appeared in the *Pacific Commercial Advertiser*:

> Fighters to receive 60 percent of the gross receipts, purse to be divided 60 percent to the winner and 40 percent to the loser; Battling Nelson and Abe Attell agree to post a forfeit of $1,000 each to operate as follows: Five hundred dollars for weight and $500 for appearance; Sam Berger, representing the Washington Athletic Club, agrees to post a forfeit of $1,000 as a guarantee of good faith and intention of bringing off the contest and straight Marquis [sic] of Queensberry rules to govern contest.[22]

Then, of course, there was the match assessment. This as printed in the *Call*:

> The match is a much better one than proposed with Joe Gans. In the case of Nelson, it will be the meeting of a sensational boxer with a man who is essentially a fighter. The match will stir up a lot of comment, as there is a wide field for argument between the adherents of the two men. Had Attell met Gans this element of doubt would not have existed, as Gans is fully as clever as Attell and the added weight would have made him an overwhelming favorite.[23]

The *Rock Island Argus* saw the battle in this manner: "This will be the dray horse against the racer, and it is hard to see where Nelson can get anything but a comical peppering. He will not be damaged any, but will be made to look much like a monkey. There is, of course, a chance for him to catch Abey, but the chance is slim."[24] Slim, because Attell's only chance of survival was to avoid Nelson. He could do that for fifteen rounds, but a longer distance would be risky.

Drawing Nelson—March 31, 1908

On the authority of the *Evening World*, "Fight fans are divided today in their opinion as to the merits of Abe Attell and Battling Nelson, who, after fifteen rounds of a red-hot, slashing fight here last night, received the verdict of a draw from Referee Eddie Smith. The decision pleased the crowd."[25]

True to form, Nelson was aggressive. Boring in, round after round, "The Dane" was unrelenting in pursuit of his opposer. However, the Battler encountered a major problem. Attell wasn't always there when he arrived. "The Little Champ" would move like the wind, avoiding Nelson's big guns that caught more air than flesh. Meanwhile, Nelson's face swelled and bled from Attell's consistent left jabs and precision right hooks. One observer stated it looked as if Nelson had "been stabbed with knives in the face."[26] When Nelson did hit his target, which appeared to be by accident, or when Abe decided to oppose a rush, it yielded enough damage to persuade Attell do one thing: run faster. The heavier Nelson weighed 131 pounds to Attell's 124, and his punching power was far superior.

According to accounts, "The coliseum was packed long before the fighters appeared in the ring for the main bout. Packy McFarland, who is here to meet Jimmy Britt, was introduced and received a warm welcome. Attell was attended in the ring by his brothers and 'Spider' Kelly, while Nelson's chief advisor was Harry Foley. In the first betting Nelson was a favorite at 10 to 7½."[27]

As for the highlights:

A quick first round found Attell landing blows, but almost slipping to his knees from a misfire. Two rights to the jaw, then a left to the face, convinced "The Little Champ" that a clinch wasn't such a good idea. Attell bled slightly from the mouth at the gong.

It was a superb second round for Attell, who sidestepped with efficiency and blocked to perfection, all while landing some nice combinations. Attell's short-arm blows were measured perfectly and enabled him to retaliate when necessary.

In the third, Nelson came back offensively, firing successfully to the face and body of Attell, while the latter struck with strong mixes. Attell, as anticipated, took the brunt of the damage at close proximity. Thankfully for Attell, his quick combinations to Nelson's face managed to keep the fighter at bay. The *Herald* noted, "The round ended with Attell landing on Nelson's face at will. The crowd cheered Attell wildly for his exhibition."[28]

A fairly even fourth saw Nelson fail at long-range sparring with Attell. Many witnesses noted, "Nelson unintentionally struck Attell over the eye with his right after the bell rang and he was vigorously hissed. It was Attell's round."[29]

The first two minutes of the fifth belonged to Nelson, while the final sixty seconds was all Attell, who even managed to bloody Nelson's nose.

A strong sixth round witnessed Attell striking at will, although Nelson appeared stronger.

The seventh was a whirlwind of fighting at close range by both boxers. Advantage Nelson early, but there was a late-round comeback by Attell.

Some powerful body blows by Nelson in the eighth prompted complaints by Attell, primarily about head butts. Attell continued to save himself from damage with precision left hooks.

In the ninth, Attell was almost sent through the ropes by a shot to the stomach, but he managed to recover. Nelson showed some solid offense before being rocked by some combinations to the jaw.

The tenth round, Nelson continued to withstand a fierce pounding to the face. As Attell's left hooks were striking with precision, Nelson did his best to strike back.

Nelson came on strong in the eleventh round with a powerful attack on Attell's body. Nevertheless, Attell continued to sidestep and weave in avoidance. Some had the round a shade to Attell.

"The Little Champ" stalled in the twelfth, but did so while taking a beating from Nelson, including a bloody nose and lip. The crowd cheered for Nelson as he nearly dropped Attell with a left to the jaw. Attell, as he had done the entire fight, countered with targeted combinations.

In the thirteenth, Attell was trying to avoid any damage but caught a solid shot to the stomach that doubled him over. Recovering rather quickly, Attell continued his machine gun combinations to the jaw that did little to slow the incoming Battler.

Nelson sensed that he had Attell close to a knockout in the fourteenth, which he did, but Attell managed to survive. According to the *Herald*, "They fought at an almost superhuman pace and as the bell rang they almost fell through the ropes from the viciousness of their efforts. Nelson seemed to have a shade."[30]

As claimed by the *Bemidji Daily Pioneer*:

Then came the fifteenth and last round of the battle. Both popped out of their corners. They met in the middle of the ring, and went at it hammer and tongs. Nelson in his eagerness missed a couple of vicious swings, and they fought at a breakneck pace at close range. Nelson has the best of this game. Attell took a hard right on the jaw and countered with a cross that staggered the Dane. Nelson's face was puffed and bleeding, and his eyes swollen nearly shut. But he fought in that last rally like a wild man. He couldn't find the finishing blow. Suddenly, in the midst of the mixing, Attell seemed to put all of his reserve energy into one last flurry of fighting. Blows fell as thick as hailstones. Attell [was] landing four [blows] to the Battler's one. And then, with the crowd on its feet in an uproar of applause the fight ended. Nelson and Attell dropped their hands and stood looking at each other, both unconvinced. Referee Smith instantly gave his decision—"Draw."[31]

For many ring analysts the turning point came in the ninth round, when a punished Nelson finally (and that cannot be overstated) succeeded in getting beyond Attell's impregnable guard. Having endured everything Attell could throw at him, his face a picture of war-torn abuse, Nelson believed it was his turn. By round fourteen, many ringside spectators cringed as they observed the bloody countenance of Attell responding to Nelson's robust body punches. Launched from an eight-pound advantage, it was clear by this time that Nelson smelled a knockout. The *Salt Lake Herald* concluded: "The fight was a most spectacular one and there was not one round during which the crowd present was not on its feet shouting for one man or the other. At the end of the contest, both men were fairly deluged with blood, Nelson's face presenting the worst sight."[32]

Still healing, Abe Attell got together with "Brooklyn Tommy" Sullivan on the evening of April 7, to sign up with Luke Marisch for a twenty-round battle at the Coliseum on April 30. As for the specifics: Both fighters were to weigh in at 5 o'clock. Attell was guaranteed $3,000, win, lose or draw, with Sullivan to receive $1,250, if the gate receipts were under $9,000, and $250 more if they were over the figure. Billy Roche was selected as referee and Eddie Graney as stakeholder. Both fighters appeared anxious for the event.

On April 16, a group of pugilists, including Abe Attell and Battling Nelson, gave a boxing exhibition in front of the university's Polydeuceam Club, at the Allston Way Skating Rink in Berkeley. It was billed as a special Ladies' Night and scheduled well in advance, but was quickly opposed by a church faction and prevented by District Attorney Brown. The group, choosing a creative solution, then incorporated. This allowed them to obtain a boxing ordinance to conduct the event. The boxers, to no surprise, enjoyed themselves as much as the spectators.

Four days later, Abe Attell was in Seattle, at Sound Beach. There he greeted the familiar mug of Eddie Kelly, the same Buffalo fighter he had dropped in seven rounds just over seven weeks earlier. Scheduled for twenty-rounds on April 20, a crowd estimated at 3,000 to 4,800 spectators turned out for what was billed as a new and improved Kelly. The trimmer boxer, who had enhanced his skills thanks to being a member of Packy McFarland's training camp, was anxious for his rematch with the champion.[33] And, although the improved Kelly did indeed look a bit better, he was still no match for "The Little Champ." Kelly, who was groggy at the end of the seventh, was dropped twice in the eighth round before the arbiter put an end to the abuse. Referee John Reid had seen enough and stopped the fight, giving the victory to Attell. The *Rock Island Argus* concluded, "Kelly not only proved unable to solve the elusive tactics employed by Attell, but he also ran into punch after punch, where his own impetus aided his downfall."[34]

In Kelly's words: "The best man won. Attell is the fastest little thing in his class. He is too fast for me now, but I intend to work hard for the next year and feel confident that someday I will be able to wrest the title from the boy. I will have to gain speed and more science."[35]

The last thing Attell needed going into the fight with Tommy Sullivan on April 30, especially after his impressive draw with Nelson and recent victories over Eddie Kelly, was the press resurrecting his 1904 confrontation with the fighter in St. Louis, when Abe was the victim of a fifth round knockout. But the *Los Angeles Herald* felt it necessary to reprint an article on the front page of the "Sporting Section" on Sunday morning, April 26, four days before both fighters were to meet again. The article, written by St. Louis scribe J.W. McConaughy, detailed his views from the West End Club's press box, and stated, "The left shot to Attell's body, which ended the battle in the fifth round, was a fair blow."[36] For whatever reason, the newspaper felt compelled to dredge up a controversial event from four years ago; the fighters had since met again only last year and fought to a draw. The recent press had been long on criticism and short on praise for Attell, with the exception of some of the local dailies. With little competition in the current class of feathers, Attell had little choice but to weigh all his options. While some warned him that the punishment he endured from a lightweight like Nelson had a cumulative effect, Attell seemed resigned to consider all offers.

Fighting at what appeared to be a suitable frequency, Attell was back home at the end of the month to meet "Brooklyn Tommy" Sullivan. You could sense from the very start that things were not right, beginning when Referee Alvie King declaring all bets off.[37]

Hopelessly outclassed, the St. Louis boxer, not to mention former champion, delivered a pitiful performance. So pathetic, in fact, that cries of "foul" could be heard from every corner of the venue. This activated *San Francisco Call* boxing writer R.A. Smythe to conduct some investigation on his own. Two days later Smythe would conclude that those who framed the match could not get their bets down and in frustration decided not to allow others to profit from their manipulation. The *Evening Star* reported:

> In the fourth round, after about a minute's fighting, Attell having drawn Sullivan into close quarters, promptly delivered a short arm right to the chin, which sent Sullivan to the mat. In a dazed condition Sullivan regained his footing. Attell went after him hammer and tongs. Twice more the St. Louis lad went to the floor, finally rolling over on his back. As he was being counted out a policeman stepped into the ring and ordered the contest stopped. Owing to a change at the last moment in the articles of agreement permitting Sullivan to weigh in at 126 pounds, the referee was instructed to declare all bets off.

Suspicion hung over the fight like a buzzard over road kill, leaving the *Call* to pen: "The betting showed from the start that the friends of Attell knew the exact status of the match. They flooded poolrooms with money and offered the most tempting odds in an effort to lure the few more dollars from the gullible public. In their eagerness to get in the ultimate dollar they were offering 10 to 2½. They even went further than this, as they offered 10 to 6 that Attell would win inside of 15 rounds."[38]

Following the event, Attell wisely decided a break was in order-a cessation of fifty-one days, to be exact.

Having not put a pair of boxing gloves on in New York City since March of 1906, and that during an exhibition, the featherweight champion was thrilled to return on June 20, at the Grand Union Athletic Club, for a short-distance affair (six rounds) against veteran Matty Baldwin.[39] A sweltering crowd seemed to enjoy the six-round display by Attell, even if it looked like the champion wasn't going all out. The sparring session entered the books as a no-decision, but most saw it as a draw. For Abe, it was simply pocket cash.

Finally, on July 11, in San Francisco, came the eagerly awaited announcement: a

"The Bunker Hill Bearcat," Mathew "Matty" Baldwin (left), along with manager Alex A. MacLean and Boston lightweight Gilbert Gallant, enjoy a training session (Library of Congress).

rematch between Owen Moran and Abe Attell had been set for Labor Day, September 7. Promoter James Coffroth would host the twenty-round battle for the featherweight title at his arena in Colma, California. The terms according to the *Albuquerque Citizen*: "Moran and Attell are to weigh in at 122 pounds four hours before the battle. There is some doubt here as to whether either of the boys can make the weight without considerable difficulty. Jim Jeffries will be the third man in the ring. The fighters will split sixty percent of the gross receipts on a 60–40 percent basis."[40] Later, Attell would demand that Jack Welsh referee and Moran's camp would push for twenty-five rounds, yet settle for twenty-three.

If you were going to make the arduous journey west, then why not pick up a fight along the way? At least that's what most fighters believed. Hopefully a strategic confrontation, one with a large purse, and who knows?—maybe some significant side interest as well. Attell found his gold mine in Sandpoint, Idaho. Taking a page of out of the marketing book for the town made famous in 1906 by the Gans versus Nelson battle, was entrepreneur Johnny Reid, who represented a contingent of businessmen interested in attracting more commerce to their little town, population under 3,000. Reid, who was always quick to point out that the town of Goldfield rose from 700 inhabitants to 7,000 by reason of the Nelson-Gans fight, was actually hoping to grab "The Durable Dane" himself for a bout at some point, but just hadn't had the opportunity to speak with Nelson. His current focus had been on his latest promotion, a ten-round affair between the featherweight champion and Seattle fighter Eddie Marino scheduled for July 29.

Born Angeleo Marino in Italy, the young fighter fought under the alias Kid Meringo and his notoriety up to this point—at least what could be verified—was based on a twenty-round draw with the popular Chicago fighter Eddie Santry. Five days before the fight Marino stated, "I do not know whether I will win this fight, but if I do it means a great deal of money for me and I will do my utmost. I will fight all the way and he will have to put me out to defeat me."[41] Ticket sales, as well as wagers, were heavy for this fight and the out-of-town interest was living up to expectations.

Unhesitant to share their observation, an unforgiving press printed it as they saw it: "FEATHERWEIGHT KING BEATS ANOTHER DUB," read the headline of the first column piece that ran in the *Los Angeles Herald*. Subtitled "Abe Attell Rakes in Bunch of Easy Money at Butte by Whipping Unknown Kiddo in Ten Rounds of Alleged Fighting.[42] For ten rounds at Sandpoint, Idaho, Seattle's Eddie Marino, stood off Abe Attell, the featherweight champion of the world—in front of a crowd estimated at between 1,200 to 2,000 spectators." The newspaper also reported that it was originally scheduled for twenty rounds, then altered to ten just prior to the fighters' entering the ring. The *Spokane Press* concluded: "For eight rounds the champion played with Marino, then went at him viciously in attempt to put him away in the last two. Marino was knocked to the floor five times in those two rounds but each time he came up ready for more. Attell was given the decision."[43]

Clear by the action was that Attell wasn't going to let him coast the ten rounds, leaving questions as to what round was the money on? Perhaps a better question might be: what was the motivation behind altering the distance only moments before the fight? It was no secret that the greater part of the betting was waged on Marino's chances of going the distance. As for the young fighter, he would go on to defeat Billy Lander, the lightweight champion of Canada, at Calgary. There was also chatter, at least between Reid and Marino, for a match with Attell in Calgary on Christmas Day. The champion's camp was without comment. In a sign that maybe things were not everything they appeared to be, it was learned on August 21 that Attell, who supposedly had "a lot of money and plenty of influential backers, has not yet been able to raise the $10,000 forfeit for his coming match with Owen Moran, and has asked for more time to get the money together."[44]

23 Skidoo, September 7, 1908

Two major boxing events, held on September 7, created two contrasting headlines in the following day's sports sections across the United States and even the United Kingdom. The *San Francisco Call* perhaps illustrated the dichotomy best: "Attell and Moran Engage in Farcical Combat at Colma," and "Papke Gives Ketchel Awful Beating for Twelve Rounds."

Elaborating on the first, the *Call* stated: "The featherweight championship of the world is still a mooted question. Abe Attell and Owen Moran, champions of America and England, respectively, received something like $8,000 yesterday afternoon for leaving that particular question undetermined. Both are willing to tackle the problem again as soon as another $13,000 worth of public curiosity can be aroused."[45]

Now, to the second statement by the *Call*: "Stanley Ketchel of Montana, former middleweight champion of the world, was knocked out in the twelfth round at Jeffries' Vernon Arena at 4 o'clock this afternoon by Billy Papke of Illinois, who is now middleweight champion of the world. Ketchel was a 2 to 1 favorite in the betting."[46]

If you were a fan of boxing, but didn't attend either bout, it became clear which fight you should have spent your hard-earned dollar on.

Back to the Attell versus Moran battle, the *Call* concluded: "The fight-going public has been stung again. It fell for a world's championship contest to be determined in 23 rounds by men who had gone 25 rounds to a draw. The public put up $13,303 at the gate, and for its money was treated to a splendid exhibition of Abe Attell's ability consistently to avoid anything like fighting through 23 rounds, and possibly half as many more."[47]

Reporters covering the fight debated a few quick observations: Attell was "stalling through 23 rounds," and "in only five of the twenty-three rounds did he make even a pretense of fighting." Secondly, the decision was "a bit tough on Moran, who did all the fighting the fans got, and who had an edge on a sufficient number of rounds to entitle him to a decision," so Moran "must be held blameless." Finally, "Referee Jack Welsh's draw decision was the best feature of the world's championship contest."[48]

In retrospect, the *Call* concluded: "There was no thrill, no excitement, nothing to give intense interest to the battle, though before the men entered the ring everything pointed to a typical championship mill. There was the immense crowd, the lively betting and the perfect weather. The fighters spoiled all this with their indifferent work."[49]

Abraham Attell believed the decision was unjust and stated so:

I always get the worst of it in my own town every time I fight here. I had a clear lead throughout the fight and certainly was entitled to the decision. I asked Referee Welsh when he visited me a few days ago at my training camp what was he going to do if the fight went the limit. He said he would call it a draw if the fight was close, but if either man had a decided advantage he would give a decision. I am willing to fight Moran again under the same conditions at 20 or 25 rounds, but I would not fight my mother over a distance of 45 rounds.[50]

Referee Welsh believed it an even fight throughout and claimed:

There was no other verdict but a draw decision which I could render and be fair to both men. The battle was evenly waged throughout and to decide a championship on such a close margin would not be right. Attell had a slight lead, as he did the cleaner work. He was the cleverer boxer and scored cleanly. Moran, however, evened it up by his aggressive tactics and his willingness to mix it at any time. There was no time in the contest that either fighter appeared to be in trouble and as there was not a knockdown scored during the contest a draw decision, to my judgment, was fair to both men.[51]

Owen Moran claimed victory, stating:

Why, Attell never led during the fight and I forced the fighting all the way and I don't see how Referee Welsh could call it a draw. Attell did not outbox me, as I met him blow for blow and when a man leads and forces the fight and takes a chance of being knocked out he should be given the decision. I injured my right hand in the second round on Attell's hip when he jumped into the air and I could not use that hand with good effect in the remaining rounds. I will stay here for some time and will take Attell on again, but I would like to fight him 40 rounds or more. I am willing to fight any man they want to bring.[52]

The battle was a lesson on the art of defense, a craft often dismissed by the uneducated follower of the sweet science as cowardly. Moran could not mount the offense required to defeat Attell, thus the draw. Had Moran been the offensive fighter he claimed he was, he would have made the necessary adjustments to take the fight beyond a draw. Elite fighters, such as Attell and Moran, utilize their strengths and compensate for their weaknesses. On the rare occasions when they fight each other, this task must be conducted at a level of precision beyond that of their opponent, which means every level of detail must work to their favor from the weight of the gloves and length of the fight, to training and making weight. It's a chess match, and one wrong move could cost you a victory.

Here's a better observation as noted by the *San Francisco Call*: "Several times during the fight Moran measured Attell with his left and then sent the right over to the jaw. This was the most effective punch that he had, but it didn't seem to carry a great deal of force. Abe soon became alert for the blow, but not until it made him look like a busher a couple of times."[53] Since his most effective punch lacked the necessary power, then that was a weakness of Moran's training. And what did his opponent do? After noting his deficiency, Attell compensated for it with his movement. The ability to effectively counter an offensive action was why Abe Attell was a champion.

To be thought of as a talented boxer by the public is one thing, but when a legendary fighter such as Jim Jeffries singles you out for fighting prowess, that creates an entirely new level of acceptance. While Attell was setting his sight on Freddie Welsh, Jeffries, who was never far from a reporter, made his views known: "There are four white fighters before the public that I have great confidence in. They are Billy Papke, Battling Nelson, Abe Attell and little Johnny Coulon. It makes no difference when this quartet starts, you are sure to get a run for your money."[54]

Jeffries went on to applaud Papke for his brains, Nelson for his record, and Coulon for his quick development. Jeff concluded with: "Then take Attell. The Hebrew boxer is a wonder. There is no other way that I could express my opinion about Attell. He is clever as they make them. His record is what we might call a dream when it is looked over."[55]

Abraham Attell Versus Freddie Welsh—November 25, 1908

Word came on November 2 that Abe Attell and lightweight Freddie Welsh would meet the night before Thanksgiving at the Jeffries Athletic Club in Vernon, California, for a fifteen-round battle.[56] According to the *Herald*: "Attell will get $3,000 for his end, win, lose or draw, and Welsh, who will have to make 130 pounds at 2 o'clock the day of the fight, will take 30 percent, win, lose, or draw, figured upon the total receipts of the attraction."[57]

It was no secret that Attell, the lighter of the duo, wanted only a ten-round affair, while Welsh was hoping for twenty and that a weight compromise needed to be worked out. Both parties came to agreement with little problem and affixed their signatures to the contract. The *Herald* also claimed: "Welsh is the cleverest man in the lightweight division today. Nobody in that division classes with him in cleverness and speed any more than the featherweights of the world class with Attell. These boys are in a class by themselves."[58]

The Attell family was also thrilled to learn that Monte had been selected to meet Mike Kutchos for fifteen rounds as part of the second preliminary, or the semi-windup; the boys wore to weigh in at 116 pounds at 2 o'clock. Monte came down to Los Angeles on the Owl, or evening train, on November 11 to assist his brother in training. As for Abe, the *Herald* reported that he went hunting with Harry Burt first, before later turned his attention to fight preparation: "He killed one duck, and Harry got another, and both returned to Los Angeles with the story that they had killed their limit. They forgot to mention the further fact that one apiece is more than the average limit for them. According to those who enjoyed the sport as spectators, neither could hit a duck with a stick if the duck was tied to the post."[59]

Freddie Welsh, lightweight champion of the world (1915–1917), debuted in 1905 and fought until 1922 (Library of Congress).

The final workouts for both fighters drew big crowds, as the anticipation for the fight was huge. The *Herald* continued to document each stage of the battle: "Attell will do absolutely nothing from now on [November 24] that resembles hard labor, for he is right on the edge and could go into the ring at any minute prepared to put up the battle of his life. Welsh, on the other hand, still has a couple of pounds in the line of excess baggage, and today will taper this off in order to be at weight tomorrow."[60]

While the betting was slow, interest in the fight continued to increase. As stated by the *Herald*:

According to Jeffries club officials the demand for seats exceeds that recorded for the Papke-Ketchel Labor Day fight, and indications for a house exceeding $12,000 are bright. Never before have the fans in this section of the country been presented with such a classy bout, and as the racing men are all scrap enthusiasts a crowded house is sure to greet the featherweight champion and England's premier lightweight when they crawl between the Vernon ropes tomorrow to engage in their all-engrossing argument.[61]

In his pre-fight statement, Attell confirmed:

You can say for me that I have not been beaten in four years and I have no idea of taking a beating this time. Of course, I know that I am tackling no ordinary lightweight when I meet Welsh, but I have proved many times that I can go out of my class and win, and I expect to do so again when I meet the cleverest lightweight in the business. My condition is highly satisfactory and there is nothing lacking that I could wish for that would be of any aid to me unless it be that I would ask for a few more pounds. I prefer to fight a good one, rather than a dub [a jab at the *Los Angeles Herald*], any time, and I know that is Welsh wins I will not lose any prestige, as I am going out of my class to meet the cleverest and speediest lightweight in the ring. I shall make the fight of my life and am in condition to do it.[62]

In his pre-fight statement, Welsh announced:

I am pleased at the opportunity to box Attell because I believe I will defeat him and am frank to admit that to do so would add materially to my prestige as a boxer, as I would be the only lightweight in the business with that record, and as Attell recently held Nelson to a 15-round draw, a victory for me over Attell would put me in a position to force Nelson to recognize my claims upon his attention. There is nothing lacking in my conditioning and I am delighted with the results of the training period. I have developed my speed and punch and never felt so confident of winning a hard battle in my life. I know positively that he cannot beat me and I feel absolutely certain that I shall win. I will be under the weight when we step on the scales, and it has been decidedly easy for me to do the poundage without affecting my condition or dulling my speed. This is a great opportunity for me and I intend to make the most of it.[63]

General admission tickets to the fight were priced at $2, while reserved seats could be had for $3, $5, and $7.50, with box seats at $10. A ticket bought you two good preliminaries along with the main event: "Hobo Dougherty vs. Kid Arcy, ten rounds, catchweights, as curtain riser at 8:15 o'clock, with George Blake as referee. Semi-windup, Monte Attell vs. Kid Kutchos, fifteen rounds, for bantamweight championship of [the] Pacific Coast; weigh in at 116 pounds at 2 o'clock the day of the fight with Tommy Walsh as referee."[64]

A special streetcar service, from downtown districts to the arena, was furnished to attract attendees. The cars ran down Spring Street from Temple block to Seventh, then on to the arena without a change. All the cars were marked "Direct to Jeffries Vernon Arena," the service beginning 45 minutes before the doors opened.

The morning newspaper boldly proclaimed the result: "WELSH DECISIVELY DEFEATS ATTELL IN FIFTEEN ROUNDS."[65] This two-line synopsis in the *Los Angeles Herald* told the story, but so did the details: "Fight fans were satisfied last night in their years of longing to see Abe Attell whipped, as Freddie Welsh decisively trimmed the featherweight king in every one of their fifteen rounds of whirlwind boxing and earned a most decisive victory—one that was both popular and beyond question. Welsh outboxed and outfought Abe at every turn in the road and proved himself at least as good a ring general."[66]

By the way, Monte won his fight.

Taking a look at the fight by rounds:

In round one, Attell declined to shake hands with Welsh, therefore establishing the undercurrent for the battle. He then dispatched some lightning jabs to the Welsh Wizard's stomach, followed later by some short jabs to the gut. Welsh sent some light left jabs, a few kidney punches, a left to the face, followed later by some stiff lefts to the abdomen and nose. Both fighters were cautious and measuring their punches. In round two, under a light rain, Attell posted some hard punches at close quarters including two lefts to the jaw. Welsh mailed two lefts to the face and repeated lefts to Attell's nose. An early clinch in round three found Welsh landing a left on the jaw during a breakaway. Attell addressed numerous blows to the stomach while Welsh consigned numerous left jabs to the face and two long left overhand blows to the jaw—a punch that had proven effective against

"The Little Champ." Attell exhibited marvelous defensive moves while remaining vigilant with his offense. Round four began with Welsh dodging a vicious lead by the feather. Attell directed some outstanding short-arm jabs to the jaw, and continued to remain circumspect. Welsh forwarded numerous sound combinations to the chest and face of Attell, but the Californian did not appear hurt. Two long jabs to Attell's stomach opened round five. Attell was furious at the abdomen assault and fought back viciously, but many of his punches were blocked. He later transmitted a right to the face of Welsh at the bell. Welsh conveyed a stiff uppercut to Attell's jowl and exhibited some outstanding defensive prowess.

Welsh continued his assault to Abe's jaw in round six. Attell phoned a hard left to the face, followed later by several stiff blows to the same area. Two Attell shots that looked low prompted an immediate warning by the Referee Charlie Eyton. Welsh wired more lefts, followed by some firm combinations to the jawbone. He continued to work Attell's kidneys, especially in clinches, while looking strong defensively. Round seven opened with an Attell assault to the body. The Californian telegraphed a right to the stomach and later received another warning about low blows. Welsh sent two lefts to the jaw, some nice mixes to the face and some solid uppercuts that appeared to rock "The Little Champ." Two more solid lefts to the jaw by Welsh infuriated Attell, who did his best to retaliate. Attell's mandible continued to get pummeled in round eight. In clinches, Attell still went to the kidneys and later dispatched some good overhead blows to the head. Welsh posted some rigid stomach punches, but broke ground in three clinches. Again, Welsh hammered on Attell's jaw in round nine. Attell mailed some concrete body blows including numerous stomach punches. Welsh, who was giving a clinic on defensive moves, addressed three huge wallops to the jawbone of Attell, then a fusillade of uppercuts found Attell's face. The ring was slippery in round ten. Attell consigned several blows to his opponent's countenance. Welsh directed a left at Abe's head, before mounting another aggressive stomach strike. This he followed with more combinations to the face. As Welsh slipped on the wet canvas, Attell sent some well-directed shots to his face and body.

There was a bit of apprehension regarding the footing of both boxers on the wet canvas in round eleven. Attell forwarded another gut assault, followed later by several left leads to Welsh's nose. Welsh transmitted stiff lefts to the mug of Attell three times without a return, before pounding him with combinations. He later targeted Attell's jowl once again. The feather had noticeably slowed near the end of the round and was punching only in clinches.

Round twelve belonged to Welsh, who took control of the fight. Attell conveyed several lefts to the face, but could not mount much more. Welsh phoned a crushing right straight to the mandible of Attell, before landing with combinations. Welsh continued with his machine-gun left jabs. Both Welsh and Attell were warned of low blows. Suddenly dancing and scoring at will, Welsh was also laughing, to the cheers of the crowd, when he returned to his corner.

Attell started by pounding Welsh's face in round thirteen. Both fighters threw numerous punches at close range, but the long-range artillery belonged to Welsh, who was scoring at will to Attell's head. The feather complained of head butting by Welsh, while he himself was landing some questionable blows. When the gong sounded, Attell's face was red and puffed from his opponent's assaults, and he was starting to look like a beaten man.

Welsh went to Attell's body at the beginning of round fourteen. Staying in the center of the ring where it was dry, Welsh unloaded with a barrage of facial punches, stunning his opponent. Still, Attell took the blows and did not break ground. Slipping a few times, Attell managed a rally, but Welsh's defense was superb—only about half of Abe's punches hit their mark.

In round fifteen, the gladiators shook hands to begin the final act. Abe rushed aggressively, but Welsh held him harmless in the clinch, before backing him up with a succession of punches to the jaw. Attell tried to smother Welsh in the clinches and go to his body, but Freddie would dance away. Both fighters were assaulting the body, but it proved too little, too late.

As for Attell's performance: "It was too big a task for him to beat an opponent who was his equal in all the fine points of the game and yet had height, weight and reach added to make the handicap almost impossible."

It could have been a wake-up call, but it wasn't, nor was it a title loss.

Speaking of losses, Attell was struggling with his from a financial perspective. On December 7, he filed his answer to a suit brought against him in the Superior Court for the collection of $504.75 claimed to be due the assignee, R. Milligan, of the claim of Ransom & Company, alleged proprietors of a New York gambling house. According to the *Evening Bulletin*: "Attell admits giving his note for $304.75 and a check on a San Francisco bank for $200, but evades responsibility for making them good by declaring that both were in payment of gambling debts and therefore void. About the same time with the filing of his answer, Attell filed with Sheriff Hammell a bond for the release of an attachment of his share of the gate receipts at the Attell-Welsh fight at the Jeffries Club two weeks ago."[67]

Taking a quick break from the ring, Attell returned to his training on December 7, four days before he was scheduled to meet Ad Wolgast for ten rounds in front of the Pacific Athletic Club, at Naud Junction.[68] Baron Long, matchmaker for the Jeffries Athletic Club of Los Angeles, made the match that was originally planned for twenty to twenty-five rounds. Attell liked the deal, which guaranteed him $2,000 for his end, win, lose, or draw, but not the distance. The feather champion reiterated that he did not need much work and that he had no fear of losing his title to Wolgast.

Wolgast, who was coming off a strong performance against Kid McCoy, was becoming a lightweight force. A student of the Battling Nelson school of survival, Wolgast was all offense; leading with his head, he was as relentless as he was indefatigable. His team trained at Doyle's camp at Vernon and it included sparring partner Jack Sullivan.

Attell was training at the Eastside quarters with sparring partners Dick Hyland and Fred Corbett.

The *Herald* documented the fight preparation: "Yesterday Attell went on the road in the forenoon, and later in the day he took up his regular ring work, and did not stop until an hour had been devoted to his workout. He boxed six rounds with Hyland and two with Corbett. He looked to be in fine trim after his exercise, and the color which he lacked when he fought Welsh had come back to his skin, and he seemed fit to defend the title which he has held so long against all challengers."[69]

On December 11, Abe Attell and Ad Wolgast fought for ten rounds to a no-decision, which was permitted under the law. One daily reported: "There was a division of sentiment regarding the verdict. However, Wolgast rushed the fighting in every round, backing Attell all around the ring and landing frequent heavy swings to the stomach that shook the champion severely. In the rallies, Wolgast fought Attell to a standstill and often forced the champion to break away from the clinches by his fusillade of blows to the body."[70]

Ad Wolgast boring in during his fight against Tommy Murphy on February 22, 1913 (Library of Congress).

Wolgast's heavy blows, to both the jaw and stomach of the champion, shook Attell. Like a marble in a pinball game, "The Little Champ," fighting at 122 pounds, was being bounced about the ring by his challenger. The consensus opinion, indicated by the hoots and hollers ringside, was that Attell did not try his best and was simply going through the motions. Despite the criticism, the *Los Angeles Herald* saw it as Attell's fight, as he outpointed his opponent in eight out of ten rounds.

Eighteen days later, on December 29, Attell would end his year in New Orleans battling against Cincinnati clubber "Biz" Mackey for ten rounds at the Southern Athletic Club.[71] Both men were to weigh in at 122 pounds ringside.

More than 3,500 spectators witnessed Abe Attell utterly dominate eight rounds against a much weaker "Biz" Mackey, as he pummeled the Ohio fighter unmercifully. It was as though Attell had woken up in the eighth, as he sent Mackey to the floor for the first time. The *Herald* printed: "The referee counted eight before Mackey rose. The Californian then sent him down with a right-hander and the Ohioan allowed seven to be counted before he got up. For the third time Attell sent him to the floor, but Mackey got up before the gong. As a last effort Attell went at him furiously with both hands and sent him down, but just as the referee counted ten the Ohio boy again tried to struggle to his feet, but he was out."[72]

Contemplating his fate, Abe Attell was considering going abroad, specifically to Melbourne, Australia, where a purse had been hung up for a match between him and Johnny Sommers. Domestic offers he had been receiving, including one from Jeffries to meet Jem Driscoll, just were not meeting his needs.

In Monte's Corner

Comforting, at least to Abraham Attell, was looking into his corner on New Year's Day, in one of the biggest fights of his life, and seeing brothers Monte and Caesar, along with Battling Nelson and Kid Farmer, as his seconds. Monte, who was certainly a factor in his brother's training and success during the year, also managed to log eight fights during eighty-six rounds of solid boxing. His fifteen-round draw with Jimmy Walsh eliminated any doubt that he was one very serious contender for the bantam title.

Alterations of lineal champions in 1908: Jack Johnson became the first African American world heavyweight champion by defeating Tommy Burns at Sydney, Australia, on December 26; world middleweight champion Stanley Ketchel lost his title on September 7 to Billy Papke by a 12th-round technical knockout at Vernon, California, but regained it on November 26 at Colma, California, where he knocked out Papke in the 11th

The Galveston Giant Jack Johnson and his first wife Etta Terry Duryea. All of three of his wives were white, a fact that caused considerable controversy at the time (Library of Congress).

round; Mike "Twin" Sullivan vacated the world welterweight championship, and Battling Nelson took the world lightweight championship from Joe Gans, who was floored nine times, with a 17th round knockout at Colma on July 4.

For the world featherweight champion, he clashed for 144 rounds in 12 fights, while successfully defending his title six times and battling four members of boxing's elite class: Owen Moran (twice), Battling Nelson, Freddie Welsh and Ad Wolgast. Worth noting: The combined career record of the aforementioned boxers alone was an amazing 262–51–43, with 144 victories by knockout. It was nothing short of a monumental year for Abe Attell, arguably one of the finest in the history of the sport.

CHAPTER EIGHT

Two Champions, Two Divisions and One Family, 1909

"Rumor has it on good authority that Attell and his wife are living on the fat of the land at the Goldfield hotel, and that Abe is doing only make believe training in the afternoons for the benefit of spectators who congregate daily to see him box a few short rounds."[1]—Tonopah Daily Bonanza

Boxing shared much of its popularity in 1909 with baseball. The Pittsburgh Pirates (NL) defeated the Detroit Tigers (AL) to win the 1909 World Series by 4 games to 3. And while boxing had the Attell brothers, baseball had Harry and Howie Camnitz, who pitched for the Bucs. Years before we knew anything about genetics, it was clear that some families seemed to possess remarkable physical qualities. Those who followed the sweet science, especially fans living in San Francisco, knew all too well that the Attell brothers boxed, but just how well would be confirmed in 1909.

The bold type on the front page of the *Tonopah Daily Bonanza*, from Tonopah, Nevada, on the morning of January 15, 1909, read: "Abe Attell Stopped Weeks In Ten Whirlwind Rounds." Even more impressive than the size of the headline was that it appeared in the hometown paper of Freddie Weeks, since both Tonopah and Cripple Creek claimed the defeated fighter. The pair fought a fast and furious ten-round battle before the Goldfield Athletic Club, in a place healing from an identity crisis, thanks to the sport of boxing. Goldfield had reached a peak population of about 20,000 people only three years earlier when it hosted a lightweight boxing championship match between Joe Gans and Oscar "Battling" Nelson. Now it needed only sustain itself, or so it was thought, with other magnetic battles like this between Attell and Weeks; Goldfield is about twenty-five miles south from Tonopah, as the crow flies.

As for the fine print of the twenty-round championship battle, the *Ogden Standard* noted: "Five ounce gloves and soft surgical bandages were allowed under the agreement; Marquis [*sic*] of Queensberry rules were to govern and the men were to break at the order of the referee; Each of the principals and Tex Rickard put up $500 cash as forfeit and the men were to weigh in at 122 pounds ringside."[2]

As for the spectators from near, and not so far, the local daily observed: "Seven coaches and eight automobiles arrived from Tonopah, Round Mountain, Rhyplite, Reno and San Francisco, containing 800 people. About 500 came from Tonopah, mostly Weeks admirers, headed by Louie Polin and a brass band."[3] Both fighters were in superb condition, with pre-fight wagering at 10 to 7 in favor of Attell. These odds were despite the partisan views being expressed by the local broadsheets, including the *Tonopah Daily Bonanza*, that gave this account: "After a few rounds the altitude will begin to affect Abe. The ring in the Goldfield arena is only a trifle over sixteen feet, while Attell is used to twenty-four foot rings—which is also in the favor of Weeks.... That Tonopah may be the home of the man who is to lower the colors of the one-time invincible Attell is the wish of every fight enthusiast in the city."[4]

San Francisco referee Eddie Graney oversaw the battle. The large Tonopah contingent included Bob Givan, W.S. Johnson, Dave Holland, Phil Allen, and Newt and Grant Crumley. They, like others, sat placing their bets right up to the fight time. Attell entered the ring first, followed by Weeks, the latter drawing the bulk of the applause. "Graney stepped into the ring at 9:45 and commenced to give the fighters their instructions, after which the men were introduced, posed for their pictures, and the fight was on."[5]

Looking at the highlights:

In round one Attell staggered Weeks with two quick lefts to the neck. Weeks assumed a rushing philosophy in round two, landing a solid combination to the face of Attell and winning the stage. A stiff left drew blood from Weeks's nose and later the fighter slipped to the floor in a third round most believe even, and Attell gallantly assisted Weeks to his feet. Attell turned up the offense and danced defensively to pick up round four. Both fighters appeared tired in round five, as Weeks delivered some nice lefts to the face of Attell before winning the go-round.

In round six, Attell posted some hard lefts to the stomach of Weeks before sending him to the ropes. The champion took the stage; Attell opened a cut over Weeks's left eye, causing the fighter to bleed badly in round seven. From this point forward, Attell took command of the fight. Weeks was losing control of his punching and weakening. Though Attell took round eight, Weeks did manage to swap some good punches. Weeks slipped to the floor for a second time and Attell, again, helped him to his feet; In round nine, Weeks dropped for a four-count while bleeding badly. Both fighters appeared tired. In round ten, the *Bonanza* observed: "Both men stall for [an] opening. Attell puts Weeks down with a hard left

American boxing promoter George Lewis "Tex" Rickard was the leading promoter of the day and even the builder of the third incarnation of Madison Square Garden in New York City (Library of Congress).

to the jaw. Weeks is down again. Weeks is put down for the count with a hard swing to the jaw and is unable to rise. Freddie did the best he could but was completely outclassed by the clever Attell."[6]

Words from the winner, as reported by the *Bonanza*: "I could have ended the fight in the third round had I so desired, as Weeks was practically unable to protect himself at one time in that round. Weeks is a good little man and has a fairly hard punch, yet he is no match for me. I had some money bet that the fight would not go over nine rounds."[7]

Words from the loser, as recorded by the *Bonanza*:

> I done my best from the start and can only say that the best man won. It was my intention to make a short fight of the affair and I started in the first round to either get Attell or get licked. But he was too much for me. He is one of the cleanest fighters in the ring today, and it is my opinion that he will keep the championship belt for some time to come. Tell my Tonopah friends that I appreciate the rousing reception they gave me when I entered the ring, and I say I done my best; but it was of no avail.[8]

Even with an impressive start to the year, a critical press wasn't short of jabs for the champion. Thankfully the fight with Weeks managed to alter a few views, if only for a while. This analysis was given by the *Hawaiian Star*:

> The foxy Abe Attell has been under suspicion recently of playing with his opponents and being content to win by decision rather than by the knockout route. This may have been due either to a cautiousness brought about by the lack of training or by a desire to obtain matches more easily by "pulling" and thereby giving the impression that he had gone back. Whatever the reason may have been for his lack of enthusiasm when inside the ropes his attitude made him extremely unpopular with ring-goers and resulted in some very unkind things being said about the little Hebrew scrapper. That he considered it high time to change his tactics are [sic] evidenced by his knocking out Freddie Weeks.[9]

Knockouts are to boxing what home runs are to baseball. Finishing blows, momentum killers or the coup de grâce—as binary as a light switch. It's not that the game is "a damage for dollars affair," as boxing fans certainly do not want to see someone hurt. It's just that spectators desire the best possible performance. That satisfaction level had often been attained through offensive prowess. Taking the art of defensive boxing to an entirely new level, Abe Attell's ring efforts were still being misinterpreted. It was a shame, actually, as defense is as much a part of the game as a sound offense. Once you followed Attell, you learned how to appreciate his skills, and could definitely tell when he was or wasn't on his game—or wasn't trying, as some discerned. In boxing there is a phrase, "Penny wise or pounded foolish," and Attell knew the difference.

Word went out on February 1: Attell intended to meet English champion Jem Driscoll—at 124 pounds at 6 o'clock of the night of the fight—before the first New York club to present him with a sound offer.[10] The fight, however, must be held between February 18 and February 24. A fighter ahead of his time, Driscoll, with his rigid, upright style, cast far from an elegant appearance, until he blended it with his precision movements. It was then that his ability could quickly make a good fighter look careless, even off-balance. Attell wisely specified the title would not be on the line. Driscoll, who happened to be in New York, stated that his current schedule wasn't conducive to the offer, so fight fans would just have to wait. The incertitude was like handing a child an ice cream cone on a hot summer day, then taking it from him before the first lick.

Secrets had a short life on the American frontier, especially when it came to the sweet science. The champion had aroused some curiosity when he was out in Goldfield,

Featherweight Jim or "Jem" Driscoll (left) posing with fellow boxer Eddie Johnson. Driscoll was British featherweight champion and won the coveted Lonsdale belt in 1910 (Library of Congress).

and it took less than two months for it to end up in print. The *Fergus County Democrat,* of Lewiston, Montana, ran the piece called "Attell Loses His Money."

> Abe Attell picks up easy marks in the boxing game, but he certainly is the easiest kind of mark for the "gamblers." Abie throws all of his coin away at the bookies and the manipulators of other games of chance at every available opportunity. A letter received from Goldfield states that although the classy Hebrew took a flyer over at Goldfield and cleaned up $2,500 for boxing Freddie Weeks, he, in the meantime, realizing what a snap he had, tried his luck bucking the wheel in Tex Rickard's gambling hall. The result was that when it came time to settle up, Tex found that he had Abe boxing for the fun of it. Pretty soft for Tex. He could afford to pull off a show every night on this sort of layout.[11]

Leaving the mining town of Goldfield, Attell was scheduled next to meet the familiar face of Chicago fighter Eddie Kelly in New Orleans, "The "Little Champ's" first battle in the city. The ten-round event was scheduled for February 4 at the Southern Athletic Club and was expected to draw a fairly large crowd. Having knocked out Kelly twice before, Attell knew his opponent well enough to enjoy some of the French and Spanish Creole architecture of New Orleans between training sessions.

The fight, as anticipated, proved an easy win for Attell, as Kelly's seconds threw up the sponge in the seventh. The *Call* noted: "Kelly stood up with his opponent with fairly well divided honors until the sixth round, when Attell made his attack more vigorous and landed a number of lefts to the face and body, and gave Kelly plainly the worst of it. When Kelly came up for the seventh round Attell sent him to the floor four times in quick succession, and his seconds, seeing that he could not last longer, gave up the fight."[12]

Now back to the proposed match with Driscoll. It took until February 16 before an agreement could be finalized between the champion and the Wales featherweight. Hastily scheduled for February 19, the ten-round affair would take place before the National Athletic Club. It was agreed to at 125 pounds, weighed in at 6 o'clock the day of the fight, and each fighter posted a forfeiture of $500 in case he failed to make the bar. Expectations remained high despite the conditions: it was a short-distance battle in New York State, where no decision could be rendered in a boxing contest.

As confirmed by those close to the sport, these were the two best boxers or the best matched pugilists in America at this time. There was no chance whatsoever, at least in the eyes of many, of a one-sided contest.

The predictions came true: it was one of the most scientific displays in boxing history by two of the ring's foremost experts on defense. Driscoll dazzled the audience with his ability to counter Attell's moves, efficiently ducking and sidestepping the champion's controlling left. The pugilist from the capital of Wales, "Jem"—or is it gem, as he was brilliant in the ring—danced magnificently. Keeping his opponent at bay with his straight left, Driscoll was impressive with his command. The dazzling no-decision brought Driscoll, or as gunman Bat Masterson called him "Peerless Jim," to the forefront of the division.

Attell, who comfortably danced with his British combatant for the duration, even had a few believing he bettered the Englishman. Most felt that only a distance battle, say, of twenty or twenty-five rounds, could enable one fighter to shine over the other. Driscoll was 10 to 8 favorite before the contest, but the odds went even just before the fighters entered the ring. Charles Seger, Al Lipsco, Al McMurray, and Jimmy de Forest seconded Attell, while Jimmy Johnson, Charlie Harvey and "Boyo" Driscoll looked after Peerless Jim. The *Herald* penned:

> Driscoll's left jabs were frequent and he landed them in one-two and one-two-three fashion on Abe's face, raising a lump over his right eye in the fifth round. At in-fighting the American proved better, sending in some hard body punches that staggered the Britisher. In the sixth round Attell landed a hard, swinging left on the head, which sent Driscoll staggering to the ropes. In the seventh Attell reached the face and stomach with telling effect, but Driscoll was willing to mix things, and landed some hard ones over the kidneys. A short right just over the heart made Driscoll look weary as he went to his corner at the end of the round. Honors were even in the eighth, with both men looking as though they could continue for an hour. In the ninth and tenth rounds Driscoll had the advantage in the number of blows landed.[13]

Returning home to his wife (the couple maintained a residence at 135th Street in New York City) after the fight, Attell made no comment to the press. Later, however, some remarks leaked out that claimed Abe thought he had earned the victory. In stark contrast, Driscoll attended a barn dance given by St. Raymond's Church, up in West Chester, after the fight. He had little time to sway or pirouette, however, as he was sailing for home in the morning aboard the *St. Paul*. Driscoll did state that Attell was the best man he ever fought.[14]

Looking at how some of the spectators viewed it: Bat Masterson believed Attell won without question. "Driscoll did little or no forcing. Attell had to do it all. His punches were the harder, too." Joe Humphries claimed, "It was a nip and tuck thing. A draw about hits it." Young Corbett stated, "I think Attell won," and according to Owen Moran, "Driscoll won. Attell was bad."[15] Since only members of the National Athletic Club could purchase tickets, access to the bout was limited.

Following the Driscoll match, the only thing on the minds of most fight fans was a distance rematch. But frankly speaking, "The Prince of Wales" had confirmed what Attell feared, that someone just as clever could counter his systematic moves, and do so with precision. A match between the two just wasn't a priority for "The Little Champ." And besides, Attell continued to receive some sound challenges. Owen Moran, who had fought two draws with the champion, posted $5,000 to bind a match. Following his bout with Driscoll, Abe was a bit more mindful of his vulnerability and an eyewitness to the improvements in the defensive skills of the European fighters. Balking at most offers, Attell decided to head south.

Philadelphia, a short and convenient train ride from New York City, was where Attell was scheduled for back-to-back contests against Young Pierce of Germantown. The duo's first contest, a six-rounder, was slated for March 1, in front of the Washington Sporting Club. A black boxer who "had paid his dues in the Philadelphia area," Pierce had been matched against some decent fighters including Harry Baker, Al Delmont, and Jimmy Walsh. He had also gained a level of notoriety as a victim of an eighteenth-round knockout by Owen Moran in the United Kingdom in August 1907. The *Rock Island Argus* noted:

> For the first three rounds he [Pierce] frequently stood toe to toe and exchanged straight left-hand punches and right-hand body blows with the great master of the featherweights. In the fourth and fifth rounds Attell drove Pierce to the ropes, and while the latter was standing with both legs straight under his body Attell beat a wicked tattoo with rights and lefts on his opponent's body. Once he drove his nimble opponent through the ropes by this vicious onslaught.[16]

Picking up a considerable amount of Philadelphia money, Attell sailed to a relatively easy no-decision over Pierce. As the main event to a strong boxing card, few were surprised by the impressive draw; hundreds were unable to gain admission. Attell did not train hard and got noticeably winded after the third round. As with similar Attell matches, the media was quick to remark, with a line that was becoming all too familiar: "The contest was one of the fastest and most scientific ever seen in the city."[17] The only damage reported was "a slight bleeding at the mouth by Pierce."[18]

A fifteen-round rematch, this time at the Olympic Club at Essington, was scheduled for March 10. Attell, wasting no time, knocked out Pierce in the sixth round. The Philadelphia fighter was no match for a resolute Attell at any level and did not land an effective blow the entire confrontation. Which raises the question, why take both fights? Money (purse and side bets), exposure, and proximity were all factors; after all, we are talking about the featherweight champion of the world.

Defining a Champion

Many believe that boxing champions aren't born, they're made. But there were instances when the Attell boys, and not just Abraham, seemed cast from the perfect genetic mold—a solid frame enhanced by extraordinary muscle and motor development. Stir in some proper training and you have the two major factors that affect athletic performance. Like all boxers, Abraham and Monte were shaped by their experiences, a reflection of their time and surroundings. And, in their case, it was a champion's environment.

Champions seize the moment because they accept that it is their time. They will stay champions for as long as they think, and act, like champions. By refining his skills, from a knockout artist to a clever defenseman, Abraham's actions exemplified a championship mindset, even if his maturity, at times, did not.

Champions understand they are expected to win. After all, the ring is their domain and once inside of it, confidence becomes the supreme belief. Victory, a champion understands, is his only option. But this realm had parameters, such as choice of opponent, risk of the title, payment, weight, and length of confrontation, and his team needed to bear in mind each and every variable. It's one thing to be on top, another to stay there. Attell, only a few years into his reign, was picking up his master's degree.

Great pugilists also acknowledge their past. Following in the footsteps of Ike Weir, Torpedo Billy Murphy, Young Griffo, and George Dixon, along with Frank Erne, Solly Smith, Dave Sullivan, Ben Jordan (Great Britain), Eddie Santry (Great Britain), Terry McGovern and Young Corbett II, as featherweight champion of the world, suited Abraham Attell just fine, but these were big shoes to fill.

While both Monte and Abe understood that it was the small wins that gave them the credence to claim their title, they knew as champions that it was easy to become complacent or overconfident. That fine line between peak performance and overtraining needed to be mastered, as did their opponent selection. The competition a fighter selects paints his portrait, and a champion must remember that he has the brush. Abraham was still struggling with where, when, and how to draw the line. And even when the lines were drawn it was difficult to stay between them.

Champions see their life as a gift, not an obligation. This is hard for some boxers who may not love every minute of the journey, every photograph with a fan or autograph during dinner, but they are conscious that attitude fashions skill, or polishes the bust of a Hall of Fame fighter. Abe, despite his public exposure at places like the racetrack or baseball field, valued his privacy. Not only did he not like his dirty laundry hung out to dry, he didn't even want people to know he did laundry.

So what separates the great champions from the good ones? Their faith is greater than their fear. It is their passion and purpose that will overcome any challenge they may face, and that is completely understood. They grow from their miscalculations to become stronger, wiser and better fighters. They don't make excuses when they don't win, and they watch their mouth when they do. The best days of their life, champions know, are always in front of them. Abraham Washington Attell believed that, in this his third full year atop the featherweight division.

Gauging the Competition

Bearing in mind his title, a dollars-per-round approach was not out of the question for Abe Attell, nor was there a law against it; better a crucifixion in the press than in the ring, or so many thought, including Attell. For any champion, the ring can be a delicate balance between pride and temptation. The fact that Abe would not face a fighter with over twenty official wins until Biz Mackey at the end of April was painting an image of fighter unsure how far down the food chain to make a match. This was where a fighter needed the guidance and skills of a sound business manager. When, or should I say if, he finds one, he has to listen to him.

Staying in town on March 18, Attell took a ten-round skirmish with Patsy Kline at the Whirlwind Athletic Club in Harlem, both boxers doing battle at 122 pounds. Kline,

(From left) Italian Gengro Pasquale, a.k.a. Patsy Kline, Harry Stone, and Italian featherweight champion Battling Reddy (Library of Congress).

who had been fighting out of New Jersey, was thrilled at the chance to enter the ring with the champion. Attell, who took every round in the ten-round no-decision, toyed with the fighter, and while he had many opportunities to end the fight, he chose to ignore them. I know what you're thinking: a hearty side bet may have played a part. Those who attended the fight, or Attell's $1,000 performance, weren't too happy. An account in the press two days later claimed:

> A sporting man known to everyone in New York came down from Abe's dressing room just before the fight and whispered some interesting information. "Abe got his money and sent it home and Klein [sic] is to go ten rounds," said the sporting gent. That's just what happened. As an all around, plain sewing or fancy stitch faker Abe Attell has few equals and no superiors. Abe's ring work is so crooked that he often meets himself coming into the ring just as he steps out of it to go back to the dressing room.[19]

Again, the expectations of a champion are to win, and win decisively. Therefore, anything short of such a performance will be subject to suppositions. Ring rumors, too, have to be taken with a grain of salt, as more than one journalist had been crossed; sour ink can be sweet retribution.

Less than a week later, it was back to the familiar face of Frankie Neil.[20] It took only two lines to sum up the engagement in the *Norwich Bulletin*: "Abe Attell outboxed and outfought Frankie Neil of San Francisco in a fast ten round bout at the Bedford Athletic Club in Brooklyn tonight. The champion had Neil's face cut to ribbons with straight lefts and right hand smashes."[21]

On March 20, three days before the Neil encounter, Attell was matched with neophyte Frankie White of Chicago. The two were scheduled to meet for twenty rounds, in Dayton, Ohio, on March 26. The featherweight championship, for the third time this year, would be put on the line in front of the Dayton Athletic Club.

Eight rounds of work were all it took for Attell to deliver White to the canvas. The *Call* confirmed: "The end was not unexpected, as the Californian had his antagonist groggy practically throughout the whole mill. Just after White went down from a hard blow on the point of the jaw, James J. Corbett, who was has been playing at a local theater, was introduced. He and Attell did a little fancy shadow boxing to the delight of the spectators."[22] The latter instance proved more interesting to some than the main event.

Catching many people by surprise was word that Big Jim Jeffries's Athletic Club, located in Vernon, California, which is five miles south of current downtown Los Angeles, was facing closure. Baron Long, who had come from Fort Wayne to Los Angeles a year and a half earlier to start a fight club, had been losing money—the figure quoted in the newspaper was $15,000—on his promotions and has been attempting to sell the club.[23] Nevertheless, despite interest in the sport, there had been no takers in the venue. It was Long who interested Jim Jeffries in the enterprise and persuaded him to lend it his name. Having promoted some of the best fights of the previous year—including McFarland v. Welsh, Papke v. Ketchel, Attell v. Welsh—it simply could not sustain itself.

Acknowledging the importance of the three major railroads running through the region was the attraction of the city of Vernon. Rail was a marketing asset the sport of boxing used to attract industrialists from the East Coast to travel there—hopefully enjoy themselves enough to want to relocate parts of their operations to Vernon. The Vernon Avenue Arena, under the control of entrepreneur Jack Doyle, had opened up the previous year (1908). While it hoped to fill some of the void left behind by the club closure, it remained to be seen.

The featherweight division was turned upside down on April 26 with the news: "Attell Breaks Hand And Takes Lay-off, Will Not Be Able to Fight for at Least Six Months."[24] It took only one misplaced blow, a right hand in the third round that floored his opponent Biz Mackey for a count of seven. The Columbus crowd could sense something was not well. In championship fashion, however, Attell would not relent, but went on to continue the fight and knock out Mackey with machine-gun lefts to the face in the eighth round. The *Salt Lake Tribune* noted the damage:

> The injury will cost the featherweight champion many thousands of dollars. He would at least box once a month, and his fights would net him $500 to $1,000 with the ordinary men, and a match with a topnotcher would bring much more money. Attell says that he will do light gymnasium work in order to keep himself in good condition, and will give his hand plenty of time to heal up. He believes that six months ought to be enough, and at the expiration of that time he will meet any man in the world at his weight.[25]

Promoter James Coffroth, perhaps the most aggressive impresario in the business, was among the first to alter his plans. It was mentioned that he had secured a deal with Attell to be matched at his club—preferably with Owen Moran in a 45-round bout at Colma—in a big fight over the summer.[26] Naturally, the Attell injury sent the feather division into a tailspin, as contenders scrambled among one another while waiting for the champion to heal. Coffroth would instead focus on another Attell, namely Monte, by trying to match him with little Johnny Coulon in June. A battle between both gladiators would do much to clarify the ambiguous bantamweight championship.

With regard to Moran, Attell had a sole condition, and one that Coffroth may have overlooked, be it intentionally or not: that a battle between the adversaries not to go beyond ten rounds. As champion he could set such parameters, mindful that Moran's only chance at beating him was at a longer distance. But a promoter may or may not want such a short contest, especially with regard to a championship fight. If Attell held his ground, he was certain Coffroth could deliver acceptable articles at a beguiling price.

When it came to knowing what was going on in the fight market, a promoter such as Coffroth had more ears than a cornfield. Aware of the financial needs of both fighters, not to mention the ticket prices his market could bear, Coffroth was in no hurry; the only way any serious contender could stay in the championship mix was to be matched against Attell, so let the champion heal. Understanding this, Moran returned home to England during the first week in June to await a respectable offer.

While healing, Attell attended to things at home, engaging in some private training sessions for young boxers and hitting the racetrack. Painfully, he would also have to read the hyperbole being spouted by his peers. "I don't see how Abe Attell can claim the title," stated Owen Moran in London. "I will fight Attell for $1,000 a side at his own weight—122 pounds—any number of rounds from 20 to 45."[27]

For the champion, his period of convalescence was a mere 114 days outside of a ring—an impressive term for anyone, if of course it was successful. To test his mitts, Attell met tomato can Harry Stone in Saratoga, New York. The two New York fighters sparred to a ten-round no-decision in front of the Saratoga Athletic Club. Inside Convention Hall, a crowd estimated at 2,000 watched as Harry Stone waited until the final two rounds to mount any sort of attack. While the fighter weakened the champion, it was far too little too late. For Abe, it felt good to be back in the ring regardless of the competition.

Next stop Pittsburgh, on September 6, where Abe Attell jumped into the ring for a six-rounder against boxer Eddie Kelly. It was the second time that year—the two, as you recall, had met back in February in New Orleans, where Kelly was knocked out in the seventh round. This fight, conducted before the New American Athletic Club in Luna Park, was held in a building formerly used as a cafe when the venue was in its glory. Appearing not to be bothered by his healing hand, Attell used his trademark left jab to control the fight that went the distance to a no-decision. Kelly, although trying to put on a good showing, was clearly outclassed; the Buffalo fighter was nearly knocked out in the third round.

Philadelphia's Tommy O'Toole wasn't prone to fighting out of town, but if it meant a shot at the champion, well, why not? So it was off to Boston (Attell was smart enough to know not to take on the fighter in a Philadelphia distance match), where the fighter would meet "The Little Champ," for twelve rounds at the Armory Athletic Association. For the champ, it was his longest bout since he broke his hand, and as it turned out, the most prolonged battle of the year. Over 2,000 spectators watched as O'Toole had the better of the contest, according to most, but Referee Charles White gave the decision to Attell. As the *Tacoma Times* witnessed, "In the final round, O'Toole hammered Attell all over the ring and had blood pouring from his face when the bell rang."[28] The *Herald* saw it this way: "The fifth round was the hardest fought of the bout. Attell drove O'Toole to the ropes with smashing rights and lefts to the head, but O'Toole came back and sent Attell staggering to his corner. The round closed with Attell repeating his first charge, forcing O'Toole to cover. Attell closed O'Toole's right eye in the eighth. Up to the final round honors were about even."[29]

Next, two quick six-round (no-decision) affairs awaited Abe Attell in, of all places, Philadelphia. In the first, on October 6, he outpointed Philly's own Buck "Twin" Miller. The *Salt Lake Tribune* wrote: "Attell had the better of every round. Toward the end of the third round Attell staggered Miller with a succession of swings to the head, and at the finish had the local boy in bad shape. Early in the last round Miller did his best work. He succeeded in landing several jolts on the champion's chin. Apart from this flash Miller was at the mercy of Attell."[30]

At the Nonpareil Athletic Club on October 8, Attell, with little exertion, defeated Newark fighter Patsy Kline for his second victory of the week in the city. As the *Washington Times* saw it:

Attell handed Kline a fierce walloping last night, and came within an ace of finishing the Jersey boy in the second round. He sent Kline down with a hard right, and the same round opened a cut in Kline's nose. The count of eight was imposed on Patsy while he was trying to get himself together on the ropes. From then on to the finish it was all Attell. The little champion landed whenever he pleased. In the last round Kline was in such bad shape that Attell looked over to the referee, thinking he would stop the bout. Kline was game enough to take the beating, and it went the limit.[31]

Ever since Jack Johnson won the world heavyweight crown—stopping Tommy Burns in Sydney, Australia, the day after Christmas the previous year—every promoter had been hungry to match the black champion with the retired Jim Jeffries. It was on that day, sitting at ringside, that novelist Jack London, covering the bout for the *New York Herald*, sounded the cry for Jeffries to come out of retirement and defeat Johnson, with his now famous words, "Jeff, it's up to you." Well, few beyond the Bay Area realized that the Attell family also put an offer on the table and the *Call* noted it: "I, Caesar Attell, will bid $60,000 for the Jeffries-Johnson fight. My brothers will back me and I will post $30,000 as soon as my bid is accepted. My brothers and I have four pawn shops in San Francisco and we think we can handle the fight if we get it."[32]

The *San Francisco Call* printed the offer on October 28, and added: "Now here is a chance for Jeff and Johnson. They can't lose anyhow. If they don't get the money for fighting, they can attach a few watches, unredeemed diamonds and a carload or two of misfit coats and pants. Keep on bidding Caesar. So long as you have a few hock shops to back you up, there is always an out for you."[33]

Finishing off his ring year in the beautiful city of Memphis, Tennessee, the featherweight champion would engage in two eight-round fights—the legal limit. The first was against Moran, that's Brooklyn's Johnny Moran, at the Phoenix Athletic Club. One has to sense that there was an amount of enjoyment from the members of the press who could print, "Attell Finally Meets Moran." Both fighters agreed to the weight of 122 pounds at 6 p.m. and began training hard in the area for ten days.

As the *Call* saw it, "Not until the fifth round did Attell extend himself. From then on he made a chopping block out of his rugged opponent. Moran possesses a vicious right swing, but only once, in the second, did he drive it home reaching Attell's head. The blow nettled Attell and he fought to a clinch, displaying the speed and science that has given him the title he now holds."[34] Attell was given the eighth-round decision, but only after Moran exhibited a bit of speed, science and stamina.

Charley White, a fighter whom Battling Nelson picked as the boy who could wrestle the title away from Attell, would complete the champion's year, as the two tangled on December 6.[35] Similar to Attell, White hailed from a fighting family—his brothers Jack White and Billy Wagner were also boxers. Now fighting out of Memphis, via Chicago, White was undefeated in over twenty fights and on his way to becoming one of the sport's great left hook artists. But the eighteen-year-old did not live up to expectations and lost the eight-round decision; the fighter would later claim that Attell's demand that he make 122 pounds ringside weakened him. White did, however, prove himself a worthy opponent and one with some sound defensive skills. Not surprisingly, he wanted to fight Attell at twenty rounds or more, believing that despite his loss, his height, weight and reach advantage would work to his favor in a longer contest. The *Desert Evening News* noted the damage: "Attell was the first to show blood, a vicious right uppercut landed flush on his mouth. Not until the last round did he draw blood from White's nose and mouth. It was on Attell's superior infighting that Referee Barry based his decision, which was hooted by many in the crowd."[36]

Between the two Memphis contests, the press was working Attell hard to match not only with Owen Moran, which appeared unlikely, but also Ad Wolgast. Finally, Abe piped up, stating: "If Ad Wolgast wants my game I will put up a forfeit of $2,000 to be a side bet, and will be there on time. I will fight him at 122 pounds, ringside."[37]

Meanwhile, promoter James Coffroth was about to arrive in London, where he would try his hand at matching Jem Driscoll with Attell back in San Francisco. Owen Moran, who had just arrived in the United States on the *Lusitania* from England, hoped to match not with Attell, but Battling Nelson as a preliminary to the Jeffries-Johnson contest on July 4, 1910.

Attell was scheduled to do battle with Chicago fighter Tommy Mowatt in Kansas City, Missouri, on December 27, but the fight was canceled; no reason was given by promoter C.B. Nelson.[38]

In Monte's Corner

Unfortunately, there are no continuous records of the early days in the bantam division, only facts such as American Charley Lynch's claiming the title in 1856 by defeating Simon Finighty in 43 rounds, at 112 pounds. From 1870 to 1890, many individuals took claim to the title, but it was George Dixon who set the mark at 112 pounds when he defeated Nunc Wallace in 1890. The weight would advance from 112 to 115, and finally rest at 118, where it is today.

When undefeated champion Jimmy Barry retired, Terry McGovern took the bantams to the eve of the succeeding century by defeating Pedlar Palmer in 1899, but the following year McGovern vacated the title to join the featherweights. The title then began fluctuating like the tides, as Harry Harris took the crown by outpointing Pedlar Palmer in 1901, before moving up to the feathers, like McGovern. In 1902, Harry Forbes's claim to the title was universally recognized, then solidified when he beat British champion Andy Tokell. In 1903, Frankie Neil knocked out Harry Forbes. British champion Joe Bowker outpointed Frankie Neil in 1904, but then outgrew the division. Both Digger Stanley of England and Jimmy Walsh of Boston then asserted ownership of the title. Walsh then defeated Stanley in 1905, and lay claim to the title. But he too outgrew the division. In

1907, Kid Murphy claimed the title by beating Johnny Coulon that year and again the following year. But the legitimacy of Murphy's ownership was seriously questioned by many in the division who were still battling each other and even bouncing between divisions, boxers like Frankie Neil, Johnny Reagan, Jimmy Walsh, Frankie Conley, Johnny Coulon and George Stanley. For example, Jimmy Walsh was battling Abe Attell for the feather crown in September 1907, before defending his bantam title, which he claimed he never gave up, in March 1908. Jimmy Reagan then beat Walsh in January 1909 for the bantam crown.

On February 22, 1909, Jimmy Reagan put the world bantamweight championship on the line at 115 pounds inside the Mission Street Arena and lost a twenty-round decision to Monte Attell. In his next three fights, Monte defeated Harry Dell, Bobby Johnson, and Jockey Bennett before Frankie Neil claimed the title, which was still vacant at 116 pounds. Monte Attell then knocked out Frankie Neil, at 116 pounds, in the eighteenth round of their title bout in Colma, California. And, just to be sure, Monte defeated Jimmy Reagan again on August 11, in Oakland, at 115 pounds. He then went on to defeat Percy Cove and Jimmy Carroll twice. Monte also put his title on the line three times against Danny Webster, and fought to a draw in each battle. Monte Attell had never looked or fought better than he did as world bantamweight champion.

The only change of lineal champions was that of the bantams, but there were some notable fights during the year. In the longest battle of the twentieth century, Joe Jeannette knocked out Sam McVey in round forty-nine on April 17, in Paris. As fate, or a promoter, might have it, all the other significant battles of the year took place in Colma, California. Battling Nelson retained his lightweight crown with an impressive knockout of Dick Hyland in round twenty-three of their May 29 confrontation. On June 26, Dick Hyland floored Leach Cross 15 times en route to a kayo in round forty-one. Stanley Ketchel, with a broken right hand, defeated Billy Papke in twenty rounds on July 5, and Jack Johnson floored Stanley Ketchel in round twelve of their October 16 battle.

Mention of title bearers begets the question: At what age is a pugilist of championship caliber at his best? According to the *East Oregonian*:

> Many of the ring experts insist that between the ages of 25 and 35 the best fighters are in their prime, an assertion that appears to be backed up by the records of the great boxers of America, England and Australia. Jeffries, probably the greatest pugilist the world has ever seen, was 24 when he won the heavyweight championship from Fitzsimmons. He was 28 at the time he knocked Corbett out in ten rounds at San Francisco, and he was considered then to be at his best.[39]

The article goes on to note that John L. Sullivan was 24 years of age when he won the championship from Paddy Ryan; Jack Johnson, the new champion, was 31; and George Dixon lost his feather crown to Terry McGovern at the age of 30. The Attell brothers, as champions, fit perfectly into the range quoted. The question being: how long can they stay there?

In 1909, the world featherweight champion battled over one hundred rounds, in sixteen fights, and did not suffer a loss. Defending his title three times, he fought one member of boxing's elite class, Jem Driscoll. After breaking his hand, he entered the ring again 114 days later, to fight seven times before the end of the year.

Brothers Abraham and Monte Attell made history in 1909 by becoming the first pair of brothers to hold world titles simultaneously. In so doing they placed the name Attell in the pantheon of boxing history. Together they fought over 25 battles in over 150 rounds, and did not suffer a single loss!

CHAPTER NINE

A Champion's Pace, 1910

"His brains work faster than his hands and his hands move more quickly than those of nine-tenths of the men he meets. His fights are usually poor ones to watch, but he goes on gathering the change just the same, because he never wastes an effort and has a brain that takes quick advantage of every opportunity."[1]—Evening Times

Man, in his most primitive form, was only steps from the sport of boxing. Inasmuch as fighting with fists has always been an option, it was a primordial factor of survival. Transforming an action, or reaction, into a game would require thought. It was not until controls were implemented that it became less of a barbaric act and thus less offensive, not to mention a sport that required no equipment.

It was boxing's visceral nature, however, that made it a social stage, complete with the sovereignty to legitimize it as such. If a voice could not be understood on the street, or in the courtroom, then it could be given a forum in the ring. Boxing became a sociological petri dish, a mirror for who and what we were. And never was it more indicative as such than on July 4, 1910, in Reno, Nevada, when the first African American world heavyweight boxing champion, Jack Johnson, met an undefeated white champion, James J. Jeffries, who stepped out of retirement to answer the call of engagement. One-sided from the very start, the fight lasted fifteen rounds, more out of a fear by Johnson than out of need. And when it was over, the champion—who sent Jeff to the canvas three times in the fifteenth round—was still champion. However, to say he was the undisputed champion was a lie: the fight triggered race riots across the country, with many humiliated whites unable to acknowledge Johnson's victory. The fight was such a mirror of our society that many states and cities banned the exhibition of the fight films, even motivating Congress to ban distribution of all prizefight films across state lines in 1912. In truth, if the candle of racism had always been here, it took boxing to light it.

In taking a look at boxing's reigning featherweight champion, this is how one outlet saw it: "Abe Attell still bosses the feathers. However, he is not a popular champion, owing to his Shylock tactics and his insincerity. He does not care about going against tough game and his fights during the year have mostly been against men of ordinary class."[2]

Attell has taken some heat from promoters, most notably the managers of the Phoenix Club of Memphis, who not only questioned his sincerity, but also banned him from all future events—an action that had begun to haunt the fighter. A statement the *Evening Times* supported: "Attell is a splendid boxer and a sure enough champion at the featherweight limit, but he is lacking in ambition and energy. He has lost a small fortune on the ponies and at several other games of chance and is at the present time flat broke, yet he is still convinced he can beat them."[3] For Attell, such obtuse criticism was simply part of being a champion.

Enjoying some of the charm of Savannah, the oldest city in the state of Georgia, Abraham Attell, for only the second time in his career, had a fight, or should we say an altercation, on New Year's Day. According to the *Spokane Press*: "Abe Attell, featherweight champion, gave Eddie Kelly of Buffalo, New York, a terrible beating in five minutes of fighting here tonight. The police stopped the fight in the second round."[4] Not only had Abe been taking heat for his choice of opponent, but some of his regulars, like Eddie Kelly, haven't been far from criticism. "Eddie Kelly, whom Abe Attell carries around the country as an opponent when they can get away with it, looks for all the world like a map of Ireland."[5] As this was the fifth time "The Little Champ" had used Kelly for target practice, spectators weren't sure what point, if any, Attell was trying to make.

It was announced on January 31 that James Jeffries, Stanley Ketchel, Battling Nelson, Abe Attell, Frank Gotch, Dr. F.B. Roller and Sam Berger (Jeffries's manager) were to tour the world. This would only be if Jeffries was successful on July 4 in his battle against Jack Johnson for the heavyweight championship. The news came from theatrical agent, producer and director Harry Herbert Frazee, who was also the current promoter of the Jeffries-Gotch-Roller show.[6] Frazee knew a hit when he saw it and planned to show the company for sixty days in this country, then sail for England on September 10. The following is an extract of a letter received by George W. Lederer, manager of the Colonial Theater, from Frazee, who had been in Jeff's training camp for over a month. It was printed two days before the big fight: "Jeff is a sure winner. His condition is wonderful and the colored champion don't look good to anyone here. No Johnson money here at all, but plenty of Jeffries money."[7]

As they say in Boston, "'Nuf Ced."

The giant Cunard liner *Mauretania* pulled into port in New York with a distinguished list of passengers, including wireless wizard Guglielmo Marconi, fight promoter Jimmy Coffroth, the Duke and Duchess of Manchester, and William K. Vanderbilt. The *Bridgeport Evening Farmer* noted the return of the promoter:

> Jimmy Coffroth, who, according to his own story, has a bet of $1,000 that he will create a new record from London to San Francisco. He bet [boxing celebrity] Eugene Corri that he will land in San Francisco before midnight on February 8 and he leaves overland this afternoon. Coffroth while abroad matched Jem Driscoll and Abe Attell to fight in California and he will announce a date for the match very soon. It is also rumored that he is hurrying westward because of the reported row between the promoters of the Johnson-Jeffries fight. On that subject Coffroth had little to say although he asked for the details.[8]

As for the Attell match, the champion would await the promoter's confirmation.

It was back home to New York on February 24, as Attell met another familiar figure in San Francisco warrior Frankie Neil, for ten rounds at the Long Acre Athletic Association. Neil absorbed the worst of Abe's cleverness and scarcely landed a dozen clean blows during the contest. This was the way the *Tribune* saw it: "A snappy left jab to the face started Neil's nose bleeding in the second round, and Attell jabbed the injured member during the entire round. The last two rounds produced the most action. Attell constantly trying for a knockout. In the ninth Attell cut loose and soon had Neil in a bad way. Right swings to the body and jaw had him dazed and the bell was welcome to him."[9]

Charley Harvey (left) with America's first big-time boxing promoter, James Wood Coffroth (Library of Congress).

Attell dropped Neil twice in the tenth, but the dazed battler hung on to make the distance. The fight entered the book as a "ND10." For Frankie, this was not only the last time he would meet with Attell, but his next to last professional fight. Frankie and Abe always shared a passion for the ponies, which was no doubt one of the reasons for the association. After retiring, Neil planned on investing the bulk of his earnings in a large stable of horses.[10]

Turning back to promoter James Coffroth, it was reported on February 12 by the *Times*: "[He] made a record run from London of nine days, six hours and thirty-five minutes [to his San Francisco office at midnight February 8], thereby winning $2,000 wagered with Eugene Corri [English fight referee] and other London sporting men [members of the Eccentric Club of London] that he could make the trip in ten days."[11] Enhanced considerably by the Southern Pacific's star train, the Overland Limited, which transported the promoter to his hometown, the publicity stunt achieved its goal. Coffroth, or the Phineas Fogg of Frisco, also claimed that he had matched Jem Driscoll to meet Abe Attell on July 2.

On February 28, the same evening that Tommy Murphy of New York took a twenty-round decision from Owen Moran in San Francisco, Abe Attell knocked out Harry Forbes in the sixth round of a contest that took place in Troy, New York. Watching Forbes take an unmerciful beating in the sixth round finally compelled his seconds to throw up the sponge.

And as if the beating weren't bad enough: "Later Forbes was arrested by a United States marshal on a charge of using the mails to defraud during 1907. He had been indicted at Council Bluffs, Iowa."[12] Harry would get his house in order and manage to stay in the bantam mix, however, even taking on Johnny Coulon the following year. As for Team Attell, Troy was about as far north as Abe hoped to extend himself. Staying in New York suited him just fine.

The Unimaginative

New York State had become the epicenter of irresolution. Five consecutive ten-round no-decisions—from nearly the beginning of the spring until summer, the last taking place in Los Angeles—would keep "The Little Champ" occupied until the end of August. Decision or not, even a champion needed a paycheck.

"The Streak of Indecision" began on March 18, at the National Sporting Club, where Attell met the rugged lightweight Johnny Marto for ten rounds. The New York boxer was no walk in the park for Attell, as Marto claimed that he had never been knocked out. The *Herald* noted, "Marto was a dozen pounds heavier and in much better physical condition than Attell. For six rounds, Attell showed his usual cleverness and had the advantage of scientific points. But then he became weary and Marto by incessant rushing and heavy slugging evened the score and forced Attell to show his cleverness. If a decision had been rendered it might have been given to Attell on points."[13]

Fourteen days later, on April 1, Abe Attell met Owen Moran of England, whom he had drawn in two previous California encounters, and fought ten rounds to a no-decision. The betting was even going into the fight that was held before Wilson's Fairmount Athletic Club. Attell entered the battle, billed as a grudge match, several pounds lighter than Moran. As the *Call* saw it:

> In the first round Moran poked a stiff right into Attell's left eye, but Attell came back strong and the round was his. The second also went to Attell, but Moran outpointed him in the third. Attell retaliated in the fourth, fifth—in this round he drew blood from Moran's nose—and sixth rounds. Fighting was hot in the seventh, eighth and in the ninth Moran had his turn at drawing blood with a blow over Abe's eye. In the final round Moran, in a rush, surged against the ropes. As he bounded back, he fell against Attell and both men rolled over on the floor. Moran finished strong and was fighting hard at the close.[14]

While the last round was probably the most exciting, the public wasn't buying it, and as anticipated, the battle did not live up to expectations. This was nothing more than a repeat performance and proof that both fighters needed a finish fight in order to claim superiority. To say Attell's official record was getting redundant would be an understatement. The *Call* was quick to note the participants' schedules: "Moran will leave for California within the next few days. He is matched to fight Tommy McCarthy at San Francisco before Jim Griffin's club on April 29. Attell probably will remain around New York and Philadelphia in the hope of getting another match."[15]

According to the *Spokane Press*, before Moran left New York he had a verbal run-in with Attell at a local cafe. Upon entering the bistro, seeing his recent opponent, Moran greeted him warmly. Attell stated, "I don't think I ought to shake hands with you. You roast me behind my back and besides you have been saying a whole lot of things about us Americans.' Moran denied it and called the assertion a lie. He then stated his willingness to bet $5,000 that Driscoll could whip the champion. Attell remarked, 'I have $250 with me, which I will post right now as part of the bet.'"[16] Moran, who didn't carry money with him, noted that Driscoll was not coming to the United States to meet Attell—a play on just who would be matched with whom. Moran would not meet Driscoll until 1913, and Attell would never again meet the "peerless" feather.

Before his next ring battle, Attell and fellow boxer Leach Cross, who also happened to be a dentist, took part in a vaudeville stint in New York. A quick diversion, the avocation was also a way to line their pockets. The act began with Abie coming into Cross's dental office with a toothache. The two chat, tell a few jokes, like: What is another name for a dentist's office? Answer: A filling station. After the applause dies down, both boxers spar a few rounds to the delight of the crowd. The show was a wonderful opportunity for many to see the champion in a different light and witness his skills far closer than a General Admission ticket might provide.

Attell's next two ten-round no-decisions came from back-to-back confrontations with Tommy Murphy.[17] The first was held on April 28 before the Empire Athletic Club, over on West 155th Street, in New York. The bout, taken at catchweight, saw Attell easily grabbing the first seven rounds, but things quickly changed. Murphy, who had at least a twelve-pound advantage, took the eighth and ninth, even sending Attell down for the count of three with a hard right to the face in the latter. Such an assault, as everyone who followed Attell knew, meant one thing: retaliation. Attell was furious when he arose, and he let loose in the tenth, pounding Murphy around the ring. Had Murphy taken his action a round sooner, he may have found the canvas in the tenth.

The rematch on May 20 was held at the National Sporting Club. Attell, who forgave few and forgot nothing, picked up his game a bit. Bear in mind, it was Murphy who wanted the second match, but in a different club, and the champion, being the champion, approved. As one daily saw it: "The first six rounds were all Attell's. He was faster, cleaner and cooler. In particular his left jab to the face was puzzling and damaging. In the seventh and eighth Murphy worked to close quarters and did some wicked infighting. They were his only rounds. With a burst of speed, Attell let loose all he knew in the ninth and made Murphy look almost like an amateur. In the tenth, the champion was content to hold a safe lead."[18]

An interesting appraisal of Abe's skills appeared in the *Evening Times*, on May 6, as the reporter tried to understand why Attell was still boxing and so many other fighters his age were not: "Attell boxes just as little in every engagement as possible and still gets by with

Lightweight Leach Cross, a.k.a. "The Fighting Dentist," was one of the many boxing Cross brothers (Library of Congress).

it. Once he was a knocker-out, now he just eases his way by. If the bout goes ten rounds Abie figures that he must be on his feet for thirty minutes, and every second of that time consumed in stalling, feinting or putting the other chap to a disadvantage."[19]

So how did the audience view his actions? In most cases it seems, according to this writer, they saw Attell as a fighter who expended only the energy required, conserving the rest for his next fight. Also, the reason why Attell was still atop the division: "His brains work faster than his hands and his hands move more quickly than those of nine-tenths of the men he meets. His fights are usually poor ones to watch, but he goes on gathering the change just the same, because he never wastes an effort and has a brain that takes quick advantage of every opportunity."[20]

Word came on May 26 that Pal Moore gave Jem Driscoll the worst drubbing of his life in Philadelphia the previous evening, this during a six-round affair. It caught more than a few by surprise, but the eighteen-year-old Moore had been turning heads on the East Coast, and he turned even *more* that night at the National Athletic Club. The local boy was landing two for every one of the English feather's punches. The trouncing of Driscoll sent the division into another tailspin.

Seems Caesar Attell had the fight bug again. Not having fought since March of 1907, the featherweight had decided to once again enter the prize ring. "Believe me," says Abie in discussing Caesar, "he used to be a wonder in a short battle. But I want Caesar to stick to the coast, for they don't treat me right around New York, and I know he wouldn't get any better treatment. Let me show them a thing or two when I meet Driscoll. That's all."[21]

Attell's streak of five straight no-decisions would come to an end in Los Angeles, where the champion would meet Owen Moran once again. Why not? The money was good and it just might prompt the right promoter to offer a distance affair. Objections, and there were always some when these two stubborn pugilists met, were quickly cleared up with the exception of weight—that decision was left to the club. The *Herald* was quick to note McCarey's skills as an arbiter:

> It did not take Manager McCarey fifty seconds to render his decision as arbiter in the squabble between Owen Moran and Abe Attell regarding the weight they must make and the hour at which they must make it for their ten-round newspaper decision affair of June 24. Although he had all night to become impressed with the dignity and responsibility of his position as arbiter, he did not lose any sleep over it and when he came to town yesterday morning he promptly notified the squabblers that the weight would be 124 pounds and that it must be made at 5 o'clock the afternoon preceding the fight.[22]

Both boxers accepted McCarey's decision, as both had foreseen his response and were even training for the weight.

The fight, as anticipated, took place at the Naud Junction Pavilion. According to the *Omaha Daily Bee*:

> In spite of Governor Gillett's stand against prizefighting and his instructions to District Attorney Frederickson to stop last night's fight [June 24], Abe Attell and Owen Moran fought their ten-round bout as scheduled, Attell being given the newspaper decision. The district attorney did not interfere on the grounds that it was a "sparring bout" strictly within the law and not a prizefight. It was a hairline verdict. With two such clever men in the ring, the bout could well have come under the designation of a "sparring contest," but there were periods when it approached dangerously near to prizefighting.[23]

Though not the distance battle the fans had been endlessly clamoring for, it satisfied some of the ring thirst of Junction fans. Many had grown accustomed to making their own decisions with regard to who won the fight, so just seeing these two great gladiators scrap was a thrill.

Following the encounter with Moran, Attell and company made plans to head east toward Reno, Nevada, for the Johnson versus Jeffries fight on July 4. In fact, Attell met with Jeff out at his training camp in Moana Springs, where it was noted by the *Arizona Republican* that the two chatted for over an hour:

> Jim bent over the little fighter, listening to every word he uttered. It was an important talk for Jeffries. Abe Attell was in Jack O'Brien's corner when the latter met Jack Johnson in Philadelphia less than a year ago. The featherweight told the undefeated heavyweight today that O'Brien made Johnson "look foolish" on many occasions during the fight. Attell illustrated with his own fists the blows he would have Jeffries deliver and Jeffries watched with attention concentrated.[24]

Back on May 19, 1909, a 205-pound Jack Johnson evened a 162½-pound Philadelphia Jack O'Brien at the National Athletic Club in Philly. Had a decision been permissible in the six-round battle it would likely had been a draw. The *Call* saw this way: "O'Brien's marvelously fast foot work and his superior blocking saved him from damage in several close mixes, and three times he was forced to his knees by the great strength and weight of Johnson in the clinches."[25]

The *Call* reported, "After the talk Abe declared that he was utterly taken by surprise at Jeffries' appearance. He said that he had been misled by pictures of the former champion and before seeing that fighter in the flesh had thought Johnson a 2 to 1 favorite. 'Now,' Abe declared, 'I think there is nothing to it, but Jeff.'"[26] Jeff respected Attell and knew that if there was an angle, "The Little Champ" could find it. Jeffries's support system included not only Attell, but Jim Corbett, Jack Jeffries, Joe Choynski, Bob Armstrong, Sam Berger, Dewitt Vancourt, Tod Boyer, and Roger Cornell, all of whom followed the fighter into the ring against Johnson.

"The Fight of the Century" had been covered from every possible slant, or so it was believed. Close examination often yields a forgotten soul, and that is where our attention turns: to the announcer, Billy Jordan, who had introduced more fighters than any man in the world. Reflective of the rampant racism of the day, this was his partisan pre-fight opinion as printed by the *Call*:

> "When I turn loose the 'Let'er go' at this battle it will start away the greatest contest at which it has been my good fortune to be present in the capacity of an official. I really believe that it will be the real climax in battling in the heavyweight division in many decades. Naturally I fancy my old pal James J. Jeffries. He is going out to bring the championship back to the white race, where it belongs, and naturally my sympathies are with him. His work has been cut out for him, however, and I realize that this speedy Negro will be a hard individual for any fighter to beat. But Jeff will come down in front after the race has gone about 15 rounds. He will take little punishment, but he expects that. He's game and will win."[27]

On July 4, 1910, James J. Jeffries, having been lured out of retirement for all the wrong reasons and enduring a brutal training regiment, was battered relentlessly by Jack Johnson. The champion, who taunted the Jeffries team and the crowd, was himself incessantly insulted before retaining his title. Jim Jeffries had emerged from his alfalfa farm only to validate the golden smile radiating from Jack Johnson's untouchable face.

The offers kept rolling in to match Attell: first, against Seattle's Pete McVeigh on July 26, or Eddie Marino in Calgary on August 22, then four matches in Australia from Hugh McIntosh, the Sydney promoter. In view of the growing anti–prizefight sentiment Attell was weighing all his options regardless of venue.

On August 10, 1910, the first African American world boxing champion of the 20th century, Joe Gans, who reigned continuously as world lightweight champion from 1902 to 1908, died of tuberculosis. Some, like boxing historian and *Ring* Magazine founder Nat Fleischer, believed he was the greatest lightweight boxer of all time. When Abe Attell heard the news he was in Spokane, Washington. The press reported his remarks as, "Gee! Isn't that too bad!" The impromptu remark sounds obvious and trite until you understand the circumstance. Attell confirmed that he "heard from his bedside daily, but hoped against hope that he would pull through."[28] The champion fully understood how grave the circumstance had become. In his words: "Joe Gans was the greatest lightweight that ever entered the ring. In his prime no fighter of his weight was his equal. When you think of his ability throw out those two Nelson fights, for he was only a shadow of his former self. Consumption had him in its grasp even then."[29]

Abe Attell should know, because he assisted in training the "Old Master" for his last fight with Nelson on September 9, 1908, in Colma, California. It was the final fight of their great trilogy, of which Nelson took two out of three from Gans. The *Evening Star* noted, "Abe is ranked as one of the cleverest men in the game, yet in training with Gans the featherweight title holder was no match for the scientific colored man."[30]

From Spokane, Attell left for Calgary, Alberta, Canada, where he met Seattle lightweight Eddie Marino at catchweight on August 22. The fight, Attell's first outside of the United States, was scheduled for fifteen rounds. The conflict promised to be of interest, as both fighters, having fought each other back in July of 1908, were familiar with each other's style.

The reports from Calgary, however, were conflicting. An on-site report by a Salt Lake newspaper claimed: "From the sound of the first gong it was apparent that Merino [sic] had no chance and before the opening round was over, he went down, and Attell repeated the performance twice in the second round and again in the third, when Merino's seconds threw up the sponge."[31]

The Canadian Mounted Police were there to ensure order and insist on clean breaks. The *Tacoma Times* reported, "The fight was staged in an open air arena under the most adverse weather conditions [drizzling rain]."[32]

A United Press leased wire story, likely composed prior to the conflict and used in order to meet deadlines, especially those on the East Coast, claimed Attell won the fifteen-round decision.

Settlers, and there were many between 1896 and 1914, flocked to Calgary from all over in response to the offer of free "homestead" land. As agriculture shaped the "working man's economy," many activities began to cater to its participants. Not only would boxing become extraordinarily popular in Calgary, but so too other activities. The world-famous Calgary Stampede that began in 1912 would become known as the "greatest outdoor show on earth."

Former Canadian lightweight champion Billy Lauder was next to meet Attell in Calgary, on September 5. Outclassed by the champion, Lauder, who hailed from Medicine Hat, Alberta, was "knocked out in the seventh of what was intended to be a ten-round contest."[33]

Both Mr. and Mrs. Attell returned to the United States, specifically Milwaukee, for two ten-round conflicts: Charley White on September 16, and Frankie White on October 7. As if that were not enough challengers of the same surname, Attell would battle Jack White in Winnipeg on October 10. Charlie and Jack were brothers and part of a fighting family that included another brother named Wagner White, who fought under the name of Billy Wagner. The family lived and fought out of Chicago.

On September 16, it was Charlie who battled Abe to a ten-round no-decision. It was claimed that Abe's fast work in the final two rounds was what garnered him the newspaper decision. According to an *Evening Standard* account, "Abe was sent against the ropes in the first but came back smiling and landed a hard left to White's face, followed by another to the stomach. In the second round, there was some in-fighting with a good exchange at long range."[34]

White landed a solid combination to the face of Attell in the third round. Many saw it even by the gong. "The fourth was a repetition of the third."[35] Both fighters went to the face in the fifth, with Attell landing a bit better. The *Standard* went on to confirm the result: "The sixth was another even break and both slowed down in the seventh. Abe had a shade the better of the eighth. He landed one [punch] that brought blood to White's nose and sent in a rain of short arm jolts to Charlie's stomach. He devoted his time in the ninth to getting to White's body and then sent a hard left and right to the face. The champion did all of the fighting in the tenth and would have won the decision on this if nothing else."[36]

Two days later, the *Herald* noted:

Charley White came from a fighting family; his brothers Jack White and Billy Wagner were also boxers (Library of Congress).

> Jim Griffin, manager of the Broadway Athletic club, announced tonight [September 18] that he had matched Abe Attell and Ad Wolgast to fight twenty rounds in Dreamland Rink on the night of October 31. Griffin said a referee would decide the contest and that if there was any interference on the part of the authorities he would be prepared to meet it. Attell is presently in Milwaukee and Wolgast is at his home in Cadillac, Michigan. Arrangements for the match were made by wire.[37]

The goal of the promoter was to make the most cost-effective match imaginable, thus making it as easy possible for the participants to say "yes" to the deal. As champion, you can drive a tough bargain, but things can change radically once you are not. Though it was an attractive match, Attell understood that to endure twenty rounds with Wolgast, a lightweight champion, would be extremely difficult. The men who had always given Attell trouble in the ring had been clever chaps, boxers like Moran, Driscoll and soon Kilbane, and not the sluggers who bore in. As it would prove, the fighters would sign at 133 pounds at ringside, but had to wrestle with the purse. Like any boxing deal, it wasn't finished until the opening bell.

On Friday night, October 7, the champion featherweight fought lightweight Frankie White of Chicago in a ten-round no-decision bout before the Badger Athletic Club.

Looking at the fight by rounds: Attell took round one thanks to an accurate and effective straight left. A strong defense, combined with a dominant left jab, gave Attell round two. Attell's left gave him round three as White slipped to the mat. By ducking leads and catapulting lefts, Attell took round four. Machine-gun combinations to the head and body of White gave Attell round five. A slight advantage to Attell in round six was courtesy of his dominant left. White got wild in round seven as Attell stayed defensive until just before the gong. White's aggression in round eight was blocked by Attell's skilled defense. White led often in round nine but failed to deliver any real punishment to Attell. White brought the crowd to their feet in round ten with a combination to the face of Attell, but received several in return. "A decision was not necessary, even if the law permitted one, as opinion was unanimously in favor of Attell. The boys fought at 130 pounds," reported the *Wenatchee Daily World*.[38]

On to Jack on October 10, the third White in the surname trilogy. Fifteen snappy rounds led to a draw in Winnipeg between the champion and Jack White. The *Tribune* noted, "In the fourth round White got in eleven good body blows and it looked as though he could get a knockout at any moment. However, in the fifth Attell came back strong and put it all over White. Attell began to warm up in the thirteenth round and had his man dazed."[39]

Making noise in the Midwest was a twenty-one-year-old fighter out of Cleveland, Johnny Kilbane.[40] The champion wanted proof for himself, so it was off to Kansas City for a ten-round meeting with the youngster on October 24. John Patrick Kilbane was born on April 18, 1889, in Cleveland, and turned pro in 1907. He had, or so it seemed, been rattling the cages of featherweights ever since. With a solid build (he stood 5'5" high with a 68" reach), clever hands and good footwork, Kilbane had been under the tutelage of feather Jimmy Dunn, and together they had been systematically climbing the ranks of the division. And now, Kilbane faced the champion, and while he knew it wouldn't be easy, he also knew it would be an education. Immediately the youngster showed his cards: he made Attell go after him. And he boxed with "The Little Champ," because unlike Attell's previous opponents, he knew he could. Kilbane was the fastest fighter Abe had seen in some time, in and out like a flash. Although he couldn't match Abe's infighting, or his ability in the clinch, the young man showed some nice artillery at long range. The *Spokane Press* observed, "Referee Leo Shea gave Attell the verdict, but the crowd declared it was a draw and a good draw. So did the newspapermen present. Shea, they said, was blinded by the radiance cast by a champion when he lifted Attell's hand after ten rounds of milling."[41]

Three days after the date with Kilbane, Attell was back in New York, at Brown's Gymnasium, to fight Cleveland's Biz Mackey. As you recall, in his last battle with Mackey,

Attell broke his hand. Mackey's stock in the division had since been falling a bit, despite sound victories over Al Delmont and Willie Houck. As the *Spokane Press* reported, "'Biz' Mackey was elected to the Lemon club today [October 28] by unanimous vote of fight fans who witnessed his fight last night with Abe Attell. Mackey is being declared the biggest lemon of them all, for he was absolutely helpless in the hands of the clever Hebrew."[42]

For an assessment with a little less Vitamin C was this from the *El Paso Herald*: "After Attell had floored the Cleveland man three times in the sixth round, the latter's seconds crawled into the ring and hauled Mackey into his corner. A clean hard one to the body knocked Mackey down the first time in the sixth and as he rose, a right hand swing to the jaw toppled him over again. A right to the jaw ended the battle."[43]

Following a good night's sleep, Abe Attell once again took to the road with Eddie Kelly, this time in Amsterdam, New York. Why not, as it seems the pair had met everywhere else in the country? After putting Eddie to sleep in four rounds proved no problem, it was off to Philadelphia to meet the now superfluous skills of Owen Moran for the third time this year. With very little interest, the two fighters scrambled to their fourth draw, in a six-round defensive effort before the National Athletic Club on November 9. As the *Spokane Press* printed, "Both were bloody when the final gong rang, but a draw was the only possible decision."[44]

The Attell versus Moran saga was really wearing on the media by this point. Their fatigue no better exemplified than by a comment by the *Spokane Press,* on November 19, ten days after the fight: "The annual farce between Abe Attell and Owen Moran, in Philadelphia, filled the house, netted a goodly sum for the chiefs, and proved as exciting as a funeral."[45]

It was Frankie Conley who took the belt from Monte Attell, in their forty-two-round championship fight in Vernon, California, back on February 22. Now it was up to Abraham, or so he believed, to avenge that loss. Attell headed to New Orleans to do battle with Conley, holder of the bantamweight title, on November 13, in what was scheduled for twenty rounds—the city limit—under the auspices of the West Side Athletic Club.

Under pressure by Abe's camp, the distance was amended to fifteen rounds. Attell weighed 124 pounds, while Conley was three pounds lighter. Chicago Referee Dave Barry handled the fight. Attendance was strong, with some claiming it was the largest to witness such a contest in twenty years. As observed by the *Salt Lake Tribune*, "While Conley landed the most blows, few of them were damaging. Nine-tenths of the blows landed by both fighters were jabs or short-arm hooks in the clinches. Conley's style was to cover his head and rush in with swift blows to the face. Attell did not seem to mind these and for the first five rounds played a waiting game, always guarding against body punches with his left."[46]

Another observation was this from the *Spokane Press*:

> Conley had all the better of the first 13 rounds, and the crowd was greatly dissatisfied when the referee declared the scrap a draw at the end of the fifteenth. Even though Albie got a draw, however, whether it was deserved or not, it was clearly shown by the battle that in a finish fight Conley would prove the master. Frankie is not only a clever boxer, but he has the punch as well, and when he lands on Abe a few times, if they try the long route, the Hebrew will quit cold, and the finish will come soon afterward.[47]

The champion, who retained his title, received $1,500 for his end and transportation both ways.

For his final bout of the year, Abe Attell would be utilizing the services of three sparring partners—Danny Goodman, Jimmy Carroll and Lew Powell—to whip himself into shape for his battle against Pal Moore on November 30 at the Fairmount Athletic Club in New York.[48] The action no doubt was taken as a result of the strong showing Moore gave Driscoll back in May.

If preparation was the answer to consternation, then the champion should have entered the ring with confidence. And that's precisely what he did. In a rather one-sided ten-round contest, Abe Attell outclassed and severely beat his opponent. The *Washington Herald* saw it this way:

> Pal Moore, the eighteen-year-old Philadelphia pugilist, gave a wonderful exhibition of courage. With his right eye closed tight Moore kept on fighting against tremendous odds until the crowd that packed the building cheered him incessantly. Moore weighed about five pounds more than Attell, who again showed that he is one of the greatest boxers in the world. He made Moore look like a green novice practically all the way, hitting him with both hands incessantly, until in the fourth round the Quaker was knocked down with a hard right-hand swing on the jaw. Moore got on one knee and took a count of nine before resuming, but Attell did not appear overanxious to finish him then and there.[49]

The *Barre-Daily Times* noted this interesting incident: "Moore surprised the crowd in the seventh by putting Attell down with a right swing. Abe sat in the middle of the ring with his legs crossed laughing, waiting for the count of nine, when he sprang to his feet."[50]

Bantamweight Paul Walter Von Franzke, a.k.a. "Philadelphia Pal Moore," fought from 1907 until 1922 (Library of Congress).

In an interesting contrast, here is Abe Attell before the fight to the *Evening World*: "I feel good. I trained for the fight. When I train I'm good; when I don't train I feel worried. I weigh about 123 pounds and I feel fine—strong, in fact, never better. If Moore beats me, why, he's the better boy. All I have now is my chewing gum-my pal."[51] Here is the champion after the fight: "Moore is one of the nicest, gamest and cleanest 'little' fellows I've ever fought. He can hit, too. He beat me to a right hook in the seventh and I went down. I could have jumped right up, but what was the use? It counted as a knockdown anyhow. Moore caught me many a nice left-handed punch in the mouth and cut my lip. I took a lot of punches thinking I would take his steam away. Moore is O.K."[52]

As champion, Abraham Attell took plenty of criticism, so it was particularly nice when a newspaper paid him a tribute. Such was the case before his last fight, when the *Spokane Press* ran an article titled "Abe Attell One of Wonders of Ring." To extract a few quotes: "When the history of the ring is written, Attell will have to be one of the heroes; he's one of the most remarkable boxers that ever pulled on a glove.... Attell has met and beaten every good feather weight of his time.... Attell has led his league all this time and he is still the champion; and his record will stand favorable comparison with any boxer the world has ever seen."[53]

Attell was very close to boxing Packy McFarland at the Fairmount club in New York on December 19, but later demanded that the fight be moved. He also added that he was done fighting big men and would continue to defend his title at 122 pounds. The fight, as they say, smelled funny to begin with, and Attell could sense it, thus his decision. In a bout with contrition, Attell also admitted "he has been forced to fight under wraps time and again, because he was heavily in debt to the promoters, as the result of his weakness for gambling."[54]

In Monte's Corner

Monte Attell lost the bantamweight title to Frankie Conley on February 22, 1910, in forty-two very hard-fought rounds in Vernon, California. It was an even battle until Conley happened to catch Attell rushing in with a left hook to the jaw. The fight would become the longest title fight under Queensberry rules to end in a knockout.

Monte would go on to fight nearly another one hundred rounds during the year, while claiming a version of the bantam crown. But the loss, as expected, weighed heavily on his shoulders. Diminishing the burden somewhat would be a solid ten-round victory over Jimmy Walsh in November and a points victory over Billy Wagner in December.

In other news: Ad Wolgast outlasted Battling Nelson at Point Richmond, California, to win the world lightweight championship, in a fight that was stopped in round forty; and world middleweight champion Stanley Ketchel was shot and killed at Conway, Missouri, by Walter Dipley, a jealous farm worker. This left a division title vacant and an enormous void in the heart of the sport.

Two other notable engagements: Owen Moran shocked Battling Nelson in the eleventh round, flooring him five times, the last for the only ten-count of Nelson's career on November 26 in San Francisco; and Freddie Welsh defeated Jem Driscoll by a foul in the tenth round of their battle in Cardiff, Wales, on December 20.

Fighting over 170 rounds in nineteen fights, the world featherweight champion continued to successfully defend his title whenever he chose to put it on the line. He did not lose a single contest. Attell continued to distinguish himself by battling against members of boxing's elite class, including Johnny Kilbane and Owen Moran, the latter three times. The champion also fought for the first time outside the United States. The interesting events of the year were five straight ten-round no-decision bouts, three consecutive opponents with the surname White, and drawing the man who took the title from his brother. As champion he remained under constant scrutiny, but nevertheless steadfast in his defense.

CHAPTER TEN

From the Comfort of Home, 1911

"When Attell talks about dissipation he doesn't include drinking or smoking. He never did either, and about his only bad habit was gambling. He used to love to play the races, and up to a year and a half ago he had won and lost fortunes on the racetracks. He says he hasn't made a bet on the ponies since 1908 at Saratoga. Now he plays cards, just social games, now and then, but no big stakes ever figure in the play."[1]—Evening World

It was a year of discovery, as Norwegian Roald Amundsen led the first expedition to reach the South Pole; Hiram Bingham, an American historian, discovered the Incan city of Machu Picchu; and British physicist Ernest Rutherford discovered the structure of an atom. For the battling Attell brothers, realization in their line of work was not so succinct. For Monte, it meant finding and fighting his way back into the bantam mix, while for brother Abraham, protecting one of the most coveted of all boxing titles was about staying above the criticism through prudent decision-making.

A reflective view of the previous year, printed in the *Omaha Daily Bee* on New Year's Day, really struck home for Abraham: "The defeat of Jeffries and [Battling] Nelson marked the passing of all except one of the old guard fighters of the decade. Abe Attell, the featherweight, stands alone on the pinnacle to which he battled his way over some of the greatest little men the sport ever produced—Gans, Erne, McFadden, McFarland, Lavigne, Fitzsimmons, Corbett and McCoy, all good fighters—have passed out."[2] Not overly sentimental, but wise before his years, "The Little Champ" appreciated the recognition.

For Abe Attell, maturity lent itself to simplification. This meant employing a new strategy: "The Little Champ" would fight close to home. New York State, with its no-decision policy and short distance limit, was a security blanket, or a title preservation tactic. At this stage of his career, it just made sense, unless, of course, somebody made the champion an offer he just couldn't refuse. To dance ten rounds under the ceiling of the Empire State was to waltz to wealth, or so Attell believed.

Besides, interests outside a square ring were playing a greater role in his life. A newspaper had this to say regarding the champ's first conflict of the year:

In one of the cleverest exhibitions of boxing ever seen in the city, with a rushing, slashing, banging finish in the tenth round. Joe Coster (122 pounds) fairly smothered Abe Attell (124 pounds), the featherweight champion in a ten round bout in front of the Vanderbilt Athletic Club, Brooklyn last night [January 9]. Coster was a surprise party, one of the disagreeable kind to Attell. Abe, much to the surprise of everybody, lacked his old cleverness. Whether he was "pulling" only the foxy Abe can say.[3]

As for the highlights: In round one both fighters cautiously measured their punches before mixing in a clinch. Attell's defense attempts—lefts and uppercuts—failed as he endured a facial assault. Coster continued to attack Attell's physiognomy in round two, as the champion worked his adversary's body against the ropes. Attell began executing his jabs successfully in the third while mounting an attack to Coster's countenance. Coster came back hard and fast in the fourth and landed successfully to Attell's head. Some nice combinations by Coster damaged the champion as he was sent to the ropes in round five. The blood began flowing from Coster's claret as Attell's facial campaign resumed in the sixth. Coster countered strong in the seventh with solid blows to Attell's face. Both fighters persisted with their attacks to the head in round eight. Coster continued to endure Attell's left to the body, as he countered with jabs to the champ's physiognomy in the ninth. This is how the same source viewed the final round: "Coster jabbed Attell's face so many times in the tenth that it was impossible to

Born Giuseppe Agnello in Italy, "Joe Coster" began fighting out of Brooklyn in 1906. Later, he became a New York boxing judge (Library of Congress).

count the blows. He made a whirlwind rally near the end of the round and sent Attell nearly through the ropes. The second rope alone saved Attell from falling on the floor. While in that position he jabbed Abe until the latter was dazed."[4]

It was a consensus opinion that Coster had outpointed Attell, even if the damage assessments differed. Attell didn't duck the criticism—he looked out of shape—but he requested a rematch. He was a 1 to 2 favorite coming into the battle and would likely have similar odds when he met Patsy Kline before Tom O'Rourke's club on Friday night.[5]

In Bob Edgren's column in the *Evening World* on January 10, 1911, the writer answered a reader's question regarding Attell: Had he ever been put to the mat with a knockout? Yes: it had happened back in 1904, when Tommy Sullivan sent Abe to the heavens in the fifth round of a battle in St. Louis. But what was interesting was Edgren's recollection of another confrontation, one that didn't make it into the record books: Abraham Attell was knocked cold by boxer Tony Bender on March 7, 1906, in New York City. It happened during a three-round event at Elmer's, a little gymnasium over at Forty-second Street and Sixth Avenue. Elmer's was owned by Bill Elmer, the noted philanthropist, who, like many in his capacity, had a passion for the fight game. Elmer, who had once been partnered in the gym with Kid McCoy, was running the place and decided he would match Attell against Bender. Naturally, there was an enticing gentlemen's agreement between the parties—these one-off challenges were as much a part of the game as speed bags and jump ropes—with Attell opting only for the three round route.

Bender, a lightweight, was a Jersey boy, lean and hungry, and could pack a punch. As the bout began, Bender was cautious, while Attell, under complete control, worked him with his trademark left jab. This was fine for a while, but became just plain irritating when Bender could not defend against it. To Bender's credit, however, he kept moving and observing, like a lion at a watering hole. Then, seeing an opening in Attell's defense, Bender uncorked a solid right directly to Abe's chin and sent him horizontal. It was a marksman's shot, and Bender took it. The referee, seeing Attell out cold, stopped counting at three and went over to congratulate Tony. When Attell came to, he was still all in. Bender then continued to drop "The Little Champ," almost at will, and Albie kept getting up. However, by the third round, Attell had regrouped, and he took control of the fight. This was just one of numerous confrontations that never found its way into the record books. And it's why you often hear of a fighter during this period bragging that he has fought hundreds of fights, even if they weren't accounted for.

The *Evening Star* was quick to summarize the champion's next encounter: "Patsy Kline shoved Abe Attell down the championship ladder at the National Sport Club last night [January 13]. The work that Joe Coster began early in the week Kline finished. He beat the featherweight champion in a close boxing exhibition of ten rounds by a small margin, but it was sufficient to give him a [newspaper] victory."[6] Even if the press saw it that way, the fight was obviously registered with the requisite no-decision.

Having admitted the previous year that he may have pulled a few punches here and there, Attell now found himself forever associated with another disputable issue, and it would surface here.

Did Abe "pull"? Fatigue, which can at times mirror pulling a punch, may have been an issue, but tiredness was not synonymous with pulling punches. Most observers felt Abe was there the first three rounds, but noted a decline from that point onward in his defense. Kline took control in the fourth and did not relinquish it until the eighth round, landing most of his punches at will and even having Attell dazed in the sixth. As the *Evening Star* saw it: "Twice Kline had Attell on the ropes in a bad way. But Patsy, just as he had an excellent chance to end the bout with a knockout, weakened and missed his triumph. Abe was able to stall along in the last two rounds, and make a fairly good finish. But that was all. Kline, though he had failed to land the sleep producer, had won on points (according to reports) with good wallops in the middle sessions of the boxing."[7]

Kline, a Newark featherweight who had recently fought well against Joe Coster, Benny Kaufman and Young Pierce, was far from a tomato can. If he had the chance to put away Attell, as some viewers believed, he would have taken it. And that's what separates a contender from a champion.

A Lesson in Subjectivity

Now to the world of newspaper decisions, or subjective assessment based on the knowledge of the appraiser—which the gamblers believed was better than none at all, and what the boxing community had grown to acknowledge as gospel. Although it was hoped that regional bias played no role in these interpretations, research, in some instances, may prove otherwise. Prejudice in favor of, or against, one person is difficult to extract. Using this fight as an example—in the land of indecision, or New York State— here is how the experts saw it, according to the *Tribune*:

> For Attell: *New York Tribune*—Attell still a master boxer, easily outpointed Kline; *Herald*—Attell has little trouble with Kline; *Times*—Attell cleverly outpoints Kline in ten-round bout; *Telegram*—Attell defeats Kline, showing absolute mastery; *American*—Kline's wallop fails to find the wily Attell; *Press*—Attell wins by shade from Patsy Kline; *Evening Telegram*—Attell too clever for Patsy Kline in a ten-round bout; *Globe*—Attell far from his old self, but wins easily; *Mail*—Attell, on downgrade, defeats Kline, but generalship saves him; *Evening Sun*—Attell shows old form in bout with Kline; and *Evening World*—Attell outpoints Kline, but Kline does all the fighting.
>   For Kline: *World*—Kline too sturdy for Abe Attell in fast bout; and *Evening Journal*—Attell, under a pull, loses bout to Kline.
>   For a draw: *Sun*—Only a draw for Abe Attell with Newark boxer.[8]

While the majority clearly saw the fight for Attell, there were some who viewed it differently. This could be for any number of reasons, such as unfamiliarity with the sport, lack of acquaintance with how a fighter handles a no-decision fight, a personal vendetta— you just don't know. As a champion and in a major market, Attell had plenty of media coverage and established support—familiarity, however, breeds expectations. Fighting away from such a major market could limit media exposure and reduce, if not eliminate, any advocacy. More than one champion has regretted leaving his "comfort zone," or fighting in a market that cost him his title.

A New York State of Mind

A product of Ontario, and the featherweight champion of Canada, Billy Allen was now making his home in central New York. On January 23, "The Little Champ" would make the roughly 215-mile journey to meet Mr. Allen, at the legal limit, inside the Alhambra. Located at 275 James Street, at Pearl Street, in Syracuse, the Alhambra was built in 1900 to replace the original Alhambra, built sixteen years earlier. It was a multi-purpose facility hosting everything from boxing and basketball to bingo and roller skating (the second floor was used as a roller skating rink). The bout, refereed by Tom Cawley, promised to be an exciting affair—for a champion like Attell to be in town was quite a treat for central New York fight fans. The *Daily Missoulian* noted, "With the exception of a few rounds Allen did most of the leading, but his showing was marred by frequent attempts at 'covering.' In the fourth round Attell injured his right hand by coming in contact with Allen's elbow. Attell was not forced to extend himself in any of the rounds."[9]

The lackluster affair, to little if any surprise, was Attell's third straight no-decision. The western jaunt to Syracuse happened to be along his journey to Cleveland, where Attell, against his better judgment, would take a fight against Tommy Kilbane on January 31. Abe had hoped to act as chief advisor to his brother Monte when he faced "Young Britt" in a 15-round encounter in Germania Maennerchor Hall in Baltimore on that date, but it could not be arranged.

Tommy Kilbane (no relation to Johnny Kilbane) hailed from Cleveland, Ohio, and was an erratic fighter turned punching bag, who had a propensity to devour novice fighters, draw average scrappers, and lose to good boxers. Kilbane would enter the fight weighing

127 pounds to Attell's 119. Attell knew it was a dangerous proposition, but took the fight anyway. This is what one daily printed: "The fight between Abe Attell, featherweight champion, and Tommy Kilbane, here, in which Attell broke his right shoulder bone, was declared no contest by referee Will McKay.[10] The injury to the champion proved more serious when it was learned that the left arm was injured, the tendons being badly strained and bruised."[11]

Some fighters can just sense when something doesn't feel right, and Attell knew he should never have left New York. Having fallen to the floor during a clinch with his adversary in the fourth, which landed Kilbane atop of Attell, the champion immediately sensed something was wrong. An attending physician, Dr. J.V. Gallagher, believed Attell could be in a position to fight within two months, which was a blessing for those who believed the injury far more serious. The Doctor also believed Attell's "skills would not be impaired by the accident."[12] It was not a pleasant night for the Attell brothers, as Monte lost his fight in Baltimore.

Back home in New York, a confident champion stated to the *Courier*: "I feel from what my surgeon says, that I will be able to start work in time to go through with a match with Driscoll late in March. I am anxious to meet him on the terms suggested by the representatives of McIntosh and Britt, as I understand Olympia is really the center of the boxing game abroad and good money is assured a man who can win."[13]

As for his account of what happened, Attell claimed to the same source, "Kilbane threw me down and I landed on my right shoulder and dislocated it. While lying helpless, with my left elbow on the floor with his hands covering my side, Kilbane fell on me, placing his knee on my left arm between the wrist and elbow in such a way as to fracture a small bone above the elbow joint."[14] The incident appeared to take its toll on many fronts, as it entered some record books incorrectly as a KO by 4.

A Rare Glimpse at the Champion

Writer Vincent Treanor wrote a complimentary piece about Attell for the *Evening World* on February 4, 1911. The insight was the first in some time to reflect on the life of the fighter.

> Abe Attell, featherweight champion of the world, is the wonder of wonders in the prize ring. He has seen champions of all classes come and go during his career, yet today he stands supreme—practically invincible at the head of the featherweight division, and few are they among the lightweights who can defeat him. Within a period of thirteen years, during which he has been fighting, Attell has cleaned up more than $200,000. No matter what happens now, he is beyond want for the rest of his life, and the members of his family, living in San Francisco, are all in comfortable circumstances, thanks to the earnings of Abe.[15]

The article then takes the reader through the young man's life, his fight with the famous George Dixon, then on to his current position:

> Most of Abe's winnings, up to the time he was married five years ago to Elizabeth Margaret Egan, a San Francisco girl, went home to his mother. Today, his mother owns three houses in Frisco; his brothers are in the loan business and doing well. In addition Abe himself owns a house and lot in Los Angeles, which he paid $10,000 for five years ago after he beat Frankie Neil. The property is worth $18,000 now and the house rents for $70 a month. His wife has two pieces of valuable property in Frisco and Abe has $45,000 of the $200,000 he has earned with his fists stowed away.[16]

The illuminating work goes on to mention that his sixty-five-year-old mother lives an active life, and the fighter credits his success during the last five years to his Irish wife, stating, "She has kept me on the strait and narrow path, and I have had no time for dissipation. I have known her for twelve years. She went to school with my sisters out home."[17]

The champion then acknowledges his vices as the article continues: "When Attell talks about dissipation he doesn't include drinking or smoking. He never did either, and about his only bad habit was gambling. He used to love to play the races, and up to a year and a half ago he had won and lost fortunes on the racetracks. He says he hasn't made a bet on the ponies since 1908 at Saratoga. Now he plays cards, just social games, now and then, but no big stakes ever figure in the play."[18]

Naturally, as champion, Attell dislikes criticism, as a citrus lover as was quick to state: "If I fight a so-called lemon and fail to knock him out, I am accused of pulling. The other fellow gets no credit for being a good man. If I knock out a man in two rounds, the papers say, 'Attell picks another lemon.' It's awful hard on a champion."

"The Little Champ" went on to defend his ring tactics; explain the evolution of the fight game and how much easier it is to get hurt, like breaking a hand, because of the improved defensive strategies; and even explain the difference between stalling and just waiting for the right moment. The reporter concludes with, "Attell realizes he can't go on forever, and it was for that reason he has decided to retire and go into some business at the end of the year. Just now he is dickering for the sale of property in the vicinity of the new American League ballpark."[19]

A Presumptuous Return

In a tremendous display of heart, Abe Attell battled ten quick rounds against Frankie Burns to a no-decision at the National Sporting Club on March 31. Those who witnessed the contest called it, according to the *Rock Island Argus*, "scintillating with brilliant boxing."[20]

In a more detailed review, the newspaper printed:

Twice during the mill, in the ninth and tenth round, Attell knocked Burns to his knees, but try as he would he was unable to administer the sleep producer to the fast little Jersey boxer. Attell boxed the last six rounds with a left arm that was helpless. In the fourth round Burns hit him hard twice. One blow landed on the arm near the point of the elbow and the other struck him on the shoulder. Those blows hurt his broken collar bone and shoulder—an injury he had received in a bout in Cleveland with Kilbane.[21]

Attell's arm was virtually useless by the fourth round, however he didn't want to flag Burns of the injury so he used it sparingly into the ninth. It was clear he was a one-handed boxer by the final round. Thankfully, Attell's powerful right not only kept Burns at a safe distance, but also dropped him to the canvas. To think the caliber of boxer it takes not only to re-enter the ring two months after a serious injury, to engage with a fighter like Burns—a fighter who held newspaper decisions over Charley Goldman, Johnny Coulon and Tommy Hock—for ten rounds, speaks for itself.

Badly hurt, Attell fought Burns to a standstill, but now it would cost him weeks of healing time. Understanding that not only his incredible determination but also his trademark stubbornness, many weren't surprised that he entered the ring too soon, but how do you tell that to a champion? How do you convince a fighter who was not only atop his division, but one of the best who ever fought there? Couldn't he have picked an easier target than Burns? Certainly, but he did not.

The law said prizefighting shall not be permitted in New York, so just how had they been dodging the issue? Well, spectators could attend boxing matches, not fights, thanks to Manhattan's fight impresario named Billy Gibson (a name that will surface again in association with boxer Gene Tunney), who was granted a permanent injunction by a New York Supreme Court. The problem was police interference, so Gibson went to Justice Seabury for a restraining order. Seabury complied, and athletic clubs were then allowed to conduct matches before club members. Now, if a police officer attempted to enter a club, he could face six months for contempt.

The police constantly challenged the issue. For example: "Magistrate Murphy, in the West Side Court, today refused the application of Captain McNally of the West Forty-seventh Street police station for warrants for the arrest of Abe Attell and Frank Burns, the principals, and others in a boxing bout at the National Sporting Club last night [March 31]."[22] Because the captain was unsure that an admission fee was charged to those who saw the contest, Magistrate Murphy could not assist him. "Magistrate Herman declined an urgent invitation to participate in a fishing expedition which was tendered to him today by Acting Captain Gilmartin of the East Twenty-second Street station. The object of the expedition was to fish for evidence that the Horton law had been violated...."[23] Warrants could not be issued because there was no evidence that the law had been broken.

With his injury healing, it was reported that the champion was to pass the time, and incidentally pick up a little jingle, by going into vaudeville as a monologist. If you can't walk the walk in a ring, then talk the talk outside of one. Abe, like many pugilists, loved the spotlight.

Unable to train, "The Little Champ" also used some of his free time to share some stories with the

Jersey City bantamweight Frankie Burns debuted professionally in 1908 and ended his career in 1921. He stood 5'4½" tall with an impressive 67½" reach (Library of Congress).

press. It was unusual for the champion to comment about the practice of deception, but he did in May to the *Calmut News*, and it was about the many ways boxers cheat the scales: "Oldest of all and one that is still tried but seldom worked successfully, is the trick of putting a wad of gum on the underside of the 100-pound weight. That used to fool many greenhorns and sleepers but nowadays no boxer goes to the scale without first grabbing the weight and inspecting the underside."[24]

Attell also spoke of how they used to replace the lead or iron of a weight with shoe-maker's black wax, trusting that once hardened it would appear like the metal. The champ confirmed that most fighters caught on to the fix and started using their fingernail to scrape the metal for wax. He also mentioned, an example: "One manager I knew long ago had a special 100-pound weight made for him, with every detail correct, but so filled with lead that it was eight pounds to the bad. If a man weighing 140 pounds was weighed with that dicker iron his poundage registered 132. See the idea?"[25] The man became an expert at slipping the weight on and off the scale without its being recognized.

The champion continued his disclosure:

> Out on the coast they have a clever trick. If your man is overweight leave the scale alone. Take him right up there. There will always be a jam around the scale, everybody looking at the weights and the beam to see you don't monkey with them. Let your man hook a finger into the coat pocket of a friend standing by. It will throw off all the weight upon the friend and the scale will not budge. In 99 cases out of 100 nobody will get wise—everyone will be rubbering at the beam or weights.[26]

Hey, with the shelf life of a pug at about seven years, some would do whatever it takes to prolong a career.[27]

By the last week in May, Abe was getting restless and agreed to match with Knockout Brown before the National Sporting Club on June 8. This was, of course, if he was healed and the terms were accepted; the weight was to be 132 pounds at ringside.

By June 2, however, it was obvious to Attell that he had not sufficiently healed and the champion was forced to call off the bout. The following month, the press—forever presumptuous and always willing to bury a champion—were running articles speculating that Abe was near retirement. If so, who might claim his title? Later it was rumored that Patsy Kline and Johnny Kilbane were part of an elimination bout to see who might fight the champion if a match could be made. In the interim, Abe convalesced, on tenterhooks as usual.

Word came cyclically, as it does in boxing, of another rising star. This time it was a featherweight named Jose Rivers, who was fighting out of Tom McCarey's club in Los Angeles. According to McCarey, Attell was assuredly *the* champion, but there were a great many who looked upon Rivers as the impending champion, or Attell's successor. Rivers's pompous yet optimistic manager, Joe Levy, was already billing the boy as the world's champion featherweight—the heir apparent to Abe's supreme reign.

When you are as smart a champion as Attell, you don't get sucked into these scenarios; you play them, which is precisely what he did. Knowing McCarey like the back of his hand, Attell dropped him a telegram, according to the *Tacoma Times*, on August 12, stating: "[Attell] wants $10,000, win, lose or draw for his end of a 20-round go here [Los Angeles] with Rivers on New Year's Day." Adding, "Getting big money here to box suckers ten rounds, so must have $10,000 to fight Rivers."[28]

Later, McCarey, who had hoped to bait Attell, confirmed that he would meet with Rivers's manager to discuss Attell's terms. The snickers could be heard all the way to Long Beach, Rivers's hometown, and back. The two fighters would never meet.

As for the Ladies

A woman's boxing voice was seldom heard in the game, so when they did speak it was often from an interesting perspective. Mrs. Patsy Kline, age eighteen, shared her views exclusively with readers of the *Tacoma Times* in September. She mentioned her opinions had changed regarding fighters, and that she now found them "to be clean, big-hearted men."[29] Fully supportive of her featherweight husband, she didn't get nervous but admitted her anxiety would end if she could be allowed to see the fight and sit in her husband's corner. She then told a brief story: "I will never forget January 13, 1911, when Patsy defeated Abe Attell, the featherweight champion. I have never seen Attell fight, but I have heard of his wonderful cleverness. When both boys entered the ring I took my old place outside the clubhouse. When the crowd poured out I asked the first man who had won and he told me Patsy Kline by a mile, and it made me jump with joy."[30]

The article prompted a question: Should a prizefighter marry? As might be expected, there were differing opinions. A look at the list of those who were hitched included Abe Attell, Tommy Burns, Frankie Conley, Jim Corbett, Bob Fitzsimmons, Jim Flynn, Joe Gans, Jack Johnson, Al Kaufman, Johnny Kilbane, Kid McCoy, John L. Sullivan, and Ad Wolgast. Just the same, an equally impressive bachelor's list included Jimmy Britt, "Knock-out" Brown, Joe Coster, Stanley Ketchel, Battling Nelson, Philadelphia Jack O'Brien, and Freddie Welsh. So what did the ladies think? According to Mrs. Conley, who also spoke to the *Times*:

> I believe that Frankie has become 25 percent better since we were married. He has shown more desire to win than before and his training has been almost perfect. He leads a quiet home life, with regular meals and sleeping hours and is perfectly contented. Nothing is permitted to worry him and I have noticed during the last month that he is stronger and quicker in his ring work. We are happy and our happiness has been a factor in putting Frankie in his present condition. We live modestly and are saving money.[31]

Mrs. Conley then added: "I think that a fighter who does not live a fast life and who marries a nice girl and settles down to make a home and become a permanent member of society should be given credit for what he does, as he is doing the proper thing both for himself as a fighter and as a member of society at large."[32] It certainly made for an interesting topic. There was no comment made by Mrs. Attell, or Abraham for that matter.

Perhaps worth noting, since "Kid McCoy," or Norman Selby, was on our list, maybe the answer lay in just how many times one was married. The "Kid" had just taken wife number eight, an heiress from the northern part of New York State, and had married five women, one of them three times.

Mended Mitts

The announcement came on September 11: George McDonald, manager of Matt Wells, the English lightweight champion, in conjunction with Harry Pollack of the Madison Square Athletic Club, proclaimed that he had made a match with Abe Attell, the featherweight champion. The boys would fight at Madison Square in New York on September 20, likely weighing in at 135 pounds at 5 o'clock in the afternoon. The match was a surprise to some who believed Wells, boxing at that weight, was one of the cleverest fighters around and perhaps too clever for Attell.

The concern was a valid one. At the conclusion, most reporters saw it Wells by a shade. Wells controlled the ten-round no-decision from the start, exhibiting great foot-work, clever feinting, and sound judgment. The *Evening World* viewed it this way:

> In a very business-like way Wells began jabbing and hooking at Abe's chin. He was as accurate as a rifleman. He missed very few punches, and Abie, to his own surprise, was unable to block the swift little Englishman's blows. Almost at will Wells shot them through Abe's guard. While the punches were snappy they didn't have much gunpowder behind them. There was nothing in the knockdown line delivered during the entire ten rounds.[33]

Ever mindful of his strategy, when Attell realized he couldn't hold his own at a distance, he went inside. But Wells adjusted by dropping back a bit, and continuing his success with his punishing left and uppercuts. Wells was quicker, and Attell's ring rust became noticeable less than halfway through the bout. The *World* noted:

> It was a fairly even thing until the beginning of the third, when Wells cut loose and drove Abie back on his heels with hard punches delivered as fast as he could drive his hands in. Abe's eyes, nose, and mouth began to show distress signals. He reared a little under the attack, but rallied, and the crowd cheered uproariously when Abe, featherweight champion, scored a few blows. Abe did not have the accuracy that Wells showed. Wells developed a trick of dancing and feinting and drawing Abe's lead, and then beating him to the punch. He did it handily.[34]

Attell rallied in the sixth, but Wells outlasted him. The seventh was a similar round, but Attell's rally was shorter and Wells's assault was stronger, forcing the champion to place emphasis on his defense. The pace of the fight then fell off during the final three rounds. As the *World* viewed it: "Wells seemed content with his big lead, and he didn't try to add to it or to score a knockout. The ninth was slow, and in the tenth Abe didn't start his usual finishing rally until within the last ten seconds. Even then, Wells put on a little more steam and held him easily. Aside from his weight advantage, about thirteen pounds, Wells was faster, more accurate and even trickier than Attell. He had no trouble in winning."[35]

British fighters were well aware of the value the New York market, and the exposure did Wells some good. The following day San Francisco promoter James Coffroth telegraphed the British fighter's manager with two offers: $5,500 for a bout with Packey McFarland, or $7,500 for a contest with Ad Wolgast, the lightweight champion.

As for Attell, his current manager (Abe went through managers like tissues) John J. Reisler had announced on September 11, the same day the public learned of the Wells bout, that Attell was prepared to meet Johnny Kilbane, Attell's foremost rival. But that fight would have to be in New York City at 123 pounds—a ten-round, no-decision affair. Kilbane, having knocked out Joe Rivers, was now at the forefront of division contenders. Meanwhile, Team Attell was about to travel west to Buffalo on October 28, for a fight with Herman Smith.

From Frank Erne to Rocky Kansas, Buffalo, New York, was a hotbed for lightweight boxing talent from 1899 until 1926. Names like Harry Coulin, Jake Schiffer, Joey Mendo, Lockport Jimmy Duffy, Elmer Doane, George Erne, Kid Black, Teddy Meyers, Harry KO Mueller, Jimmy Goodrich and Herman Smith all added to the city's rich boxing heritage. In his first professional year as boxer, Herman Smith didn't have his master's degree yet, but knew enough to stay away from Abe Attell for ten rounds. As the champion chased,

California-born Alberto DeNave, a.k.a. "Joe Rivers," debuted professionally in 1929 and ended his career in 1938 (Library of Congress).

Smith ran so fast Attell had difficulty catching him. But Attell outclassed Smith in every department on the way to a newspaper decision.

Three days later came word that Johnny Coulon, who claimed the bantamweight championship of the world, had turned down an offer of $3,000 for a fight with Abe Attell. It was a noteworthy offer out of New Orleans and one that would have made life for the Attell brothers a bit interesting. Johnny's manager, his brother Ben, didn't want him moving up to scrap with the feathers; Coulon was as content at 116 pounds as Attell was at 123.

Back home, Abe Attell's next antagonist was Young Cohen on November 15. Taking three fights in less than ten days, Attell made it a goal to fight himself into shape. Cohen was a clever English fighter whom some compared to Jem Driscoll, which was an exaggeration. Here's how one source viewed the scrap: "Attell gave the Englishman a terrible beating, but Cohen took all the champion could give and came back for more. In the fourth round Attell shook Cohen up with a hard jolt to the jaw, but was unable to land a knockout."[36]

Five days later, it was inside the Olympia Athletic Club of Harlem for a ten-round encounter with Brooklyn's Willie Jones. Clearly over his head, Jones, who had managed some good outings in his last eight fights, landed scarcely a dozen clean punches. The *Tribune* reported: "Attell knocked him down and almost out in the fifth round, but took his time in following the lead and let his rival recover. It was merely a case of a courageous novice fighting a past master of the game. Jones had little outside of a rush and wild swing for the head. The crafty champion lay back, swaying away or leaping in quickly shot his punches home with rare precision."[37] Please note the use of the word "rival" here connotes opponent, and not "equal."

The champion continued to show signs of healing as he sliced and diced feather-weight Leo Johnson with his trademark left jab inside the Malvern Athletic Club on November 23. In the fifth round, when Johnson's manager could no longer tolerate the facial deconstruction of his fighter, his corner threw up the sponge. The *Bridgeport Evening Farmer* noted: "The climax to the one sided [New York] affair came after Attell cut Johnson's face with a series of left jabs and connected with several rights to the stomach. Johnson showed a yellow streak from the start, resorting to hold tactics from the time the gong unleashed the contestants until the bout was stopped."[38] It was Attell's relentless and unanswered assault, or cumulative damage, that put away his opponent.

The report continued, "In the second and third rounds Attell had Johnson almost stowed away, the negro swaying from side to side under a fusillade of jabs, swings and hooks. Had foxy Abe so desired he could have put the haymaker across before the gong sounded for the end of either of those sessions, but Attell stalled and gave Johnson a chance to remain."[39] The champion finished the month strong by undertaking two more ten-rounders before also concluding his year.

Newspapers often poked fun at Attell's longevity—and not just his, but any boxer who had exhibited prolonged success over his division. That is, until another pugilist decided to come out of retirement to show the youngsters "how it is done." Comebacks, as common to boxing as autumn leaves are in New England, are always treated with a degree of skepticism, as they are seldom successful. This time it was Joe Choynski, who had been a boxing instructor at the prestigious Pittsburgh Athletic Club. "Chrysanthemum Joe," the son of a Jewish Polish immigrant who settled in California in 1867, had last fought in 1904. Having taken great care of himself—not drinking tea or coffee and watching his diet—the former fighter, with a right hand so powerful he drove one of Jim Jeffries's teeth into his lips, believes: "The fighters of today are a lot of sluggers who lack science, and he thinks a man handy with his left and lively on his feet could outpoint them. Choynski is ambitious enough to believe that he can demonstrate that he is entitled to match with Jack Johnson."[40]

The fighter announced that he had arranged a six-round scrap with Buck Crouse, so the public must now wait and see if there was anything left in "The California Terror's" tank. Choynski, a brilliant Jewish boxer, certainly had nothing to prove, as he was already one of the most respected fighters in history.

For Attell, and spectators for that matter, the final two fights, both back-to-back, were lackluster, as he danced and outclassed Patsy Kline for ten rounds on December 1 at the Navarre Athletic Club in Brooklyn, and did the same against Willie Jones at the Gowanus Athletic Club in South Brooklyn. The *World* reported: "Kline hardly scored a punch during the entire ten rounds. Attell might as well have been shadow boxing for all the opposition he received. The best thing that Kline did was to swing from the floor every now and then. He swung all his might, too, but at the time the blow should have struck something substantial Attell was many feet away, sneering."[41]

In much of the same tone, but this time against Jones, the *Tribune* concluded: "Standing off and measuring the rushes of the plucky little Jones, Attell met him with a tantalizing left jab to the face that had Jones wild and worried. The latter was game, but totally outclassed. Only his aggressiveness made it look other than a boxing lesson from the old master to a presumptuous youngster."[42]

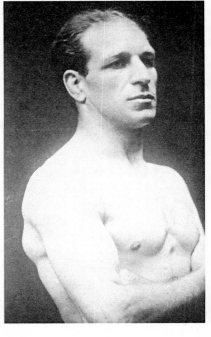

San Francisco–born heavyweight Joseph Bartlett Choynski, whose greatest victory came in 1901 when he knocked out future heavyweight champ Jack Johnson in three rounds (Library of Congress).

On December 4, Attell was to meet Joe Clarke in Wilkes-Barre, Pennsylvania, but the bout was called off. According to one source, "Owing to the receipts not being sufficient to pay Attell's guarantee" was given as the reason.[43] Team Attell then headed back home for a scheduled meeting against "One Round" Hogan, scheduled for December 18 before the Madison Square Athletic Club. Hogan was expected to do 133 pounds at 6 o'clock in order to battle for the featherweight championship. As "The Little Champ" prepared for Hogan, he received good news, which was confirmed by the *Evening World*:

> Abe Attell and Johnny Kilbane, the great little featherweight fighter of Cleveland, have at last been matched to meet in a twenty-round bout for the featherweight championship of the world. They will battle in the open air before the Pacific Athletic Club of Vernon, California, on Washington's Birthday afternoon for a purse of $10,500 for which Attell is guaranteed $7,000 and Kilbane the remaining $3,500. Kilbane held off for some time for $4,000 for his end, but finally gave in when Tom McCarey, who was promoting the fight, telegraphed him that he could not give out that amount.[44]

The news certainly secured a fine holiday for both fighters, knowing that a pot of California gold was awaiting them early next year in Vernon.

Now back to the Hogan bout. Always at risk due to the weight clause, the confrontation was looking grim by December 11. It was looking as if Hogan couldn't make 133, so Attell briefly agreed to 135 pounds before threatening to call off the fight if Hogan could not shed the extra two pounds. Then, when it looked as if Hogan might be able to make weight, the bout was postponed until December 29 at the request of Attell, who was said to have lamed his hand in a practice bout. But the story Hogan told was that Attell roughed it up with a doorkeeper who wouldn't allow the champion admission to a sporting club. Attell and Hogan would never do battle.[45]

With Kilbane inked in for February 22, 1912, Attell was hoping for one, or possibly two, ten-rounders at home before traveling out to California. On December 15, there was talk of a match with Chicago fighter Jack White before the West Side Athletic Club of New Orleans on January 14. This would be an afternoon match, with the weight stipulated at 122 pounds three hours before the twenty-round battle. Attell would receive $1,500, while White's cut was $1,000. However, this wasn't fitting into Attell's training plans, so more offers needed to be considered.

The end of the year also meant a review of the fight game. A time for advocates to expose the virtues of the game, a period for critics and curmudgeons to espouse the iniquities of the sweet science. On December 16, this is how columnist W.W. Naughton of the *San Francisco Call* summed up the champion: "Abe Attell is doing a full share toward making the pugilistic outlook as dull as ditch water. He is certainly an average character. Always a shrewd matchmaker, he never hesitates to hook up with men far bigger than himself as his matches with Matt Wells and Battling Nelson will attest. He argues, no doubt, that a defeat by a bigger man never acts as a setback."[46]

Naughton then asserted: "Attell avoids promising youngsters of his own poundage as he does a pestilence. Right now we have Johnny Kilbane, the survivor of a series of featherweight contests in which Joe Rivers, Patsy Kline, Joe Carter and Frankie Conley were the other contenders. Kilbane is Attell's logical opponent for the featherweight championship and is not only ready but eager for the fray."[47]

Attell's Advice on How to Box

At the end of 1911, Abe Attell took some time out of his busy schedule to write four pieces on "How to Box." They originally appeared inside *The Day Book*, from December 26 to December 29. Originally targeted toward young boys, to teach them the art of self-defense, they nonetheless are invaluable to anyone who desires such advice.

In Lesson One, Attell advises: getting control of your temper; and positioning— standing with the left foot from eight to twenty inches in front of the right to establish your balance. Your left glove, your greatest asset, should reach the opponent's jaw, while the right, your power supply, should protect your ribs and stomach. To avoid injury, a proper fist finds the fingers fitting snugly into the palm, with the thumb over the middle joint of the index finger—never place the thumb on top of the fist. Watch your man constantly, as every muscular move betrays his intentions. Learn to judge distances, and don't try to knock out an opponent—use your head as much as your hands and wear him down. Also, be cautious, attentive, and alert.

Attell also stated, "I never let a man hit me when I can prevent it," and "I hit every time there is an opening."[48]

The defensive master shared three methods of defense in Lesson Two: blocking, ducking and sidestepping.

To block a blow, use your right arm and catch your opponent's punching arm, under the forearm, which will lift the arm from its course; keen sight is necessary for blocking. You must learn how to block and punch simultaneously.

Ducking is used to dodge blows aimed at the head, so you must move quickly and recover fast while always keeping your jaw covered against an uppercut.

Sidestepping is a fine art used to avoid rushes. The movement is accomplished by placing the toe of the right foot in a direct line back of the left heel. In sidestepping to the right, the right foot is carried quickly to the right. To sidestep to the left, the left foot is carried to the left.

Keep your stomach drawn in, which will assume a crouching position and make it harder for your opponent to hit you.

Lesson Three points out some of the mistakes made by boxers, before including the champion's recommendations.

Of the mistakes, Attell cites failing to use judgment and standing in a position where your opponent can easily hit you.

The champion's advice: never waste a blow; put your weight behind a punch; take advantage of every opening; don't pass up an opportunity to deliver a punch; find your opponent's weakness; learn to feint effectively, making your opponent believe you are going to hit him in one place, thus drawing him off guard, leaving an opening for your real punch; and keep in motion and deliver with quickness.

Finally, in Lesson Four, the champion describes the four fundamental blows: the straight left to the face, the straight left to the body, the straight right to the face and the straight right to the body. All other punches are simply an outgrowth from these. Atell also described other punches and counter measures.

To deliver a straight left or right, straighten the arm to its full length, step in and put your weight behind your fist. You aim for either the face or the body. Always stiffen your arm and hit hard, true and fast. These are the knockout punches.

Jabs are quick, snappy blows, with the elbow partly crooked, used to wear down an opponent or to position him for another punch. The one-two punch is merely the delivery of a double blow.

If your reach is short, which is a disadvantage, throwing your shoulders forward will add some length. A clinch, which spectators dislike, is used when a boxer is tired or backed into a bad position. Always slide out gradually from a clinch, as too quickly can you leave open to a breakaway punch. To do this, let your hands slide down from the other fellow's shoulders, slipping gradually off his hands.

With these four lessons, "The Little Champ" was trying to cover some of the rudimentary points of boxing. His finer points would take volumes.

In Monte's Corner

Fighting your way back into a title mix has never been easy for a boxer, yet Monte Attell tried valiantly to do so in 1911. Fighting many of the same opponents he had fought the year before—Young Britt, Patsy Branigan, Jimmy Carroll—he managed to accumulate over a hundred rounds in sixteen fights and took just four losses, two of which came at the hands of Al Delmont. Had Attell beat Frank Burns on October 23, he would have had a title shot at Johnny Coulon; it was, however, a unanimous newspaper decision for Burns.

Above: Toronto-born bantamweight champion (1910–1914) Johnny Coulon, who later owned and operated a gym in downtown Chicago for nearly fifty years. *Right:* London-born lightweight Matt Wells debuted professionally in 1905 and ended his career in 1922. Wells competed at the 1908 London Olympic Games in the lightweight division (Library of Congress).

Noteworthy fights of 1911, which also acknowledged title changes, included: Johnny Coulon won the bantam title from Frankie Conley in a twenty-round decision on February 26 in New Orleans; Matt Wells defeated Freddie Welsh in a twenty-round decision for the British lightweight crown on February 27 in London; Billy Papke knocked out Jim Sullivan in the ninth round of their battle in London on June 8; Ad Wolgast posted a rare knockout of Owen Moran in the thirteenth round of their July 4 brawl in San Francisco; and Fireman Jim Flynn picked up a ten-round no-decision in a bloody brawl with Carl Morris on September 15 in New York.

The featherweight champion of the world fought over one hundred rounds, in a dozen fights, in 1911. However, Abe Attell did so at the cost of injury. "The Little Champ" fought to all no-decisions, with the exception of the no-contest battle against Tommy Kilbane and the knockout he gave to Leo Johnson. Although he was under constant criticism for his choice to fight under a New York State umbrella, it was a wise decision by a very smart champion. Attell was playing his cards like a master. The question was for how long?

CHAPTER ELEVEN

Losing the Title, 1912

"There had to be a goat, and I was the goat. The commission could not prove I had stalled, yet because it wanted to make an example, it picked me out and said I had made misstatements about the doctor who cocainized my sore hand and gave me an overdose ten minutes before I entered the ring to meet Knockout Brown."[1]—Abe Attell

A testament to her creators, she was as majestic as she was palatial. She was the British ocean liner RMS *Titanic*. A buoyant marvel, destined for infamy, she departed from Southampton, England, on her maiden voyage to New York City on April 10, 1912. The ship, under the command of Edward Smith, carried some of the wealthiest people in the world, as well as hundreds of emigrants from Great Britain and Ireland, Scandinavia, and elsewhere throughout Europe seeking a new life in North America. Five days later, the ship sank at 2:20 a.m., taking with her the lives of nearly 1,500 people. Eight days later, the Cunard liner RMS *Carpathia* arrived in New York City with all that was left, *Titanic*'s just over 700 survivors. The unthinkable, to the unsinkable, had become plausible.

There were times, like following the San Francisco earthquake and the sinking of the *Titanic*, when Abe Attell thought a lot about fate. Was destiny a matter of chance or a matter of choice? Most who knew "The Little Champ" would state it was the former. But there were times in the life of Abe Attell, like during his upcoming title fight with Johnny Kilbane, when it appeared to be the latter. The year would be all about change, for whether you win or lose, change always figures into the equation.

For the champion, it looked like his year would begin in New Orleans, against Jack White, on January 14. But that fight was canceled and replaced with a ten-round fight, scheduled for January 18, at the National Sporting Club in New York. His opponent, whose intimidating moniker may have stretched the imagination of some, was "Knockout" Brown—let's face it, it's hard to frighten anyone with the first name of Valentine (Braunheim).[2] As you will recall, Attell was supposed to face Brown in June of the previous year, but the fight was canceled. Having fought Leach Cross to a draw about a month earlier, Brown was a pigeon-toed southpaw who at first glance didn't look like a fighter. But the New York scrapper could pack a punch. Attell, well aware of Brown's skill set, turned on the engines. The champion's impenetrable defense allowed him to dominate the one-sided no-decision. By the second round Attell had already closed one of Brown's eyes and badly damaged the other, as the half-inch smaller lightweight could not mount a defense. The *Topeka State Journal* printed: "The fourth round was the most sensational of the bout. Brown swung hard at Attell and the latter stopped him with a straight left. Brown landed a solid left swing, sending Attell to the ropes. Just before the end of the round Brown landed lefts and rights and Attell appeared in bad shape, but at the bell the featherweight champion went jauntily to his corner."[3]

A minute's rest allowed Attell to regroup, as he dominated from this point forward, landing his jab at will. As the *Journal* continued: "Brown appeared tired in the tenth round, while Attell continued jabbing mercilessly. The fight ended with a fierce mix-up, from which Brown emerged groggy and bleeding from the nose and mouth. By popular verdict it was Attell's fight."[4]

The fight appeared so one-sided that it brought the skeptics out in force. On January 22, the boxing commission agreed to conduct an investigation of their own; they wanted to know whether or not the champion stalled during the encounter. Attell appeared before the commission, and the dailies, including the *Bridgeport Evening Farmer*, noted the results:

> Attell offered as a unique excuse for his poor showing: that "cocaine" was injected into his knuckle. After an hour's questioning Attell bedecked in his Sunday clothes, cool as an icicle, stuck to his narrative that he was "doped" by an overdose of cocaine injected into a knuckle of his left hand a short time before he entered the ring. He declared his mind became a blank, his legs stiffened and he knew not when his opponent rained blow after blow on his body. He accused various persons of playing a trick on him and scorned Tom O'Rourke, who is connected to the National Sporting Club, where the bout was staged.[5]

New York–born Valentine Braunheim, a.k.a. "Knockout Brown," debuted professionally in 1908 and ended his career in 1916 (Library of Congress).

The admission caught everyone by surprise. The champion's answers were delivered in his customary forthright manner, although many of the newspapermen in attendance were quick to note when he contradicted himself. The same source stated, "Altogether he made it appear he had fought the best he knew how and was oblivious of anything that would taint his name with crookedness."[6] After an hour of testimony by Attell, the commission released him so that he could catch a train for the coast to battle Johnny Kilbane. The matter could have ended there, but it did not. Which raises the question, why not?

Attell's testimony before the State Athletic Commission was contradicted by six of seven witnesses who appeared before the board at their Park Row offices on January 24. The six who disputed the champion's claims were Dr. Joseph Safian, the club physician whom Attell said gave him an overdose of cocaine to deaden pain in his thumb; Valentine Braunheim, a.k.a. "K.O. Brown"; Danny Morgan, Brown's manager; Tom O'Rourke, the National Sporting Club's manager; Patsy Haley, referee; and Charles Doesserick, managing director of the club. Only Danny Goodman, chief second for Attell, adamantly defended the champion.

According to the *Tribune*, Dr. Safian testified, "On the night of the bout, at Attell's personal request, he had treated him for his sore thumb by giving him an application of 1 percent of a solution containing one-fifth of a grain of cocaine in twenty drops of water and that the amount had no effect on Attell's mind or body."[7]

"Knockout" Brown believed Attell fought as hard as in any of his previous bouts—this a fighter's observation, as he had never met Attell before. He also proclaimed that there was no secret arrangement made between the two men and declared he had a strong resentment against Attell because of an insulting remark.

Daniel Morgan confirmed he noticed nothing unusual about Attell the evening of the fight and that he did not appear drugged. He stated, "Attell was a joke fighting Brown that night. He was afraid, and simply fought on the defensive to stay the distance."[8]

"Tom O'Rourke declared that it was 'nonsense' to say that Attell's poor exhibition was due to a drug. Attell, he said, 'is going back, and in Brown he was up against a man of a different style and could make no better showing.'"[9]

Haley, who refereed the bout, corroborated further comments made by O'Rourke regarding Attell's unfair fighting tactics, but stated the champion appeared bewildered and slow in action due to Brown's fighting style. Haley, who himself had fought Attell, then added: "To watch Brown from the outside of the ring he looks like a 'bum,' but his awkward style had Attell puzzled, and Abe couldn't get to him. I don't think that Attell could knock Brown out in four months, nor Patsy Kline in a week. He has seen his best days and is slipping back."[10]

Charles Doesserick corroborated O'Rourke and other witnesses. Only Danny Goodman supported the champion's claim by stating that he did not appear natural throughout the bout—the champion could not answer his questions.

Boxing fans couldn't believe the headline that ran in papers such as the *Tacoma Times*: "Attell Ruled Out of Game" was the news that hit the wire on Friday, January 26. "The New York State Athletic Commission on Thursday [January 25] suspended Abe Attell, featherweight champion, for six months for faking his recent fight here with Knockout Brown."[11] The move, however, would not affect his upcoming engagement with Johnny Kilbane.

The *Washington Times* added more detail:

Back row, from left: Cleveland featherweight Johnny Kilbane, Lancaster's (Pennsylvania) Leo Houck, Philadelphia lightweight Sam Robideau. Front row: noted Philadelphia referee Jack McGuigan (left), Johnny Loftus, all members of the National Athletic Club of Philadelphia (Library of Congress).

With bills in the [State] Legislature to abolish the commission and end boxing, it is conceded on all hands that fighting in this State is on trial, and that rigid action will be necessary to preserve it. A few more fights in the order of the Attell-Brown mix-up would surely kill the game. An investigation of the National Sporting Club, to learn if it was in collusion with Attell in the fake fight, is underway. The commission exonerated Brown and his manager from any part in the fake.[12]

Attell arrived in San Francisco on February 1, none too happy with the news.[13] Even if he declared he was ready to quit the game, he footnoted it by stating that before he retired he would like to meet Johnny Coulon and Knockout Brown in San Francisco. How serious he was about retiring remained to be seen, but he did mention he wouldn't mind settling down in a different line of business in 'Frisco. With regard to his suspension, the *Topeka State Journal* stated that Attell quipped: "There had to be a goat, and I was the goat. The commission could not prove I had stalled, yet because it wanted to make an example, it picked me out and said I had made misstatements about the doctor who cocainized my sore hand and gave me an overdose ten minutes before I entered the ring to meet Knockout Brown."[14]

The Loss

In Vernon, California, the speculation—be it on the streets, in the pool halls, or at the newsstands—was that when Abe Attell met Johnny Kilbane for twenty-rounds on February 22, his title just might be in jeopardy, in spite of initial odds in Attell's favor. The Cleveland fighter had posted an impressive string of victories including Charley White, Patsy Brannigan, Frankie Conley and Joe Rivers. Kilbane had also drawn both Jimmy Walsh and Monte Attell. Many sources even speculated on the outcome: "Kilbane fought [Abe] Attell ten-rounds in Kansas City a year ago and lost, although those at the ringside say he earned a draw. It is known that Attell frequently wins by a narrow margin, to get a return match and bigger money."[15]

Ad Wolgast, who some believed had won more money in the past two years from betting than any other boxer, let it be known that he was wagering $1,000 that Attell would beat Kilbane. Wolgast believed the talk about Abe's hands being in poor condition was exaggerated.

Team Kilbane, which included Johnny Coulon, Tommy Kilbane (no relation), and Manager Jimmy Dunn, trained at Venice, near Los Angeles. Johnny had defeated Tommy, but the latter boxed Attell, as you recall, and broke his shoulder.

Many periodicals, such as *The Day Book*, commented on Kilbane's performance: "It was not until Johnny knocked out Rivers [September 4, 1911] that he became a national figure. Rivers won a decision over Kilbane [May 6, 1911] in one bout but refused to meet him again until he saw Kilbane just shade Patsy Kline. While watching this bout he decided Kilbane would be easier and fell into a cleverly baited trap, set by Jimmy Dunn."[16]

So it was, on this Thursday, February 22, 1912, that the gate of defeat opened and Abraham Washington Attell walked through it. He was not pushed, nor did he fall through the egress; he held his head high and sauntered to the other side. The invincible champion, defined by more victories than most field generals, proved vulnerable on his twenty-ninth birthday. It was as if it was meant to be: a decisive victory, but not by knockout. Kilbane had systematically taken nearly every round.

A capacity crowd of nine thousand people—the venue ordinarily seated 8,400—

Manager Jimmy Dunn (left) with his talented featherweight Johnny Kilbane (Library of Congress).

witnessed the event, with an estimated 5,000 spectators turned away at the gates. The *Evening Times* proclaimed: "It was the greatest crowd that had ever viewed a prize fight in Los Angeles. The receipts amount to approximately $25,000. The men fought for a purse of $10,000, of which Attell was to receive $6,500, win, lose or draw, and Kilbane $3,500. Besides they agreed to divide evenly 50 percent of the moving picture money."[17]

For Attell, the cleverness that had defined him seemed to vanish at the opening bell. He was outfought, as his fans found it difficult to find a round in which he dominated. While his defensive prowess may have been forgotten, his survival tactics were alive and well: the crowd berated Attell when he held Kilbane's arms in a clinch, "heeled" his opponent in the third round, and tried to bend Kilbane's left arm back in the eighth. Boos and hisses increased as the rounds progressed, sounding a warning, like a foghorn, as the champion's ship approached danger.

Kilbane, who entering the ring as an underdog, was on his game, lightning fast.

The *Evening Times* noted the speed: "A straight left jab to Attell's nose or sore left eye was his favorite blow. He would send this in and then like a flash cross with his right to the other side of Attell's head and jump back out of harm's way."[18]

A look at the battle, round-by-round:

Round one began with both men walking cautiously to the center of the ring. Kilbane dispatched a hard right to the jaw and a combination to the jaw. No notable offense by Attell, only some misses. Confirming distances, the champion understood, was always a first-round objective. The round finished even.

Apprehension fueled round two as both fighters staked out their territory. Attell posted no offense. Kilbane mailed a vicious left to the jaw, a number of unanswered combinations, and a straight left that drew blood from Attell's mouth. He followed with two hard lefts to the face and a sharp right to Attell's bad eye. It was Kilbane's round.

Round three began with a complaint. The challenger was claiming that Attell had bent his arm. The champion just smirked, appearing stupefied by the assertion. Attell addressed no offense, choosing again to mount what was viewed as a strategic defense. Kilbane consigned a hard right and a combination to the face. Attell was warned of "heeling" in the pair's second clinch. The men were clinching as the bell rang. Again, it was Kilbane's round.

Round four opened slowly. The champion directed only defense despite being hit by three punches to his every one. Kilbane forwarded two quick opening jabs, a hard right and a stiff left to the head. As Attell was warned for holding, jeers arose from the crowd. At one point the champion motioned Kilbane inward, but the Clevelander was much too smart for the prompt. The round finished even.

Round five saw Attell's bad eye, his left, swollen and nearly closed. Again the champion transmitted no offense to speak of, which found him a victim of the crowd's dissatisfaction. Kilbane conveyed primarily jabs to Attell's bad eye and he continued to display his quickness. It was another even round.

As round six opened, Kilbane jabbed relentlessly at Attell's eye. The champion phoned a stiff left to Kilbane's mouth—his first hard blow—followed by a hard left to the jaw. Kilbane wired little more than his jabs, as the balance of the round was one long clinch. Round even.

The champion finally forced the fighting in round seven. Relieved, his fans at ringside could now take a deep breath. Attell telegraphed a left to the jaw of his adversary. Kilbane sent a nice combination to the face of the champion and a solid straight left to the jaw. Both exchanged body blows in clinches. It was Attell's round by a shade.

Attell rode the bike in round eight, and Kilbane just could not catch him. Attell, face swollen, dispatched no effective offense. Kilbane posted a nice combination to the head, followed by another amalgam to the face that began blood flowing afresh from Attell's mouth. Near the end of the round, Kilbane sent a terrific left to Attell's jaw.

Round nine was a sparring session. It was Kilbane's round by a shade.

Round ten began with a rush by both fighters. Attell mailed nothing but complaints to Referee Eyton that Kilbane was holding. Kilbane addressed a solid left to the mouth, a right to the ribs, then four machine-gun rights to the jaw. Again, it was Kilbane's round by a shade. With the fight half over, it was a fresher-looking Kilbane ahead on points.

Round eleven began with the champion rushing head-down to the center of the ring. Attell consigned a low left that received a warning, followed by a right to the jaw. Kilbane directed some solid rib blows, but not much more. It was the slowest round of the fight. Honors even.

In round twelve, many spectators began yelling "Kilbane." The champion forwarded a rigid right to the jaw. Kilbane transmitted a left to the jaw and a good combination to the ribs. Through his chewing-gum smile, Attell was overheard telling Kilbane that he was hard to hit. Round even.

It was a talkative round thirteen, according to sources, as Attell said, "You knocked Rivers out, didn't you? Well, come on and make it two."[19] Just as Attell said the word "two," Kilbane phoned a hard left to the jaw that silenced the champion. Attell returned a hard right to the jaw. Kilbane then phoned a nice combination to the face. The two were fighting toe-to-toe as the gong sounded. It was Kilbane's round.

Kilbane appeared to come on a bit stronger in round fourteen. Attell wired no offense.

Kilbane telegraphed a hard left to the nose, and a nice combination to the face. Sources noted that "Kilbane brought a roar from the spectators by imitating the 'Texas Tommy' around the referee."[20] Kilbane's round.

In round fifteen, Attell, sensing he was losing the fight, picked up his foot speed a bit, but not his assault. Where was his offense? The fans were now screaming at the champion to deliver something. Attell sent nothing but a rhetorical comment to a fan. Kilbane dispatched two lefts to Attell's sore eye, a left to the head, and a right to the ribs. It was Kilbane's round.

As round sixteen opened, Kilbane went right for the face. "Referee Eyton grabbed Attell and motioned Kilbane to his corner. Taking a towel, the referee rubbed the grease from Attell's body."[21] Seeing their fighter taking some solid body blows, Attell's seconds were making every possible effort to reduce any impact. Attell posted a head butt in a clinch that started blood flowing from over Kilbane's eye. The crowd was furious at Attell's actions. Kilbane then mailed a left to the jaw, and numerous body blows.

Ferocious fighting began round seventeen. The champion complained of holding, while being cautioned against butting. Attell sent virtually no offense. Kilbane dispatched a number of good lefts and a powerful right to the stomach. It was Kilbane's round. Even if Attell realized he was losing the fight, which he certainly did, he could do little about it.

Rounds eighteen and nineteen saw Kilbane in complete control; Attell could only manage to defend himself.

In round twenty, "Kilbane fairly smothered the champion in this round, at the conclusion of which Referee Eyton promptly awarded the verdict to the Cleveland fighter. It was a popular decision."[22]

The *Daily Bonanza* described the scene: "The decision of Referee Eyton was received with a wild whoop. Kilbane was carried from the building on the shoulders of his friends. 'I want to telephone to Mary,' he said, meaning Mrs. Kilbane. Attell, tired, his face drawn and bleeding, left the ring alone. As he reached the edge of the platform, he said to a friend, 'Well, I had to stand for it: I couldn't do any better.'"[23]

Three days after the Kilbane loss, or a month after his suspension and the fallout from it, Abraham Attell was lauded in newspapers across the country. "To look back over his fourteen years in the squared circle is to view accomplishments which such as can be accredited to no other man," was just one line of a syndicated article from the *San Francisco Call*.[24] It pointed out that Attell had likely fought 250 times or more; defended his title against all comers at 122 pounds; fought perhaps 3,000 total rounds; had not a mark where a glove touched him; never used tobacco in any form or tipped a goblet; had been modestly rich; had pawned his wife's diamonds; and had plunged beyond reason but had learned how to quit.

Attell, who hardly ever grinned, was affably reflective in the piece—even when talking about the money he lost, the former champion just smiled. He stated how Young Corbett showed him how to parlay his money in Denver. He then told the *Call* reporter of the biggest bet he ever made, on a horse named Prince Armor running at Yonkers:

> [Attell] talked freely, grammatically, rarely peppers his conversation with an oath, and has no trace of either the Frisco or New York dialect. The deep parenthesis scored on either side of that mighty nose give him the look of a cynic, but when he talks one must note the air of complete maturity. He has lost his joys and enthusiasms; he is a pessimist, rather than an optimist, and pugilism is a profession rather than a sport with him. Also, when he gets into the green tights and begins to slam things around, one notes the complete efficiency with which he does the slamming. The old angler always makes less noise than the green fisherman.[25]

Attell issued a statement about the Kilbane fight on February 24. In it he denied telling anyone that he had been "robbed" by Referee Eyton. The *Daily Missoulian* described the former champion's feelings:

> I want another chance at Kilbane and am not going around talking "robber." All I said was that Eyton told me two days before the fight that he wouldn't allow Kilbane to hold my hands. This was all I asked. There seems to be some difference of opinion as to who did the holding, but I knew it wasn't me. I never held Kilbane cheaply. I always knew he was a hard man and that I would have to go the limit to win. I still think I can beat him, and am ready to cover any forfeit he names for a return match. As champion he will, of course, be in position to dictate terms, but terms make no difference to me. I always gave men I defeated another chance. I know of nothing that should prevent him from doing the same. There is no hard feelings between us, and I am sure there never will be.[26]

As for the new champion, he told sources, "I don't think Attell deserves another chance. The public knows he has no chance with me, and it would hurt the game."[27] Kilbane, who had accepted a theater engagement, now focused on being champion outside the ring rather than in it.

On the day that the fight's moving pictures were brought from Los Angeles up to San Francisco (March 5), Attell was back home in Frisco, hard at work at his old training quarters at Millet's. The former champ was training for his next fight, which was in town on March 9, against Tommy Murphy. He was disregarding a warning from his physician that he had better nurse his wrenched shoulder muscle. As boxer Jack Dillon was also in Millet's, training for his mix with Walter Coffey across the Bay in Oakland, hundreds came to watch both scrappers, many noting Attell's bandaged left shoulder. The fight pictures were viewed the following evening in San Francisco, as the city of Los Angeles had an ordinance prohibiting their exhibition. They would soon be distributed per the fight agreement.

Interesting was the manner in which the fight film was promoted. In May, the Princess Theatre, in the state of Washington, was running an ad for the film (admission twenty-five cents) that stated:

In addition to showing the twenty rounds of the contest that gave to the world a new champion in the featherweight class, the picture-makers went into the training quarters of both men and got an intimate impression of the methods of both fighters while preparing for the fray. In the sixteenth round, Attell is shown fouling the Cleveland boy very plainly. The clinch is shown followed by Kilbane's merciless tattoo on the face and body of his opponent, and then the foul occurs. Attell, butting with his head, opens a great gash over Kilbane's eyes, from which blood is spurting. Referee Lyton [*sic*] also figured in the sixteenth round by stopping the fight for a brief interval while he rubbed Attell's body with a towel. It was seen to be covered with a greasy substance. The twentieth round shows the vigor of the new champion. He sent a shower of blows to Attell's head, of which the camera shows all faithfully and again the camera shows how he changed his footwork in that round. In this round, Attell nearly went over the ropes and a clinch is shown in which each exchanged vicious blows. Kilbane's last crack at his now weakened opponent, was a hard right to the head and a clinch just as the gong sounds ending the fight. It is claimed by boxing experts that this is the fastest and cleverest exhibition ever caught by the motion-picture camera, and will be reproduced in its entirety at the Princess Theatre, tonight.[28]

As for criticism of his performance in the film, Referee Charles Eyton went on record February 28: "An offer to bet $5,000 that the motion pictures of the battle will uphold his stand. Eyton proposes to select three well-known referees who did not see the contest, give for them a private exhibition of the films and let them decide. He already has deposited $1,000 to bind the bet and has intimated that his defi is directed particularly at Ad Wolgast and Jim Jeffries, who are quoted as having taken exception with Eyton's decision."[29] Jeffries would later deny he took exception. As for Wolgast, he just wasn't prone to losing a bet.

Speaking of bets, it was also learned on February 28 that "Attell was so confident of winning from Kilbane in Los Angeles on Washington's birthday, it is said, he sold his interest in the moving pictures for $1,500 and wagered the money on the result of the fight."[30]

According to Jimmy Dunn, Kilbane's manager, and printed in the *Day Book*: "We heard from Cleveland that Morris Bloom, Attell's old manager, and Emil Thiry, manager for Packey McFarland, went to Cleveland with $10,000 of Attell money and bet it with admirers of Kilbane. They learned that Cleveland fight fans had sent about $3,000 to $5,000 to Los Angeles to bet and they wired Attell, who raised more money and covered these bets."[31]

"This statement as to the heavy wagers made by Attell is partly corroborated. Mrs. Attell is also said to have told a woman friend in Los Angeles something to the same effect. She gave the figure, however, at $3,000 as the sum that Abe sent back to Cleveland to be placed on himself," according to the *Day Book*.[32] The publication also speculated that Attell was flat broke.

Murphy's Law

The *Salt Lake Tribune* described the results: "Today when Tommy Murphy got through with him, Abe Attell's face was a picture of hard luck and usage. His left eye looked like a new buttonhole and his countenance generally was out of plumb. If Abe did not sport a cauliflower ear, it was because there was no room for one, all the available space being occupied by other tributes to Murphy's punching power. Murphy weighed 133 and Attell 122."[33]

At the end of twenty rounds, Tommy Murphy had picked up a decision over Abe Attell, the former featherweight champion, in Jim Coffroth's Arena at Daly City, California. *San Francisco Call* columnist W.W. Naughton proclaimed, "Battle proves decisively that the former king of featherweights never can 'come back.'"[34]

Attell's friends actually thought he had pulled out a draw because the fight looked that close until the nineteenth round. In the concluding round Attell was not striving to win, only to survive. Dog-tired Abe Attell wanted to impress Referee Jack Weiss with something, anything, but could only stall through the final round. The *Tribune* noted, "Murphy was the most persistent of the two all through the contest, but whenever Attell cut loose with might and main he evened the score. Abe simply gave flashes of his old-time form. In some of the rounds, he ducked in a way that bewildered Murphy and brought cheers from the crowd."[35]

The boxers traded rallies, as if they were wind-up toys, each taking his turn. In uncharacteristic style, Attell allowed his arms to drop when being assaulted by Murphy, giving an appearance that he was on the verge of collapse. Though it ignited the crowd, it wasn't to be, as the fighter would then regain his self-control. His marvelous footwork, an Attell trademark, was nowhere to be found, as he allowed himself to be easily cornered. A defenseless posture also surfaced during clinches, where Attell had no solution to Murphy's infighting.

The final two rounds turned the fight toward Murphy. The *Tribune* documented round nineteen: "Murphy was at it like a winner when the nineteenth opened and time and again sent Abe's head bobbing with short-arm rights and lefts. Attell retaliated with body punches that carried no sting with them. Desperate milling at close range wound up the round, with Attell very tired."[36] And in round twenty:

> They fought like a pair of tigers at close quarters, each trying to secure a decisive advantage. The crowd yelled encouragingly at each fighter. Murphy sent Attell's head back thrice and Abe stalled and clinched. It was all Murphy and the crowd cheered again and again. Attell was a very tired boy and seldom landed a blow. The fight ended with Attell covered with blood and holding desperately to his belligerent antagonist. Referee Welch promptly declared Murphy the victor. The decision was roundly cheered.[37]

Attell made no statement as his seconds tried to put him back together in his dressing room. Ad Wolgast, who was sitting ringside, shook his head saying, "Too much weight."[38] While Wolgast was impressed with Attell's ability to take the beating, it was his feeling that the battle was lost on the scales. For the loss, Attell received thirty-five percent of the gate receipts, or $1,940.05, and Murphy took home thirty percent, or $1,662.90.[39]

Two days later, on March 11, the accusations began flying, as it was reported in the *East Oregonian* that Attell offered both Murphy and his manager $4,000 to lay down, or lose on a foul, and they "double crossed him."[40] Attell denied the allegation. Adding to the claim, according to Murphy and his manager Jim Buckley, was that gamblers dropped $150,000 on the fight, believing that Murphy had been fixed to lose. The following day, the *Topeka State Journal* reported that promoter James Coffroth admitted he had heard the inside story hours before the fight and took steps to protect the public: he spoke to Referee Jack Walsh and informed him of what he had heard. Upon hearing this, Walsh suggested that all bets be declared off, but Cofforth stated, "I advised him not to do this, but to watch for low blows early in the contest, and if in his judgment the fight was being faked, to call off all bets and declare it a no contest."

Then, on March 15, the *Washington Herald* stated: "Abe Attell, erstwhile featherweight champion, today filed suit for $20,000 against Jim Buckley, manager for Harlem Tommy Murphy, because Buckley is alleged to have charged Attell with having offered Murphy $4,000 if he would 'lay down' in the recent fight between Murphy and Attell. The action was filed in Superior Court."[41]

Abe also entered into a contract to appear in a San Francisco vaudeville theater for one week, starting the next Sunday. Which is probably good, as Mrs. Attell was seen sobbing after the Kilbane fight. Not long before, she had stated, "I can't stand Abe being beaten up this way. If he loses the fight with Tommy Murphy he shall never step into the ring again."[42]

Columnist Naughton, never short of salt for Attell's wounds, had a different view. He shared it in his editorial titled "Attell Preferred Poker Table To Punching Bag," which was published on March 23 in many newspapers including the *El Paso Herald* and *Salt Lake Tribune*:

> To criticize Abe Attell harshly, at this stage of the game, savors largely of throwing water on a drowned rat. Attell through his indiscretions is in bad standing in the three biggest boxing centers in the United States, namely New York, San Francisco and Los Angeles. His defeats by Johnny Kilbane and Tommy Murphy have lowered him terribly in the pugilistic scale, and, instead of pulling out of the game in a blaze of glory he is leaving behind a reputation for crookedness.[43]

Naughton then turned to the vices: "Aside from all questions of impaired fighting ability, there is something that has contributed to Attell's downfall more than the ravages of time. It is his deep-seated love of gambling. His nearest friends now declare that for years he has lacked the power to desert the poker table long enough to train properly."[44] Naughton did not name the nearest friends.

He then went on to quote a letter from a Los Angeles businessman who had the inside scoop on the Attell training camp. The letter was quoted as saying: "Attell sat up all night playing poker the night before he fought Kilbane. His training for that event was a joke."[45] Naughton slapped Attell hard, not only scolding him for not training, but for his incorrigible attitude. To think that such an unwarranted and unsubstantiated editorial came from the pen of San Francisco columnist was unfathomable.

Exactly a month later, on April 23, Attell was back in a Sacramento ring and the *Call* was there: "In a fight that was disgustingly slow and tedious, Abe Attell, once featherweight champion of the world, dropped Jimmy Carroll in the seventh round of a scheduled twenty-round bout before the Capital Athletic Club tonight. Two body blows, a right and then a left, sent Carroll in agony to the floor for the count. Sol Levinson refereed."[46]

Dispatches from the fight were not kind to Attell, stating that he was charitable to his opponent, appeared out of condition, and stalled. The stalling criticism at this time nothing short of overused. If he deserved greater respect, which many believed he did, he did not receive it. If what fight fans had seen of Attell so far this year was his worst, then he was still a better boxer than ninety percent of those fighting. The *Call* printed:

> The stream of blood that flowed from Attell's nose and a cut over his eye in the sixth made many think that Attell was being severely punished, but it was not so. Attell, when he desired, beat a rapid tattoo on Carroll's stomach until the latter winced. As the seventh round opened he shot a hard right

over Carroll's heart and Jimmy went down for the count of eight. When he came up, Attell slammed a left to his stomach, and the fight was over.[47]

It had been over 150 days since his last knockout (Leo Johnson), 153 to be exact, and Attell felt good picking up the "KO7."

The press, including the *Evening Star*, perhaps in a bout with themselves for their unfairness, stated:

> How the boys do like to pan Abe Attell and especially since the title was taken away from him. Talk about that old houn' dawg and his troubles; it wasn't a marker to the way they kick Abe around these days. Only last week the former champion met and knocked out Jimmy Carroll, the California featherweight. Attell is now accused of being a party to a fake and all because Carroll put up a bad fight. At this distance, it would seem the critics ought to suspend judgment in the matter or until something tangible in the way of evidence was produced. Abe was a hard proposition to get along with in the old days, and never very popular with the rank and file of sports and newspaper men, but there is a limit to all these things, and besides I don't believe in kicking a man just because he's down.[48]

These words came from a newspaper columnist for the *Sunday Star*, who just happened to be a former boxer, James J. Corbett.

Longevity was never a given when a boxing manager chose to work with a fighter like Abe Attell. A very wise and wily Billy Nolan—the man who helped guide Battling Nelson to the championship—understood this from the start, but like his predecessors, believed he would be different. Nolan marched to his own drummer. Although the veteran feather may have thought he needed some well-deserved time off, not only to rest a bit, but to give some old bruises time to heal, his new manager had a different idea. It was time, Nolan believed, to take Abe Attell to the mountains, to the manager's 1,200-acre Lake County ranch, and prepare him for a comeback. A rustic country life was what Attell needed—trapping, hunting and fishing for his meals, splitting firewood, you name it—in order to rebuild himself and his reputation. The former champion had given Nolan full power to make all his matches and to bring him back into proper physical condition. And true to form, Nolan took it. As Attell was getting into shape, Nolan was spinning the press and just trying to land his fighter some key matches, like Ad Wolgast, one of Nolan's first targets.

By mid–May, Nolan had pictures of Attell on horseback and chopping wood, the usual public relations spin to support his claims that Attell was a new man. As for Attell's reaction: "I changed my city clothes and put on my new regalia—the overalls, spiked shoes, soft shirt and hat. I felt queer for a time, but soon got used to it."[49] Nolan understood this was going to be a hard sell, especially after all the bad press Attell had been receiving, but it needed to be done. Admittedly, it was difficult for many who knew Attell to buy into the "cowboy image." Nonetheless, Nolan had a proven track record, as did Attell, so maybe, just maybe, it might work.

By the end of May, Nolan was dropping notes to the press telling them, "Abe Attell lives the simple life now." Some bought it, others not so much. The *Seattle Star* printed, "Nolan has proved a hard trainer. He has routed Attell from his couch on the porch at 5:30 every morning, forced him to ride horseback, tramp through the mountains and to keep regular hours. That it has done Abe a world of good is proved by his present weight— 135 pounds, which is more than he ever weighed in his life. And it isn't fat—it's good muscle."[50]

Such was the view of the Seattle press. A bit further south, in San Francisco: "Abe has not drunk a cup of java or tea, let alone eaten pastry of any description. Seems rather strange for the boy who has been used to the cafe and the bright lights for the last ten years. His sincerity can be reckoned by his actions and the result from his now rugged and much improved appearance."[51]

With his customary brilliance, Nolan played the press. For example, he wanted a strong match for Abe's comeback. So he told reporters that he had been wired by a few big-name promoters, like Tom McCarey, asking if Abe was ready to meet, say, Johnny Kilbane or Joe Rivers, at a place like Vernon, on a key date, say, July 4. This would get a rise out of the press, even induce some to contact McCarey to verify the claims. Newspaper accounts would be printed, the public aroused, then Nolan would use it—to leverage another fight, or even better, force the issue with McCarey.[52] By late June, Nolan was playing every angle trying to match his fighter against the lightweight champion Ad Wolgast, or even a rematch with Harlem Tommy Murphy—the latter of which was targeted for July 4. But nobody was buying it. When negotiations tanked with both fighters, Attell agreed to box ten rounds with Eddie Marino before the Tacoma Athletic Club, the event to take place at the clubhouse, or old Glide rink, on Wednesday, July 3.

Attell was just feeling like his old self. "It was a clean scientific battle, rather devoid of gore and might have been staged in a parlor. Taking all things into consideration, it was the best boxing exhibition ever staged at the [Tacoma Athletic] club."

Attell wanted to put on a splendid display, and he did exactly that against the familiar face of Seattle fighter Eddie Marino. Granted, Marino had been a punching bag since the two last met in August 1910, but Attell put on a brilliant demonstration of speed and accuracy. Defensively, he blocked and shifted in ways many hadn't seen in years. The *Tacoma Times* wrote: "When Referee Frank McGeehan held Attell's hand aloft, awarding him the decision at the end of the tenth round, Attell had not drawn a deep breath or worked up a sweat. He had carried the fighting all the way and had worked hard but he was not ruffled. Only a sore right hand kept him from disposing of Marino any time after the fifth round, and he apparently protected the wage earner as a mother would a young child."[53]

Following the Marino bout, Attell issued a challenge to box Wolgast for the lightweight championship of the world—the former feather king also noting his willingness to wager $10,000 on himself. Not long after that challenge, the first signs of trouble between Attell and Nolan began to surface. As Attell was making his northwest tour, the fighter was trying to pick up an "easy money" exhibition in Portland on the eve of his scheduled fight with Tommy Murphy. Needless to say, Nolan objected to such an unwise move. Attell then stated he wasn't going to fight Murphy, after Nolan had already posted a $1,000 forfeit.

By August, it was time for the rematch with Tommy Murphy, something Attell's guileful manager Billy Nolan was able to secure before his own dismissal—more on this after the fight. Originally scheduled for July 4, it had been moved to August 3. It was scheduled for twenty rounds at Coffroth's Arena over in Daly City, the same place as their previous encounter. The *Call* noted the affair:

> The margin of superiority in the boxing abilities of Abe Attell and Harlem Tommy Murphy was too slight for Referee Jim Griffin to decide yesterday afternoon after the pair of boxers had gone 20 rounds, and he waved both hands in the air as an announcement that his verdict was draw. It was decision that met with popular approval, as the difference in the merits of both fighters was so close that it would have been an injustice to either to declare against him.[54]

Both fighters had stepped up their game and fought solidly until the end. Attell finished with his usual flurry, but Murphy swapped wallops to assure the equal measure.

The heavier of the two by at least ten pounds if not as much as twenty, Murphy tried, where he could, to use it to his benefit, but to no avail. Neither fighter was distressed the entire fight and there were no knockdowns. While the battle was interesting, it wasn't thrilling, despite the gore, because Attell wisely chose to box strategically; slugging it out with Murphy, he realized, could prove disastrous. Surprisingly, Attell, when he entered the ring, was a 10 to 6 choice with betters. According to the *Call*:

> Murphy appears to have Attell sized up pretty well and knows how to fight him. He kept meeting Attell's straight lefts with the same kind of blow and often he beat the former featherweight champion to the punch. His best work was scored when he led with his left. Sometimes he would fail to land, but he would never tear right after Attell and continue to let go lefts. Attell seemed unable to get away from Murphy when he started these rushes.[55]

The final round proved to be the most exciting of the encounter, as what was left in the tanks of both fighters was utilized. The *Call* printed, "Both men tore after each other. Attell used that [controlling] left to the head and frequently whipped it to the body, and these blows seemed to hurt Murphy. In the clinches, both men swung both hands, Attell directing all his blows to the stomach, while Murphy whipped up several uppercuts in a vain effort to score a knockout. Had he landed one of those blows he might have won the battle decisively."[56]

Marching to his own drummer was not only the Attell approach, but the Nolan way as well—some would say whimsically that they were meant for each other. Nolan was a born car dealer before cars, able to make a match and drive a hard bargain equally to his pleasure. According to Nolan, as he told the *Call*, his "contract to handle Attell's affairs called for 35 percent of his earnings of the former featherweight champion, which shows that the astute manager was by no means a piker."[57]

Originally, Attell and Murphy were to meet on July 4, and Nolan signed up to fight on a percentage basis, but Coffroth couldn't obtain a permit. So new articles were drawn up and figures amended, such as a guarantee for $3,500. But then, Attell fired Nolan and called the battle off. Coffroth then talked Attell into the battle. Attell then took a turn preparing new articles and signed them himself. The *Call* confirmed, "From good sources it is learned that Attell was guaranteed $2,000 with a privilege of 35 percent of the receipts. From these figures Attell's end of yesterday's fight was about $2,100, as the house looked to be about $6,000."[58]

Nolan, who never left a deal quietly, told the press he was suing Attell: "First for 35 percent of the $1,000 which he obtained for boxing a bush fight in the North on July 4 [actually it was July 3, against Eddie Marino] and for 35 percent of $3,500, the contract which he signed when he was Attell's manager. Figuring the different expenses which Abe has undergone, he will owe himself money after everything is settled."[59]

Back in New York City

With little fanfare, and his suspension now complete, Abe Attell returned to New York City. On September 13, inside Madison Square Garden, he met British boxer Harry Thomas at the all-too-familiar distance of ten rounds. The Englishman, who outweighed Attell by almost two pounds, also outboxed the former champion by a slim margin. Attell seemed a bit slow, lacking the vitality of his previous battle, and didn't display the snappy defense he exhibited with Marino. The *Farmer* noted: "Thomas scored numerous points with the left hand. He flicked it into the American's face again and again before Attell had a chance to block or step away. Attell possessed the harder wallop, but he could not land it with effect. As the bout drew to a close Thomas' superior stamina told the tale. Attell slowed down in such a manner that the result was clear to all."[60]

Only a small crowd turned out, due to higher ticket prices, not to mention a sheriff and twenty deputies looking on should the exhibition turn into a prizefight. Thomas was considered a rising star in the ranks—not a Jem Driscoll, but slowly working his way up the ladder—and it was hoped that he would have drawn better. As for Attell fans, they too were there, having not forgotten their suspended hero, or was it mountain cowboy?

The media continued to attack Attell, as if he were a geriatric gladiator: "The only visible effect of the once great little fighter's attack was when he opened a puff under Thomas's right eye in the seventh, drawing a flow that looked much worse than it really was."[61] Both fighters appeared relieved when the ten-round no-decision concluded.

Fighting a New England pugilist on his own turf was never easy, but neither was battling a former champion. On October 24, Attell fought Boston's Jimmy Walsh to draw during a fight that consisted of twelve two-minute rounds before the Pilgrim Athletic Association. When Attell declined to get on the scales—the articles calling for both men to make weight—Walsh's manager insisted on the shortened rounds. The fans howled, but few left, as the fight went on. The press noted, "Attell took a lead in the early part of the contest by his infighting, frequently getting Walsh in a corner and beating a rapid tattoo on his stomach. After the seventh round Walsh kept the Californian at a distance with stiff left hand punches to the jaw."[62]

An eight-round tussle with Oliver Kirk in St. Louis, Attell's final battle of the year, was not intended to be significant, but it was. When the gong sounded at the end of the sixth round, in what was to be an eight-round affair, something was clearly wrong. The headline the following day, November 28, sent shock waves through the boxing community: "Abe Attell Quits in Midst of a Battle."

The *Evening Standard* printed: "Instead of retiring to his corner Attell stepped to the ropes and announced that he had enough-that he had given 'the best that was in him,' but that he was now through with the fight game forever. He was badly outpointed in the six rounds."[63] The 3,000 spectators witnessing the contest stood dumbfounded as Attell repeated, "I'm all in as a fighter, boys. It ain't no use, it ain't no use."[64]

Stupefied by the proclamation, the press printed eulogies of the fighter: "Abe Attell was Marvel," claimed the *Evening Standard* on December 7, and "Attell One of The Greatest Fighters," printed the *Evening Times* on December 13. The year was being summarized as a changing of the guard, as not only had Attell lost his feather crown, but Wolgast the lightweight title to Willie Ritchie on a sixteenth-round foul. That fight was held at Coffroth's Mission Street Arena in Daly City, California, on November 28. Others, including bantam Johnny Coulon and heavyweight Jack Johnson, had approached the danger zone with their behavior both in and out of the ring. All this while, it took Attell until December 15 to say wait a minute, "I'm still in game."[65]

Three days later, Attell, contradicting himself, told the New York press he was thinking about managing. He also went on record stating to the press, "In the first place my match with Murphy was fixed. I fixed it with Murphy's manager, Buckley, myself, hoping to make an impression that would force Kilbane to meet me again. Murphy was to lie down on me—take the knockout in the sixth round. When the sixth passed I found that I had been double-crossed."[66]

"And, now I am through," confirmed the twenty-nine-year-old Attell, who was now back at home in New York City.[67]

In Monte's Corner

In what some might view as a systematic approach, Johnny Kilbane completed his destruction of the fighting Attell family on December 3, when in the ninth round of his bout in Cleveland, the police had to step in to prevent a knockout of Monte Attell. The *Evening World* noted the devastation: "Attell went to the mat five times, and the last time was sent cleanly through the ropes. The police picked him up from the floor of the stage and kept him out of the ring."[68]

The best one-line summary you will ever read in a boxing biography: If it were not for Johnny Kilbane, the Attell family would have had a better year. Both brothers, each having fought over 100 rounds, added three losses to their official total—the surname of Kilbane common to both. And both Attell brothers finished their year with a loss. The big question now was: had both slipped from the championship picture for their weight class? That, however, remained to be seen.

The end of the year also found the New York State Athletic Commission introducing a new scale of weights: paperweight, 105 pounds; bantamweight, 115 pounds; featherweight, 125 pounds; lightweight, 135 pounds; welterweight, 145 pounds; middleweight, 155 pounds; commission weight, 175 pounds; and heavyweight, above 175 pounds.

Of notable ring battles: Boxing's

Oliver Kirk of the United States was a bantamweight and featherweight professional boxer who won two gold medals in two separate weight divisions boxing at the 1904 Summer Olympics (Library of Congress).

Johnny Kilbane, the man who ended the featherweight championship reign of Abe Attell, spent much of his life in the public eye. He is pictured here with his wife and daughter. Kilbane defended the featherweight title for over a decade and, in retirement, became a senator in the Ohio State legislature (Library of Congress).

most famous "double knockout" sees champion Ad Wolgast fall to the canvas atop Joe Rivers in the thirteenth round of their battle on July 4, in Vernon, California. A far from impartial Referee Jack Welsh then helps Wolgast to his feet while counting out a fouled Joe Rivers, and Luther McCarty surprises heavyweight contender Al Kaufmann by knocking him out in the second round of their October 12 conflict in San Francisco.

To hide and feel guilty would be admitting defeat, and Abe Attell knew better. Granted, losing a title that had become synonymous with his name was nothing short of devastating, but there were options: Taking a page out of the George Dixon playbook, Attell could chart a course toward reclamation. Not an easy path by any means, but it was a direction. And, yes, there were some obstacles to overcome—he was suspended for six months for "faking" a fight, and his association with such travesties, unfortunately, now preceded him. But, reclaiming the title, he knew, could fix that as well.

"The Little Champ" fought 115 rounds in nine fights, winning only one, drawing two, with two "no decisions," while losing three fights in one year, two of which were back-to-back. In what could be the end of a remarkable career, he quits—a nonexistent word, let alone action, in the vocabulary of any Attell—in the sixth round of his fight with Oliver Kirk. Attell also fired manager Billy Nolan during an unsuccessful comeback bid and admitted attempting to fix his March fight with Tommy Murphy, a boxer who would "double-cross" the former champion. His recent behavior did not reflect the champion he had been, nor was it conducive to his resurrection.

CHAPTER TWELVE

The Thrill Is Gone, 1913–1919

"Johnny Kilbane is the man I want to box. He should give me an opportunity to meet him again. I beat Johnny in a ten-round bout in Kansas City before he won the title from me. I want Kilbane to treat me the way I treated him. I gave him another chance."—Abraham Attell[1]

1913

In New York City, a rebuilt Grand Central Terminal reopened as the world's largest train station. The sport of boxing, like other professional sports, cringed when the 16th Amendment to the United States Constitution was ratified, authorizing the federal government to impose and collect income taxes. A former New Jersey governor, Woodrow Wilson, succeeded William Howard Taft as the 28th president of the United States. All this took place before Abraham Attell, presumed retired, decided to once again enter a New York boxing ring.

Hanging up the gloves remains the toughest decision a professional boxer faces. It is the process of coming to terms with time that can envelop the soul. Unlike a rail terminal, a boxer cannot be rebuilt to perform at the level of proficiency he once had; history bears witness to such attempts. And there is no bell to toll to end a career. To be an elite champion, such as Abraham Attell, was incomprehensible to most, making such a solitary decision even more difficult. Part of every champion will forever be trapped inside the ropes; Abraham understood this, even if he didn't accept it.

New Year's Day typically included an assessment of the fistic world in newspapers across the country. Willie Ritchie of San Francisco, and Johnny Kilbane of Cleveland, took much of the praise for their new titles, while some, like Attell, took more criticism. The *Evening Times* penned:

> The downfall of Abe Attell furnished the surprise of the year. The little fellow had reigned supreme among the featherweights for so long a time that it seemed impossible for him to be beaten. Such men as Harry Forbes, Frankie Neil, Joe Gans, Bat Nelson, Joe Wolcott, Stanley Ketchel, Bob Fitzsimmons and Jim Jeffries won titles and passed into the discard during the regime of Attell and it seemed that he was destined to retire unbeaten, but the midnight oil will get the best of them and it finally landed Abe and today he is but the shadow of the great unbeatable featherweight that smiled at those clamoring for his crown.[2]

Later, there was this appraisal and comment, from the *Tacoma Times*: "Abe Attell, once featherweight champion, is not going to desert the ring game—just yet—according to

163

the announcement of the veteran today. 'No more long, grueling contests for me,' said Abe, 'just these little, four-round sprints. I can get plenty excitement out of them.'"[3]

Thinking beyond his own career, Attell was still focusing on putting together a solid stable of fighters. The *Salt Lake Tribune* noted:

> Abe Attell, a former featherweight champion, produced a sensation tonight [March 13] known as "Louisiana," a 119-pound boxer, whom he brought from Philadelphia. "Louisiana" surprised the fans at the Forty-fourth Street Sporting Club by his cleverness, punching ability and dazzling speed. He won with ease from Jimmy Murray of Brooklyn in a ten-round bout. The new wonder's name is Joe Biederberg. He is anxious to take on Champion Johnny Coulon or any other top-notcher at 117 pounds.[4]

A Sense of Vindication

On January 2, Oliver Kirk, the St. Louis boy who was believed to have made Abraham Attell quit boxing, lasted just

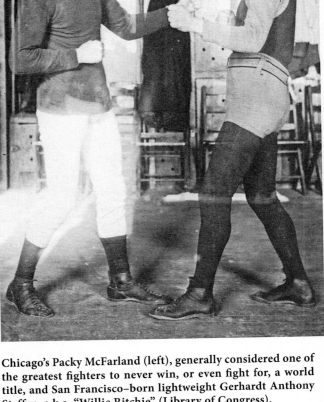

Chicago's Packy McFarland (left), generally considered one of the greatest fighters to never win, or even fight for, a world title, and San Francisco–born lightweight Gerhardt Anthony Steffen, a.k.a. "Willie Ritchie" (Library of Congress).

one round and a half before champion Johnny Kilbane sent him to "Neverland." The champion literally shredded the hometown boy against the ropes before Kirk's attendants had to carry him from the ring. Thankfully, Kirk would have plenty of time to heal before his next fight: he would meet Abe Attell on Wednesday, March 19, in the feature bout at the Forty-fourth Street Sporting Club in New York.

The venue, formerly the National Sporting Club, was also utilizing Attell's services as a promoter. Landing the bout, Attell assumed, was nothing short of perfection: first by fighting, and hopefully by defeating Kirk, he would vindicate himself from his last ring performance. Secondly, a decisive victory, if it could be had, would draw instant comparisons to Kilbane, and hopefully a public outcry for a rematch. A Bridgeport newspaper reported, "Many admirers of Attell are anxious to learn if Abe can show anything near his former form. Attell insists he can, and says that if he fails to get the popular verdict over Kirk he never again will don the mitts."[5]

It was a re-emergence with a vengeance as the former featherweight champion pummeled his St. Louis opponent to a standstill in the third round. In what appeared to be a sure knockout, Referee Stanley Kelley stepped-in to intervene. Oliver Kirk, floored twice by Attell, was almost helpless, meandering about the ring when Kelley waved it off.

The articles of agreement had called for 128 pounds at ringside. Attell scaled at 122¼, while Kirk tipped the beam four pounds to his advantage. In the first round, Kirk chose to fire distant artillery to confirm his reach, while Attell started with the body and worked to the head. Attell got the jab working early and took the first segment. In round two, Kirk spent far too much time working his jab, while Attell got serious in the exchanges. The *Sun* recorded the confrontation:

> When the third round opened Kirk resumed his left-handers and he landed a dozen of them cleanly in Attell's face before the latter began to wake up. With a sudden right hand swing on the jaw, Attell made the Missourian stagger to the ropes. Another right-hander in the same place, delivered with all the strength he possessed, enabled Attell to floor Kirk in a heap. The referee started to count, but Kirk jumped up and began to run. He was unsteady on his pins and had practically no defense. Attell followed him closely and drove him to a corner, where Kirk was a target for a blinding volley of swings and uppercuts. He tried in vain to cover up, but Attell got under his guard with solid hooks, which straightened Kirk up. Then came left and right hand swings on the neck and jaw, Kirk sprawling on the canvas, groping for the ropes.[6]

Kirk rose at the count of nine, only to be hammered at will by Attell. The referee had to twice yank the former champion from his adversary who appeared seconds from a knockout. The crowd loved the action and Attell followers piled over the ropes to embrace the winner. It was Attell at his finest, the perfect performance.

Ironically, Attell's battle with Kirk almost didn't take place. Promoter James Coffroth was looking for an opponent to face Harlem Tommy Murphy on Washington's birthday after Ad Wolgast failed to sign articles. Coffroth was trying to decide between Bud Anderson of Medford, Oregon, and Attell. The latter had done his best to sell the promoter, but didn't get the bid. Thankfully, the Kirk fight worked to Attell's favor. Also, Wolgast later agreed to the fight.

Murphy, who fought twenty rounds to a draw with Wolgast on February 22, would later compliment Attell by stating after the fight, "Not for a million dollars would I go through that fight again. It was by far the toughest scrap of my career, and after it was over I almost decided to quit the game."[7]

Five days later, Attell was back in the press gloating over his victory and looking toward the future. The *Calmut News* quoted him as saying, "After I've had a few more fights and demonstrated that I still have the 'goods.' I want to take on Johnny Kilbane, the title-holder. I feel sure I can regain the championship that I lost to him more than a year ago."[8]

The spin was on. Now it was up to Kilbane to take the bait.

Less than a month later, Attell was back inside a New York ring for a ten-round bout against Jimmy Walsh—the fifth meeting between the pair—at the Forty-fourth Street Club. Slow, not to mention uneventful, or so it initially appeared, the bout on Thursday, April 3, disappointed many who were anticipating a view of the Attell of old. The *Standard* observed: "Attell appeared in splendid form and at times showed a slight return of the speed that once made him famous, but at the end of each round he slowed up and Walsh seized the opportunity to even things up. At the finish neither showed any outward evidence of having been in a match. Ringside weights were: Walsh 124; Attell, 123."[9] A lackluster, not to mention redundant, no-decision was not what Attell needed, especially after the Kirk fight. And to make matters worse, it wasn't over.

Five days later, news came out of Syracuse, New York, where Walsh was fighting Bobby Pittsley at the Alhambra, that Eddie Keevin, Walsh's manager, had filed charges with the New York boxing commission against Attell for the latter's alleged "eye pecking" tactics the previous Thursday. This move came as a surprise to most, as only a few sources acknowledged such an injury. The *Bridgeport Evening Farmer* noted: "Jimmy was outboxed, but outside of a slight bruise over his right eye, he fared little the worse for the lesson."[10] Keevin, who claimed Attell was using his thumb to purposefully blind Walsh, wanted the former champion suspended for all time. Under the Frawley law, if found guilty, Attell could indeed face such a penalty.

Looking back at their meeting, the *Sun* reported: "Attell was fighting hard in the fifth round, which was much in his favor except the last few seconds, when Walsh staggered him with a right hand swing on the jaw. As the sixth round began the thumb of Attell's left glove was accidentally pushed into Walsh's right eye, so that he could not see a thing and had to take a painful thumping."[11] This report claimed that Walsh had recovered the following round and even rallied against Attell. The accusations against Attell appeared contrived and unjustifiable.

Proof that when it rains, it pours, another unusual incident struck Attell. A week later, on April 15, the former champion traveled to Atlanta to meet Philadelphia fighter Benny Kaufman. Everything appeared normal in the scheduled ten-round clash, until the second round. From that point forward, Kaufman didn't box but danced, avoiding Attell at all cost. Atlanta police commissioners, having seen enough, stopped the encounter in the seventh round and announced the bout was "no fight." The Orpheum Theater crowd, sensing something was obviously wrong, was stunned when promoter Henry Norton stepped forward to support the view of the commissioners. Any momentum Attell was trying to build along the comeback trail was slowly leaking around the foundation.

With the momentum from the Kirk fight virtually destroyed by his last two encounters, Attell needed a course correction, and quickly. Less than two weeks later, in Baltimore on April 28, "The Little Hebrew" was given a decision over George Chaney at the end of their fifteen-round dust-up.[12] However, reviews of this Empire Theater fight contradicted the decision, some claiming it one of the worst in Baltimore ring history. "Only a half dozen body blows were struck. Both men exchanging a succession of blows to the face."[13] Chaney, who had knocked out Young Britt in the second round of his previous fight, had shined in his last six straight contests and had all the appearances of a southpaw contender. But the referee saw it differently. Even if Attell's southern swing didn't look that bad in the record books, it didn't smell sweet, as they say. It was time, he thought, to head home and regroup.

By Memorial Day, the feasibility of an Attell comeback was becoming harder to sell, both to the public and promoters. Mexican lightweight Joe Rivers, who had sparred with the former champion, was one of the few who stood behind Attell. The fighter remarked to the *El Paso Herald*: "You can't tell me that Attell can't come back. I saw him fight on the coast when he was champion, and I feel no hesitancy in saying that he is every bit as good now as he was then. I think he can lick all the featherweights. I feel so certain of it that I'd bet $2,500 on it, providing, of course, that Attell trains as he should."[14]

One last big score, Attell believed, was what was needed, either to rejuvenate his career or to end it. And that meant only one person: Johnny Kilbane.[15] Team Attell swung into action trying desperately to land a match. But word finally came on June 14 of the verdict. This version was printed in the *Seattle Star*: "All negotiations for a match the later part of the month between Johnny Kilbane, the featherweight champion, and Abe Attell are off. Announcement to that effect was made here [San Francisco] today by Promoter Jim Griffin following a conference with Jimmy Dunn, Kilbane's manager. Dunn, Griffin said, wanted a stiffer guarantee than he could afford to give."[16]

The announcement didn't end it, however, as both parties continued negotiating throughout the remainder of the year. Attell took on new management, in the form of Herman Morse, to pressure Kilbane into a rematch, but to no avail. Despite finding it difficult to locate opposition at his terms, the champion simply had no desire to face Attell.

Attell didn't climb back between the ropes until July 24. It was then that he took a fight with Willie Beecher in front of the Atlantic Athletic Association over at Rockaway Beach in Queens. The *Day Book* noted:

Abe Attell was outpointed in a ten round bout at New York last night by Willie Beecher, but won an easy decision over the referee [Charles Draycott]. The former featherweight champ was wild in his swings and several times accidentally landed on the referee. In the fifth and sixth Abe swung wild rights to the referee's dome, flooring him, and in the seventh, in trying to escape from Beecher, rammed the arbiter in the stomach, putting him down for the count of eight.[17]

The event was a fiasco, something that should have been avoided if Attell was serious about his comeback.

Let the Record Show

To think that the great Daniel Mendoza, "The Fighting Jew," could be mentioned in the same breath as Abraham Attell, exhibits the prominence "The Little Hebrew" had attained. And that was precisely the comparison that was being drawn to show how far back the Jews have been in the fighting game and the tremendous gains they had recently achieved thanks to battlers like the Attells. The *Day Book* noted:

Abe certainly did some remarkable milling in his day, as his splendid record shows. You all know that Abe's brother, Monte, is also quite a ring battler. The Ghetto district of New York City has turned out quite a number of famous fighters of the Jewish race including: Dolly Lyons, who became a sparring partner for George Dixon; Mike Harris, who stood off Wolcott for four rounds; Joe Bernstein, who battled Terry McGovern, and Leach Cross, or Dr. Louis Wallach, a dentist, who has some strong pull (no joke) on the great East Side.[18]

Heir to the legacy of all this talent, a youngster by the name of Benjamin Leiner, who was born on April 7, 1896, sharpened his boxing skills in an area gym. Benny Leonard, as he would be known, would arguably become not only the greatest Jewish fighter ever, but one of the very best to ever wear a pair of boxing gloves.

None other than Attell himself confirmed that a match had been made with Kilbane and set for November 12. Promoter James Coffroth would be finalizing details in the coming weeks for a twenty-round featherweight title bout to be held in San Francisco on February 22, 1914. Later, Attell would attest to Kilbane's aggressive negotiations that included, according to Abe, a $4,000 guarantee and thirty percent of the gross receipts. Attell, who had vaudeville obligations, planned to leave for San Francisco on December 31. It was also noted by the *Day Book* that "Attell is not in good financial condition."[19]

For Monte Attell, the year was his second in a row without a victory. He fought in seven contests, possibly eight, although it can't be confirmed, against only three opponents: Ad Zotte, Cal Delaney and Roy Moore. Of the three adversaries, Zotte, a Mexican-born fighter hailing from Stockton, California, provided the most entertaining display. At this point, it's clear that Monte had essentially fought his way out of contention.

As for brother Abraham, it would prove to be his final full year of professional boxing. While Attell intended to step aside soon, following his presumed match with Kilbane, and try his luck at retirement, he would have more bouts with reconsideration than with opponents.

1914

In January 1914, as the Ford Motor Company announced an eight-hour workday and a minimum wage of $5 for a day's labor, Abe Attell had just one thing on his mind: a match with featherweight champion Johnny Kilbane. If his fight with the popular Cleveland boxer drew as anticipated, Attell stood to make more money in one day than a worker at Ford Motor Company earned in one year. Attell confirmed to the *Bridgeport Evening Farmer*, "I can beat anybody that is afraid of me and I know that Kilbane is afraid of me. I want to win back that title. I feel lost without it, and, believe me, I'll do everything in my power to succeed."[20] The intimidation tone was new to Attell, even if his promise was not.

The fight game amounted to big money, and Attell was constantly reminded of it. A recent article in the *Washington Times* listed Owen Moran's earnings for his five fights with Attell, which totaled nearly $15,000. With the average annual income of a U.S. worker at $577, Attell couldn't imagine—partly because he hadn't had to for many years—earning a living in any other manner. With a male life expectancy of 52 years, it was, however, a concern.

The Attell versus Kilbane championship battle, scheduled for February 22—also March 20, July 4, October 13, October 15, October 16, November 1, and November 20, to name only a few dates—would never take place due to adverse circumstances. From copious Kilbane injuries, to fight and family commitments, a date could not be secured. For the former champion, there would be no graceful ending, no memorable swan song to which to attach a memory.

Johnny Kilbane did fight 12 times in 1914, against foes such as Eddie Moy, Frankie Daley, Joe Mandot, and Willie Houck, but not a single adversary could hold a candle to Attell, nor would any ever be included in a conversation of boxing's elite fighters. Kilbane was also taking some heat in the press that year for having yet to fight an international battle, along with what would become a redundant observation: his failure to put his championship on the line. But pressure or no pressure, the featherweight titleholder still had his crown.

In between training for his potential battle with Kilbane, Attell took the stage. Local advertisements would read: "Special Announcement, To Lovers of Real Boxing, Abe Attell, For 12 Years Undisputed Featherweight Champion of the World, Will Box Three

Great Rounds, With the Best [insert city] Boxer at the [insert venue]." Interviews with the local newspapers were common, and they would always ask Attell about the championship. The exposure proved to be a wise decision on the fighter's part; he needed to stay relevant while he waited for Kilbane.

On May 14, the former featherweight champion caused a bit of a stir when he was spotted walking with Evelyn Nesbit Thaw, the popular American chorus girl and artists' model, along the streets of, of all places, Grand Forks, North Dakota. Immortalized by artists James Carroll Beckwith, Frederick S. Church, and notably Charles Dana Gibson, who idealized her as a "Gibson Girl," Evelyn's face had found a home on nearly every form that could be printed since the turn of the century. To most, however, Evelyn Nesbit was known as the subject of "The Trial of the Century," as her jealous husband, multimillionaire Harry Kendall Thaw, shot and murdered Stanford White on the rooftop theater of Madison Square Garden on the evening of June 25, 1906. Having

Evelyn Thaw, a.k.a. Florence Evelyn Nesbit (1884–1967), known professionally as Evelyn Nesbit, was a popular American chorus girl and artists' model whose liaison with architect Stanford White immortalized her as "The Girl in the Red Velvet Swing" (Library of Congress).

returned to the stage the previous fall in New York, she was in Grand Forks as part of a tour that would take her next to Duluth, before returning home to New York. Also in Grand Forks was Jack Clifford, her dance partner and soon life partner, who would become Nesbit's second husband in 1916.

As New Yorkers, both the Thaws and the Attells frequented Manhattan's finest establishments—city gentry took advantage of the exquisite dining, such as Rector's, not to mention the theater. For Abraham it could be a contrasting lifestyle: Rector's with the wife on one evening; Shanley's, over on Broadway, between 42nd and 43rd, with the boys the following night.[21] Even if Grand Forks was a far cry from "The City," vaudevillians enjoyed the company of each other, not to mention a bit of press.

August found Attell in London to rattle the cages of many feathers, including Freddie Welsh, of whom he posted a $1,000 forfeit. He found himself returning home "to New York on the *Philadelphia* with a stateroom all to himself, and has in his care $500,000 worth of rare manuscripts and books."[22] Seems New York book dealer George D. Smith, who had spent months in London acquiring collections, including many pieces from the Earl of Pembroke's library, needed to guarantee transportation of a large consignment of books immediately back to the States, and Attell agreed to oversee transport. As guardian of the treasures, and a good one at that, the former champion took comfort in his state-room. No word was given if Attell was able to pick up any decent card games with the score of American millionaires on board. "The Little Champ" had sailed for the United Kingdom the second week of July.

Family Matters

In addition to guarding manuscripts, perhaps "The Little Champ" should have con-sidered guarding his wife, as Mrs. Attell reported on September 2 that she had lost a gold mesh bag containing $3,000 worth of jewelry. Distraught, she told the second branch detective bureau of New York that she believed she left it in a store during a Monday shopping excursion. The *Sun* penned, "Detective Culhane went to the store with Mrs. Attell, but could find little on which to work. The valuables will be described in the next pawnshop circular, and the 500 detectives of the bureau will be ordered to look out for them. Mrs. Attell also will offer a reward for their return to her at the St. Francis Hotel, 124 West Forty-seventh Street."[23] Many of the missing items—which included a diamond-studded watch, several plain and diamond rings and a bracelet—were gifts from her hus-band during his championship days.

On September 26, 1914, Mrs. Annie Roth Attell, matriarch of the Attell family, died in San Francisco. She was sixty-four years old. As one daily put it, "Monte Attell, former bantamweight champion, was with her, but his brother Abe, the former featherweight champion, is in the east, the family does not know where."[24]

Raising such a large family, under the conditions she was dealt, was no simple task; not nearly enough credit has ever been given to boxing mothers, or wives. Yet the sacrifice they endure is incomprehensible. She was buried in Colma, California.

Word came from Chicago on December 14, inside papers such as the *Ogden Stan-dard*: "Abe Attell, former featherweight champion pugilist, was made defendant in a suit for divorce filed here [Chicago] today by Mrs. Ethel Attell on charges of cruelty. The cou-ple were married on March 14, 1907, and according to Mrs. Attell they lived happily until her husband lost his championship title."[25] Abraham learned of the suit while he was in Omaha, Nebraska, as part of a vaudeville show, and stated the following day that he would "contest the case because the charge was cruelty." He also stated, "I would not have made a contest against any other charge, but I am going to show that a prizefighter need not to be a brute in his family."[26] Both these quotes appeared in the *Ogden Standard*.

The divorce hit Abraham hard. During his stay in Omaha, when he needed an ear to bend, he turned to columnist T.A. Andrews. Attell, unlike other former champions, such as Battling Nelson, was not one to air his personal feelings to the public, so such an instance was rare. The *Herald* was one of the newspapers that carried the former champion's comments:

> I could forgive anything my wife might have done, but to state that I had beaten her is going the limit. Such a statement is bad enough with society people, but when a boxer is accused of such doings the people only smile and say, "What else could you expect from a fighter?" The story about taking away her diamonds in Chicago is true in a way, but the conditions leading up to it were not

told. If they were it would sound very different. And I did not take them in the way reported, nor did I beat or lay a hand on her."[27]

Attell continued: "I made big sums of money for the past six years and gave her everything she could desire. I loved her dearly and do still, but there are some things I would not stand for. I am sorry that there should be a parting, but I guess it will be for the best now. It hurts deep down just the same." Later, on December 29, it was announced in Chicago that the couple "have patched up all differences and the suit will be dropped."[28]

A piece titled "Tip from a Fighter" was picked up by a few dailies and even Abe got a kick out of it:

> Richard Bennett, the actor, was a prize fighter when he was a young man, and, as a result of this accomplishment, he has many friends in the ranks of pugilism. One evening during a performance in the Midwest, Abe Attell went behind the scenes and called on Bennett in his dressing room.
>
> "Are you going to play San Francisco?" asked the pugilist.
>
> "Yes," replied the actor, "I think we'll put on the play in the Greek Theater over at Berkeley for one or two special performances."
>
> "Take a tip from me, Bennett," cautioned Attell, not getting the real significance of the theater's name, "don't do that. If you do you'll lose a lot of money. There ain't enough Greeks in that town to fill a moving picture house."[29]

On the books, Attell was an inactive fighter. Although he sparred with many pugilists during the year, including Charley White—whom he assisted with his battle against Willie Ritchie—and may have picked up a few four-rounders for some pocket cash, there would be no recorded bouts. In addition to the Kilbane debacle, other matches were attempted: a bout against bantam Chick Hayes, scheduled for July 4 at Evansville, Indiana, was canceled, and two Thanksgiving Day bouts, the first against Jean Delmont and the second against "Goo" Stewart, were proposed, but neither came to fruition.

In retrospect it was an extremely challenging year for the entire Attell family; for Abraham, there were times when it seemed like his entire world was crumbling beneath him. The Kilbane mess was unproductive; the stage was profitable, but to be labeled a "former" anything was never easy; the Welsh fishing expedition in London proved unfruitful; the loss of his mother was tragic and required healing; and he abhorred his personal life being dragged into the public. Reading between the lines, one might also believe that things were still not perfect at home.

In the past, the ring had always been Abe's refuge; now it was no longer there. For the first time since 1899, he did not log a professional fight. With the loss of his mother, his mind drifted back in time, back to the days "South of the Slot," where he, Jimmy Britt, Eddie Hanlon, Dick Hyland, Frankie Neil, Willie Ritchie and Joe Thomas, fought their boyhood fights. It was the Attell family, he knew, that really drew attention to Frisco's fighting quarter, and that was thanks to the incessant support of his mother. Perhaps it was these memories that would now serve as his sanctuary.

1915

Panic struck the city of New York in January, as Mary Mallon, a cook at Sloan Hospital, infected 25 people with typhoid fever; she was placed under quarantine for life, and was known thereafter as Typhoid Mary. Jokingly, Abe Attell referred to himself as a fighter quarantined from a shot at the title, which may well have been the case. Johnny

Kilbane would fight fifteen short-distance battles—only two of his fights went twelve rounds—to the requisite no-decision verdict this year, without putting his championship on the line. This was the control a champion had. And it came at the expense of those contending for the title. For Attell, the thought of fighting Kilbane had become an obsession. Again a fight with the champion was scheduled, this time for the last week in June in New Orleans, but it too would never be realized.

While Attell believed Kilbane to be his greatest adversary, others believed differently. To his critics it was age. The *Ogden Standard* observed: "Youth is the rule in the prize ring today. Very few good men are over 30. Joe Jeanette at 35 is a Methuselah. And he has not beaten a good man for many years. Sam McVey at 30 is several years past his prime as a boxer. In lighter classes, 30-year men are scarcer still. Johnny Coulon at 25 was forced to relinquish his bantam title. Abe Attell, now 31, is out of the ring. He was only 28 when he lost his title."[30]

Articles such as this appeared almost routinely and not only irritated Attell, but forced him into a defensive mode with the press. For example, while still on the vaudeville circuit—he was appearing in Seattle during the final week in March, and the first week of April at the Orpheum Theater—he began his conversation with the press by emphatically stating that he was going to tackle Johnny Kilbane, specifics disregarded.

Making his way cross-country on the stage circuit, Attell understood he had to feed the beat writers to garnish some press. The *Tacoma Times* noted, "Abe Attell, playing at a Portland theater, says that he has made $300,000 in the fight game, is saving most of it, and that he doesn't want any benefits for him in his old age. 'I'm still going to have some when I die. It's a wonder some of the other boxers don't take Abe's tip and save a little of the come-easy money.'"[31]

After Attell's stage monologue, he would spar a few rounds not only for the audience, but also to keep in shape. The *Journal* reported:

> Eddie Flanagan, a local amateur, is nursing a jaw today as the result of an encounter with Abe Attell, former featherweight champion, on the stage of a Portland theater. After doing a monologue Sunday, Abe invited Portland fistic artists to don the mitts with him. Flanagan accepted. In the third round, Flanagan began to swing with more than sparring vigor and Abe whipped over a right jab to the jaw. Eddie went down but was quickly assisted to his feet and shaken into consciousness by the San Francisco boy.[32]

The summer would find Attell back on the East Coast, peddling a successful show. The *Bridgeport Evening Farmer* noted:

> With Abe Attell & Co., in "The Big Fight," headlining the vaudeville program at the Plaza there is little wonder that the cozy playhouse is playing to capacity audiences at every performance. "The Big Fight" is a very interesting offering and in it Attell, the man who held the featherweight championship of the world for twelve years, is assisted by Goff Phillips, the famous blackface comedian. At the finish of an exhibition, or three round bout, Attell renders a recitation entitled "The Knocker" that is enthusiastically received.[33]

Attell got a bit of chuckle out of hearing that Jimmy Clabby, the Indiana middleweight, and George Chip, from Newcastle, Pennsylvania, were called to account by the State Athletic Commission for an alleged "fake" that took place at the St. Nicholas Rink in May. The commission was following the same procedures Attell had endured during his investigation. Both principals testified that they did their best and that the poor showing was due to fatigue. The *Farmer* noted, "The fact that they had boxed three or four times before and were thoroughly acquainted with each other's style was also advanced as a reason that the men did not put on a fast exhibition. Clabby is of the clever type of boxer, while Chip is one who bores in head down, without science and only a determination to reach his opponent regardless of the result."[34]

In Gloversville, New York, of all places, Frankie Callahan became the final knockout victim of the great Abraham Attell on September 6.[35] It was, however, by accident, as Philadelphia's Tommy Houck was the original adversary. Attell refused to fight the heavier Houck, so novice Frankie Callahan stepped up and lasted three rounds before kissing the canvas. The audience was also treated to a celebrity second, as Attell had in his corner heavyweight Frank Moran. Unfortunately, the entire event was seen by some, such as the *Washington Herald*, as nothing more than a "comeback" stunt and attracted very little attention.

Boxing marriages, like those of other professional sports, are never easy, and the difficulties are often attributable to the physical demands of an athlete. A good friend of mine, who just so happened to be married to a popular fighter, used to remind me that divorce was never an option. Poisoning or stabbing the son of a bitch, sometimes, but never divorce.

Ethel M. Attell, wife of Abraham Attell, sued for divorce on September 22 in San Francisco. The suit was filed in superior court. The *Daily Bee* printed, "Failure to support her and desertion were charged in the petition. No alimony was asked. Mrs. Attell said she and her husband separated in August 1914. They were married at Santa Anna, California in 1907. Mrs. Attell was Miss Ethel M. Egan of San Francisco."[36] Even if both saw the action coming, divorce is never easy.[37]

In November, while on the vaudeville circuit out in Grand Forks, North Dakota, Attell couldn't resist the opportunity to censure the present-day boxer. The former champion was comparing the "draw boxers" of the day to the "knockout" fighters of yesteryear. The *Grand Forks Daily Herald* printed the observation: "Most of the boys in the ring today are afraid to get hit. A lot of them are pretty boys who don't like to get their hair mussed or their maps soiled. Conditions are such that they can dance through six or ten rounds and get away with it. In the old days, we fought. Look at the gang I had to tackle— Kid Broad, Herrera, George Dixon and that lot. No tango tea with those boys. It was biff, bang, slam all the time."[38]

Attell would then demonstrate as he instructed and continued his dissertation:

A fighter to hit good and hard has to "set" himself. He has to put his feet on the floor solidly and put all his weight into his punch. These boys we see nowadays are so busy bobbing around to keep from getting hit they never set. I think there is only one fellow in the ring today who hits right—hits like the good old boys did—and that's Mike Gibbons. But Mike won't go in close and take a chance. Compare some of these parlor dancers with Terry McGovern, Herrera and the like. This fellow Herrera hit Benny Yanger on the jaw one night and Yanger struck the floor so hard his shoulder bone was broken.[39]

Aurelio Herrera, whom Battling Nelson called the hardest puncher he ever faced, then became a subject for Attell's praise:

Herrera hit me on the chest one time and knocked me clear through the ropes. For a month, I could feel a heavy weight on my chest. Even now, when I take a deep breath, I think of the time the Mexican hit me. Herrera was the hardest hitter I ever faced. George Dixon was the best in all around ability. Gee, he was clever. My hardest fight was with Bat Nelson. He was a lightweight and I was a featherweight, but I signed for 15 rounds, figuring I could outbox him. Outbox nothing. We mauled one another for fair. That was a terrible night.[40]

Sometimes it takes years before stories surface, for one reason or another. The subject arose whether or not a fighter had ever counted the house (hey, if you are a fighter getting a percentage of the gate, it was your money), and Attell couldn't resist chiming in. The *Southern Herald* ran the tale:

> Abe was fighting Owen Moran, a former protege of Charley Harvey of San Francisco. Moran was tearing into him like a madman, with Attell ducking and blocking languidly as he looked around the house. Suddenly Abe grappled Moran and wrestled him over to the corner where Monte Attell, Abe's brother, was sitting. "Monte," said Abe sadly over the struggling Moran's shoulder, "I can tell you that there isn't a cent more than three thousand dollars in the house. I counted the bleachers and the boxes myself. Only three-dollar people came in after the first round." Then Abe settled down to the less important business of boxing Moran.[41]

Turning to another tale, Abe gave the press a stroll down memory lane with a funny story he recalled about Kid Broad. Apparently Broad's father told his son that if he was ever floored, to just think of his old daddy in Cleveland and get up. Bearing this in mind, Broad met the hard-hitting Aurelio Herrera, who floored him early in the battle. Well, as the referee tolled off the count, Broad simply thought of his father and got up. The wisdom of the father had prevailed. Many newspapers, including the *Tucumcari News*, ran the story: "In the next round Herrera landed another sledge hammer drive. Broad, as he lay on the floor, went through the same act, mumbling: 'Kid, think of your daddy in Cleveland and get up.' He was up in a jiffy."[42] But in the fourth round, Herrera unleashed a direct shot to Broad's jaw that dropped the fighter like a redwood. "The referee had about counted him out, when Broad, dazed and dreamy-eyed, looked up and said: 'If you want me to get up this time, Dad, you'll have to come and pull me up.'"[43]

In a year that saw the controversial film *The Birth of a Nation*, directed by D.W. Griffith (it premiered in Los Angeles in February), becoming the first film to displace that of the Johnson versus Jeffries celluloid in popularity, Abraham Attell placed one recorded fight in the record books. It was a bout with his last knockout victim, Frankie Callahan of Ohio, not to be confused with Brooklyn's tough lightweight of the same name. With brother Monte inactive, the Attell brothers appeared painted out of the ring picture.

1916

The global war, centered in Europe, that began on July 28, 1914, was threatening the involvement of the United States by 1916. It was what few had foreseen and many simply couldn't imagine. Even if turmoil was only a shore away, making ends meet was still a priority for most. The average cost of a home was $5,000, a car $400, while a staple such as a loaf of bread cost about seven cents.

A bit unsure as to what direction take, Abe Attell began his transition out of not only marital life, but out of boxing. Since his loss of the title, Attell found his voice—actually, he had little choice, in order to stay relevant—and was seldom short of words. Commenting on the now familiar "cauliflower" or "tin" ears, carried by what appeared to be nine out of ten boxers, Attell told the *Day Book*: "It's a change in the style of fighting, or rather a change in the style of not fighting. In the old days men stood more erect and picked off punches with their hands, jumped away from them or stepped inside of them. Now they bore in, head down or sideways and stop punches with their beans. A rap on the ear causes the blood to coagulate and a puffed listener is the result."[44] The phenomenon, no better exemplified than by Attell adversaries Battling Nelson and Ad Wolgast, made little sense to most. Why get hit if you didn't have to? And as the game would prove, getting hit led to far more damage than just a "tin" ear or two.

Speaking of adversaries, Johnny Kilbane would fight eleven times in 1916, putting his title on the line only once, against George "K.O." Chaney. For the champion, it was also his final fight of the year. Although Kilbane hadn't been in the ring with Attell since 1914, the memory remained fresh. "I thought when I beat Abe Attell for the lightweight title I had beaten the best left hand in the business, but I found a better one when I met [Richie] Mitchell in Cincinnati, the other day," claimed Johnny Kilbane to the *Seattle Star*.[45] The champion commented on the fighter's effective use of the left, as it was in his face all the time. While he admitted it didn't have much sting, the champion felt its use at jabbing could take Mitchell into the lightweight championship mix—a great compliment for the Milwaukee fighter.

Once again elaborating on the former champion: "Attell had a number of different ways of using his left, and it was always hard to tell what he was going to do with it. That left hand got him the championship and allowed him to keep it for 12 years."[46]

It was an interesting observation by the champion, who did not comment regarding another match with Attell, because frankly, he didn't want one. Kilbane did go on to state that Johnny Dundee "has a good left," Patsy Kline a "terrific wallop in his left," and that Mitchell "makes it impossible for an opponent to try to 'set' for a punch."[47] Kilbane was in no hurry to bring the title to the line and it frustrated the hell out of his competitors.

Talking about lefts, many fight fans still believe that Jess Willard used his far more effectively when he outpointed and outgeneraled Frank Moran on March 25 in their Madison Square Garden tussle for the heavyweight championship. The ten-round requisite no-decision saw Willard alter the topography of Moran's countenance with his snappy southpaw. Only two notable dissents surfaced regarding the observation. John L. Sullivan spoke out in favor of Moran, stating, "Willard is a counterfeit champion."[48] And Abe Attell confirmed Moran as the superior fighter.

Having made a lucrative living with his hands, Attell shifted his interest to another extremity, his feet. The *Richmond Times-Dispatch* reported, "He is fitting No. 1's to fair Broadwayites, No. 6's and selling nobby hats to frequenters of the Rialto. Abe Attell, in other words, has opened a shoe store in the theatrical district with the proceeds of his many battles in the squared arena. He says that it is a good business."[49]

But don't expect Abe to fit you personally, as he was busy fashioning his vaudeville show for the road. In places such as Bridgeport, Connecticut, Attell would perform his witty monologue, then box three exhibition rounds with local champions, during three daily performances. The *Farmer* was quick to report, "Sharing honors with Mr. Attell will be 'the girls from Mexico,' a girly, girly act with special scenic environments and a cast of 15 people, mostly girls, all of whom can sing and dance, and the comedy is of rapid fire kind and the fun is fast and furious."[50]

Sustaining press coverage for his vaudeville production meant Attell had to frequently recall an old memory or reach into his old bag of tricks. One such fable found Attell claiming he was the originator of the "bowknot trick." He used the scheme only when he was in trouble, and it was Frankie White who detected the ploy. The *Farmer* ran the confession:

The former champion would have his gloves tied on to his hands with a knot such as cowboys use with their neckties. He would be fighting until an opponent drove him into a tight place. Then, while feinting and without anybody noticing, he would pull the string and the glove would almost fall off. Naturally the bout would have to stop until the referee tied the glove back, and this gave Attell time to get his breath and resume his composure.[51]

By May, perhaps reading too many of the reports in the newspapers, Abe Attell was talking comeback. The *El Paso Herald* quoted him, "If possible, I'd like to have the rounds limited to one and a half minutes each. I realize I haven't the stamina of old, but I feel sure that in ten rounds of 90 seconds each I could earn a clean victory over Leonard."[52]

Why not?, Attell thought. The proof was right in front of him: Baseball player Nap Lajoie, at the age of 42, stole home the other day; Mike Mowry, who began playing when most readers were just toddlers, was the regular third sacker for the Dodgers; and George Moriarity, a survivor of the first great flood, topped the hitters in the American League at the beginning of the month. Attell's thought was to meet Benny Leonard, the reigning lightweight aspirant. The ten-round event, he believed, could be held in New York, while Attell's funeral, as everyone else believed, could be conducted shortly thereafter.

The press, believing he wasn't all that serious, knew his thoughts made for good copy, so they ran with it. Attell was rattling the trees to see if anything would fall out. Nothing did. Nonetheless, by October, after Joe Lynch sent Monte Attell, the last survivor of that fighting family, to the cleaners in about seven rounds, Abe was once again toying with the idea. He was in Monte's corner that night and had the unpleasant duty of tossing up the sponge for his blood-soaked brother. Word was he signed to match Lynch and was currently in training. Lynch, unimpressed by the action, believed "he can beat up the whole family."[53]

Author Jack London died at 7:45 on the night of November 22, at his ranch in Glen Ellen, California. He was a victim of uremic poisoning; at first physicians believed he suffered from ptomaine poisoning, but it was later determined to be a severe form of uremia. Born on January 12, 1876, in San Francisco, London graduated from high school before entering the University of California. Instead of completing his college studies, he headed to the Klondike during the famous 1897 gold rush to Alaska.

As an explorer he visited Japan, hunted seals in the Bering Sea, and traveled across the United States observing and noting everything around him. It would be the social and economic problems he observed that would combine with his experiences to form the foundation for his many writings. *The Call of the Wild* and *White Fang* were both set in the Klondike Gold Rush, as well as the short stories "To Build a Fire," "An Odyssey of the North," and "Love of Life." His narratives, such as "The Pearls of Parlay" and "The Heathen," were written about his visit to the South Pacific, while *The Sea Wolf* was all about home, or the San Francisco Bay area.

The struggle for survival became the prolific London's passion. He found it in his own experiences and he discovered it in the sweet science, a sport which he thoroughly enjoyed. As a correspondent he covered numerous fights, including one of the classic Bay Area clashes between Battling Nelson versus Jimmy Britt, and as a novelist penned *The Game*. Considered a boxing masterpiece by writers such as Ashton Stevens, it tells the story of boxer Joe Fleming, who meets his death in the ring.

On his passing, writer Mabel Abbott penned this about his work, and it appeared in the *Tacoma Times*: "His stories insisted on description of cold, hunger, thirst, wounds—any kind of physical suffering: of passions pushed beyond the limits which most people acknowledge; of crudity for its own sake. He knows that if he could make people shrink, they would read on, fascinated, to see if he would do it again."[54] Then, Abbott stated this about the man: "London made use of every experience, penning firsthand accounts of riding break beams, 'booze-fighting,' and the life of a wharf-rat. Self-revelation to the uttermost was part of his stock in trade. His heroes were all egotists, and they were all, to some extent, Jack London."[55] Pugilists such as Attell respected London, and enjoyed having him ringside and reading his accounts.

During a year of transition, new faces emerged, while others departed: Kid Williams, thanks to referee Billy Rocap, hung onto the bantam crown; light heavy champ Jack Dillon managed to endure against heavyweight Frank Moran; Jimmy Wilde began his seven-year reign over the flyweights; and a relatively new fighter, after suffering two broken ribs in the second round, managed to battle back soundly against heavy John Lester Johnson. His name was Jack Dempsey. For only the second time in his ring career, Abraham Attell would not log a fight during the calendar year.

1917

With the world at war—most of the fighting was taking place on land in Europe and characterized by long periods of bloody stalemate—most feared the inevitable, a U.S. participation. And that indeed happened in 1917, allowing the balance of World War I to slowly shift in the Allies' favor. All professional sports naturally took a backseat.

For Abe Attell, the end of the line came in New Orleans on January 8. The *Evening Star* reported, "The bright lights again have taken their toll. Abe Attell, former featherweight champion of the world, attempted a 'comeback' last night at New Orleans in a scheduled ten-round bout, with Phil Virgets. Attell went one round at top speed, then weakened perceptibly and in the fourth round was knocked out and was unconscious for five minutes."[56]

Limited press coverage found the event restricted to only a few sentences, almost along the lines of a filler. There were no long farewells or articles detailing one of the greatest boxing careers ever. In defense of the press, Attell had faded from the sports pages in recent years, and his attempts at a comeback were considered "old news."

Virgets, who had defeated Philadelphia Pal Moore the previous December, was a worthy opponent and was being managed by a New Orleans writer and boxing manager Fred Digby, who wisely positioned his fighter against Attell. Fred and Phil had grown up together in the Johnson Street neighborhood of the Crescent City, which made for a good story—in fact, a better one than Phil's battle with Attell. Digby was hoping to take his fighter straight to Kilbane, but others, particularly Rocky Kansas and Frankie Russell, thought differently. Virgets, whose brothers also boxed, would fight until 1921 before hanging up the gloves.

Only two lightweights looked capable of taking Freddie Welsh's crown: Benny Leonard and Richie Mitchell. Like Attell, Leonard was clever, a defensive genius. Unlike "The Little Champ," he packed a dangerous knockout punch. Mitchell had developed into a strong two-handed fighter and was now featuring a good punch. The *Bismarck Tribune* wrote: "Both of these boys had to look out for the 'bogie man,' Johnny Kilbane (Featherweight Champion). Johnny is determined to go after the lightweights and arrangements are now being made for him to meet Mitchell and Welsh. Although Kilbane will give away several pounds when he meets any lightweight, he is considered the most dangerous man in the ring at that weight."[57]

By August, it took sports writer Paul Purman to remind us how far the sport of boxing had progressed with the headline: "Pugilistic Ranks Invaded By Hebrews Who Now Hold Four Of Seven Championships!" The story said, "A list of their real names probably would not be recognized even by the most ardent boxing fan, Benjamin Leiner, Gershon Mendiloff, Al Rudolph and Battling Levinsky. Leiner, of course is Leonard, Mendiloff is better known as Ted Lewis and Rudloph fights as Al McCoy."[58] While the informative article failed to mention Levinsky's real name, Barney Lebrowitz, we won't fault him, as Purman reminded us that the four held the lightweight, welterweight, middleweight and light heavyweight crowns between them.

The story also noted:

> With the exception of the Irish, no race has produced so many good fighters than [sic] the Hebrew. The present day champions with the exception of McCoy are up to the average of the old day. Leonard certainly is greater than the two champions who came before him and unlike either Welsh or Ritchie is willing to risk his own crown now and then. Lewis is a great fighter, shifty, clever and hard-hitting. Levinsky made a name for himself as an iron man when he fought two or three times a week against the best men of his class.... Al McCoy, generally recognized as middleweight champion on account of his one-round victory over George Chip two or three years ago, manages to hang on to the title because no middleweight has been found able to knock him out in ten-rounds and Al won't play unless it's a ten-round no decision fight.[59]

Other notables mentioned included Leach Cross, Charley White, Kid Herman and Harry Lewis. They all had to be grateful to their predecessors who forged a path for those to follow, especially Bay Area boys Joe Choynski and the Attells.

So the only man to gain and lose a world championship on his birthday closed the book on his boxing career in 1917. Having held the featherweight crown from 1906 until 1912, with double-digit title defenses, he had proven himself the greatest feather of his day. Having fought George Dixon, Battling Nelson, Owen Moran, Freddie Welsh, Ad Wolgast, Jem Driscoll, and Johnny Kilbane places him in an elite class—in fact, the very first to enter the International Boxing Hall of Fame in 1990. Of his twelve fights in 1908, five were against future Hall of Famers. Although his official induction record, as impressive as it is, reads 171 bouts, 91 wins, 9 losses, 18 draws, 2 no contests, 51 no-decisions and 53 knockouts, there was far more to Abraham Washington Attell.

Closing the Book, 1918–1919

Being Abe Attell the *former* featherweight champion had never come easy for the fighter.

While imitation was certainly the sincerest form of flattery—by 1918, there were over a dozen fighters who had used a form of the name Abe Attell, from Young Attell to Abe Attell Goldstein—it was always difficult to see their names in the same sports section he once dominated.

Attell was flattered when a few of the dailies ran articles recognizing his thirty-fourth birthday. The *Farmer* penned, "The clever little Hebrew ring general who has for years been the monarch of the featherweights appeared for the last time a little over a year ago, when he met Phil Virgets in New Orleans. Virgets, unknown, unheralded and unsung, was awarded the victory over the former champion in the fourth round. The fact of the matter is that Father Time licked Abe, and not Virgets."[60] Many of the stories focused on his title loss and unsuccessful comeback instead of his reign as featherweight king, which was disappointing. Exceptions were the old beat writers, like T.A. Dorgan, known as TAD, of the *New York Evening Journal*:

> Attell was one of the most remarkable featherweights that ever stepped under a rope. One night he'd fight at 118 pounds, the next he'd take on a lightweight. Size and weight never bothered him much. He fought such lightweights as Eddie Hanlon, Tommy Murphy, Battling Nelson and Freddie Welsh, and was always there at the finish making it quite interesting for his opponent. He even fought Buddy Ryan, the welterweight champ, in a six-round affair out West, and bested him. That's more than a featherweight of today will do.[61]

Now reduced to columns such as "Today In Pugilistic Annals," "Ten Years Age In Sports," and "Scraps About Scrappers," Attell would only find himself quoted if he attended a fund-raiser, tribute dinner or training camp, and that was only if he was willing to spin a story, or predict a fight. For example, the *Tulsa Daily World* noted, "Abe Attell, former featherweight champion, while in St. Louis saw Jack Dempsey train for his recent bout with Billy Miske, and opined that Dempsey is the best looking heavyweight in the game today. 'He hits like the old-time stars used to hit,' says Abe, 'and is shifty and packs a terrific punch.' Attell says he believes Dempsey can whip Fulton and predicts he will be the next heavyweight champion."[62] For the record, Attell was right as Dempsey beat Fred Fulton by knockout in either 23 or 18 seconds (depending on the stopwatch) into the first round of their July 27 battle. Fulton was scheduled to meet world heavyweight

Abe Attell and Young Corbett "mixing it up" during a Cleveland exhibition (Library of Congress).

champion Jess Willard on July 4, 1918, but public sentiment was against a world heavy-weight championship fight taking place during World War I. Promoter Col. J.C. Miller had little option but to cancel.

On May 27, New York's sporting fraternity held a fundraiser for the Red Cross at the Polo Grounds. The *Washington Times* covered the event: "The Yankees and the Cleveland Indians returned from a flying trip to Cleveland to continue their series, which was to be preceded by field contests between the players. Boxing by Young Corbett and Abe Attell, former ring stars, and Freddie Welsh and Joe Welling, and wrestling by Tommy Draak and Yussif Hussane were added features."[63]

By July, Abe's day-to-day routine of tending to his business affairs was getting a bit redundant, so he turned his attention to becoming a boxing instructor at one of the military camps in France. Attell, who had only put in his application and expected an answer in a few days, knew that forms such as these had a way of taking their time. Other fighters, such as Johnny Kilbane, had taken this route as well.

During the second week of July, reports hit the press that Monte Attell was almost totally blind and had returned to the solace of the Pacific Coast. There his friends hoped to be able to establish him in a much safer profession. The *Sun* noted Monte's condition and stated: "While it has been claimed that the eyesight of boxers is frequently ruined as a result of heavy blows over the eyes, yet if the truth were known, defective vision results in the majority of cases from unclean hands of seconds and unsanitary methods in ring corners. Filthy gloves that have been used several times are enough to ruin the eyesight of any boxer and the wonder is that more cases of blindness do not result."[64]

Even with everything people had said and heard regarding Attell's activity, it always seemed that a contradictory blurb found its way into the newspapers. On August 23, 1919, the *Seattle Star* reported that Attell wanted a comeback. "He signed today to meet Frankie Burns, an Oakland lightweight, September 11."[65] It was to be a four-round contest. Whether Attell was inspired by Jack Britton, the thirty-six-year-old champion of the welter class who continued to baffle opponents, or simply got the bug from working with other fighters, nobody was quite certain, not even Attell. The *Sun* was quick to point out: "The difference between Attell and Britton is that the welter champion has fought steadily every year since he began his boxing career in 1905, while Attell practically retired after he was beaten by Kilbane in 1912."[66]

As people started realizing that Abe Attell had indeed hung up the gloves, more comments regarding his career surfaced. Al Lippe, who once managed the fighter, stated to the *Sun*: "Abe Attell was the greatest little fighter, in my opinion, that ever lived. He probably made more money in the ring than any other boxer and saved less. Today Abe, the idol of the fight fan, is a poor man…. He fought so often he seldom had time to train for any of his battles, but he always was in shape."[67]

John J. Reisler, promoter of the Tulsa Sporting Club—the gentleman who also happened to stage the Benny Leonard–Jimmy Duffy contest on November 17, 1919—had seen nearly every great fighter of the last three decades and had this to say regarding "The Little Champ": "The greatest fighter I ever saw was Abe Attell … as far as cleverness and ring generalship, there never was his equal." Reisler ranked Benny Leonard as the second greatest. As for Attell, he ranks George Dixon and Joe Gans as the two greatest fighters he ever saw.[68]

In a prelude to an association that would soon prove most noteworthy: Believing that he was about to be robbed for a third time by men who were raiding his crap game,

Arnold Rothstein, 35, of 355 West Thirty-fourth Street, shot two or possibly three, of eight policemen who descended upon him at an apartment in West Fifty-seventh Street and Eighth Avenue on January 19, 1919.[69] Thankfully, the police were not seriously injured. Rothstein, who had never been arrested by the police before, was charged with gambling, felonious assault and carrying concealed weapons. Nineteen other men were arrested and later released on $1,000 bail. One of those men was Abraham Attell. The police seized about five thousand dollars in evidence. The *Sun* noted, "They also found three sets of loaded dice, they said, and showed these to Abe Attell, one of the prisoners, who used to distribute wallops as a prize fighter and who told the police his bank roll had just received a knockout of $1,100 in five minutes."[70]

The *Manning Times* reported, "Rothstein, who is reputed to be a millionaire, is said to have told the police that he lost $28,000 to hold-up men who raided a crap game in Harlem two years ago, and that experience was repeated two weeks ago when he lost $11,000."[71]

On July 11, 1919, eighty-two days before the first game of the 1919 World Series, it took a parisian, in this case a writer for the local Tennessee newspaper, to remind us of the education we receive from sports:

> Sport teaches a square deal. Take it in any game of sport. It is not "good sport" to shoot a bird except on the wing; sporting blood gives the other fellow a chance always and there are laws of sportsmanship for every game that gives a square deal. Hear the fans howl when a baseball decision is seemingly unfair! The rules governing a prize fight, a horse race—any sport make them as fair as possible and any crookedness ruins a sport for a man of sporting blood.[72]

To believe that there must have been something in the air, one need only glance to the column left of the article. It dealt with business jealousy. More and more issues were being placed center stage for the general public to address. The paper claimed, "Betting and gambling have ruined sports to some degree today, and have thereby rendered certain sports taboo, but it is only a molly-coddle who thinks that there is nothing to sports except a gamble."[73]

The *New York Tribune*, Magazine and Review, became so frustrated with the issue that it ran a cover story on November 9, 1919, with the headline, "Saratoga's Choice: Famous Spa or Gambler's Mecca?" Writer Louis Lee Arms stated: "There is a fight going on in this little city which resembles in its tactical elements a military engagement. The proposition, in general terms, is whether Saratoga Springs is to put its own house in order and develop as the greatest watering resort on the American continent, or continue to play complaisant host during each August [Saratoga's one-month racing season] to the biggest and most sinister gambling interests in the country."[74] The city's preeminent bookmakers, led by John C. "Irish John" Cavanagh, would travel northwest to the placid town of Saratoga annually. The migration would take the town, population 15,000 in June, to over 40,000 by August.

The article continued, "Someone must feed these people; someone must supply the odds and ends that strike the human fancy; someone must provide that recreation which comes after racing hours. This is the Saratoga merchant; the proprietors of rooming and boarding houses and motion picture theater owners have done, in part, at an immense profit. The gambler's money is full panoplied with wings. He is a royal spender."[75]

Often making the journey north, not among Cavanagh's cronies but with his own entourage, was the businessman, gambler, racketeer and Jewish mob kingpin Arnold Rothstein. Nicknamed "The Brain," Rothstein took organized crime into places it had never dreamed of, and did so with the flair of a robber baron. The son of wealthy Jewish businessman Abraham Rothstein and his wife Esther, young Arnold, whose brother became a rabbi, proved that more than one apple could fall from the tree, and in his case, roll a considerable distance. And rolling was what got Arnold in trouble—dice, that is.

Rothstein soon became one of New York's foremost gamblers, a walking high-stakes floating dice and poker game. To walk safely in the evening streets of Manhattan required a bit of extra help, and that came in the form of bodyguards, one of whom was "The Little Champ." Attell's reputation spoke for itself, as did Rothstein's, but his fists spoke louder.

By 1910, the twenty-eight-year-old Rothstein had found a home in the Tenderloin section of Manhattan and owned a casino. It was through his business, not to mention his father's banking contacts, that he established a network that would be the envy of the finest security agencies in most countries.

Getting back to the January 19, 1919, incident and Rothstein's arrest, the *Tribune* reported:

> A motion to dismiss two indictments against Arnold Rothstein, charged with felonious assault upon Detectives McLaughlin and Walsh of Inspector Henry's staff, was granted yesterday by Judge McIntyre in General Sessions. In making his decision, Judge McIntyre criticized the District Attorney's office because "much time was spent and doubtless public money expended in an effort made to fasten the crime upon the defendant." The court also declared that "not a word of evidence appears in the grand jury minutes showing that the defendant committed an assault upon anybody."[76]

Rothstein's case was handled brilliantly by former City Magistrate Fuchs. In announcing the decision, Judge McIntyre, according to the same source, stated:

> The indictment among other things charges the defendant with having committed a felonious assault. It appears that the grand jury was engaged in conducting a John Doe proceeding covering a period of five months, in the course of which the grand jury saw fit to direct the lodgment of an indictment against the defendant. Under our system of jurisprudence, fortunately, a surmise, conjecture, or a guess can have no place as evidentiary of the commission of the crime. Why the grand jury ordered an indictment in this case is incomprehensible. It should not have been voted. It was idle to do so. The motion to dismiss is granted.[77]

CHAPTER THIRTEEN

The Black Sox Scandal of 1919, 1919–1921

"I see great things in baseball."—Walt Whitman

Postwar innocence was in full bloom as the first World Series after the close of World War I pitted the unyielding, or so it was believed, Chicago White Sox against the Cincinnati Reds.

The Reds, managed by Pat Moran, were led by outfielder Edd Roush, who won the National League batting title with an average of .321, and third baseman Heinie Groh, who hit .310 and finished three notches below his teammate.[1] Starters: catcher Ivey Wingo, first baseman Jake Daubert, second baseman Morrie Rath, shortstop Larry Kopf, outfielder Sherry Magee and outfielder Greasy Neale—all of whom hit .276 or below— rounded out the batting order. Impressive, the Reds managed to win 96 games, while losing only 44, thanks to a pitching staff anchored by Dutch Ruether (19–6, 1.82), Slim Sallee (21–7, 2.06), Ray Fisher (14–5, 2.17), Jimmy Ring (10–9, 2.26) and Hod Eller (19–9, 2.39).

The Sox of 1919, managed by Kid Gleason, were similar to the team that only two years earlier had won the World Series.[2] The American League champions were led by outfielder Shoeless Joe Jackson, who hit .351 (4th in AL), and second baseman Eddie Collins, who hit .319. Starters: catcher Ray Schalk, first baseman Chick Gandil, shortstop Swede Risberg, third baseman Buck Weaver, outfielder Nemo Leibold and outfielder Happy Felsch—all of whom hit .256 or above—completed their batting order. Imposing, the White Sox managed to win 88 games, while losing 52, thanks to a pitching staff anchored by Eddie Cicotte, who led the majors with 29 wins and 30 complete games while posting a 1.82 ERA (2nd in AL). Adding to the pitching strength of the White Sox: Lefty Williams (23–11, 2.64), Grover Lowdermilk (5–5, 2.79), Dickie Kerr (13–7, 2.88) and Red Faber (11–9, 3.83).

In 140 games, the Cincinnati Reds (.263 team average) won 8 games more, and lost 8 games less, than the Chicago White Sox (.287 team average) who scored 110 more runs over their opponents, while batting a bit better (+0.024). The Chicago White Sox, with a team ERA (earned run average) of 3.04, had two twenty-game winners in both Cicotte and Williams. The Cincinnati Reds, with a better team ERA (2.23, a difference of 0.81), had one twenty-game winner in Sallee, but two nineteen-game winners in Ruether and Eller. As good as the Chicago White Sox were, it's hard to describe them using the adjective invincible.

Left: Injuries reduced Edward Victor Cicotte to a 12–19 record in 1918, but in 1919, he rebounded to win 29 games and once again led the league in wins, winning percentage, and innings pitched, as well as in complete games. *Right:* After spending 1918 working in Navy shipyards, Claude Preston "Lefty" Williams came back strong in 1919 with his greatest performance, going 23–11 with a 2.64 earned run average (Library of Congress).

Positioning Statements

Statistics, or "dope" as it was called, tells only one story, as many were reminded by the great scribe Grantland Rice, who provided this view that appeared in the *Chattanooga News*: "In the same way, the Reds are quite likely to play much better ball than their personnel might indicate. Breaking the deadly spell of a fifty-year drought may hold them on the rampage, no matter how the White Sox work. Most of those doing the early topping have already picked Chicago by way of the man-to-man selection. But the Reds are quite likely to look better on the ball field than they do on copy paper when the post-season pot is opened."[3]

It was no surprise that league loyalty played a role in advance predictions. "The teams are so evenly matched that I look for a series that will write new baseball history," stated White Sox manager Kid Gleason.[4] This statement, printed on the very day his team entered the conflict, proved prophetic. As for his adversary, Reds manager Pat Moran, he claimed, "I know that Gleason is piloting a team that can furnish a crisis, but our boys never have fallen down and I am confident that they will rise to the occasion."

"In my judgment they are evenly matched," uttered Wilbert

William Jethro "Kid" Gleason became manager of the Chicago White Sox on December 31, 1918. In his first season, the team won the pennant but lost the World Series to the Cincinnati Reds, resulting in allegations that the White Sox had been paid by gamblers to "throw" the Series (Library of Congress).

Robinson, the respected manager of the Brooklyn Dodgers, who led his team to the National League pennant in 1916.[5] It was, however, a guarded statement that wasn't supported by the oddsmakers. The *Sun* reported,

> Chicago men are here [Cincinnati] with odds 7 to 5, but backers of the Reds say that they want 8 to 5 and even better, which on the face of it is entirely ridiculous and indicates that there is not among Cincinnati followers of baseball anything that bears even the faintest resemblance to an overpowering urge to bet on the Reds. This feeling seems to point to the fact that even in Cincinnati they recognize that discretion is the better part of valor.[6]

The Cincinnati Reds

As for those in the Reds' corner: "These games will be decided on the ball field and not in newspaper columns. I shall be pulling heartily for Pat Moran," voiced John McGraw (manager, New York Giants), a former World Series champion (1905). "I think Cincinnati can squeeze through a winner in the World Series," pronounced George Stallings (manager, Braves), a former World Series champion (1914). "While

As a manager, Pat Moran led two teams to their first-ever modern-era National League championships: the 1915 Philadelphia Phillies and the 1919 Cincinnati Reds (Library of Congress).

I think it will be a hard fought series I believe the edge is with the Reds, possibly five games out of nine," observed Hugo Bezdek (manager, Pittsburgh Pirates). "But remember breaks have often decided the series, and if Pat [Moran] can lick Cicotte in the opener I expect to see the Reds come out winners," analyzed Gavvy Cravath (manager, Philadelphia Nationals). "Moran is the most able handler of pitchers in the big leagues and his pitchers will win the series for him," Fred Mitchell (manager, Chicago Cubs), a former World Series loser (1918) was quick to remind. "The Reds have the punch to carry them through the series to victory," claimed Branch Rickey (manager, St. Louis Cardinals).[7] Not surprising, it was a partisan perspective.

The Chicago White Sox

As for the White Sox, allegiance also rang true: "I can't see anything but the White Sox. Cicotte and Williams ought to be good enough to work in four of the games," proclaimed Miller Huggins (manager, New York Yankees). "I think the White Sox will beat the Reds without much difficulty," declared Tris Speaker (manager, Cleveland Indians). "While I have the greatest respect for Moran I feel sure the Sox will win the series," observed Connie Mack (manager, Philadelphia Athletics), a former multiple World Series champion (1910, 1911, 1913). "The White Sox should win the World Series inside seven games," commented Clark Griffith (manager, Washington Senators). "The White Sox is the better team and will win," remarked Ed Barrow (manager, Boston Red Sox). "The Reds, no doubt, will put up a stubborn fight, but I think the White Sox will win," opined Hugh Jennings (manager, Detroit Americans), a multiple World Series loser (1907–1909). "The White Sox should win the World Series from the Reds," observed Jimmy Burke (manager, St. Louis Americans).[8]

Johnny Evers, called one of the brainiest players in the history of baseball, and a participant in three of the only five World Series in which the National League entry was victorious, picked the Reds to win. The *Topeka State Journal* noted:

> Many pages of figures have been written to show the superiority of the Sox, but dope based on such foundation does the Reds an injustice. In pitching, the Reds are superior to the Sox; and on the defense they are equal; in batting the Sox may have a bit of an edge. But the Reds are pinch players. They are just as surely a "money club" as the Sox. They play real baseball. They have "class" and they have one of the greatest managers in the game in command. These are the reasons I believe the Cincinnati Reds will be champions of the world when the last play of the final game is ticked over the wires.[9]

Since a majority of baseball fans were unable to attend the event, they found solace in newspaper coverage. Newsstands across the country became hubs for the exchange of information, with analysis beginning with the box score, before moving on to observation, as fans reconstructed the event. Coverage always began with the local daily. Naturally, news reports from the host cities drew the greatest attention. When fans were done reading their Chicago newspapers, they might swap it for one from Cincinnati, if they could be found; out-of-state papers, when delivered, could be days old, but still useful. In addition to the information exchange, it wasn't unusual to cast a wager or two at the newsstands. Most would read what commentary they could get hold of, or afford, then take the best odds they could find. Fans who couldn't afford a paper, such as kids, might wait nearby to grab a copy from the trash, then take it home to cut out the articles for their scrapbook or to hang on the wall. It wasn't unusual to swap issues to gain another perspective or to read your favorite columnist.

The World Series of 1919

Although most fall classics had been the best-of-seven format, the 1919 World Series was a best-of-nine series (along with 1903, and later 1920 and 1921). The new format was an attempt to capitalize on the growing popularity of the sport, by increasing both attendance and revenue.

Game Summaries: October 1, 1919—October 9, 1919

For each game a summary will be provided, including statistics, before points of interest are noted, followed by printed observations. All the material presented was available to a dedicated baseball fan.

GAME ONE

The 1919 World Series began on Wednesday, October 1, 1919, at Redland Field in Cincinnati, home to the National League Champion Cincinnati Reds. In front of 30,511 fans, the game remained close, a 1–1 tie, until the bottom of the fourth inning, when White Sox starting pitcher Eddie Cicotte, a talcum-powder ball specialist, lost control.[10] Giving up successive hits, climaxed by a two-out triple to the opposing starting pitcher Walter "Dutch" Ruether, Cicotte was then relieved by Wilkinson (4th inning), who was followed by Lowdermilk (9th inning). The Reds scored five times in the fourth and later added 3 more runs to enhance their 9–1 victory. Walter "Dutch" Ruether, who advanced 5 runners and drove in 3 runs, was the game's winning pitcher, while Cicotte took the loss.

Cincinnati advanced 19 runners, while Chicago only 5. The Reds had 14 hits to the White Sox' 6. Each team had only one error: Kopf (SS) for Cincinnati and Chick Gandil (1B) for the White Sox. Cincinnati left 7 on base, while Chicago 5.

Points of interest: Morrie Rath, the Reds leadoff hitter, let Cicotte's first pitch go by for a strike before being hit with the second pitch in the back. Later, Daubert (1B) was hit by Grover Lowdermilk. Both teams threw an equal number of strikes, 21. Two double plays were turned, both by Chicago. A grand total of 197 pitches were thrown by pitchers, 88 by Ruether and 109 by Chicago hurlers Cicotte (52), Roy Wilkinson (37) and Lowdermilk (20). After the game, Sox catcher Ray Schalk was quick to tell reporters that Cicotte had repeatedly crossed him up, or delivered a pitch he did not signal for.

Observations as printed in the *Sun*:

The first game of the 1919 series assuredly was one of the singular upsets peculiar to World's Series. It can only be compared with the first game of the 1914 series, when Rudolph, pitching his first world pennant game for the Braves, beat the veteran Athletics, 7 to 1. Chicago today was trounced even more severely.[11]

Eddie Cicotte, who piled up twenty-nine victories in the American League this year, was pounded by the Reds as though he were a busher. His famed mystery ball had nothing mysterious about it.[12]

However, he [Cicotte] received a similar trouncing once before this year. When the White Sox made their second visit to New York this year the Yankees turned on Knuckle Ball Eddie in the first game of a double header and pounded him for twelve hits and eight runs in five innings. It may be consoling news for American League rooters that two days later Cicotte recovered and shut out the Yankees.[13]

GAME TWO

On Thursday, October 2, 1919, the second game of the 1919 World Series was played at Redland Field in Cincinnati, in front of 29,690 fans. With the exception of the starting pitchers and catcher Rairden supplanting Wingo at catcher for Cincinnati, the lineups remained the same.

The Reds scored 3 of their 4 runs in the fourth inning, on the way to a 4–2 victory over the Chicago White Sox. Both teams had two double plays in a game that saw less run production and defensive efficiency; only six runs were scored, and twice as many errors were committed than in Game One. After giving up three runs, Williams pitched soundly, allowing only one additional run in his losing effort.[14]

Cincinnati advanced 10 runners, while Chicago only 6. The Reds had 4 hits, to the White Sox' 10. Chicago had one error: Risberg (1B), while Cincinnati had two: Daubert (1B) and Neale (RF). Cincinnati left 3 on base, while Chicago 7.

Points of interest: Chicago starting (and only) game hurler pitcher Claude "Lefty" Williams gave up six bases on balls but six fewer hits. He struck out only one batter. A total of 213 balls were pitched, 92 by winning pitcher Harry "Slim" Sallee and 121 by losing pitcher Williams. Reds' pitcher Salle was also charged with a balk in the sixth inning.

Chicago's Joe Jackson (CF) led all batters with three hits. On the World Series train back to Chicago, it was later learned that Charles Comiskey spoke to John Heydler, president of the National League, stating that his manager Kid Gleason believed there was funny business on the part of his players.

Observations as printed in the *New York Tribune*:

Williams was wilder today than Tarzan of the Apes roaming the African jungle from limb to limb.[15]

We have beaten Cicotte and Williams and have nothing to fear of the other pitchers on Gleason's staff, he [Moran] said.[16]

GAME THREE

On Friday, October 3, 1919, the third game of the 1919 World Series was played at Comiskey Park in Chicago, in front of 29,126 fans. It would prove to be the shortest in duration at one hour and thirty minutes. Cincinnati used the same lineup as the previous game, the only exception being right-handed pitcher Ray Fisher. Manager Gleason altered his cast of characters by replacing Eddie Collins with Nemo Leibold as a leadoff man and handing the ball to rookie pitcher Dickie Kerr.

The Sox scored two runs in the second—Chick Gandil driving in two runs—and one run in the fourth inning, as Kerr held the Reds to three hits in a 3–0 shutout.

Cincinnati advanced 3 runners, while Chicago moved 7. The Reds had 3 hits, to the White Sox' 7. Chicago had no errors, while Cincinnati had one: Fisher (P). Cincinnati left 3 on base, as did Chicago.

Points of interest: Kerr threw 99 pitches, while Reds' losing pitcher Ray Fisher tossed 81. Reds' reliever Luque hurled 13 pitches in the eighth. Each team popped eight flies and nearly an equal number of ground balls. Both teams turned one double play. Joe Jackson led all batters with two hits.

Cincinnati remained ahead in the series 2–1.

Observations as printed in the *Topeka State Journal* and *New York Tribune*:

In what little betting was reported today on the series the Reds were 8 to 5 favorites. On today's game there were some bets at even money, but in most cases the White Sox followers were demanding odds. There was plenty of Cincinnati money but few Chicago takers.[17]

Shortly before today's World Series game started, betting was 7 to 5 that Cincinnati would take today's pastime. Cincinnati backers were finding no difficulty in finding takers at those figures.[18]

Federal Judge [Kenesaw Mountain] Landis, who witnessed the Reds' first two victories in Cincinnati, adjourned court to witness today's game.[19]

GAME FOUR

On Saturday, October 4, 1919, the fourth game of the 1919 World Series was played at Comiskey Park in Chicago, in front of 34,363 fans. For the White Sox it was the return of starting pitcher Eddie Cicotte against the Reds' Jimmy Ring. The contest remained a pitching duel until the top of the fifth inning, when Cicotte fielded a Pat Duncan slow roller that got away from him. The wild throw to first resulted in a two-base error and began a one-out rally. Fumbling a cutoff throw from Jackson, Cicotte allowed Duncan to score. A double by Greasy Neale scored Kopf, making it 2–0, and that, along with some solid pitching by Ring, was enough to carry the Reds.

Cincinnati advanced 3 runners, to Chicago's 4. The Reds had 5 hits, to the White Sox' 3. Both teams had two errors: Cicotte (P) for Chicago had two, while Rath (2B) and Groh (3B) fumbled for Cincinnati. Cincinnati left only 1 on base, while Chicago left ten.

Points of interest: Cicotte cost himself the game with his errors, as his pitching statistics—balls, strikes, etc.—yield a steadier arm than Ring. The latter was a fastball pitcher who relied on White Sox pop-ups to get him through the game. Both pitchers went the distance, with Cicotte actually throwing one more strike (33) than Ring. Ring tossed 111 pitches, of which 44 were balls, while Cicotte threw 94 with only 27 balls. Wingo of the Reds led the hit parade with 2. The Sox turned the only two double plays.

The Reds led the series 3–1.

Observations as printed in the *New York Tribune*:

> The club that batted close to .300 for an entire season in the American League has earned exactly one run in four full ball games, and that lone tally resulted from a fluky triple and a fluky single linked together for a fluky run.[20]

> It will always be a mystery why the nerve of a pitcher like Cicotte, who has been through this thing so often before, should crack under the strain of the ballyhoo that goes with the World Series, while comparative infants like Ruether and Ring go into the thing as though it were just a ball game-and that is all it is, after all.[21]

> It was in the fifth inning that Cicotte lost his head and the ball game-Cicotte, winner of twenty-eight games in the regular season; Cicotte, who had been held as one of the coolest pitchers in a pinch in his league.[22]

GAME FIVE

On Monday, October 6, 1919, the fifth game of the 1919 World Series, originally scheduled for the previous day but postponed by rain, was played at Comiskey Park in Chicago, in front of 34,379 fans. It was another game that appeared as a pitching duel, between White Sox hurler Lefty Williams and Reds pitcher Hod Eller, until the bottom fell out for Chicago in the top of the sixth inning. The Reds scored four runs that inning. It was starting pitcher Eller who ironically sparked a rally when his blooper fell between Felsch and Jackson. The Reds added another run in the ninth to shut out the Sox 5–0.

Cincinnati advanced 11 runners, while Chicago only 1. The Reds had 4 hits, to the White Sox' 3. Chicago had three errors: Eddie Collins (2B), Felsch (CF) and Risberg (SS), while Cincinnati had none. Cincinnati left 3 on base, while Chicago 4.

Points of interest: Eller pitched solidly for the Reds and, once he gained the lead, seemed to never look back; he threw only five times in the sixth inning. Williams had three fewer strikes (43) and three more balls (28) than Eller, which isn't bad considering he was relieved by J. Erskine Mayer in the ninth inning. Buck Weaver (3b) led the hit parade with 2 of the Sox' three hits; Eller recorded nine strikeouts, including a then-World Series record six in a row.

The Cincinnati Reds were now only one win away from their first world championship.

Observations as printed in the *Sun* and *Evening Star*:

> Eller pitched one of the greatest games that ever won a World's Series today. He couldn't be touched, that's all. His feat of striking out six in a row will go down in World's Series history as one of the greatest achievements on a ball field.[23]

> World's Series are makers of baseball reputations, but they are also destroyers of reputation. Hap Felsch was regarded as baseball's greatest center fielder next to Tris Speaker before this series, but he will have a hard time proving it after today's game. One hit in five games doesn't help his reputation as a slugger either.[24]

> Betting on the series now is practically at a standstill. Reds' supporters are offering 2 to 1 and getting no takers, and even 3 to 1 finds Sox fans chary of risking their coin.[25]

GAME SIX

On Tuesday, October 7, 1919, the sixth game of the 1919 World Series was played at Redland Field in Cincinnati, in front of 32,006 fans. To stop the bleeding, the White Sox turned to the unlikely figure of Dickie Kerr, and although he was less dominant than in Game 3, he managed to stay on course—not an easy task when three errors allowed the Reds to jump to a 4–0 lead by the fourth inning. The Sox battled back, picking up a run in the fifth, three in the sixth, and a much-needed run in the tenth to claim the 5–4 victory.

Cincinnati advanced 5 runners, while Chicago moved 11. The Reds had 11 hits, to the White Sox' 10. Chicago had three errors: Risberg (1B) 2, Felsch (CF), while Cincinnati had none. Cincinnati left 8 on base, as did Chicago.

Points of interest: A hit parade for both clubs, as the Reds got eleven hits off Kerr, while Ruether and Ring were touched for ten. Kerr appeared to be the steadier hurler. Weaver and Neale led the hit parade, each with three. The Reds had three double plays, to the Sox' two. Dickie Kerr was now 2–0 in the series.

Observations as printed in the *Bismarck Tribune* and *Great Falls Daily Tribune*:

> Seven Cincinnati fans, business men, today bet $60,000 on the Reds winning today's World Series contest. The money was wagered in Chicago. They wagered $15,000 at odds on the first game. They doubled on the second and third games. Losing on the third game they dropped their betting to $15,000 won and then bet the $30,000 on the fifth game, which they also won. They then bet the $60,000 on the sixth game.[26]
>
> "I have every confidence that Cicotte can beat Cincinnati and may start him tomorrow, if I think he is right," claimed manager Gleason.[27]

GAME SEVEN

On Wednesday, October 8, 1919, the seventh game of the 1919 World Series was played at Redland Field in Cincinnati, in front of 13,923 fans. Despite Cicotte's erratic performance, not to mention a wealth of unfavorable rumors, Manager Gleason turned to his ace in Game 7. Cicotte wasn't brilliant, but he was steady. Threatening only in the sixth inning before losing 4–1, the Reds helped hang themselves with errors.

Cincinnati advanced only 4 runners, while Chicago moved 13. The Reds had 7 hits, to the White Sox' 10. Chicago had one error: Eddie Collins (2B), while Cincinnati had four: Rath (2B), Duabert (1B), Groh (3B) and Roush (RF). Cincinnati left 9 on base, while Chicago 7.

Points of interest: Harry "Slim" Sallee, the Reds' starting and losing pitcher, was lifted in the fifth inning—Ray Fisher relieved him for an inning, followed by Dolf Luque. Sallee now has a 1–1 record in the series. John Francis "Shano" Collins led the hit parade with 3. Dolf Luque pitched strong in Reds relief, striking out five of the White Sox batters in the four innings he pitched. Cicotte threw 120 pitches, 40 for balls, 34 for strikes and the rest as flies, grounders or fouls. The Reds turned the only double play of the game. Speculation, from those who believed the event not on the square, was rampant with regard to why the Sox won game six and seven. The first belief was that new money had entered the equation. Talk of a new syndicate of gamblers (the street now wise to the event) who favored Chicago was an underworld speculation. The second belief was that the players in on the fix hadn't been paid.

Observations as printed in the *New York Tribune*:

Between the highly fashionable hours of 2 and 4 p.m. on Tuesday afternoon the Reds were within one lone base hit of being champions of the world. This lone blow was all that separated them from the proudest title of the old game. Today they are on the verge on panic, with their big lead cut down to one game, most of their pitching staff blown to pieces and the abiding knowledge that if "Hod" Eller can't stem the rush the Sox will be champions of the world by Friday night.[28]

It's a strange thing, but the Sox have badly beaten the pitchers who defeated them before. Ruether was knocked out of the box and so was Sallee. The same thing will happen to Eller. The Sox played magnificent ball, outguessed the Reds, outbatted them, outplayed them and Cicotte outpitched them. I may start Williams tomorrow.[29]

The Sox today have tradition to back them up. Some seven years ago they opened with two drawn battles against the Cubs and then lost the next three straight. Out of five games they had failed to produce a victory. But with their broad backs to the wall they suddenly whirled and won the next four contests, a trick they now confidently expect to repeat with Lefty Williams now due, as Cicotte was, to grind out at least one victory from three starts.[30]

GAME EIGHT

On Thursday, October 9, 1919, the eighth, and deciding, game of the 1919 World Series was played at Comiskey Park in Chicago, in front of 32,930 fans. Lefty Williams gave up four straight one-out hits for three runs, in fifteen pitches, before a very disgruntled Gleason relieved him with Bill James in the first inning, followed later by Roy Wilkinson in the sixth. The Reds scored again in the second (5–0) and the fifth (6–1), before posting three runs in the sixth (9–1) and a final run in the eighth (10–1). The Sox managed to rally in the eighth to pick up 4 runs. The Reds came away with a 10–5 victory to take the series, 5–3.

Cincinnati advanced 24 runners, while Chicago only 11. The Reds had 16 hits, to the White Sox' 10. Chicago had one error: Schalk (C), while Cincinnati had two: Roush (CF) and Rariden (C). Cincinnati left 12 on base, while Chicago 8.

Points of interest: Joe Jackson hit the only homer of the Series, a solo shot in the third inning after the Reds had a commanding lead. Wilkinson, the last pitcher used by Chicago, actually had the best inning, the ninth, when he threw only seven times. Lefty Williams took the final loss, leaving him 0–3 for the series. Hod Eller picked up the win, giving him a 2–0 series record. Advance word, backed by reports from some who covered the event including Fred Lieb, was that Williams would pitch game eight and that it would be over early.[31]

Observations as printed in the *Chattanooga News* and *El Paso Herald*:

Claude Williams, twice beaten by the Reds, was sent back at them today and Kid Gleason insisted that "no ball club in the world can beat Williams three games in a row." That was one of the reasons why White Sox backers offered 6 to 5 that their favorites would win the contest.[32]

It was the anniversary of the day that Mrs. O'Leary's cow kicked Chicago over and Thursday it was Claude Williams who kicked the lamp. Williams has worked three games in this series, not one of them up to within 20 percent of his American League standard. He has thrown away two by bases on balls, by crossing his catcher and not by allowing hits.[33]

The players on the Cincinnati team, by annexing Thursday's contest and thereby capturing the series, will receive $117, 157.68, which divided into 22½ shares will net each share $5,207.01. (Three players were allotted only a half share.) The White Sox will draw down $78,104.70 and each of the 24 players will receive $3,254.36.[34]

For most baseball fans, summer ended with the final out of the World Series, which in this case occurred on October 9. For a day or two after, fans might be interested in a particular analysis or summary, but for the most part baseball had completed its annual cycle. The newspapers that fans had so much demanded only the week before, now rested in undisturbed stacks on the stand. Why spend two cents on a final edition of the *(New York) Sun* or three cents on the *New York Tribune*, when you could just grab a local daily for news?

The Early Word

Writer Wilton S. Farnsworth, writing for the *New York American*, learned on October 30, 1919, that Arnold Rothstein, the well-known gambler, was approached and informed that for $20,000 he could clean up a fortune by wagering on the Cincinnati Reds to defeat the Chicago White Sox during the recent World Series.[35] The *Times and Farmer* noted, "The alleged scheme was to 'buy' a party who would see that the White Sox were defeated. The *American* also learned that two telegrams were sent to a former champion fighter in Cincinnati from New York the day before the series opened, which were signed 'A.R.,' Rothstein's initials."[36] When approached by the former fighter, Rothstein insisted that he spurned the offer. According to the same source, "I have heard rumors that I was mixed up in such a deal," Rothstein said, "but it's a lie. I do not want to be called a 'copper,' but I feel that it is time for me to spike these reports and protect my reputation."[37]

Rothstein did confirm that he was approached and told of the details as indicated above, but denied his involvement, saying, "I replied to him as follows: 'Get away from me, you rat; I don't believe you can do such a thing, and even if you could I don't want anything to do with it.'"[38]

Rothstein then continued, the *Times and Farmer* noted: "The man, however, was persistent and said: 'I am going to Cincinnati and if everything is all right I will send you a telegram.' Again I called the man a rat and told him to move along as I didn't want to be seen in his company. A night or two later, during dinner at home, the long-distance telephone operator called, saying that this former champion fighter wanted to talk to me from Cincinnati. I told my servant to say that I was not home."[39] Again, Rothstein uses the descriptor "former champion fighter," which clearly restricts an identity selection, instead of the name of the individual.[40]

The *Times and Farmer* continued: "The 'fixer,' however, must have informed the party that was to arrange the alleged deal whereby the White Sox would lose, that I had agreed to back the plan. For I have learned that he telephoned a friend here to rush him a telegram saying: 'EVERYTHING IS O.K.,' and signed my initials."[41] The word "fixer" purposefully places the association on another individual, thus Rothstein's use of the term. He obviously knew the content of the telegram and added: "Later he must have been told to get more assurance that I was in on the deal, for this same friend sent him another telegram, the wording of which I do not know, but which was signed 'A.R.'"[42]

Some sources indicated that the sender of the telegram was "a Broadway 'grifter' (petty swindler) who recently was arrested on a charge of white slavery." Rothstein knew that the former champion was in Chicago and expected to return to New York shortly. He didn't say how he knew. "And when he gets back I'll make him tell the true story," declared Rothstein. He did not say how he would accomplish the task.[43]

Instead of having "legs," this story appeared ready to die a slow death.

A Slow Start

Enter Hugh Stuart Fullerton, one of America's most influential sportswriter of the first half of the 20th century, who really gave the story its legs.[44] Born on September 10, 1873, in Ohio, Fullerton carried his journalistic dreams to Chicago, where they welcomed his colorful style. Among the first to use player quotes in sports reports—his methodology an influence on others, including Ring Lardner and Grantland Rice—Fullerton and his approach grew in popularity. Fullerton knew baseball, having made a name for himself by predicting the White Sox over the Cubs in 1906, and he knew Chicago from all sides. Tipped off by gamblers, prior to the 1919 World Series, that the event was not on the square, he wouldn't let the story rest.

Fullerton reported on December 17, 1919, in the *Evening World*: "Charles A. Comiskey, owner of the Chicago White Sox and one of the greatest characters baseball ever has produced, a man of undoubted honesty and of the highest type of sportsmanship, has stated in Chicago that, after two months of work by detectives and others, he has been unable to find evidence that there was dishonesty among the players of his team during the recent World Series."[45]

Never bashful about his approach, with its psychological undertones, Fullerton also claimed in the same work that Comiskey had had "detectives working since the night of the second game of the series in Cincinnati, when one of the best known gamblers in the country went to him and told him the stories that were being circulated through the underworld of sport."[46]

The gambler was said to have made no accusations but did identify where the money was coming from. Fullerton was just relentless, throwing lines like Cicotte's knucklers: "The fans and the public generally will not stand for a verdict of 'not proved.' They demand to know the facts."[47]

Tenacious in his pursuit, Fullerton then had the effrontery to list the fans' two demands in the piece: "Either a verdict of guilty with a penalty of expulsion from baseball, or a verdict of not guilty, with whatever punishment may be inflicted upon those responsible for the stories concerning the series."[48] With this single statement, an audacious sportswriter altered history by demanding that a professional team owner, and a sport, account for their actions.[49]

Then, in a virtuous moment, Fullerton handed us the commandment: "It is not the seven players who are indicted by common gossip that are on trial. It is the good name of baseball and the honesty of the hundreds of players who are not mentioned."[50] Amen.

Major League Baseball, especially Comiskey, didn't need this any more than they needed nine games to prove a point. Nor did the gamblers, at least the ones who lined their pockets. "The players who are accused are entitled to an opportunity to defend themselves from the charges. And, the fans are entitled to know whether baseball is on the square."[51]

Fullerton, not Major League Baseball, then proposed Judge Kenesaw M. Landis, of the United States District Court for the Northern District of Illinois, be requested to hear all witnesses and return a verdict.[52] In addition to the players, the following people should appear before him to tell him their stories: "Karl Zork, a shirt waist manufacturer and sporting man of St. Louis; Ben and Lou Levy (Levi), of Des Moines, IA; Abe Attell, former lightweight champion boxer; Bill Burns, a former left-handed pitcher, who was with the Chicago White Sox and with the Cincinnati Reds[53]; Joe Pesch, a gambler of St.

Judge Kenesaw Mountain Landis was an American jurist who served as a federal judge from 1905 to 1922 and as the first Commissioner of Baseball from 1920 until his death (Library of Congress).

Louis[54]; a theatrical man named Redmond of East St. Louis; a gambler named, or called Eddie of Boston; and a gambler called Tim, said to be well-known in Des Moines, IA."[55]

The words from the *Evening World* continued:

> Next let him call before him Mont Tennes, chief of the gambling fraternity of Chicago, who, in spite of his business is known as a loyal lover of baseball, and Arnold Rothstein of New York, who was mentioned in connection with the scandal through telegrams to which he declares his initials were signed.[56] He then can call the detectives employed by Comiskey, Kid Gleason, manager of the White Sox, Sam Pass of Chicago, one of Gleason's friends,[57] *Collyer*, a sporting sheet publisher in Chicago, and such reporters as James Cruisenberry of the *Chicago Tribune* and Ed Wray of St. Louis.[58]

Fullerton went on to list himself, along with Ray Schalk and Eddie Collins. But many, including wordsmith Frederick G. Lieb do not believe Fullerton; others even accuse Fullerton of being one of those who lost money on the Sox. The *Sun* noted, "The Western writer asks that a lot of gamblers be summoned and asked what they know about this affair. To this one baseball man said: 'I wouldn't believe a gambler's testimony if he stood on a stack of Bibles as high as the Woolworth Building.'"[59]

Lieb, writing for the *Sun*, was quick to point out:

> In 1909, when the Pirates and Tigers took turns on winning on alternate days, there were rumors that thing was being dragged out; then in 1912 there again were stories that everything was not all right and there were stories of gamblers fixing players just as there were after the 1919 series. That is the

series in which the Red Sox had the big edge, three games to one, but the Giants came back and tied the series with two one-sided victories. The eighth game, the one in which Snodgrass made his famous muff and Merkle his famous lapse at first, resulted in a tenth inning Boston victory and enabled the Red Sox to win the championship.[60]

In the latter case, suspicion was aroused when Owner Jimmy "Loafer" McAleer refused to let Smoky Joe Wood pitch game six, a contest Boston would have won, making it four games to one, one game having resulted in a tie. Wood had already posted two impressive wins and anticipated the call. As printed in the *Sun*:

> His brother was known to have had a good sized sum bet on the game, but on the train coming from Boston to New York McAleer told Manager Stahl to pitch O'Brien, who had lost the only Boston game so far. O'Brien was knocked out of the box in one inning, the Giants scoring five runs in that frame. After the game, Wood and O'Brien had a fistfight in the Polo Grounds clubhouse and there were some ugly rumors. McAleer's argument was that he pitched O'Brien so that if Buck lost he would have an ace in the hole for the next game in Boston. This argument was generally accepted, but there were persons unkind enough to say that McAleer wasn't particularly displeased when the Red Sox lost the New York game.[61]

Leib mentions the telegrams that Abe Attell was supposed to have sent to Arnold Rothstein, and the stress met by the Forty-second Street gambling fraternity, but points out: "At the Latonia track the day before the Series, a hot tip was put out by some of the 'regulars' to go heavy on the Reds for the first game, the story having got out that Cicotte was not right."[62] He also described a supposed effort to get two of Moran's pitchers drunk before the start of the series, then points out: "But if it is true that the Sox were fixed, the element which attempted to 'liquor up' Moran's pitchers evidently was working the other way."[63]

1920

In between attempts to keep the baseball conspiracy story alive, newspapers were slowly realizing just how incredibly talented a now retired boxer was. The *Times* noted, "Abe Attell was one of the greatest feathers the ring ever produced. He thought nothing of tackling the best lightweights and holding his own with them."[64]

Just over three weeks after the printing of the assessment above, Attell again made the *Tribune*, and not in the way one might expect: "Fifteen witnesses have been summoned to appear before the extraordinary grand jury today in connection with inquiries growing out of the investigation into rumors that money was passed to bring about the liberation of Arnold Rothstein, gambler, who was charged with shooting two detectives."[65] A rumor to the effect that $32,000 had been split between former city magistrate Emil Fuchs, a member of District Attorney Swann's staff, and a newspaperman, came to the attention of the mayor's office. Fuchs stated there was no proof substantiating the bribe rumor. Abe Attell was one of those subpoenaed.

Meanwhile, Attell was being tried in the court of public opinion. The former boxer was evicted from the 4th Regiment Armory in Jersey City, during the Benny Leonard and Johnny Dundee fight (their eighth meeting) for flashing a roll and offering to lay odds on the main event. According to the *Tribune*: "The house was jammed at the time and Abe, uttering loud protests, was pushed through the crowd."[66] The behavior, by the way, was not unusual at such an event. The newspaper was quick to point out: "The

Jersey police ejected some of the known gamblers whose names were mentioned in connection with the alleged World Series scandal."[67]

On Wednesday, April 14, 1920, Lefty Williams picked up his first win of the season in the very first game, as the Chicago White Sox defeated the Detroit Tigers 3–2. Manager Kid Gleason's batting order on this day: Nemo Leibold (RF), Buck Weaver (3B), Eddie Collins (2B), Shoeless Joe Jackson (LF), Happy Felsch (CF), Ted Jourdan (1B), Swede Risberg (SS), Ray Schalk (C) and Lefty Williams (P). The only notable difference in the lineup, when compared to last season's "Opening Day," was the absence of a now retired Chick Gandil, who had been replaced by Jourdan.

Also garnering press was "The Little Champ's" namesake: "Abe Attell Goldstein, who is making quite a reputation as a classy bantamweight in the East, is being cleverly handled by Willie Lewis, the old middleweight boxer."[68] One can only hope that he too wouldn't be subject to such public humiliation.

Attell was saddened to learn of the suicide of one of his former sparring partners, Domenico Santora, known as Monte Tyler, on July 3. The body of the bantamweight boxer was found in Chicago hotel room.

From a positive perspective, the *Times* offered:

> There's another prospective champion up in the Attell family. The new Attell's name is Gilbert. He is fifteen years of age and is a nephew of Abie, of Monte, and of course, also of Caesar. Gilbert Attell was one of the Columbia Park boys who were returning home from the Orient. On the Fourth of July a show was given on board, with boxing as a feature. Gilbert volunteered to take part in one of the bouts, and his skill with the gloves surprised all onlookers. Now, before long, we suppose Gilbert will be heard from among the regular local boxers, though as yet he has not intimated that he has ambitions for a prize ring career.[69]

The Initial Investigation

Four hundred and two days after Wilton S. Farnsworth penned his article for the *New York American*, H.H. Brigham, foreman of the Cook County Grand Jury investigating alleged baseball gambling, informed the public that they now had some names.

On September 24, 1920, the headline was front-page news in the *New York Tribune*: "Grand Jury Finds World Series 'Fixer.'" H.H. Brigham told newspaper reporters that the name of the man who "fixed" the 1919 world's series for Cincinnati to win had been given to the grand jury. This man, Brigham stated, acted as a representative of a ring of gamblers, who offered Chicago White Sox players money to throw games to the Cincinnati Reds.[70]

Testimony, according to the article, had prompted the grand jury to subpoena: "Arnold Rothstein, of New York, millionaire turfman and controlling owner of the Havre de Grace racetrack; William Burns, former Chicago American and Cincinnati National League pitcher; Abe Attell, former featherweight boxing champion, and several other well-known sportsmen."[71]

The word printed by some sources, including the *Chattanooga News*, claimed: "Hal Chase [one of the other well-known sportsmen] approached Abe Attell to see if the boxer had a connection that would pay $100,000 to have the Series 'fixed.'[72] Attell was said to have approached Rothstein, who declined. Attell was alleged, however, to have reported to Chase that the deal had been made."[73]

The piece continued: "The members of the White Sox who were involved were to be paid $15,000 after the first game was lost, and the balance in regular installments until the series ended. Attell is said to have obtained backing for his scheme by interesting a number of well-known eastern gamblers who came to Chicago before the World's Series, established betting headquarters, and won heavily by taking all the Chicago money offered on the White Sox."[74]

It was also noted: "Verification of disclosures naming Abe Attell, former featherweight champion, and a number of New York gamblers in connection with the $100,000 bribe with which the 1919 World's Series is alleged to have been 'fixed' in favor of Cincinnati, was received today from Charles A. Comiskey, owner of the White Sox."[75]

The *Chattanooga News* printed: "Comiskey admitted that in his investigations after the Series last fall, he had received reports similar in every detail to those now before the grand jury. He refused to make a detailed statement regarding them, however, until the grand jury completes its investigation."[76]

Mr. Brigham, speaking for the Cook County grand jury, stated "positively that there had been 'crooked work' in organized baseball."[77] The statement came at the same time that Charles A. Comiskey "criticized Ban Johnson, president of the American League, for failure to cooperate in the investigation of charges of crookedness leveled against the Chicago teams."[78]

The grand jury, which was to be dissolved on September 30, would be retained as a special inquisitorial body to probe further the charges of crookedness in baseball. It was also noted that New York Giants pitcher Rube Benton made sensational charges "that a pool of $100,000 was paid to certain White Sox players by a Pittsburgh gambling syndicate for the 'throwing' of the world's series [*sic*] between the Chicago White Sox and the Cincinnati Reds."[79] Heine Zimmerman, Eddie Cicotte and Phillip Hahn all denied Benton's claims.

Ban Johnson also reported a rumor "that the same gambling syndicate which is said to have operated so successfully last year had threatened certain White Sox players with exposure unless they agreed to 'throw' games this year."[80] Also disclosed was the investigation of the mails for possible misuse, and that a number of new witnesses would be called, including George M. Cohan, theatrical producer, who is said to have lost $30,000 on the series; Mont Tennes, believed to have lost $80,000 in the same manner; and John A. Heydler, president of the National League.

It was reported on September 27 that several members of the Chicago White Sox will be asked questions by the Cook County grand jury about reports that Fred McMullin, a White Sox utility player and friend of Abe Attell, distributed mysterious packages, perhaps containing money, to other members of his team during the last week of the World Series. The *Washington Times* reported: "Charles Weighman, president of the Chicago Cubs, has reiterated charges made last fall that the outcome of the inter-league contest was a foregone conclusion as early as August of 1919. He based his statement on a 'tip' he declared he received (while in Saratoga, NY in August) from Mont Tennes, Chicago gambler, who is said to have lost $30,000 betting on the White Sox."[81] Weighman went on to state: "I know Rothstein would bet his shirt if he thought he was right. He has a lot of money and bets freely, but I doubt whether he would permit himself to be mixed up in an affair like this. I think he is on the square."[82]

In another twist, United States Attorney Charles F. Clyne stated to the *Tribune*: "The baseball pool that is sold in every large city in the United States is put out by a syndicate

American League club presidents: (standing, from left) Frank Navin, Detroit; Benjamin S. Minor, Washington; Frank Farrell, New York; (seated) Charles Comiskey, Chicago; Ban Johnson, AL President; Joseph Lannin, Boston (Library of Congress).

in Greencastle, Indiana. These pools have a very bad effect on the baseball public. Thus the fans get accustomed to baseball betting."[83]

The previous year, not only had there been a clash of baseball talent, but two opposing cliques of gamblers are said to have vied with one another in trying to make certain the losses of the teams they were betting against. The *Washington Times* ran the front-page news: "EIGHT WHITE SOX BALL PLAYERS INDICTED" was the headline on September 28, 1920.

Indictments against eight members of the Chicago White Sox for alleged crookedness in the 1919 World's Series were voted this afternoon by the Cook County grand jury, which has been probing conditions in organized baseball. The men indicted are: Chick Gandil, former first baseman; Fred McMullin, utility infielder; Happy Felsch, center fielder; 'Swede' Risberg, shortstop; Eddie Cicotte, pitcher; Joe Jackson, left field; and Buck Weaver, third baseman. The true bills charge conspiracy to commit an illegal act.[84]

Three hundred and fifty-five days had passed since the final pitch of the 1919 World Series.

Former prizefighter William Maharg was one of the witnesses likely to be subpoenaed. His reported confession in Philadelphia that he and Bill Burns, former White Sox pitcher, were involved in the conspiracy soon became the latest sensation of the probe.[85] The *Times* reported:

Maharg's confession that the White Sox were bribed to throw the Series for $100,000 but they received only $10,000 and his charge that Eddie Cicotte, the pitcher was the Sox player who made the offer to "throw" the Series has aroused a storm of interest. According to Maharg's story he met Bill Burns, an old friend, in New York, and Cicotte approached Burns in a room at the Ansonia Hotel with an offer to "throw" the Series if Burns could find someone to put up $100,000. Burns talked it over with Maharg and then went to Arnold Rothstein, New York gambler, with the proposition.[86]

Maharg then names Attell, according to the *Times*:

Rothstein, Maharg said, turned the scheme down but later Burns telegraphed him that Rothstein had "gone through." Burns afterward told Maharg, he says, that he had encountered Abe Attell and that Attell had "fixed things" with Rothstein. Attell came to Cincinnati, Maharg said, with a bunch of gamblers and established headquarters at the Sinton Hotel. Burns and Maharg went there to get the $100, 000 from Attell to turn over to the White Sox players. Attell "stalled them off," Maharg said, claiming that they needed the money to bet on games. Attell finally gave them $10,000, Maharg said, but the remaining $90,000 was never paid. Maharg charges that Attell and his friends cleaned up a fortune but "double crossed" the Sox. Burns and Maharg, the confession says, lost large sums betting on the third game of the Series, which the White Sox won, under the belief that it also had been "fixed" for Cincinnati to win.[87]

Immediately after his eight players were indicted, Charles A. Comiskey, through his attorney, Alfred S. Austrian, sent the following message, which was printed in the *Tribune*, to each player:

You and each of you are hereby notified of your indefinite suspension as a member of the Chicago American League Baseball club. Your suspension is brought about by information, which has just come to me directly involving you and each of you in the baseball scandal (now being investigated by the present grand jury of Cook County) resulting from the world series of 1919. If you are innocent of any wrongdoing you and each of you will be reinstated; if you are guilty you will be retired from organized baseball for the rest of your lives, if I can accomplish it. Until there is a finality to this investigation it is due to the public that I take this action, even though its costs Chicago the pennant.[88]

The column to the left of the Comiskey letter in the *New York Tribune* read: "Attell Angry, Will Expose Series Plot, Ex-Pugilist Declares He'll 'Raise the Lid Sky High' With Story of Deal at Astor." Abe Attell, none too happy with the accusations being made by Billy Maharg, said he intended to "shoot the lid sky high."

Finding Attell near a scoreboard in Times Square, where he was chatting with friends, the boxer responded: "You can say that the story placing the responsibility upon me for passing the $100,000 to the White Sox is a lie. It looks to me that Rothstein is behind these stories, and I am surprised at this, because I have been a good friend of Rothstein."[89]

Attell took a breath and continued positioning himself to the *Tribune*: "You can see that someone is trying to make it appear that I was responsible for the 'deal' at the Astor. Well, I can tell you that I was not responsible for it. I will tell what I know about it at the proper time. Rothstein, I know, is trying to whitewash himself. Nobody can pass the buck to me. Maharg's story of the fake telegrams and all the rest, as far as I am concerned, is all bunk. I am not ready to tell you what I know just yet."[90]

According to the "*Trib*," Attell then returned to Rothstein: "I have done many things for Rothstein, and when he didn't have a cent I fed him and boarded him and even suffered a broken nose in defending him from a bootblack in Saratoga. We have not been on the best of terms for the last year, but I didn't think he would open up this way."[91]

A member of Rothstein's family spoke on his behalf from a residence at 355 West Eighty-fourth Street, as Arnold Rothstein was unavailable for comment: "You can say that Maharg's story with regard to the meeting in the Hotel Astor is substantially correct.

Arnold Rothstein was never in on the deal at any stage. He told me he was much surprised when the proposition was put to him, and declared to Burns and the other man present that he didn't even think it could be done. The other man, Arnold said, was a stoutish fellow of medium height, and he didn't know if it was Maharg or not."[92]

The family member then addressed Attell:

> A few days after he turned these fellows down Arnold was approached by Attell but again he refused to have anything to do with the proposition. Arnold never sent any telegrams to Attell at Cincinnati during the World Series, and if Attell says that he received any money or telegrams from him at that time you can say that Arnold Rothstein says its untrue. Why should he be sending telegrams when he didn't have a thing to do with the matter? As for Attell's statement that the present stories originated with Arnold, I am sure from what Arnold told me that Burns and Attell themselves did the talking.
>
> Rothstein simply wants it known that he had nothing to do with the proposition at any time.[93]

When the indictments hit, the confessions followed. The Illinois State Attorney soon had signed confessions from Jackson, Cicotte and Williams, with Felsch professing his guilt to members of the press. The *South Bend News-Times* penned: "Cicotte, according to the court attaches, told the grand jury he received $10,000 from gamblers, finding the money under his pillow when he returned to his hotel room on the night before the first game at Cincinnati. 'I refused to pitch a ball until I got it,' they quoted him as saying. Jackson, it was said, testified he was promised $20,000 by 'Chick' Gandil, but received only $5,000. Claude Williams, according to witnesses, got $10,000."[94]

Cicotte himself, according to the piece, was trying to put the picture together: "The court officials also quoted Cicotte as saying that the players had believed that 'Chick' Gandil had 'double-crossed' them and that Maharg's story was the first intimation they had that Attell had 'held out' on them."[95]

On September 29, two more indictments were handed down: Those indictments were of "Sport" Sullivan, a Boston gambler, accused by "Lefty" Williams of fixing players; and a companion of Sullivan's named Brown of New York.[96] Assistant State's Attorney Replogle, in charge of the grand jury examination, believed both Sullivan and Brown, an alias, were agents for Arnold Rothstein and associates of Abe Attell.

Felsch spoke of Attell to the *Sun and New York Herald*: "Who was responsible for the double-cross I can't say. I suspect Gandil, because he was the wisest one of the lot and had sense enough to get out of baseball before the crash came. But I have heard since that it was Attell. Maybe it was Attell. I don't know him, but I had heard that he was mixed up with the gamblers who were backing us to lose."[97]

Williams fingered Brown and Sullivan as the linchpins for the enterprise, according to the same source, and added: "I was supposed to get $10,000 after the second game when we got back to Chicago, and I didn't get this until after the fourth game, and then he [Gandil] said that the gamblers had called it off, and I figured then that there was a double-cross some place. Gandil informed me in Cincinnati that Bill Burns and Abe Attell were fixing it so that we could get $100,000, making $20,000 more. That I never received."[98]

Attell, through his retained counsel, William J. Fallon, insisted that he was not the head of the gambling ring in the fixing affair.[99] Mr. Fallon stated, according to the *Tribune*, from his office in the Singer Building:

> Mr. Attell has done nothing dishonorable. He has absolutely nothing to conceal, and in due time his story will be fully told. While stories issuing from Chicago do not place Mr. Attell in as satisfactory a position as might be hoped, the fact is that at least two of the so-called important witnesses have

Left: The distinctive smile of Charles Arnold "Chick" Gandil. It was in his first season with the Senators that he met bookie and gambler "Sport" Sullivan. *Right:* Joseph J. "Sport" Sullivan (1870–1949) was an American bookmaker and gambler from Boston who was a pivotal player in the 1919 Black Sox Scandal (Library of Congress).

deliberately lied where they touched on my client's connection with the matter. We shall offer proofs to show they were absolute falsehoods. They have done my client a grave injustice, but you can rest assured he will be vindicated.[100]

Attell told a reporter for the *Evening World*: "I never acted as a 'fixer.' There is some mastermind, which has evolved and operated the whole scheme; of course he was assisted by several others. His name and their name I know. But I do not care to reveal them at the present time. To the best of my knowledge, ten gamblers made at least $250,000. Later, I shall give names and particulars."[101] Attell then dropped out of sight and was reported to be somewhere in Philadelphia on September 30.

Meanwhile, Fullerton would not rest and penned for the *World*:

What man financed the disgrace of the American National sport? It was not Bill Burns.... It was not Abe Attell.... Attell has had money in large amounts, but never that large, and during the last few years up to a time a day or two prior to the World Series he was rated as being 'close to the cushion.' It was not Maharg.... It was not the St. Louis manufacturer whose name has been freely mentioned. It was not the Des Moines brothers who have been mentioned ever since the deal. The ball players, eight of them, received, according to their stories, $65,000. It is charged that Chick Gandil got away with about $50,000, according to ball player estimates, and that it was given him to divide among the players....[102]

Fullerton then laid it on the line by noting: "Plainly, allowing for the turnover of money won and the betting on credit, there was more than $300,00 actual money needed to finance the plot. It is not enough to convict and disgrace a bunch of ball players. To cleanse the game the authorities must get the man or the men at the top. FIND THE MAN WHO WIRED MONEY TO ATTELL AND BURNS."[103]

According to State Attorney Maclay Hoyne: "I am convinced that the whole affair grew out of the gigantic pool-selling schemes that have been prevalent for some time. If we could get at the bottom of these we could have clean baseball."[104]

The prosecutor also commented on penalties to the *Tribune*: "The crime of gambling or conspiring to gamble is a misdemeanor in Illinois. If the players received bribes to throw the 1919 Series they could be punished under a law prohibiting conspiracy to gamble. The penalty is a small fine or jail for not more than six months. Indictments for general conspiracy would make possible a ten-year term."[105]

On October 2, 1920, it was stated that District Attorney Swann had three subpoena servers hunting for Abe Attell. Word came on October 15 that Attell was residing in Montreal, Canada; he had been living there, it was believed, since the investigation began. Also, the Cook County grand jury investigating the baseball scandal issued a subpoena for Arnold Rothstein of New York, and three St. Louis men: Harry Redmond,[106] Joseph Pasch (Pesch)[107] and Thomas G. Kearney.[108]

By October 22, it was printed in the *Morning Tulsa Daily World*:

> Indictments against 13 persons believed to have been implicated in the 'throwing' of games in the 1919 World Series were returned by the special Cook County grand jury, which has been investigating the baseball scandal for more than a month. Judgments against 10 of the men named today previously had been voted, but were revoted to overcome legal technicalities, while the other three—Abe Attell, Hal Chase and William Burns—had only been unofficially mentioned in connection with the investigation. All the indictments charge conspiracy to commit an illegal act, a crime for which a penitentiary sentence can be given under the laws of Illinois.[109]

On October 26, following the testimony of St. Louis American League second baseman Joe Gedeon, someone believed to have been at the wrong place at the wrong time, and Arnold Rothstein of New York, both men were exonerated from complicity in the throwing of games in the 1919 World Series.[110] That was the word out of Chicago. For the record: Rothstein said he lost $6,000 on the series, while Gedeon said he won $600.

Attell gave out a statement from Montreal on October 29 that appeared in the *Farmer*:

> The Chicago players received $60,000 or $70,000. Where did it come from? At the time of the World Series I was broke. Five days before, I sold my wife's platinum and gold wedding ring for $125 to a man in Chicago. When I went to New York City to borrow money, I was given the information about the Series by Hal Chase and Bill Burns. I first met Burns in Philadelphia, where I was watching a double-header with Cincinnati. At this game he and a prizefighter named Mohawk had Chase throw four games to Philadelphia, and I myself lost $4,000. At that time there was a boy on the field betting for Chase and Burns. The boy's father kept the hotel where Burns and Chase and all the players were staying.[111]

Attell then added more to the Burns pitch:

> Burns had been told that I was a friend of Arnold Rothstein, and after the game he came to me and told me that if he had known who I was he wouldn't have let me down. He added that some time he would see that I get even. It was because of this that when I met him at the Polo Grounds in New York he told me to get as much money as I could together and bet it all on Cincinnati to win the World Series. He said that it was all fixed, and that gamblers had been all over the country arranging it.[112]

Attell then pinpointed the source: "Joe Gedeon, Bill Burns and Mohawk arranged the whole thing. They went town to town to get as many gamblers as they could to put up money and lay bets. I spoke to Rothstein about the proposition, but he knew of it already and told me so. Bill Burns, who had been to him with a proposition, had already warned him."[113]

To elaborate on Rothstein, Attell added:

Rothstein is worth about $4,000,000 or $5,000,000 which he has got by his wits. He has always been a gambler, and has financed anything or everything. District Attorney Swann of New York says he has evidence against Rothstein that Rothstein told men Chicago would win the series and that he then sent his men to bet on Cincinnati. In New York City, Rothstein said he lost $70,000 on the World's Series, but before the Grand Jury in Chicago, he says he lost only $6,000. Between twenty-five and thirty persons went down to Mr. Swann's office in New York simply to say what a fine fellow Rothstein was. Mr. Swann himself asked: What did they do for it?[114]

Attell then recalled the January shooting, according to the *Farmer*:

At the time of a certain shooting scrape in New York last year I was in the room. Everybody knew who shot the two policemen. After the shooting everybody was in an uproar, and the man who did the shooting said he thought they were holdup men. He told inspector Henry not to get excited and he told the two policemen that were hurt that he would look after them and give them enough, so that they should not want for anything. Consequently, in court afterward the testimony of the police against this individual was laughable. They eased down on him and never told what they had been offered.[115]

In summary, Attell stated to the press:

Chicago has exonerated Rothstein in regard to the baseball scandal. In the grand jury room they indicted Hal Chase, who is broke and hasn't got a dollar. They indicted me, and I'm in the same position. They indicted Bill Burns, who had a little money, but who had not a big enough stake to put up. Rothstein told my lawyer that he would keep his mouth shut and on my lawyer's advice I came to Canada. It was not my wish, and I am going right back to Chicago anyway, even if it is against legal advice. I don't need to be extradited. I want to clear myself with the public. Rothstein made between sixty and seventy thousand dollars out of the World's Series besides expenses.[116]

Abe Attell voluntarily arrived at the office of Acting District Attorney Talley in New York on November 16, and was quick to state, "I certainly will not be the goat."[117] On January 24, 1921, the *New York Herald* provided some insight into the delayed actions of the court. The headline read "Indicted Sox May Never Be Forced To Face Trial, New State Attorney in Chicago Is Making No Effort to Push Cases, Papers are Pigeonholed, Probability That Indictments Will Be Stricken Off Calendar, says Official." The *New York Herald* noted comments by the new state attorney: "'The indictments are a lemon,' declared one of the assistant prosecutors of the State's attorney's office today. 'If this case is ever set for trial, and I don't think it will ever see the light of a criminal court calendar, the result is inevitable; it will be acquittal for the whole lot of them.'"[118]

On March 17, 1921, the state of Illinois dropped the cases against all of the former Chicago White Sox baseball players indicted for the alleged throwing of the 1919 World Series, except Chick Gandil. The action was taken after Judge William E. Dever had refused to grant a continuance of more than sixty days in the case. The state demanded six months on the grounds that it would take that length of time to gather new evidence, which would give the prosecution a chance of conviction.[119]

Robert E. Crowe, State's Attorney, immediately announced that an attempt would be made to gather new evidence and indictments would be sought against the men. Apparently, the change in the office of the Illinois state attorney had led to the misplacement of numerous related documents including the confessions of Cicotte, Jackson and Williams.

The Second Investigation

On March 26, 1921, one hundred and forty-four indictments naming eighteen men were returned by the Cook County grand jury as a result of the second investigation into the alleged throwing of the 1919 World's Series to Cincinnati by Chicago White Sox players. Eight separate indictments against each person were returned. The indictments named the thirteen men indicted in the first investigation, and also five men—Carl Zork,[120] Ben Franklin,[121] Ben and Louis Levy (Levi),[122] and David Zelcer[123]—charged with taking part in arranging the alleged conspiracy.

A review of the re-indicted: Eddie Cicotte, pitcher who confessed to receiving $10,000 to throw games; Claude Williams, pitcher who confessed to receiving $5,000; Joe Jackson, outfielder who confessed to receiving $5,000; Fred McMullin, utility infielder; Chick Gandil, first baseman; Swede Risberg, shortstop; Oscar Felsch, outfielder; Buck Weaver, third baseman; Hal Chase, former major league first baseman; Bill Burns, former major league pitcher; Abe Attell; Rachel Brown, alleged gambler; and Joseph J. Sullivan, alleged gambler. Five hundred and thirty-four days had passed since the final pitch of the 1919 World Series. According to the *Evening Public Ledger,* "Each indictment today contained three counts charging conspiracy to defraud, obtaining money under false pretenses and conspiracy to do an illegal act. Bonds were fixed at $3,000 for each indictment, or $24,000 for each man."[124]

Abe Attell surrendered himself on May 10, 1921, to Detective James J. Coy on the indictment found against him in Chicago. The *Tribune* reported:

> Attell, arraigned before Magistrate Ten Eyck, gave his age as thirty-eight and said he lived at 850 Seventh Avenue (New York). As soon as the former pugilist had been placed in custody, William J. Fallon, his counsel, obtained a writ of habeas corpus from Justice McAvoy in the Supreme Court. Magistrate Ten Eyck committed Attell, whereupon the prisoner was taken before Justice McAvoy, who held him in $1,000 bail, which was furnished. Justice McAvoy will hear arguments on the writ of habeas corpus Saturday.[125]

A writ of habeas corpus directs a person to produce the prisoner and justify the prisoner's detention. If the prisoner argues successfully that the incarceration is in violation of a constitutional right, the court may order the prisoner's release. On May 13, Governor Small of Illinois signed requisition papers for the return of Attell to Chicago to stand trial. Six days later it was noted that Attell was making overtures to turn state's evidence, or to testify for the state.

In a strange twist of events, on May 20, 1921, Attell was freed, and then rearrested. A magistrate dismissed the short affidavit on which Attell was being held, before he was rearrested, by Detective Coy, based on the governor's warrant calling for extradition. The *Herald* noted: "William J. Fallon, counsel for Attell, still insisted that because no one is on hand to identify his client as the Attell mentioned in the Chicago baseball indictment he should be set free. He went to the Supreme Court and secured adjournment until Wednesday of argument on a writ of habeas corpus already applied for when Attell was first arrested."[126]

On May 25, argument in the case of Abe Attell was temporarily halted. Three days later, Attell was in front of Justice Tierney on the writ, as a result of his arrest in New York. William J. Fallon, counsel for Attell, contended that the Abe Attell mentioned in the Chicago indictment was not the Abe Attell he represented and denied that his client conspired on October 3, 1919, as the indictment charged, to defraud one Samuel W. Pass—the complaining witness before the Cook County grand jury that indicted Attell—of the People's Gas Company of Chicago out of $500.[127] "The first count of the indictment charges Attell, and other individuals, with taking $500 from Pass."[128] According to the *Tribune:*

Attell while on the stand, denied that he knew Cicotte, Williams, Jackson and others of the White Sox players who are charged with throwing games to the Cincinnati Reds, except by name. Justice Tierney decided that if it could be proved that the Abe Attell mentioned in the Illinois warrant, on which the former pugilist is held, was the Abe Attell under arrest here, the court would have no alternative but to dismiss the writ and let the law take its course with regard to sending the defendant to Chicago.[129]

On June 10, in New York, Attell counsel William Fallon announced that he would have several of the indicted Chicago White Sox in court willing to testify that Abe Attell was not the Attell indicted. Their testimony would corroborate that of Samuel Pass, who was responsible for the expose, and who said that, so far as he knew, Attell was not the man whom the Chicago authorities were seeking.

Finally, on June 25, Abe Attell was discharged by Supreme Court Justice Donnelly, following an argument by his counsel William Fallon. The *Evening World* noted: "During the habeas corpus hearings held before Supreme Court Justice Tierney, Mr. Fallon said, not one witness had been able to identify Attell as one who had taken part in the conspiracy."[130]

The complaining witness, identified in this account as Samuel Pass, swore that he had never seen Attell until he was pointed out to him in court during the hearings before Justice Tierney. Pass, in his testimony before the Cook County Grand Jury, claimed he had heard one Abe Attell had been one of the parties in the conspiracy. Six hundred and twenty-five days had passed since the final pitch of the 1919 World Series.

Meanwhile, in Chicago, with the case of the eighteen men indicted in connection with the 1919 World Series scandal set to begin on Monday, June 27, George E. Gormon, assistant state's attorney, was quick to point out that Attell's discharge in no way affected the state's case. It simply meant that Attell would not stand trial, and that consequently there would be one less man in the penitentiary when this case was finished, or so he believed.

On July 9, the prosecution in the case stated that it would "demand the maximum penalty of $2,000 and five years' imprisonment for each man found guilty."[131] The announcement came on the same day that former heavyweight champion Jack Johnson was released from Leavenworth Federal Prison after serving ten months of a year's sentence for violation of the Mann Act. His wife Lucille Cameron Johnson arrived the day before to assist securing the release and seeing to it that a fine of $1,000 was paid. It was noted that Johnson had received many lucrative fight offers and that a homecoming reception was being planned in Chicago. A prospective juror (only four had been selected thus far for the White Sox case) hoped his possible jury selection wouldn't interfere with his plans to attend the Johnson reception.

Postscript

On August 2, 1921, the seven former White Sox baseball players (Weaver, Felsch, Risberg, Gandil, Williams, Jackson and Cicotte) and two others (Carl Zork and David Zelcer, a.k.a. Bennett) were found not guilty by a jury. The jury took only one ballot. The verdict was reached after two hours and 47 minutes of deliberation but was not returned until 40 minutes later, since Judge Hugo Friend was out of court when the decision was reached.[132]

The announcement of the verdict was greeted with cheers from the several hundred who had remained in court for the final decision. "Hurrah for the Clean Sox," was heard over the cheers of relief as the flashbulb photographs recorded nearly every smile in the courtroom. The *Arizona Republican*, among others, printed: "Bailiffs vainly pounded for order and finally noticing Judge Friend's smiles, joined in the whistling and cheering. Hats sailed high in the air, papers were thrown around and the court room was the scene of the wildest confusion in any recent Cook County criminal case."[133]

Taking a closer look at the case:

The indictments upon which the defendants were tried contained 12 counts, but the state dismissed three after presenting its evidence.

Attell was discharged; Hal Chase was arrested in California but never brought to Chicago; Ben Franklin became ill and could not be brought to trial; Fred McMullin was not apprehended on the second indictment; Rachel Brown and "Sport" Sullivan were never apprehended.

Rothstein's name was invoked and it was charged that he financed the conspiracy that was consummated in the cities of Cincinnati and Chicago. Bill Burns—the prosecution's star witness, who turned state's evidence—corroborated that William Maharg accompanied him on all of his alleged dealings between the players and the gamblers. The *Republican* printed:

> Burns asserted Cicotte and Gandil were originators of the scheme to throw the Series for $100,000. According to Burns, Abe Attell, who was supposed to be the lieutenant of Rothstein, double crossed the players and gave them $10,000 of the promised $100, 000. During the trial the defendants' attorney contended that Ban Johnson, president of the American League, had instigated the prosecution because of a feud with Charles Comiskey, owner of the White Sox. During the trial it became known that the original confessions said to have been made by Cicotte, Williams and Jackson, along with the immunity waivers that they had signed, had been stolen from the state's attorney's office. It was charged eastern gamblers had made up a pot of $10,000 to obtain these documents.[134]

As for the waivers, the same source reported: "All indictments remaining against the acquitted ball players will be quashed, it was announced by State's Attorney Robert Crowe. 'As far as I am concerned the case is a closed book,' said Crowe. Investigation of the disappearance of the waivers of immunity signed by Cicotte, Jackson and Williams which are said to have been sold to eastern gamblers for $10,000, is still going on, the state's attorney said."[135]

In an attempt to offset the damage, Judge K.M. Landis issued a statement on August 3, 1921:

> BLACK SOX BANNED FROM ORGANIZED BALL
>
> Regardless of the verdict of jurors, no player that "throws" a baseball game, no player that undertakes or promises to throw a ball game, no player that sits in conference with a bunch of crooked players and gamblers where the ways and means of throwing games are planned and discussed, and does not promptly tell his club about it, will ever play professional baseball.[136]

Six hundred and sixty-four days had passed since the final pitch of the 1919 World Series. It only took three hundred and ninety days to build the Empire State Building.

This was the way in which the event played out before the public and a scenario that has since been lost in translation. The entire incident, which was nothing short of a travesty, will remain an eternal scar for every person involved, or validation of the old Oscar Wilde quip, "The truth is rarely pure and never simple."

CHAPTER FOURTEEN

Misdeeds and Mishaps in the Roaring Twenties

"Why don't they pass a constitutional amendment prohibiting anybody from learning anything? If it works as well as prohibition did, in five years Americans would be the smartest race of people on Earth."—Will Rogers

The Roaring Twenties

With a nationwide constitutional ban (via the Eighteenth Amendment) on the sale, production, importation, and transportation of alcoholic beverages, or Prohibition, life as we had known it in the United States was dramatically changed. From 1920 to 1933, we became a society of "wets" versus "drys," the "moral" versus the "immoral," all at a time when economic prosperity—often just a sip, bottle, or barrel away—polarized society, yet brought it an alluring and distinctive edge.

As the government stepped in with their Federal Prohibition Bureau to stamp out alcohol, organized crime stepped up to set up an informal organization, most notably in New York and Chicago, to correct, at least in their minds and wallets, the supply chain. The result was the birth of the American Mafia, an organized crime network with operations across the United States, not to mention a black market for liquor, and an increase in drunk driving and alcohol poisoning. The illicit liquor trade came at the perfect time for gambling and prostitution houses that were looking to expand their criminal ventures. As the organizations grew in sophistication, so too did their skills in areas such as smuggling, money laundering and bribing public officials.

Enter John "Papa Johnny" Torrio, born Giovanni Torrio on January 20, 1882, and the nephew of Victoria Moresco, the wife and business partner of "Big Jim" Colosimo. "Big Jim" was an Italian-American Mafia crime boss who immigrated from Calabria, Italy, in 1895, and built a criminal empire in Chicago based on prostitution, gambling, and racketeering. As the owner of more than 100 brothels, Colosimo soon found himself in need of assistance on a variety of fronts. It was then that he invited Torrio to Chicago in order to deal with extortion demands, known as the "Black Hand," from outside his organization. Torrio eliminated the extortionists and stayed on to run Colosimo's operations and to organize the criminal muscle they needed. In 1919, when Torrio needed a bouncer for one of his brothels, he found one, thanks to Brooklyn gangster Frankie Yale, in Alphonse Gabriel "Al" Capone.

Prohibition: New York City Deputy Police Commissioner John A. Leach (right), watching agents pour liquor into sewer following a raid during the height of prohibition (Library of Congress).

"Big Jim" Colosimo was killed outside his restaurant on May 11, 1920, allegedly by Al "Scarface" Capone. Just how "The Fixers" of the 1919 World Series—whoever they may have been—managed to Waltz into Colosimo's backyard to conduct business remains a mystery, or do black hands wear black sox?

On Being Abe

As if it weren't difficult enough being Abe Attell after 1919, even pretending not to be became a challenge. A newspaper noted, "Abe Attell, alias Joe Wellar, or Joe Wellar, alias Abe Attell, was held in $500 bail for special sessions today by Magistrate George W. Simpson in Washington Heights courts. The charge was ticket speculating, but what Abe, or Joe, really tried to do was to get into the Polo Grounds to see the Yankees play the White Sox."[1] Denied admittance into the ballpark, Attell had purchased a ticket at the ticket window. Detective James Cummings then witnessed Abe trying to resell the 75-cent ticket. He was arrested and charged with violating the penal code that relates to ticket speculation. At the time of the arrest he gave his name as Joseph Wellar, of 162 East Fifty-fourth Street, in New York. Attell had been barred about a year ago from attending Yankees games, for nothing more than his association with the ongoing 1919 World Series scandal. Hoping memories were short, Attell simply decided to try his luck.

Turning back to the ring, Abe decided he was going to lend a hand to Baltimore battler Danny Frush by giving him a few pointers for his upcoming battle with Johnny Kilbane. The fight was scheduled for twelve rounds in Cleveland on September 17. Attell, as many understood, had been away from the ring for some time, but having lost the featherweight crown to Kilbane, he certainly could provide Frush with some valuable insight. And that perspective began with an understanding that dethroning a champion is no simple task.

Inactive in 1918, Kilbane fought ten times in 1919 and only seven times in 1920. The champ met Freddie Jacks in Cleveland on May 25 and fought him to the requisite no-decision for ten rounds. Still taking heat for seldom making the title available, the champ did draw the line with Frush.[2]

In addition to becoming the poster child for the 1919 World Series scandal, Attell, not to mention the entire event, fueled a rash of anti–Semitism. The *Dearborn Independent*, for example, ran disgraceful articles such as "Jewish Gamblers Corrupt American Baseball." It read: "There are men in the United States who say that baseball has received its death wound and is slowly dying out of the list of respectable sports. There are other men who say American baseball can be saved if a clean sweep is made of the Jewish influence which has just dragged it through a period of bitter shame and demoralization."[3]

The article's deplorable first conclusion:

To begin with, Jews are not sportsmen, this is not set down in complaint against them, but merely as analysis. It may be a defect in their character, or it may not; it is nevertheless a fact which discriminating Jews unhesitatingly acknowledge. Whether this is due to their physical lethargy, their dislike of unnecessary physical action, or their serious cast of mind, others may decide; the Jew is not naturally an out-of-door sportsman; if he takes up golf it is because his station in society calls for it, not that he really likes it; and if he goes to collegiate athletics, as some of the younger Jews are doing, it is because so much attention has been called to their neglect of the sports that the younger generation thinks it is necessary to remove that occasion of remark.[4]

The article spun into a "Who's Jew" of the scandal, including insults regarding Abraham Attell:

Then next in the gallery of notables in the background of baseball is the Jew gambler, Abe Attell, whose connection with sports has been of questionable character ever since his dethronement from his pugilistic pedestal. Attell is known as the "king bee" of the scheme to "throw the games" in the World Series. He knows all about underhand "throwing" of contests, because he has thrown his own fights, now feigning to be beaten when it involved gambling bets, and easily winning when the same reasons prompted.[5]

It was this level of anti–Jewish prejudice that Attell endured. These weeds of bigotry, as a result of the scandal, are often forgotten—swept under the carpet as quickly as Attell himself had been, once tried in the court of public opinion. This tendency has never been finer analyzed than by the eldest of the three Brontë sisters, Charlotte, who quipped, "Prejudices, it is well known, are most difficult to eradicate from the heart whose soil has never been loosened or fertilized by education: they grow there, firm as weeds among stones."

Just when it looked like the surname of Attell could slip quietly from the headlines, an unforeseen bulletin appeared in the *Evening Herald* on the final day of the year: "Bond Robbery Disclosed by Three Arrests, Former Wife of Abe Attell Is Held in Connection with $1,599,000 Theft."[6]

It had happened the previous July, but only became known on December 31 with the arrest of Mrs. Abe Attell (using the name Ethel Bruce), Sam Gould and Harry Cohen, a mail theft of more than $1,500,000 in bonds.[7] According to the *Herald*:

> The bonds were stolen somewhere en route from the Federal Reserve Bank, New York, to the treasury at Washington. Some were cancelled by perforations, and others stamped "paid," but the stamp was removed with chemicals and many of them were passed. Mrs. Attell, who said she divorced the boxer five years ago, is charged with attempting to pass altered government bonds. The detectives found Mrs. Attell in an apartment last night with Gould and Cohen. The inspectors said they found a complete opium set in the apartment.[8]

Back to Boxing

The fight game in the New York or Tri-State area had three notable bouts in 1921: Benny Leonard's six-round knockout of Richie Mitchell on January 14 was a display of courage. Leonard, in a resurgence of strength, dropped Mitchell three times in the first, which was a remarkable feat considering he was nearly counted out. One of boxing's premier series came to a conclusion on February 7, as Jack Britton retained his welter title with a win over Ted "Kid" Lewis. The duo had fought 22 times. Finally, the big boys fought over in Jersey City on July 2. In Rickard's, and boxing's for that matter, first million-dollar gate, light heavyweight champion Georges Carpentier stunned Jack Dempsey with a right to the chin, but true to form, Dempsey came roaring back to knock out his opponent in the fourth round.

The Roaring Twenties belonged to Jack Dempsey, heavyweight champion of the world, who held the title for seven years and two months during the raucous days that followed World War I. The "Manassa Mauler" stood six foot one inch tall, with a seventy-seven-inch reach, and his chiseled features were as if the gods themselves took turns at hammering out the perfect image. It was these movie-star looks, not to mention a bit of pugilistic prowess, that provided Dempsey with boundless appeal. He disposed of ring adversaries and ducked punches faster than anyone alive, barring Alphonse Gabriel Capone. Like most champion pugilists of the day, Dempsey was also a lady's man—every woman wanted the elbow of the champ, from Broadway stars to cigarette-smoking tramps, regardless of the admission charge. Love was cheap in the twenties, even if the drinks weren't.

As dry as it was, if of course you didn't know the right people, it was one of the most exciting times to be alive and everyone knew it, especially Abe Attell. The number of millionaires jumped four hundred percent over the previous decade and nowhere was that more evident than in New York City. This newfound wealth, some of it a result of clandestine activities, created lavish lifestyles that were difficult to ignore. Everyone seemed to be having a good time, and those who weren't, wanted to. Never hesitating to dress or act the part, "The Little Champ" lived life to the fullest. Understanding that there were those who loved him for his ring expertise, and those who abhorred him for his associations, could not have been easy. Yet Attell persevered, the dichotomy acting more as a stimulant than deterrent, as most understood he was someone to know in New York City.

1922

Winning a championship is one thing, but holding on to it, especially in boxing, is another. On February 22, 1922, the sport of boxing celebrated the tenth anniversary of its current featherweight titleholder, Johnny Kilbane. Ever since his victory over Abe Attell in Vernon, California, back in 1912, Kilbane had held on to the crown tighter than anyone thought imaginable, even Abe Attell. The closest he had ever come to losing it happened a year after winning it, in a bout against Johnny Dundee. The fight went to the limit, twenty rounds, and it took Referee Charlie Eyton to stare both men in the eyes and call it a draw.

In 1917, with no feather competition on the horizon, Kilbane tested the waters with the lightweight class and met Champion Benny Leonard. But "The Ghetto Wizard" was a step beyond the reach of many, regardless of weight class. Suffering the only knockout of his career, Kilbane saw stars in the third round.

Knockout artist George Chaney gave Kilbane a battle, at least until the third round when Kilbane put his lights out. Only the year before, spunky Danny Frush took his bout with Kilbane for only training expenses—he was that sure of himself, thanks in part to Attell. Kilbane delivered him in seven rounds and went home with $60,000 lining his pocket. Kilbane's record reign, which had yet to surpass that of the great John L. Sullivan, was still intact and likely to stay that way.

On March 21, in Philadelphia, Mrs. Ethel Goodwin, the divorced wife of Abe Attell, was arrested and charged with being a member of a band of thieves that had been targeting large fur stores. Using information supplied by alarm company employees allowed the bandits to be successful—yep, crooks were that smart back then. She was held on $3,000 bail and had a hearing set for March 31.

It seemed that not a month would go by without a newspaper contacting Attell about his career. The result was often a blurb like the one that hit Damon Runyon's April 1, 1922, column, for example: "Speaking of Attell, his notoriety in other fields has caused many persons to forget the fact that he was a really great little fighter when he was in his prime, perhaps one of the greatest we have ever had. Dividing the ringmen into three classes (the fighter, the boxer and the fighter-boxer) it seems to us that Attell was one of the two greatest of the last class—fighter-boxer—produced in many years. Joe Gans was the other."[9] But this was the Twenties, when a blurb could also have a bite.

On May 21, Abe Attell and E.M. Tausend, who were business associates in the Ming Top Bootery at 1656 Broadway, were quizzed by Fire Marshal Thomas Brophy about the condition of their shop, which was found gasoline-soaked early the day before by two watchmen and a patrol officer.

The police awoke Abe Attell in his Oregon apartment at Fifty-fourth Street and Seventh Avenue and questioned him for two hours at the Forty-seventh Street station. Attell denied all knowledge of the attempted arson, as did Tausend, who also went to the station.

While Attell was convinced the attempted arson was the work of one of his enemies, Tausend said he wasn't aware of any enemies. Attell stated to the *Herald*: "I believe this thing was done by some enemy to make it look as if I was preparing to burn the place. I don't think whoever soaked the place with gasoline really intended to set it on fire."[10]

Attell believed that whoever did the damage likely entered through a trap door leading to the Cafe Maurice. The shoe shop was situated in the Broadway Central Building, over the cafe, and adjoined the building that housed the Roseland dancing palace. Attell told the *Herald*: "As a matter of fact there is no reason why I should set fire to the store. We are making money and the business is in good financial condition. There is more than $2,800 in outstanding obligations, and there is stock worth $15,000 on hand, not to mention the value of the business itself. We carry $16,000 insurance."[11]

It was a Cafe Maurice watchman who had discovered gasoline dripping through the ceiling of the cabaret. Chief Brophy had no doubt that an attempt at arson had been made. Attell added: "The plan was obvious. They left oilcans and they saw to it that the leaking cans would be discovered before the fire started. They are bent on ruining me. I might have gone to the Hall of Fame if it wasn't for the baseball scandal. Instead, I went into business and tried to live it down. I haven't been to the races or a ball game in more than a year and I don't go around the cabarets, but these people are still trying to ruin me."[12] Attell provided his fire insurance policy and detailed records to Marshal Brophy.

As Abe danced, ducked and feinted from his adversaries, others came to his rescue. Sometimes it takes another fighter's opinion, especially that of a champion, to help set the record straight. Leave it to James J. Corbett, another Bay Area Boy, to chime in about his neighbor in a piece that appeared in the *Great Falls Daily Tribune*:

> It's really pathetic that the ring greatness of Abe Attell should be obscured by his later-day connection with gambling scandals. They know him only as an alleged tool of gamblers—not as one of the real ring marvels. Attell wasn't merely a master ringman—he was a super-fighter. There was nothing that any great fighter did that he couldn't do just as well. And there were many, many things which he did better than any little man that ever lived.[13]

Corbett went on to praise the fighter for his brains, speed and cleverness, while also comparing him to Joe Gans with regard to stamina: "He knew every trick of the game; he never had a peer as a ring general. His fights were full of action and fire; he usually gave the crowd a run for its money—and then a whole lot more. It'll be many a year before there'll be another fighter such as Abe Attell. And it's too bad that what he has done—or what has been charged against him—has caused the world to remember him only as he is, and not as one of the wonders of the prize ring."[14]

The year 1922 was another solid year for city boxing: Jack Britton barely hung onto his welter crown when he drew Dave Shade on February 17. The unstoppable Harry Greb—having fought successfully in the middleweight, light heavyweight and heavyweight ranks—broke Gene Tunney's nose on the way to the American light heavyweight title on May 23. Mickey Walker took Jack Britton fifteen rounds, then took his title.[15] Attell's eyes and ears were never far from the fight game, or his wallet, if the situation called for it.

1923

In Los Angeles, on March 2, 1923, heavyweight champion Jack Dempsey put on an eight-round exhibition to benefit Monte Attell, whose eyesight was failing. The receipts were used to assist Monte, who was setting up a little cigar store in San Francisco. Dempsey, who would soon transform the town of Shelby, Montana, from a ghost town facing bankruptcy to an overnight sporting hub, was delighted to assist one of his own.

Joe Jackson, with the assistance of attorney Ray Cannon, sued the Chicago White Sox for the back pay he felt the club owed him following his acquittal in the Black Sox scandal. Jackson felt cheated, misled by Harry Grabiner, secretary of the White Sox, who he believed took advantage of his illiteracy to obtain his signature on his three-year contract. At first the jury sided with the ballplayer, but Jackson's deposition, when produced by Sox attorney George M. Hudnall, contrasted so greatly with current testimony that the judge threw out the initial jury award and charged Jackson with perjury. Jackson eventually settled with Comiskey for an undisclosed amount and returned to his home to Georgia.

Attell had the travel bug in 1923. He arrived back from Europe on June 14, on the White Star liner *Homeric*. In the days when noted passengers found their names in the newspapers, Attell had good company aboard ship, including Colonel Charlton, British military attaché; Cyrus H. McCormick of Chicago; and Mrs. W.K. Vanderbilt and her daughters Muriel and Consuelo Vanderbilt. Attell then headed back to Europe on August 11, aboard the White Star liner *Majestic*. Also aboard the liner were Mr. and Mrs. Florenz Ziegfeld; J. Augustus Barnard; and Lady Helen Herbert of London. The exact nature of his travel, other than pleasure, was not disclosed. However, he was rumored to have been back-dooring some fight deals, or circumventing the usual channels to avoid major issues or stumbling blocks.

A banner year for New York boxing, 1923 saw some of the best matches the sport had to offer: A determined Gene Tunney avenged his loss against Harry Greb on February 23 to regain the American light heavyweight title. France's war veteran Eugene Criqui knocked out twelve-year feather titleholder Johnny Kilbane in the sixth round of their June 2 battle. Jimmy Wilde endured a brutal beating from Filipino Pancho Villa, who took the flyweight title on June 18. A prolific and resolute Johnny Dundee then grabbed the feather crown with a fifteen-round decision over Eugene Criqui on July 25. In the most memorable event of not only the year, but perhaps in all of boxing history: Jack Dempsey, floored in the opening seconds of the fight, got up to drop Luis Firpo seven times. Firpo then arose and catapulted Dempsey between the ropes and out of the ring. And this was just the first round. A reignited Dempsey then delivered a combination to the jaw of Firpo in the second that sent him to the heavens. Big Jack still had his heavyweight title.

1924

Many a boxer, past and present, was on hand to witness the fight between Harry Wills, who was regarded as the foremost contender for the world heavyweight championship title, and Bartley Madden, the rugged West Side Irishman, on June 9, 1924, at the Queensboro Stadium in Long Island City. Those in attendance included Georges Carpentier, Sam Langford, Jack McAuliffe, Tex Rickard, John Ringling, Senator James J. Walker, and Attell. Wills just pounded Madden about the ring, but the rugged Irishman, whose countenance was nearly unrecognizable after fifteen rounds, managed to go the distance. Wills may have taken the decision, but the hearts of the 17,000 spectators were with the Irishman. Attell mingled about, threw a few verbal jabs at old friends like Rickard, and chatted with any press interested in his forty-year-old perspective.

For Albie, it had been a relatively quiet year of business as usual until summer. On July 23, New York State troopers in the woods near Ausable Chasm, a sandstone gorge and tourist attraction located in the village of Keeseville, New York, arrested him in a vehicle containing fifty cases of Canadian ale. Attell gave his name as Albert Knoeher of 325 Riverside Drive, New York City.[16] Attell told reporters he had been visiting a friend in nearby Plattsburg, New York, and accepted a ride as far as Albany to save some money. He and driver James Hanlon, also of New York, waived examination and were held in $1,000 bail each. The pair was charged with illegal possession and transportation of intoxicating liquor.[17] Such an event was not uncommon during the era, especially for those who had related business interests, as did Attell.

1925

At the end of January 1925, the boxing world learned of the passing of James "Peerless Jim" Driscoll (also known as Jem Driscoll) at the young age of forty-four. Driscoll had already made a name for himself, taking a couple British feather titles, before arriving in the States.

In 1909, he fought a no-decision match with Attell, then the world featherweight champ, at the National Athletic Club in New York. Though Driscoll failed to knock out Attell, he dominated the fight and caught the attention of everyone around the fight game. Both gladiators, tremendous defensemen, put on quite a show, with only Attell showing any signs of damage after the encounter. Afterwards, Driscoll claimed that he and Attell had agreed that the title would change hands based on the newspaper decision, or the unofficial vote by ringside reporters. But such would not be the case.

It was chilling, at least for some, when word came that United States Attorney Emory R. Buckner was initiating padlock proceedings against thirty supper clubs, cabarets and restaurants. The news came on October 21, 1925, and included some of the best-known, most expensive and exclusive after-theater nightlife sections of midtown Manhattan. These weren't the bottle-smashing raids that became all too familiar in newsreels, but Prohibition agents and deputy marshals just doing their job.

For many, including Abe Attell, these were popular places like the Strand Roof Restaurant on Broadway; Club Cameo, at 288 West Fifty-second Street; and the Game Cock Restaurant at 56 East Forty-first Street. The authorities also targeted the Del Fey Club at 107 West Forty-fifth Street. Hostess Texas Guinan knew everyone by name and passed out announcement cards that stated, "It is New Year's Eve every night at the Del Fey." There, stage and screen stars were as common as foul balls at the ballpark, with dignitaries, such as Prince de Metrie, Lord and Lady Mountbatten, and Harry K. Thaw, always, or so it appeared, only a table away. Admission was by card only, unless of course you were known, like Abraham Attell. On October 12, while a sting operation was going on, Attell made the mistake of carrying a case of champagne into the club—a majority of the liquor came through a cellar pipeline—and it cost him a $500 bail, and later a $200 fine.

Champagne was the drink of choice at the Del Fey, a way perhaps to justify the $3 cover. Liquor, though frowned upon, could be had; Prohibition agents proved that by purchasing a pint of whiskey at the joint for $10.

If you knew the owners of the club, and not only were there often multiple owners but owners of multiple clubs, entrance and perks were a bit easier. All the owners carefully monitored their clientele, which only made sense, as a bust and a padlock often meant closing for a year. If, however, the owner consented to a padlock without going to trial, it could reduce his closing to only six months. Naturally there were exceptions—lots of them, in fact.

The Birth of the Blues—1926

Abe Attell was said to have a stake in a few joints. One was the Peacock Club, at 147 West Forty-eighth Street. A decree was issued for it on November 4, 1926, and it was ordered padlocked for a year. Attell didn't deny being in the joint—a Deputy United States Marshal had seen him there—but testified he had no financial interest in the place. When an establishment was padlocked, owners disappeared faster than a Houdini rabbit. Also padlocked in the Peacock Club bust was the Club La Boheme, at 117 MacDougal Street in Greenwich Village.

It was no secret that Abe loved the speakeasy atmosphere. Old friends would routinely drop by to share stories, swap leads, or perhaps toss out a wager or two. And, yes, Abe took his share of good ribbings, be it a pop about a Harlem Tommy Murphy or Frankie Neil bout, or even kidding that it was easier to get a shot of whiskey than to get Kilbane to put the belt on the line. Everybody had a tip, a favorite drink or an angle, and it was all in good fun. And, yes, it was a phallocratic culture, intent on finding a stiff shot and a skirt to go with it.

The City saw a couple of memorable battles: In an extremely close decision, Tiger Flowers took the middle title from Harry Greb on February 26. On October 12, close to 45,000 spectators jammed into Ebbets Field to witness thirty-eight-year-old Harry Wills disqualified in the thirteenth round of a fifteen-round match against Jack Sharkey. Wills, who conceded 26½ pounds to Sharkey and had been repeatedly warned by Referee Patsy Haley about holding, finally let go of a backhand punch, more out of frustration than desire, across Sharkey's face that initiated the call. Waiting for years in the bigoted boxing world for a title shot, Wills, the world colored heavyweight champion, survived by fighting the best black fighters of the era. Would Dempsey have fought Sam Langford eighteen times? Yes, but once or twice would probably have been enough. Would Dempsey's management let him? No.

The fight of the year came on September 23, inside Sesquicentennial Stadium in Philadelphia. Boxing scholar and ex-marine Gene Tunney, unbothered by the inclement weather, stunned heavyweight champion Jack Dempsey early with a right to the jaw—a preview of coming attractions. Briefly shaken in the fourth round, Tunney then took full command from that point forward, marching to an unquestionable ten-round decision. Dempsey had been a prohibitive favorite until about a month before the fight, when the New York money shifted heavily in favor of Tunney.

Attell, having made his presence known at Tunney's training camp in the Poconos, and even in Tunney's dressing room after the bout, appeared to cast a disconcerting shadow on the event. The former champion, like many around the sport, was friends with Tunney's manager Billy Gibson.[18] As unmerited as it was, Abe—whom Tunney simply tolerated because of his manager's relationship—seemed not to give it thought. Attell knew a champion when he saw one, and had a respected voice that New York money followed. And that perspective believed Gene Tunney had an excellent chance at being the next heavyweight champion. As the rain fell, a plethora of soggy celebrities sat ringside: Mayor W. Freeland Kendrick of Philadelphia, Mayor Walker of New York, Secretary of the Navy Curtis D. Wilbur, race car driver Barney Oldfield, Peggy Joyce, Gertrude Ederle, theatrical producer William A. Brady, Charlie Chaplin, Tom Mix, John McGraw, Jacob Ruppert, Wilbert Robinson, over a handful of state governors, and even (as if the odds ever were) gambler Arnold Rothstein. The latter had recently come under fire to the tune of $336,768 in a lawsuit filed by George C. Sprague, a trustee in the bankruptcy of the property of Edward M. Fuller. The suit was brought to recover money given to Rothstein by Fuller in the payment of bets on baseball games and horse races. Just in 1919 alone, the complaint alleged, Fuller lost $15,000 on baseball.

How Long Has This Been Going On?—1927

A pair of boxers, all too familiar with "The Little Champ," passed on in the month of April 1927: Aurelio Herrera and William J. Rothwell, a.k.a. Young Corbett II. Herrera, who had battled a prolonged sickness, was only 49 years old. His death was followed a few days later by that of Young Corbett, whom he met on a few occasions. Herrera lost to both Abe Attell and Battling Nelson in 1904, but two years later knocked out Young Corbett in the fifth round of a Los Angeles battle.

Another practitioner of the defensive arts, Freddie Welsh died on July 29, 1927. The crafty boxer rose to prominence in the United States in 1908, thanks to a couple of bouts with then invincible and undefeated Packey McFarland. He lost the first contest but fought to a 25-round draw in their second encounter. A 15-round decision win over reigning featherweight champ Attell, in a non-title fight, was the icing on the cake. Stepping up, he won the British lightweight title in 1909, and in his first defense he faced Jem Driscoll, who was disqualified in the 10th round. Later, Welsh managed Buffalo lightweight Jimmy Goodrich.

Over five hundred people attended the Boyertown Funeral Chapel at Eighth Avenue and Forty-third Street for Welsh's funeral service. Attell acted as a pallbearer, along with Benny Leonard, retired lightweight champion; Johnny Dundee, former featherweight champion; Mike McTigue, Humbert Fugazy, Jimmy Johnston, Willie Beecher, Benjamin Brooker and Dan McKettrick. As Welsh served as a captain in the United States Army, he was accorded a military funeral.

Taking a fancy to a promising young kid named Marty Goldman, Attell couldn't resist the opportunity to manage the fighter. Goldman, born on March 7, 1910, was a lightweight who took his first pro fight at the age of eighteen. As Marty fought out of venues such as the Broadway Arena, Ridgewood Grove and the Ice Palace, Attell's connections eventually landed the youth on some nice cards, even a few at Madison Square Garden. It was at the latter venue that Abe's east side protégé scored a victory over Jersey City lightweight Harry Carlton in an interesting six-round bout on December 14, 1928. The record Garden crowd of 21,630 also witnessed youngster Al Singer battle to a draw against former world's featherweight champion Tony Canzoneri.

Attell honed Goldman into a solid and very competitive boxer. The following year Goldman managed victories over Bulldog Gonzalez and Billy Lynch, and by 1931 had added the names of Eddie McKenna and former Bantamweight Champion Eddie "Cannonball" Martin to his list of victories. But by March 1931, Goldman was beginning to fade. Perhaps the most memorable event for the fighter happened on May 16, 1932, when Goldman was knocked out in the second round of a battle with former world lightweight champion Benny Leonard, the "Ghetto Wizard," who was mounting a comeback.[19] Goldman would finish his career with three times as many victories as losses in over 300 rounds.[20]

None too happy with Gene Tunney, Jack Dempsey issued a challenge to his adversary: to tell the truth regarding the fight a year earlier in Philadelphia. Issuing veiled charges against Tunney, Dempsey claimed "The Fighting Marine" used both Max "Boo-Boo" Hoff and Abe Attell to attempt a "fix," in this case by hiring a referee favorable to Tunney.[21]

Dempsey's charges were contained in a copywritten open letter published in a special edition of the *Chicago Harold-Examiner*. Tunney, unruffled by the assault, simply referred to the matter as classless and a plea for public sympathy. A stunt to save face is how Tunney's manager, Billy Gibson, saw it. Unable to resist temptation, Gibson countered, claiming Dempsey had deliberately planned to foul Jack Sharkey in their bout of July 21.

Tunney just laughed when asked to deny the charges. Gibson believed it nothing more than propaganda. As for Dempsey's sportsmanship, he didn't deny being whipped on the square by Tunney, just not the undertones and hearsay that came with it. He also felt Tunney owed the public an explanation of his relationship with Hoff. Dempsey's team had heard rumors of possible chicanery on fight night—something certainly not uncommon with fights of this caliber—rumors that Tunney planned on stealing the title. It was all in the choice of referee, in Dempsey's mind, and what conditions would be enforced.

Dempsey then spoke to the odds, on how some heavy money was being placed on Tunney, until the Boxing Commission named Tommy Reilly as referee. He also was notably rattled by Tunney's association with Attell, almost frightened at the thought of collusion. Just how Tunney viewed his relationship with Attell and Hoff became a Dempsey preoccupation. The Manassa Mauler saw Hoff as a Philadelphia political powerhouse and wanted to know how the pieces fit.

Dempsey quoted a document made public stating that Gibson borrowed money from Hoff and agreed to pay it all back—if Tunney did not win the fight.[22] But it contained a particular clause that if Tunney won the fight, Hoff would receive a bonus. Dempsey then questioned Tunney on the monetary value of the title.

Dempsey added an additional attack: against Jimmy Bronson, Tunney's chief second at Philadelphia, believing him responsible for inspiring the charges of "draft dodger" that were hurled at Dempsey. In response, Bronson simply dismissed Dempsey's charges as being a bit dated.

As for Hoff, who had a contract with Tunney, he threatened to sue the fighter, and then did, for $350,000.[23] Tunney claimed the contract invalid.[24] Many of those around the incident, especially those monitoring ticket sales for the fighters' next engagement, scheduled for September 22 in Chicago, called the quarrel nothing more than a marketing stunt by Tex Rickard to boost fight sales.

"The Battle of the Long Count" witnessed Jack Dempsey put Tunney to floor in the seventh, only to fail to remove himself immediately to a neutral corner. This allowed Tunney at least four extra seconds, although some will claim even more, in recovery time before Referee Dave Barry began his count. At "nine" a wise Tunney arose, having been down far longer, to drop adversary Dempsey in the eighth en route to his first successful title defense.

In the eighth round, and often forgotten: Tunney scored a left to the left side of Dempsey's face, followed by a right to the left side of Dempsey's neck. This resulted in Dempsey's dropping to his right knee, as Tunney missed with a left. Recovering so fast that his left knee never hit the canvas, Dempsey began to stand while the referee already had his right hand extended for the count. Tunney, who had barely moved, and was certainly not in a neutral corner, watched as the referee's hand came down to begin the count, "One." Referee Dave Barry, who was a last-minute replacement for a Capone-favored arbiter, should never have been counting. In boxing, the more you see, the less you are certain of.

Arnold Rothstein made his mark as a gambler, but he was far from the stereotypical gambler, or a loud-mouth braggart or petty poker-faced chip counter. He was a well-dressed man, polite and soft-spoken, with an extraordinary ability, it would soon become clear, to compartmentalize. As a numbers man, he had a God-given, purse-driven knack at counting. If he counted, he always understood where he stood, and just how he could move one step further. He didn't just think he was smarter than everybody else; he knew he was.

Impressed by few, Rothstein respected only those who knew enough not to challenge him. And if that was the case, he wanted to know why. As a gambler he didn't like the idea of being a "social outcast," but that was what he was. And he was good at it. Ironically, being cleared of complicity in the throwing of the 1919 World Series would prove his moment of immortality—this stealing nothing from F. Scott Fitzgerald's use of his image as Meyer Wolfsheim, a Jewish friend and mentor of Jay Gatsby.

Rothstein was the son of orthodox Jewish parents, destined for success, no doubt, in his father's dress goods business. But his nervous energy saw no bounds, only solace, in a pair of dice. As the perfect association—dice have eyes on all sides, as did Rothstein—it drew him to his own kind. Rothstein was mentored by "Honest John" Kelly and Richard Canfield, and while he didn't necessarily like the style of either, he knew if he could steal, I mean borrow, pieces of each, he could mold himself into the proper image—to draw respect but not attention.

Rothstein was said to play fair—his definition perhaps a bit different from most—because he knew the odds and only played when they were in his favor. Dice brought him to faro, roulette to poker, and finally the races. He even once played pool for thirty-two hours, primarily because he was always up—define this as you may. In 1910, Rothstein opened his own gambling establishment on West Forty-sixth Street. It would become famous for being the place where Charles G. Gate, son of "Betcher-Million" Gates, lost $40,000 in just one evening.

The murder of well-known gambler Herman Rosenthal put a damper on establishments and forced Rothstein into the nomad strategy of moving his "floating craps games." He was indicted, as you recall, in 1919 on a charge of felonious assault that was later dismissed.

Rothstein even once feuded with equestrian August Belmont, who tossed him from the track. But later, and true to style, Rothstein persuaded Belmont to reinstate him. In 1924, his federal income tax return drew some attention, and he was accused of "concealment and perjury." His case never reached a court decision. As his notoriety began to precede him, his friendships grew and enabled the gangster to recruit interest in his various enterprises. As a real estate mogul, he owned numerous buildings, even the Fairfield Hotel, at 20 West Seventy-second Street.

After the assault charge, Rothstein no longer carried a gun. He did, however, continue to use bodyguards. His relationship with Attell, his one-time guardian, fell apart following the 1919 conspiracy.

Arnold Rothstein was shot and mortally wounded during a business meeting—he had hoped to settle gambling debts of more than $300,000 with "Jimmy" Meehan—at Manhattan's Park Central Hotel at Seventh Avenue near 55th Street on November 4, 1928. He died the next day at the Stuyvesant Polyclinic Hospital in Manhattan without disclosing who had shot him.

New York City continued to dominate the fight scene with a number of memorable battles. The undroppable Tommy Loughran fell not only once, but twice, in the first round of his January 6 battle against Leo Lomski. Loughran, the light heavy champ, then battled back to take the fifteen-round decision. Jack Sharkey kayoed ex-light heavy champ Jack Delaney in the very first round of their April 30 bout. Lightweight title holder Sammy Mandell boxed brilliantly in a 15-round points victory over welter Jimmy McLarnin. Tunney, in his second and final heavy defense, knocked out Tom Heeney in the eleventh round of their July 26 clash, and James J. Braddock stunned the boxing world by knocking out contender Tuffy Griffiths in the second round of their November 30 encounter.

The lawless twenties were drawing to a close, but not before four unidentified men, two of them dressed as Chicago police officers, visited a Chicago garage. Seven members of the North Side Gang (among them optometrist Rheinhart Schwimmer and mechanic John May) were then murdered. The killers' primary target, gang leader George "Bugs" Moran, was not one of them. The St. Valentine's Day Massacre effectively ended the five-year gang war between the Chicago Outfit and the North Side Gang. Later, Chicago Outfit hitmen Albert Anselmi and John Scalise, two of the men suspected in the murder of North Side Gang leader Dean O'Banion and fellow mob boss Joseph "Hop Toad" Giunta, were both killed during a lavish party held at Al Capone's residence. Capone beat them to death using a baseball bat.

CHAPTER FIFTEEN

The Great Depression and Beyond

The Roaring Twenties came to a fast and furious ending on Tuesday, October 29, 1929, as over 16 million shares on the New York Stock Exchange traded at an astounding rate, wiping out thousands of investors and billions of dollars. Investors had little to do but to watch as America and the rest of the industrialized world spiraled downward into the Great Depression (1929–39). The period would begin the deepest and longest-lasting economic downturn in history to that time. The results were devastating, as in every direction you turned, the global economic collapse was there to greet you. By 1933, nearly half of America's banks had failed, and unemployment was approaching 15 million people—that's about thirty percent of the workforce.

Attell, like others, watched as the banking system fell into a complete state of chaos. Banks couldn't collect from Wall Street investors, and when they did all they found were certificates worth little or nothing at all. With bank depositors' money in the stock market now depleted, panic ensued as customers rushed to withdraw every cent they could. Banks began failing faster than water over Niagara Falls.

Not only had the economy shrunk, but so too the speakeasy—many reduced in size to avoid detection. When nationwide prohibition began, on January 17, 1920, the sale of alcoholic beverages became illegal, but alcoholic drinks were still available. Large quantities of alcohol were smuggled into the United States from Canada, over land, by sea routes along both ocean coasts, and through the Great Lakes—a fact Attell, like other speakeasy owners, knew all too well.

The reduction in square footage of drinking space also contributed to owner attrition. Only a handful of places, like the Landmark Tavern over on 626 Eleventh Avenue, managed to make it through Prohibition without a raid. And it became difficult, not to mention expensive, to drown your sorrows. The Stork Club, on East 53rd Street, remained perhaps the most popular celebrity hot spot during the early 1930s. It was there that gossip columnist Walter Winchell fed his newspaper columns on a regular basis. The Casa Blanca Club, over on 33 West Fifty-sixth Street, held on until owner Larry Fay was gunned down on January 1, 1933. The repeal of Prohibition was finally accomplished with the ratification of the Twenty-first Amendment on December 5, 1933.

Stormy Weather—1930

As the distance grows between a fighter and the ring, the rounds, or the years if you will, appear to get shorter. Anniversary salutes, once the most frequent form of recall or recollection, slowly and almost comfortably are replaced by the obituary of an old friend. The memories came flooding back in the spring of 1931, when Attell learned of the death of J.G. "Johnny" Croll, founder of Croll's Gardens in Alameda, California. Croll's was a favorite training place of some of the biggest names in Fistiania. From Fitzsimmons to Choynski, to later Gans and Attell, everyone who was anyone trained at the site before it closed in 1915.

The baseball world mourned on October 16, 1931, when they learned of the death of Charles Albert Comiskey at his summer home in Eagle River, Wisconsin. He was 72 years old. Comiskey had been confined to his home for weeks, and it was heart and kidney complications that finally took his life; he was in a coma for twenty-four hours preceding his death. Comiskey had been an American League fixture since the very beginning and had grown his franchise into the most valuable property in Major League Baseball. Comiskey, who retired from active management following the 1919 World Series scandal, was deeply hurt when he learned of his players' treachery. He insisted that that all of them be expelled from organized baseball for all time.

Nearly a year and half later, on January 2, 1933, William J. Gleason passed away in Philadelphia. He had managed the White Sox until 1923, before heading to Philadelphia to coach under Athletics' manager Connie Mack. There, Gleason won two World Series championships with the Athletics, in 1929 and 1930.

A story picked up by the media claimed Kid Gleason ran into Abe Attell at Dinty Moore's over on West 46th Street back in 1920. The midtown pub, owned by James Moore, took its name from the popular comic strip *Bringing Up Father*. Infamous for turning a blind eye to Prohibition, the dive attracted many a celebrity, including ballplayers. It was there that Attell was said to have divulged to the Sox skipper not only Rothstein's involvement, but also his own personal financial woes. Writer James Crusinberry, a reporter for the *Chicago Tribune* along with Ring Lardner, overheard Attell's intemperate admission—which casts an aura over the incident—but neither wordsmith did anything with the information for fear of libel. However, it would later surface in Crusinberry's "A Newsman's Biggest Story," inside the September 15, 1956, issue of *Sports Illustrated*. That a loquacious Attell may have said something surprises few, but the circumstance was a bit suspect. James Russell Lowell said, "As life runs on, the road grows strange,/ With faces new, and near the end,/ The milestones into headstones change,/ 'Neath every one a friend.'" Attell would agree with the former, not so much with the latter, however.

The Fireside poet also quipped, "Let us be of good cheer, however, remembering that the misfortunes hardest to bear are those which never come." On April 11, 1933, Monte Attell, blind for years—the injury attributed to an eye infection—went before the police commission to request a permit to sell peanuts in front of the local auditoriums. A quarter century ago, Monte ruled the bantam class, but had been reduced physically due to injury. The commissioners proudly voted him a free license.

Monte was only a few months older than sportswriter, author and playwright Ringgold Wilmer "Ring" Lardner, who died on September 25, 1933, in East Hampton, Long Island, New York. Lardner realized his ambition—thanks to Hugh Fullerton—when he began writing and traveling with the Chicago White Sox. In 1919, Lardner left the *Chicago Tribune* to join a newspaper syndicate and moved to Great Neck, Long Island. It was from there that he published a number of books and even wrote his first play. It was no secret that Lardner didn't care for Attell, and that Abe's sheer presence seemed to send shivers up the writer's spine. Lardner believed that there was no way Dempsey could lose to Tunney in a fair fight; therefore he always doubted the legitimacy of what he saw, both inside and outside of the ring. But the risk of a libel suit would never allow him to print what he believed regarding the heavyweight championship.

Nationwide, Prohibition ended with the ratification of the Twenty-first Amendment, on December 5, 1933. It was the hopes of many legislatures that repeal would not only generate enormous sums of much-needed tax revenue, but also perhaps even weaken organized crime.

Cheek to Cheek

Abe Attell turned fifty in 1934. Was he wondering where the time had gone? He stared at a countenance that remained incredibly handsome thanks to his defensive skills, while pugs like Nelson and Wolgast were tackling with bouts of resurfacing from their noses to their ears. Since his reign over the feathers, "The Little Champ" had watched—somewhat silently, but not in every case—while Johnny Kilbane, Jem Driscoll, Eugene Criqui, Johnny Dundee, Luis "Kid" Kaplan, Dick Finnegan, Benny Bass, Tony Canzoneri, Andre Routis and Bat Battalino made their claims. He even witnessed a new generation of fighters like Tommy Paul, Kid Chocolate, and Freddie Miller rattle the cage of the featherweight division. Those who were lucky enough—although that likely depends on your perspective, as Attell was a tireless teller of a pugilistic tale—got a chance to listen to "The Little Hebrew" spin stories about training at places like Croll's, or life "South of the Slot," not to mention more than his fair share of old-school wisdom.

Staying involved, by supporting functions such as the Commodore Dutch Association (CDA), which had carried on since 1901 the tradition of the old-time Chuck Connors ball, worked well for Abraham. It kept him young and gave him an opportunity to relive so many priceless memories. His other CDA committeemen included George M. Cohan, Jack Dempsey, Jimmy Durante, George Jessel, Al Jolson, Benny Leonard, Patrick Sullivan and Mickey Walker.

Speaking of words of wisdom, Attell listened to some of his own and took the hand of a charming and beautiful woman. The marriage of Abe Attell, 56, New York promoter and former featherweight boxing champion, and the former Mae O'Brien, 36, of New York became known on March 13, 1939, and took place in Miami, Florida. Mae, who brought three stepchildren, Walter, Mary Ann and Dorothy, to the couple's relationship, was also said to have brought a much-needed stability into Abraham's life. From all signs, the two made the perfect pair. Attell would eventually honor Mae with an establishment of her own at East 55th Street and Second Avenue in New York.

A World at War

The most universal, calamitous, and consequential conflict in history, the Second World War (1939–1945) seemed to affect everyone in some fashion, and the city of New York was no exception. When war broke out, the Attells witnessed firsthand a cosmopolitan city, at first unsure of its commitment, transform itself into a patriotic epicenter with the attack on Pearl Harbor. New York quickly became the principal port of embarkation for the warfront. From every corner of the city, troops, not to mention refugees, could be seen and overheard. Wartime industries thrived and the dispatch of fleets became front-page news. The city took on a military atmosphere, as harbors and military installations were fortified and security became as important as finding a parking space.

On Tuesday, October 5, 1943, Abe Attell was hit by an automobile on Broadway, between Fifty-second and Fifty-third Streets at five o'clock in the morning.[1] He was transported to Roosevelt Hospital where he was reported in "fair" condition.

The motorist who struck him fled the scene, only to turn up an hour later at the West Fifty-fourth Street Police Station. In a bit of irony, the man who hit him, Sam Bortz of 355 East 187th Street in the Bronx, claimed he once fought Attell under the name of "Sam Butts." This is entirely possible, considering the sheer number of Attell's regular fights, one-offs and exhibitions. Bortz was devastated when he learned the identity of the victim and openly wept.

"The Little Champ's" right leg was fractured and his head severely cut, but he was expected to recover. Bortz, released on $500 bail, would appear in court on November 5.

Though Attell was now retired, many had grown to know the fighter through his ventures outside the ring, including Abe Attell's Restaurant and Cafe at 1677-A Broadway, a popular "Steak and Chops Bar & Grill." Abraham and his wife lived at 434 East Fifty-Second Street, off First Avenue. The restaurant business wasn't easy, and even harder when your name was attached to it. However, Attell was a gracious host—which was the best part of being an owner—but the hours were long, often late into the evening or early morning, and the problems always appeared never-ending. There was often no glory for a mop-wielding or dishwashing owner, but it was part of the job. Attell would kid his friends that training for a title defense was easier than running a joint and a lot more profitable. And speaking of old acquaintances—bar owners are never short of old friends—when they dropped by, for whatever reason, the stories flowed like cheap whiskey. Even if he was adorning an apron or behind the bar, you could always catch Albie striking a pose while spinning a tale.

Speaking of establishments, if you wanted to see a celebrity in New York during the forties and fifties who didn't own his own place, you could head to a restaurant and lounge owned and operated by Bernard "Toots" Shor at 51 West 51st Street in Manhattan. Toots made the place, and the place shot him into celebrity status. From Hemingway to Sinatra to Jackie Gleason, and of course Attell, all sought the solace of Shor's. Toots never charged for crying on his shoulder.

Jack Dempsey's Restaurant, the original on the corner of Eighth Avenue and 50th Street, across from Madison Square Garden, was also a hub for the fight game. Dempsey moved the restaurant to Broadway in 1947, where you could have caught Attell sitting down in a red leather upholstered booth facing the front window. Dempsey and Attell had their moments, but it was Jack's place and he knew the fighter was there to reclaim some old memories. Besides, Abe found it tough to resist the cheesecake, and Dempsey found it difficult to refuse a customer.

Judge Kenesaw Mountain Landis died on November 25, 1944, in St. Luke's Hospital in Chicago. He was 78 years of age. For twenty-four years he presided over Major league Baseball, and made many very difficult decisions to preserve the integrity of the game. While most versions of his obituary mentioned the barring of eight members of the Chicago White Sox, player names were not mentioned. Most did state that all eight had been tried and acquitted on indictments.

"It's not that you spend all your time reading obituaries when you get older, it's just that you want to know if you're going to need a fourth for your Saturday tee time," a wise relative once told me. All kidding aside, Abe did stay current with the news, and attended the funerals of many of his fellow pugilists. He had developed a wonderful way of comforting people in their time of need, and his offers of assistance were always genuine.

Benjamin Leiner, a.k.a. Benny Leonard, passed on April 18, 1947. A service that attracted over 2,000 visitors was held for him at the Riverside Memorial Chapel on April 20, 1947. Six hundred people squeezed into the chapel, while 400 additional spectators overlooked from the balcony up above. Attell was one of the many pugilists in attendance. Also paying their respects were Billy Gibson, Leonard's manager, along with Johnny Dundee, Harry Balogh, Sam Taub, Max Baer, Barney Ross and many others. Leonard was buried in Mount Carmel Cemetery, Cypress Hills, in Queens.

Less than a month later, Attell attended another funeral, this time for William "Kid" Broad. The feather and light boxer was born in Cornwall, England, and grew up in Cleveland. Not only battling with Attell, Broad also tackled the likes of Young Corbett and Aurelio Herrera. Following his ring days, he could be seen as a Wall Street messenger or among friends whom he often turned to for support.

The Fabulous Fifties

A luncheon was hosted by the International Boxing Club, at Toots Shor's on August 23, 1951, in honor of middleweight champion Randy Turpin. It was there that Turpin received from Nat Fleischer, publisher of *The Ring*, the magazine's championship belt. The luncheon was an opportunity for many well-known boxing figures to gather, including Don Cockell, Johnny Dundee, Jack Kearns, Johnny Kilbane, Joey Maxim, Bob Olin, Barney Ross and Abe Attell. The latter naturally had more fun than anyone, other than obviously Turpin. Abe ribbed Maxim, who had his left hand bandaged, regarding his recent fight with Bob Murphy, chatted with Cockell about the British boxing scene, and joked with Kilbane. The older fighters enjoyed the attention, shared a few laughs and welcomed the opportunity to meet the new middleweight champion.

Afterwards Turpin established a training camp at Grossinger's Catskill Resort Hotel in the Catskill Mountains. Located near the village of Liberty, New York, the venue was one of the largest Borscht Belt resorts. A kosher establishment that catered primarily to Jewish clients from New York City, it also became a favorite with the fight crowd. Fighters like Rocky Marciano and Dick Tiger trained there and loved the hospitality, not to mention the beauty of Sullivan County. Abe and Mae also enjoyed the area and made it there as often as they could. Grossinger's was about ninety miles southwest of Saratoga, New York.

The first issue of *Sports Illustrated*, featuring Milwaukee Braves star Eddie Mathews at bat and New York Giants catcher Wes Westrum in Milwaukee County Stadium, hit the newsstands with a cover date of August 16, 1954. It seemed only inevitable, as the wheels of sports journalism turned, that at some point the magazine would feature a perspective on the 1919 World Series, and it did. In the September 17, 1956, issue, Arnold "Chick" Gandil gave his interpretation of the event to Melvin Durslag, in a story titled: "He Kept Baseball's Blackest Secret for 36 years.... This Is My Story of the Black Sox Series." The article featured a photograph of Attell, to the left of an image of Arnold

Rothstein, on page sixty-five with a caption stating that the former pugilist played a role and likely profited from the event. Gandil did not place Attell at the epicenter of the conspiracy, reserving that for both Sport Sullivan and Arnold Rothstein. A complementary article titled "A Newsman's Biggest Story," by Chicago sportswriter James Crusinberry, accompanied the report. As an eyewitness, the *Tribune* penman recalled Attell's rather indiscriminate behavior in hustling Chicago money, his conversation with Sam Pass, and overhearing the conversation aforementioned between Kid Gleason and Abe Attell.[2] As anticipated, the recollections sparked renewed controversy; it was almost if a new wave of conspiracy theorists had attached themselves to the event. The Black Sox Scandal, despite its age, was once again center stage.

"The Little Champ" couldn't have been happier to view the beautiful piece penned by Joseph C. Nichols for the *New York Times* on Sunday, February 17, 1957. Titled "'Little Champ' Will Be 74 on Friday," the article went right to Abe's heart. It featured a nice photograph of Attell, decked out in his Sunday finest, top hat, tux and all, inset into the middle of the work. A biographical article, it spoke not only to a successful boxing career, but touched on his life with Mae and, as expected, his thoughts on the current state of the sport.

Five days later, the Boxers Benevolent Association of New York held its annual dinner at the Park Sheraton Hotel. The honored guest, dressed to match his recent *Times* article, was none other than the oldest living ex-champion, Abe Attell. The organization focused on the needs of other former boxers, as well as charities such as the Nephrosis Foundation of New York and New Jersey. It was fighters assisting their own and their community, something Attell took pride in.

Johnny Patrick Kilbane died of cancer at his home on May 31, 1957. The former world featherweight champion (1912–23) was 68 years of age. At the time of his death, the one-time fighter held the post of Municipal Clerk of Courts in Cleveland, a position he had filled since 1952. Prior to that role he conducted training camps, taught boxing, and even became a state senator (1941–42). Most forget Kilbane was the world featherweight champion everywhere but in New York State, where they vacated his title in 1922 for his failure to do battle with Johnny Dundee. Outside of the Empire State, however, he was known as the champion who lost his title to Eugene Criqui in 1923.

When Dr. Joyce Brothers, a twenty-nine-year-old psychologist, took the top prize on the Columbia Broadcasting System's (CBS) popular program *The $64,000 Challenge*, Attell was there. (Later, when the show was mired in controversy, Attell would take considerable heat for his presence.) Not only was "The Little Champ" present, but he was part of a boxing team that included Sixto Escobar, Paddy DeMarco, Tony Galento, Billy Graham, Ralph "Tiger" Jones and Tommy Loughran. That's right, Dr. Brothers took out Loughran to defeat the team—what was Tommy thinking? His mind was on the dame, one of his teammates believed. And Dr. Brothers did so by knowing that the fourth round was when Archie Moore knocked out Bobo Olson for the light-heavy crown in 1955.

The $64,000 Challenge (1956–1958) was a popular spinoff show from *The $64,000 Question*. Most of the big winners became instant celebrities and household names, including Brothers. She later appeared in dozens of television roles, usually as herself, but from the 1970s onward was frankly just grateful for the attention. Dr. Brothers earned her Ph.D. in psychology from Columbia University and conducted her undergraduate work at Cornell University. All the boxers, including Attell, enjoyed her company and thought the world of her. Some even recalled her as the color commentator for

CBS during one of the boxing matches between Carmen Basilio and Sugar Ray Robinson.

Abe was hospitalized with the flu on March 5, 1959. As you get older you are at a greater risk of serious complications from the flu, and the Attells wisely understood this. While Abe was certain that being a professional athlete contributed to his longevity, he also knew the odds, and wasn't going to take any unnecessary chances.

The boxing world faced another loss on December 9, 1959, that of multiple-division champion Tony Canzoneri. A heart attack claimed the champion at the age of 51. Over 400 people turned out for a funeral service at the Frank E. Campbell Funeral Church at Madison Avenue and Eighty-first Street, including Paul Berlenbach, Ruby Goldstein, Rocky Graziano, Phil Kaplan, Lee Oma, Barney Ross, Danny Terris and Attell. The eulogy was delivered by Joey Adams, a comedian; the pair had worked together as a popular nightclub act. Canzoneri was buried at Mount Olivet Cemetery at Maspeth, Queens.

Sixties Smiles

"Wrinkles should merely indicate where the smiles have been," Mark Twain once quipped. And that's the way the Attells, Mae and Abraham, approached the decades that followed. It was their time and they wanted to fill it with the enjoyment they shared together.

Like so many other boxers, Abe just shook his head in disbelief when he learned they were leveling St. Nicholas Arena to make way for a television office building. That's right: the old shed on West Sixty-sixth Street, just off Columbus Avenue, had run its course. Since 1906, and only ten years after it opened as New York's first icehouse, it had hosted thousands of fights. You name 'em, they fought at St. Nick's, from the Sams (that's Langford and McVey), to big Jess Willard and Stanley Ketchel. They all fed the pigeons that flew down from the rafters. And like every pigeon that climbed between the ropes, ringside had the odds, and the gamblers always took home more cash than the pugs.

On Sunday, January 14, 1961, Abe Attell joined many luminaries inside the Serta Room of the Waldorf-Astoria for the annual dinner of the New York State Boxing Writers Association. Seated among the boxing talent: Carmen Basilio, Paul Berlenbach, Melio Bettina, Jim Braddock, Joe Brown, Billy Conn, Tony DeMarco, Frankie Genaro, Ruby Goldstein, Billy Graham, Rocky Graziano, Emile Griffith, Harold Johnson, Doug Jones, Gus Lesnevich, Tommy Loughran, Rocky Marciano, Bob Montgomery, Willie Pep, Barney Ross, Sandy Saddler, Lou Salica, Sid Terris, Jersey Joe Walcott, and many others. The group gathered this year to pay tribute to the NBA middleweight champion from West Jordan, Utah, Gene Fullmer. Utah Senator Frank E. Moss presented Fullmer with the prestigious Edward J. Neil Plaque.

Coming from a fight family, Attell respected how the Fullmers—Gene, Don and Jay—not only put Utah on the pugilistic map, but stirred up the middle and light divisions. They were simply an incredible fight family, one of boxing's best. In four attempts, Sugar Ray Robinson only walked away with one victory against Lawrence Gene Fullmer, and as Attell would note with the Benjamin Franklin line, "Well done is better than well said."

In Jersey City, on April 11, 1961, came word of the passing of Frankie Burns, a leading contender for the bantam title before World War I. Burns was 71 years old. For many years he operated a restaurant at 57 Sip Avenue in Jersey City, and it drew its fair share of the boxing crowd. Burns fought some tough battles, not only with Attell, but also against Johnny Kilbane, Johnny Coulon, Kid Williams and Pete Herman, to name just a few. Serving as New Jersey State Boxing Commissioner, a role that kept him between the ropes for years, he remained in contact with many fighters.

Also in 1961, Attell felt it necessary to again proclaim his innocence: "Abe Attell Talks-Never Before Told! The True Story of The World Series Fix." The bold headline graced the front cover of the October 1961 issue of *Cavalier* magazine. Launched by Fawcett Publications in 1952, the periodical has continued for decades, eventually evolving into a *Playboy*-style men's magazine. Rumor, and that's the way it will stay, has it that Abe might have taken a bit of heat for the type of magazine his words appeared in, but nonetheless he obviously felt a need to clarify—if such a word even exists in the vernacular of Black Sox buffs—his position with regard to the conspiracy.

A Cavalier Attitude—Reviews, Analysis and Interjection

Commanding the attention of virtually everyone in the United States was a new system for transmitting visual images and sound that was reproduced on screens. The number of television sets in American homes, according to most research, topped over 50 million. The popular new technology was quickly becoming a mass medium for advertisement, education, entertainment and news. Adding to the mix was a new form of reporting called investigative journalism, or a form of news coverage in which reporters deeply investigate a single topic of interest, such as serious crimes, political corruption, or corporate wrongdoing. One of the individuals at the forefront of this form was David Howard Susskind, a talented New York television host, personality and producer. As a former communications officer on the attack transport USS *Mellette*, Susskind saw action in World War II at Iwo Jima and Okinawa and was no stranger to controversy. *The David Susskind Show* was the first nationally broadcast television talk show to feature people speaking out against American involvement in the Vietnam War.

By the fall of 1961, the 1919 Black Sox Scandal, now over four decades old, was an easy target, as it had proven to be almost annually, for new rounds of investigative journalism. One of those who had his sights on the topic was Susskind, who felt it was his time to put his brand on the conspiracy. Attell, not to mention others associated with the event, cringed at the thought: the damage caused by annual newspaper articles was one thing, but repairing the devastation created by this new form of journalism would not be so easy.

As he had learned from, of all people, Arnold Rothstein, there was, as Attell saw it, only one way to deal with such an impending event: a direct assault. This Attell took through print by penning "The Truth Behind the World Series Fix," or his personal perspective, in the October 1961 issue of *Cavalier* magazine.[3] The edgy publication was an interesting choice, but one that Attell believed targeted the audience he wanted to reach; contributors to the magazine ranged from Richard Prather and Mickey Spillane, to Isaac Asimov and Ray Bradbury, and its editors included James B. O'Connell (1952–1958) and Bob Curran (1959).

The publication's editorial team met with Attell at Jack Dempsey's Restaurant in New York to set the record straight. Although initial expectations may have been high, it was uncertain as to which direction Attell, who sounded in control, would take the piece and exactly what new perspectives, if any, might be gleaned from his inside view. Clearly an attempt to get at the root of the devastation to our national pastime, the article was not an act of contrition, nor was it a confession. Instead, it was a clarification, and a commendable one at that. Attell did an outstanding job at setting the stage, explaining the times and the relationship—an association too often forgotten—between gambling and baseball.[4] From thugs and bookies to crooked cops and corrupt politicians, deception and betrayal were routine; to double-cross a fellow gambler was an astute action aimed at getting him before he got you.

To little surprise, Attell placed Arnold Rothstein where he belonged, at the heart of the conspiracy (Attell 9).[5] The big-time gambler and chronic equivocator had only one interest, himself. And Attell knew that all too well. Since Rothstein, whose moniker, as you recall, was "the Brain," was interested in the fix, then naturally he would assume as much control over the situation as he could; containment and command, he understood, were integral to success. Even though this would mean considerable attention to detail, and perhaps more exposure than the kingpin felt comfortable with, it became a necessity and a scheme that could work with the proper players. The article took on an aura of a casual conversation with the former champion, and as such provided far less detail on the art of the deal than most conspiracy theorists would have hoped.

Binding the deal, which meant financing and meeting the terms and conditions, was paramount to the "fixer." Although the players' primary concern centered on money matters, the gamblers' concern was odds.[6] Additionally, Rothstein had to protect his investment. So, just who would be the linchpin? Clear was the criterion: it had to be someone both Rothstein and the players could trust—a paradox among participants with little or no conscience. Attell was not that individual. Again, Attell was not the "fixer," or a linchpin for that matter.

However, Attell straightaway confirmed that he was a friend of Rothstein, having met the gangster back in 1905 (Attell 9). Rothstein, as many understood, not only enjoyed the sporting crowd and the company of professional athletes, but also the friendship from many a Tammany political figure, and Attell witnessed this firsthand. Abe did not elaborate on the level of trust between him and "A.R.," which has been presumed to be little.

The Democratic Party political machine known as Tammany Hall played a major role in controlling New York City and New York State politics and helped immigrants, most notably the Irish, rise up in American politics from the 1790s to the 1960s. It typically controlled Democratic Party nominations and political patronage in Manhattan. From Charles Murphy, the highly effective but quiet boss of Tammany from 1902 to 1924, to "Big Tim" Sullivan, the Tammany leader in the Bowery and the machine's spokesman in the state legislature, Rothstein forged his political foundation one crap game at a time. In the early twentieth century, Murphy and Sullivan promoted Tammany as a reformed agency dedicated to the interests of the working class. The new image deflected attacks and built up a following among the emerging ethnic middle class. In the process Robert F. Wagner became a powerful United States senator, and Al Smith served multiple terms as governor and was the Democratic presidential candidate in 1928.

Attell recalled fondly his early encounters with Rothstein at his playground, the Hotel Metropole, the first with running water in every room, and running mouths at periodic poker games. Notable Hotel residents included Nick Arnstein and Western law-man turned sportswriter Bat Masterson. "The Little Champ," who was on the vaudeville circuit at the time, enjoyed the camaraderie provided by the environment, not to mention the stakes.

Attell acknowledged his use as a conduit, a role he handled efficiently between Rothstein and "Sport" Sullivan, the latter corroborating that members of the Chicago White Sox had indicated a desire to "throw" the World Series for compensation of $100,000 (Attell 10).[7] When Attell later informed Rothstein of the proposal, "The Little Champ" claimed he was surprised at the gambler's lack of amazement.[8] The observation by Attell, someone who always had a finger on the pulse of the action, was a bit hard to understand, as the "fix" rumor, which the former champion would have heard, was as common as an August "place" bet at Saratoga.

Sensing his inability to contain the conspiracy, Rothstein's initial concerns were remarkably intuitive. The hustler wanted nothing to do with it.[9] Or did he?

Attell, who loved baseball, and even planned on attending the "fall classic," immediately headed to Cincinnati a day or two before the opening game. It was there that he noted the appearance of both Nat Evans, A.R.'s gambling partner, and Mont Tennes, the Chicago gambling king, in the lobby of the Congress Hotel (Attell 12).[10] As might be expected, the sighting left Attell with a sense of fascination. Had Rothstein taken a position? And if so, who was calling the shots? Attell almost sounded hurt or violated at the thought that A.R. had bypassed his involvement. Abe also acknowledged the presence of "Sleepy" Bill Burns, the ex-ballplayer; George M. Cohan, composer and singer; Nick "The Greek" Dandolis, a high-stakes gambler; and Remy Doyle, a New Orleans race track owner (Attell 12–13).[11] Burns confirmed to Attell that the first two games were "in the bag," leaving Attell the obvious action of parlaying a small investment quickly into a sizable bankroll (Attell 12–13). On the advice of Burns, Attell claimed he did not bet heavily on the third game of the World Series, and later delighted when he heard (no source was given) that Rothstein had lost a large sum on the game (Attell 13).

Attell did not elaborate on the geographic dominance each of the noted gamblers could provide or what, if any, role they were expected to provide in the conspiracy. Attell also did not address how he, along with many others, danced around the local (Cincinnati and Chicago) gambling syndicates.

Attell confirmed that he had nothing to do with the ballplayers and that all the stories people had mentioned regarding player meetings, moneys and fake telegrams were nothing more than fabrication (Attell 13).[12] Sullivan and Evans, as he saw it, were pulling the strings of the deal. Had Attell made a few dollars on the deal? You bet, but, and he repeated himself, that was the extent of his involvement. To Rothstein, Attell was a whipping boy, an odds pendulum and a fallback position if needed, not to mention a distraction. Sullivan and Evans were the point men, guaranteeing the safety of A.R.'s money and his wagers, not to mention some local air cover against any threatening skies, like that of the Black Hand. As to where the $100,000 fix money ended up, Attell could only venture a guess (Attell 13).

Other than his admission to his winnings, Attell did not comment on his financial condition. The fix money, not to mention the additional finances needed to make the desired profit—pocket change to a gambler such as Arnold Rothstein—was beyond the capabilities of most, including Attell, and something the players either understood or learned from the associated gamblers.

Attell noted that it was Billy Maharg who had spilled his guts to the newspapers (whether or not it was an attempt to qualify for a $10,000 reward for information put up by Charles Comiskey was uncertain) implicating many, including Attell. Cicotte, Jackson and Williams soon followed in a line of confessions that Rothstein was afraid would lead right to his door (Attell 89).[13] Enter lawyer William J. Fallon, the Great Mouthpiece, who would then coordinate, or redirect if you will, an expeditious migration: Attell to Canada, and Sullivan to Mexico. Rothstein, under Fallon's advice, then headed off to Chicago to vindicate himself. Those conducting the interview with Attell did not question him as to why he willingly accepted Fallon's services.

Placing the blame solely on Attell's shoulders, which may have been the intent all along, left the former champ little choice but to return to New York. There, under (of all things) Rothstein's instruction, Fallon took control of the situation.[14] This led to the dismissal of the case. As obvious as stitches on a baseball, Rothstein's efforts shielded both himself and Attell from prosecution. Fallon orchestrated the distraction with the same level of proficiency as Rothstein had executed the fix. Everybody had and knew his place.

At the age of 78, Abe Attell just wanted to clear his name and set the record straight. The *Cavalier* editorial team, headed by Bob Curran, did an outstanding job of letting a storyteller tell his story as it appeared, without interruption.[15] Attell was smart enough to realize that there would be those, whether authors or investigative reporters, who would try to make the pieces of the conspiracy fit even if it was clear that they did not. The old man was tired of being Arnold Rothstein's doormat and just wanted the same benefit of the doubt others involved with the case had been granted.

In 1963, forty-four years after the "Black Sox" and the 1919 World Series, author Eliot Asinof penned a dramatic and detailed account he called *Eight Men Out*. Like an oceanographer who discovers a long-lost shipwreck, Asinof evidently found the thought of what treasure lay beneath to be as alluring as it was exhilarating. Piece by piece, Asinof attempted to reconstruct one of the biggest travesties in American sports history. In what could be viewed as a repeat performance, Asinof interviewed Attell at Jack Dempsey's restaurant. Certainly, if "The Little Champ" had anything to add to his involvement, he was given a forum. As Asinof jabbed Attell, the aging champion selectively countered. It was then up to the author to select the appropriate pieces. Excavation, Asinof understood, without impacting each artifact or its surroundings, was essential. Each piece had its own tale to tell, in a story that already had an ending.[16]

The project, despite the liberties taken, was nothing short of a monumental undertaking. The complete story, as the author saw it, had yet to be told. Clearly understanding the complexity, Asinof, who was born in 1919, undertook it with a passion. Dealing with missing documents, deceased participants (Hugh Fullerton died in 1946, Joe Jackson in 1951, Fred McMullin in 1952, William Maharg in 1953, Bill Burns in 1953, Buck Weaver in 1956 and "Lefty" Williams in 1959, to name only a few) and silent survivors wasn't easy, but he managed to construct a view and to present it in the best form he could. The work, despite any criticism, was a masterful accomplishment. The *New York Times* called it "an admirable journalistic feat!" Yet it wasn't until it was turned into screenplay, and then made into a film (1988), that it really captivated its audience. It was then, during the "Romancing Jackson Era," a time that saw not only Asinof's book made into a film, but also *Field of Dreams*, an adaption of W.P. Kinsella's compelling novel *Shoeless Joe*, that people stopped and took notice.

For some, if not most, the tragedy of the Black Sox scandal rests in a flawed and inconsistent process, to say nothing of the lack of evidence.[17] It violated the sanctity of the game to become the ultimate tale of deception—a transgression against divine law, if you are a fan of the national pastime. As we approach the centennial of the event, it is only human not only to dissect the enigma, but to attempt to solve every remaining piece of the puzzle; curiosity has its own reason for existence. Not a simple task, as a quick glance at many of the outstanding resources listed in this book's bibliography can attest to. Yet I am reminded by conspiracy theorists: complexity serves to only mask the truth, and facts don't cease to exist because they are ignored.[18]

CHAPTER SIXTEEN

Clever Beyond Words

When the end finally came for Abraham Washington Attell, it was on Friday, February 7, 1970, inside the Liberty-Loomis Hospital in the community of Libertyville. He had been living in a nursing home near New Paltz, in the Catskill Mountains of New York. Even in death there was controversy surrounding Attell, in this case his date of birth: some had it as 1883, Attell himself listed it on his draft registration card for World War I as February 22, 1880, but his headstone was etched with 1884. Only days from what most would agree as his eighty-sixth birthday, Attell was recalled not by the adjective that shadowed him during his boxing career, "clever," but instead a descriptor that was prone to different connotations, that of "controversial." Boxing fans, however, knew better.

Of medium height and build, standing five feet four inches tall and weighing from about one hundred and eighteen pounds to one hundred and thirty-three, was how the pugilist described himself. Abraham had brown eyes, and black hair that diminished gradually, in time, and turned gray over the characteristic Attell family widow's peak. Then there was that distinctive muzzle, home to more punches than the average life of a speed bag. Attell's chiseled physique, with his superior arm development, was as imposing as it was intimidating. Despite a marked countenance, he was handsome, a gay blade and a man about town.

Most recalled his San Francisco days, as well they should, and his origins from "South of the Slot," the cable line trolley on Powell Street. It was one helluva neighborhood, a pug's paradise, and home to Jimmy Britt, Jim Corbett, Eddie Hanlon and Billy Uren (Dick Hyland). For the Attell boys, it wasn't so easy being Jewish in an Irish neighborhood, but it wasn't so bad either, knowing your brother had your back.

Turning professional was not only logical for Abe, it appeared as a natural transition. He was a knockout artist then, sending fifteen of eighteen competitors he faced in 1900 to the canvas. His move to Denver would prove a turning point in his career, brilliant in retrospect. Albie was never much for boxing managers, but a few are worth recalling, like "Bad Jack" McKenna, Billy Nolan, George Weedon, Jack Kearns, Dan Morgan and Al Lippe—okay, I'll also mention Tim McGrath, Zeke Abrams, Ike Bloom, and Lob Kohn, but I'll stop there. Denver brought the young fighter a trilogy with George Dixon, an early and much-needed education on the art of defense. And what a defenseman he would become.

The city of St. Louis was home to Attell's first loss (against Harry Forbes), his first "knock out by" (against Benny Yanger), and his first claim of the featherweight crown (against Harry Forbes). He would encounter two more losses there on the way to the world featherweight title, which he would take from New Englander Jimmy Walsh in Chelsea. Sure, Attell could be self-serving, erratic, even recalcitrant; there were times that authorities had a tough time looking away, but hey, that was boxing. And he, for all intents and purposes, was trying to make a living as a preeminent participant.

Abe became a marksman: he perfected a left jab so sound, that it could, and did, carry him to a decision. At angles only the best fighters dreamed of, he delivered precision blows and at a cadence that often mimicked the competition. He drew the fine line drawn between effort and excess exertion, an Attell hallmark.

Without question, the blokes from Britain gave him a run, especially Owen Moran. Nonetheless, Attell never ducked a challenge. In 1908, he fought twelve times, five of them against boxing's elite—Battling Nelson, Freddie Welsh, Ad Wolgast, and *twice* against Moran. Honestly speaking, how many fighters can claim such preeminence in a single year? And when the feather competition faded, instead of looking away, Attell looked up. He wasn't afraid to tackle Freddie Welsh, even if it proved the wrong decision.

His ten-round no-decision against Jem Driscoll quickly became a ring classic. It was held at the old National Athletic Club in New York, and everyone, and I mean everyone, in attendance marveled at the defensive prowess by these pugilists. After the fight, there wasn't a promoter in the world who wouldn't have taken a distance match between the two, if it had been a viable option.

It was a shrewd Uncle Tom McCarey who set Attell up against Kilbane. "The Little Champ" never should have left New York. He knew better, and did it anyway—it was as if the weight of the title had finally reached a pinnacle. It was his birthday, this is true, but luck, even Attell knew, could carry you only so far. He lost the twenty-round decision.

It's never easy to hang up the gloves, and victory laps weren't en vogue, so at some point "The Little Hebrew" had to call it a day. Truthfully, his career ended when he lost the title to Kilbane.

Fighting over 170 times and becoming a world champion, he inspired his brothers Caesar and Monte, not to mention the entire Attell clan. How many brothers can say they held simultaneous world championships? In doing so the Attell family etched their name into stone among boxing's greatest kinsfolk: the McGoverns, Sullivans, Leonards, Jeffries, Wolgasts, etc. And the boys did it against a wealth of adversity, to say nothing of the anti–Semitism.

Few historians point out how much Abraham did for his family, his mother specifically. They disregard his fierce and bloody battles against multiple members of boxing's elite, including Battling Nelson. They ignore his incredible dominance over the featherweight division and would rather spend time spinning hypotheticals about Attell's association with the 1919 World Series than to revisit the record of a genuine ring champion. With regard to the baseball conspiracy, Abe Attell denied the charges and nothing was proved to implicate him.

The 1919 Black Sox scandal was nothing short of tragedy, for not only Major League Baseball but for all professional sports. You can't help but to feel sorry for everyone involved. However, to be truthful, those implicated chose their fate; some were handsomely rewarded, others were victims of circumstance. There are choices in life, and if you are not careful, they can later define you. With or without Abraham Attell, the 1919 World Series would not have ended up any different!

Branded, Attell paid the price, over and over again. He couldn't escape the association. At times his brilliant boxing career even had to take a backseat, and that was unwarranted. But throughout, and true to form, Attell might have feinted, he might have ducked a few doozies, but when he had to take a punch, he did so.

Following his entrance into *The Ring* Magazine Hall of Fame in 1955, Abe Attell was inducted into the National Jewish Sports Hall of Fame in 1982; the International Jewish Sports Hall of Fame in 1983; the World Boxing Hall of Fame in 1981; the San Francisco Boxing Hall of Fame in 1985; and the International Boxing Hall of Fame in Canastota, New York, in 1990. The inaugural class included 53 elite members. Joining Attell in the Old Timer category were Jack Britton, Tony Canzoneri, James J. Corbett, Jack Dempsey, George Dixon, Jim Driscoll, Bob Fitzsimmons, Joe Gans, Harry Greb, Peter Jackson, James J. Jeffries, Jack Johnson, Stanley Ketchel, Sam Langford, Benny Leonard, Terry McGovern, Barney Ross, Gene Tunney, Mickey Walker and Jimmy Wilde.

Although he will always stand proudly among these great men, he will stand alone as "The Little Champ."

> *"If I am not for me, who is for me; and if I am (only) for myself, what am I? And if not now, when?"—Hillel,* Ethics of the Fathers, *1:14*

Appendix:
Abe Attell Official Record

Monikers: The Little Champ, The Little Hebrew
Born: February 22, 1884, in San Francisco, California
Parents: Father Max Attell, 1846–1929. Born: September 24, 1846, in Krakow, Malopolskie, Poland. Abraham's father Max passed away on February 5, 1929, in Thomasville, Georgia, at the age of 82. Mother: Anna Rotholtz, 1849–1914. Born: August 1849 in Poznan, Poland. Abraham's mother Anna passed away on September 26, 1914, in San Francisco, California, at the age of 65.
Siblings: Coleman Attell, 1868–1935; Yetta G. Michaels, 1873–1923; Joseph Attell, 1874–1946; Jacob Attell, 1874–1926; Meyer Attell, 1876–1951; Sarah Attell Bleadon, 1878–1974; Rose Attell Abraham, 1879–1968; Caesar Julius Attell, 1880–1979; Rachel Attell Glicksberg, 1883–1958; Monte Attell, 1885–1960; and Florence Attell, 1888–1967.
Died: February 7, 1970, in New Paltz, New York; Buried at Beaverkill Cemetery, Sullivan County, New York.
Attributes: Right-handed; 5'4"; weight: 122 pounds
Rated at: Featherweight
Reach: 66 in (168 cm)
Managers: Numerous, including: Jack McKenna, Jack Cohan, Ike Bloom, Harry Pollock, Al Lippe, Billy Nolan, and many others.

Notes

Since man has fought man, man has tried to regulate the battle. So if you intend to evaluate a fighter by his record, you must understand that certain laws were established and that they may vary by location. By the end of the nineteenth century, some specific legislation banned promoting and engaging in "ring or prize fights."

The Horton Law became effective in 1896, legalizing boxing in the state of New York until 1900. And as New York went, so, in most cases, did the sport. The Lewis Law then repealed the Horton Law in August 1900, making prizefighting illegal in New York State. But New York boxing clubs danced around the laws until 1911. On July 26, 1911, New York State Governor John Adams Dix signed a bill, the Frawley Act, permitting ten-round "no-decision" bouts, using eight-ounce gloves, but also adding other stipulations. The bill became effective on August 29, 1911. The "no decision" era was born, even if few accepted it.

The Frawley Act ended in November 1917, and again boxing became illegal. The New York State Senate adopted the Walker Law in March 1920, which legalized boxing and formally established the New York State Athletic Commission (NYSAC), which became the model for many other jurisdictions throughout the United States.

Also worth noting is that weight classes varied. For example, the State Athletic Commission, predecessor to NYSAC, issued a new scale of weight divisions in 1912, and revised it to the following in 1916: paperweight: 108 pounds (1912 =105); bantamweight: 115; featherweight: 123 (1912 =125); lightweight: 133 (1912 =135); welterweight: 144 (1912 =145); middleweight: 158 (1912 =155); commission: 175; heavyweight above 175. Bear in mind, too, that some East Coast clubs also had their own set of rules and regulations, some even banning "colored" boxers.

Abbreviations: KO=Knocked out opponent; KO by=Knocked out by opponent; W=Won by decision; L=Lost by decision; WF=Won foul; LF=Lost on foul; D=Draw; ND=No-Decision; NC=No Contest; EX=Exhibition; HOF=member of the International Boxing Hall of Fame; and -1, after a L, indicates the number of the loss.

* = See notes below year

1900

Aug. 15	William Schoenbeim	San Francisco	W2*
Aug. 19	Kid Lennett	San Francisco	KO2
Aug. 29	Kid Dodson	San Francisco	KO2
Aug. 31	Joe O'Leary	San Francisco	KO4
Sept. 18	Benny Dwyer	San Francisco	KO3
Oct. 4	Joe Hill	San Francisco	KO4
Oct. 10	Eddie Hanlon	San Francisco	W5
Oct. 19	Dick Collins	San Francisco	KO1
Oct. 25	Lew White	San Francisco	KO1
Nov. 2	Jim Barry	San Francisco	KO1
Nov. 8	Frank Dell	San Francisco	KO3
Nov. 18	Kid O'Neil	San Francisco	KO1
Nov. 24	George Brown	San Francisco	KO2
Dec. 4	Kid Jones	San Francisco	KO1
Dec. 8	Peter Carroll	San Francisco	KO2
Dec. 15	Kid Dulley	San Francisco	KO1
Unconfirmed	Kid Powers	San Francisco	KO2*
Dec. 20	Jockey Bozeman	San Francisco	W10–pro debut

* Notes: Number of fights–18; rounds–47. Six first-round knockouts. Fought six opponents with moniker "Kid." All Attell's fights were held in San Francisco. Established a string of ten consecutive knockouts. Knocked out 15 of 18 opponents. Schoenbeim fight recorded by the *San Francisco Call*, but not included in many sources. Dick Collins listed in some sources as Dick Cullen. It is unlikely that Attell fought Kid Powers on the day of his professional debut, as some sources indicate. Sixteen fights in above record verified by *Los Angeles Herald*, November 25, 1908.

1901

Jan. 26	Mike Smith	San Francisco	KO2
Feb. 12	Jockey Bozeman	San Francisco	Unconfirmed
Feb. 15	Kid Buck	Denver	W5
Feb. 22	Kid Buck	Denver	W5
Mar. 1	Kid Delaney	Denver	KO4
Mar. 24	Kid Pieser	Denver	KO3
Apr. 12	Scotty Williams	Denver	KO2
Apr. 26	Young Cassidy	Denver	KO2
June 26	Jockey Bozeman	Denver	KO3*
July 4	Kid Buck	Denver	W5*
Aug. 1	Kid Decker	Pueblo	KO3
Aug. 12	"Colorado" Jack Dempsey	Pueblo	W20
Aug. 24	George Dixon	Denver	D10 (HOF)
Aug. 28	Scotty Williams	Denver	KO1
Aug. 29	Johnny Kid Lewis	Denver	KO3
Sep. 12	George Dixon	Cripple Creek	D20 (HOF)

| Oct. 28 | George Dixon | St. Louis | W15 (HOF)* |
| Nov. 4 | Harry Forbes | St. Louis | L15–1 |

* Notes: Number of fights–18; rounds–128. Kid Buck was Attell's first repeat opponent, first victory outside the city of San Francisco, and the first opponent to fight in a trilogy of battles. Jockey Bozeman was Attell's second repeat opponent and first opponent he fought in two different cities. The unconfirmed fight with Bozeman, scheduled on February 12, was for ten rounds at 108 pounds in front of the Reliance Athletic Club. Bozeman broke his hand in the second round of the June 26 fight and could not continue. Colorado Jack Dempsey was Attell's first bout to exceed 10 rounds and longest of his career thus far. The fight decision was changed from an Attell loss to a win as a result of spectator pressure. George Dixon was the first member of Hall of Fame Attell fought. Dixon was the second fighter to complete a trilogy with Attell, but the first Hall of Famer to do so. Harry Forbes was Attell's first professional loss. For the third time, Abe Attell posted five consecutive knockout victories. In his first two years in professional boxing, Attell posted 24 knockouts.

1902

Mar. 20	Kid Broad	St. Louis	D15
Apr. 10	Kid Broad	St. Louis	W20
Apr. 24	Benny Yanger	St. Louis	KO by 19–2*
Aug. 25	Kid Abel	Chicago	W6
Sep. 11	Kid Abel	St. Louis	W20
Oct. 15	Aurelio Herrera	Oakland	W15
Nov. 10	Harry Forbes	Chicago	D6
Dec. 8	Buddy Ryan	Chicago	W6

* Notes: Number of fights–8; rounds–107. Benny Yanger was Attell's second professional loss and first via knockout. Both Broad and Abel bouts are a testament to Attell's willingness to rematch. Fight with Yanger was stopped at the West End Athletic Club by police in the nineteenth round, and Referee George Siler awarded fight to Yanger. This was the first year Attell reduced his fight frequency and the first year he did not fight in the city of San Francisco.

1903

Jan. 29	Eddie Hanlon	San Francisco	D20*
Mar. 12	Eddie Toy	San Francisco	W20*
Sept. 3	Johnny Reagan (Regan)	St. Louis	W20

* Notes: Number of fights–3; rounds–50. First year in which every battle was at least ten rounds. First year he did not fight an opponent with the moniker "Kid." Some sources incorrectly state Hanlon fight at ten rounds. The Toy fight was part of a benefit held for Frank McConnell.

1904

Jan. 4	Harry Forbes	Indianapolis	D10*
Jan. 25	Maurice Rauch	Indianapolis	Canceled
Feb. 1	Harry Forbes	St. Louis	KO5*
	(Claimed world featherweight title)		
Feb. 18	Kid Herman	Chicago	W6
Feb. 27	Young Erne	Philadelphia	ND6
Mar. 9	Patsy Haley	Hot Springs, AR	KO5
Mar. 23	Maurice Rauch	Hot Springs	KO6
Mar. 28	Aurelio Herrera	Chicago	W6
May 14	Young Erne	Philadelphia	ND6
June 2	Jack McClelland	St. Louis	L15–3
June 23	Johnny Reagan	St. Louis	W15
Oct. 13	Tommy Sullivan	St. Louis	KO by 5–4
	(For vacant world featherweight title)		
Nov. 19	Young Erne	St. Louis	W20
Dec. 8	Tommy Feltz	St. Louis	W15

Notes: Number of fights–13; rounds–120. First Forbes fight was essentially a sparring exhibition with seven-ounce gloves. The second Forbes fight was an attempt to avenge loss, which Attell did successfully on February 1. Forbes was also Attell's third fight trilogy. Attell was a substitute for Tommy Mowatt in the February 18 battle against Herman. Rauch battle on January 25 was canceled. McClelland fight was Attell's third professional loss. Reagan fight often incorrectly listed as twenty rounds. Sullivan battle was Attell's fourth professional loss, second via knockout. Erne fight was originally scheduled for November 17.

1905

Jan. 28	Tommy Murphy	Philadelphia	ND6
Feb. 3	Tommy Feltz	Baltimore	W15
Feb. 22	Kid Goodman	Boston	D15
Feb. 24	Eddie Hanlon	Philadelphia	ND6*
May 1	Jimmy Dunn	Sharon, PA	D12
May 10	Harry Forbes	Detroit	W10*
May 22	Battling Nelson	Philadelphia	ND6 (HOF)
Oct. 4	Young Erne	Philadelphia	ND6*
Nov. 1	*Chick Tucker*	*New York*	*EX3*
Nov. 8	Tommy Mowatt	Philadelphia	ND6
Nov. 16	Tommy Mowatt	Baltimore	W15
Nov. 23	Kid Sullivan	Baltimore	D15
Dec. 20	*Eddie Daly*	*New York*	*EX3*

* Notes: Number of fights–11; rounds–112. Forbes fight completes Attell's first tetralogy. Goodman fight was fought under a secret agreement. Dunn fight often listed incorrectly as fifteen rounds. Erne fight completes Attell's second tetralogy. Tommy Mowatt represents the sixth time Attell has fought the same opponent back-to-back. Sullivan fight likely a no-decision rather than a draw.

1906

Jan. 15	Chester Goodwin	Chelsea	D15
Jan. 17	*Tony Bender*	*New York*	*EX3*
Jan. 17	*Ralph Linder*	*New York*	*EX3*
Jan. 22	Billy Maynard	Portland	W10
Feb. 22	**Jimmy Walsh**	**Chelsea**	**W15**
	(Won vacant world featherweight title)		
Mar. 7	*Tony Bender*	*New York*	*EX3*
Mar. 13	*Artie Edmunds*	*New York*	*EX3*
Mar. 15	*Itsy Ryan*	*New York*	*EX3*
Mar. 19	Phil Logan	Philadelphia	ND6
Apr. 20	Frankie Neil	Los Angeles	Canceled
Apr. 24	*Kid Herman*	*Los Angeles*	*EX4*
May 11	Kid Herman	Los Angeles	D20
July 4	Frankie Neil	Los Angeles	W20
	(Retained world featherweight title)		
Aug. 15	Frank Carsey	Grand Rapids	W15
Sept. 3	Frank Carsey	Davenport	KO3
Oct. 30	Harry Baker	Los Angeles	W20
	(Retained world featherweight title)		
Nov. 16	Billy DeCoursey	San Diego	W15
	(Retained world featherweight title)		
Dec. 7	Jimmy Walsh	Los Angeles	KO9
	(Retained world featherweight title)		

* Notes: Number of fights–11; rounds–148. A battle with Mowatt scheduled for January at the West End Club was canceled and the Attells barred from fighting in the city. The Goodwin fight often incorrectly listed as January 16. On his birthday, Attell captured world featherweight title by defeating Walsh. Some sources incorrectly list a fight with Tony Moran on March 15, which actually involved Baltimore fighter "Kid" Attell (see

"Attell Defeated Moore," *Minneapolis Journal*, March 16, 1906, p. 14). The Herman fight was at catchweight. Some sources incorrectly list Herman fight as a title defense. Frank Carsey represents the seventh time Attell has fought the same opponent back-to-back. The Walsh clash on December 7 some record as KO8. As the undisputed world featherweight champion, he officially defends his title at least four times.

1907

Jan. 18	Harry Baker	Los Angeles	KO8
	(Retained world featherweight title)		
Apr. 3	Spike Robson	Philadelphia	ND6
Apr. 17	Tom O'Toole	Philadelphia	ND6
May 24	Kid Solomon	Los Angeles	W20
	(Retained world featherweight title)		
Sept. 12	Jimmy Walsh	Indianapolis	W10*
Sept. 21	Tommy Sullivan	Alton, IL	D6
Oct. 29	Freddie Weeks	Los Angeles	KO4
	(Retained world featherweight title)		

* Notes: Number of fights–7; rounds–60. Three successful world featherweight title defenses. Retained title twice against Harry Baker. A fight with Johnny Reagan was listed in one newspaper for September 27, at Springfield, Illinois, but could not be verified by multiple sources.

1908

Jan. 1	Owen Moran	San Francisco	D25 (HOF)
	(Retained world featherweight title)		
Jan. 31	Frankie Neil	San Francisco	KO13
	(Retained world featherweight title)		
Feb. 28	Eddie Kelly	San Francisco	KO7
	(Retained world featherweight title)		
Mar. 31	Battling Nelson	San Francisco	D15 (HOF)
Apr. 20	Eddie Kelly	Seattle	W8
	(Retained world featherweight title)		
Apr. 30	Tommy Sullivan	San Francisco	KO4
	(Retained world featherweight title)		
June 20	Matty Baldwin	New York	ND6
July 29	Eddie Marino	Sandpoint, ID	W10
Sep. 7	Owen Moran	San Francisco	D23 (HOF)
	(Retained world featherweight title)		
Nov. 25	Freddie Welsh	Vernon, CA	L15 (HOF)-5
Dec. 11	Ad Wolgast	Los Angeles	ND10 (HOF)
Dec. 29	Biz Mackey	New Orleans	KO8

* Notes: Number of fights–12; rounds–144. Attell has retained title twice against Frankie Neil. Kelly fight was stopped by police who prevented a knockout. In Kelly fight of February 28, police prevented an actual knockout. Kelly fight of April 20 billed and reviewed as a successful title defense. Sullivan fight of April 30 questionable with regard to integrity. Welsh was Attell's fifth professional loss. Five successful world featherweight title defenses. Attell has retained title twice against Owen Moran. Attell battled with four members of boxing's elite class: Owen Moran (2x), Battling Nelson, Freddie Welsh and Ad Wolgast.

1909

Jan. 14	Freddie Weeks	Goldfield	KO10
	(Retained world featherweight title)		
Feb. 4	Eddie Kelly	New Orleans	KO7*
	(Retained world featherweight title)		
Feb. 19	Jem Driscoll	New York	ND10 (HOF)

Mar. 1	Young Pierce	Philadelphia	ND6
Mar. 10	Young Pierce	Philadelphia	KO6
Mar. 18	Patsy Kline	New York	ND10
Mar. 23	Frankie Neil	Brooklyn	ND10*
Mar. 26	Frankie White	Dayton	KO8
	(Retained world featherweight title)		
Apr. 26	Biz Mackey	Columbus, OH	W8
	(Attell broke right hand—out for 114 days)		
Aug. 18	Harry Stone	Saratoga	ND10
Sep. 6	Eddie Kelly	Pittsburgh	ND6*
Sep. 14	Tommy O'Toole	Boston	W12
Oct. 5	Buck "Twin" Miller	Philadelphia	ND6
Oct. 8	Patsy Kline	Philadelphia	ND6
Nov. 22	Johnny (Jimmy) Moran	Memphis	W8
Dec. 6	Charlie White	Memphis	W8
Dec. 27	Tommy Mowatt	Kansas City	Canceled

* Notes: Number of fights–16; rounds–131. Attell has retained title twice against Eddie Kelly with identical results. The champion has retained his title twice against Freddie Weeks. Pierce represents the eighth time he has fought the same opponent back-to-back. Kelly fight was held outdoors. Eight rounds was legal limit in Memphis.

1910

Jan. 1	Eddie Kelly	Savannah	KO2*
Feb. 24	Frankie Neil	New York	ND10*
Feb. 28	Harry Forbes	Troy, NY	KO6*
Mar. 18	Johnny Marto	New York	ND10
Apr. 1	Owen Moran	New York	ND10* (HOF)
Apr. 28	Tommy Murphy	New York	ND10
May 20	Tommy Murphy	New York	ND10*
June 24	Owen Moran	Los Angeles	ND10* (HOF)
Aug. 22	Eddie Marino	Calgary	KO3
Sep. 5	Billy Lauder	Calgary	KO7
Sept. 16	Charlie White	Milwaukee	ND10
Oct. 7	Frankie White	Milwaukee	ND10
Oct. 10	Jack White	Winnipeg	D15
Oct. 24	Johnny Kilbane	Kansas City	W10 (HOF)
	(Retained world featherweight title)		
Oct. 27	Biz Mackey	New York	KO6
Oct. 28	Eddie Kelly	Amsterdam, NY	KO4
Nov. 9	Owen Moran	Philadelphia	ND6* (HOF)
Nov. 13	Frankie Conley	New Orleans	D15
	(Retained world featherweight title)		
Nov. 30	Pal Moore	New York	ND10

* Notes: Number of fights–19; rounds–178. Forbes fight was Attell's first quintet. Forbes seconds threw up the sponge in the sixth round. Attell fought three consecutive fighters with the same surname, White. Kelly fight, stopped by police, often incorrectly stated as "KO5." Marino fight, often listed as "W15," was at catchweight. Lauder bout often incorrectly listed as "KO17." Lauder fight was scheduled for only ten rounds, and with the victory Attell was said to have picked up the lightweight championship of Canada. Attell was a substitute for Ad Wolgast in fight against Frankie White on October 7.

1911

Jan. 9	Joe Coster	Brooklyn	ND10
Jan. 13	Patsy Kline	New York	ND10*

Jan. 23	Billy Allen	Syracuse	ND10
Jan. 31	Tommy Kilbane	Cleveland	NC

(Attell broke his right shoulder and injured his left arm
in the fourth round—out for 59 days)

Mar. 31	Frankie Burns	New York	ND10

(Attell aggravated above injuries—out for 173 days)

June 8	Knockout Brown	New York	Canceled
Sept. 20	Matt Wells	New York	ND10
Nov. 3	Herman Smith	Buffalo	ND10
Nov. 15	Young Cohen	New York	ND10
Nov. 20	Willie Jones	New York	ND10
Nov. 23	Leo Johnson	New York	KO5
Dec. 1	Patsy Kline	New York	ND10*
Dec. 2	Willie Jones	New York	ND10
Dec. 4	Joe Clarke	Wilkes-Barre, PA	Canceled
Dec. 18	"One Round" Hogan	New York	Canceled

* Notes: Number of fights–12; rounds–109. Attell broke his right shoulder and injured his left arm in the fourth round resulting from an immediate stoppage during the Kilbane fight. Referee Will McKay declared the fight a no contest. Some record books incorrectly score this as "KO by 4." Clarke fight canceled owing to gate receipts not being sufficient to pay Attell's guarantee. Hogan match had weight conditions that could not be met, plus Attell had no intention of jeopardizing a large deal he had signed to meet Kilbane.

1912

Jan. 14	Jack White	New Orleans, LA	Canceled
Jan. 18	Knockout Brown	New York	ND10
Feb. 22	Johnny Kilbane	Vernon	L20-6*(HOF)

(Lost world featherweight title)

Mar. 9	Tommy Murphy	Daly City, CA	L20-7
Apr. 23	Jimmy Carroll	Sacramento	KO7
July 3	Eddie Marino	Tacoma, WA	W10*
Aug. 3	Tommy Murphy	San Francisco	D20
Sept. 13	Harry Thomas	New York	ND10*
Oct. 24	Jimmy Walsh	Boston	D12*
Nov. 27	Oliver Kirk	St. Louis	KO by 6-8

* Notes: Number of fights–9; rounds–115. Lost world featherweight title to Johnny Kilbane. First time Attell suffered three losses in a single year. Thomas was Attell's first fight back in NYC since six-month suspension. Fight with Marino often listed incorrectly as July 4. The Walsh fight was 12 two-minute rounds shortened due to a weight conflict.

1913

Mar. 19	Oliver Kirk	New York	KO3
Apr. 3	Jimmy Walsh	New York	ND10
Apr. 15	Benny Kaufman	Atlanta	NC*
Apr. 28	George (K.O.) Chaney	Baltimore	W15
July 24	Willie Beecher	New York	ND10
Sept. 1	*Bert Wetherhead*	*Winnipeg*	*KO3*
Sept. 17	*Sid Knott*	*Winnipeg*	*W6*

* Notes: Number of fights–7; rounds–54. Kirk represents the tenth time he has fought the same opponent back-to-back. Atlanta police commissioners stopped the Kaufman fight in the seventh round and it was ruled "no fight." Some resources incorrectly label it a "KO7." The unconfirmed Winnipeg fights are listed in some sources, including *The Ring 1984 Record Book and Boxing Encyclopedia*.

1914

(Inactive)

1915

Sept. 6   Frankie Callahan   Gloversville, NY   KO3*

* Notes: Number of fights–1; rounds–3. A fight in Montreal against Frankie Fleming, scheduled for July 1, could not be confirmed. Frankie Callahan replaced Tommy Houck, whom Attell refused to fight because he could not make weight.

1916

(Inactive)

1917

Jan. 8   Phil Virgets   New Orleans   KO by 4–9*

* Notes: Number of fights–1; rounds–4. Virgets was a local featherweight.

Ring Totals

The record below is that accepted by the International Boxing Hall of Fame in Canastota, New York.

W	L	D	ND	NC	TB	-	KO	W	WF	Ko'd	LD	LF
91	9	18	51	2	171		53	36	2	4	5	0

Abraham Washington Attell was inducted into the International Boxing Hall of Fame in Canastota, New York, on Sunday, June 10, 1990. He was a member of the inaugural class. The IBHOF inducted 53 members on this date. He was one of twenty-one to be included in the "Old Timer" category. The others are Jack Britton, Tony Canzoneri, James J. Corbett, Jack Dempsey, George Dixon, Jim Driscoll, Bob Fitzsimmons, Joe Gans, Harry Greb, Peter Jackson, James J. Jeffries, Jack Johnson, Stanley Ketchel, Sam Langford, Benny Leonard, Terry McGovern, Barney Ross, Gene Tunney, Mickey Walker, and Jimmy Wilde.

Chapter Notes

This work, built from contemporaneous sources, allows Abraham Washington Attell to speak for himself whenever and wherever possible. Fighting in an era where accounts were partisan and records incomplete, the work presents what the author believes to be an accurate portrait. Article titles are included, as it is the author's view that they are extremely helpful in their evaluation of a contest.

Introduction

1. Bert Randolph Sugar, *Boxing's Greatest Fighters* (Guilford: The Lyons Press, 2006), p. 136.

Chapter One

1. "Has Art of Defensive Boxing Reached Highest Development," *St. Louis Republic*, November 17, 1901, p. 27.
2. Richard Barry, "Abe At[t]ell, the Elusive Feather," *Pearson's Magazine*, March 1913, p. 353.
3. *Ibid.*, p. 358.
4. The San Francisco Athletic Club, opened in 1885, was located in the neighborhood of what is now known as SoMa and was destroyed by the 1906 San Francisco earthquake and fire.
5. Barry, "Abe At[t]ell," p. 354.
6. Occasionally, a bargain show packed street boys in the bleachers at 25 cents a head.
7. "Attell Was a Messenger When He Started Career," *Evening World*, January 10, 1914, p. 6. This was the fifth in a series of articles columnist Robert Edgren penned about the "Untold Tales of the Ring."
8. *Ibid.*
9. "Amateurs Box and Bleed for Prize Medals, Nine Bouts at the San Francisco Athletic Club Draw a Crowd," *San Francisco Call*, August 16, 1900, p. 8.
10. "Some Good Boxing in Washington Square Hall," *San Francisco Call*, September 19, 1900, p. 5.
11. The nine boxing bouts held that evening were clearly labeled as amateur events.
12. Attell fought Barry at 110 pounds.
13. "Charity Bazaar a Great Success," *San Francisco Call*, November 9, 1900, p. 11.
14. Some sources list a fight against Kid Powers, KO2, on December 20, but that was the same evening as his professional debut and is considered unlikely.
15. "McConnell Knocked Out in Four Rounds," *San Francisco Call*, December 21, 1900, p. 8.
16. "A Painful Fourth for Some People," *San Francisco Call*, July 5, 1900, p. 5.
17. "Joe Angeli Defeats John Schmelter Easily," *San Francisco Call*, March 20, 1902, p. 8.
18. Today, 255 Third Street is across the street from the block that is the home to the Moscone Center and the Children's Creativity Museum. It is six blocks northwest of AT&T Park. Walking northwest from 255 Third Street, the first corner is Howard Street, followed by Mission Street and then Market Street.
19. "Referee Decides Against Parker," *San Francisco Call*, February 16, 1901, p. 5.
20. *Ibid.*
21. Some sources, such as the *Colorado Springs Gazette* saw the fight a draw.
22. "Put Out by Young Corbett," *Butte Inter Mountain*, June 27, 1901, p. 8.
23. *Ibid.*
24. On July 27, it was reported that Attell was trying to be paired against a couple of fighters, Billy Snailham of San Francisco first, second with Kid McFadden. Western promoters, noting Attell's skills, saw money in his mitts and the quicker they could ink him to a deal the better, but these pairings, as was often the case in the sport, could not be made.
25. George Dixon (1870–1909), aka "Little Chocolate," became the first black man to win a world boxing title when he captured the bantamweight crown in England and later added the world featherweight title (1898–1900); fought from about 1886 until 1906; held victories over Torpedo Billy Murphy, Oscar Gardner and Tommy White; and was inducted into the International Boxing Hall of Fame in 1990.
26. "George Dixon Unable to Get Decision Over Abe Attell in Bantamweight Battle," *Butte Inter Mountain*, August 24, 1901, p. 8.

27. "Matters of General Interest in the Merry World of Sport," *Butte Inter Mountain*, August 27, 1901, p. 8.

28. The Williams fight was on the undercard of the Young Corbett versus Eddie Santry bout hosted by the Colorado Athletic Association.

29. "Sporting News," *Topeka State Journal*, October 12, 1901, p. 1.

30. "Decision Given to Attell Over Dixon," *St. Louis Republic*, October 29, 1901, p. 7.

31. *Ibid.*

32. "Dixon to Meet Attell," *St. Louis Republic*, October 23, 1901, p. 6.

33. No matter what source one chooses, the claim of 33 straight knockouts can't be supported.

34. "Has Art of Defensive Boxing Reached Highest Development," *St. Louis Republic*, November 17, 1901, p. 27.

35. *Ibid.*

36. *Ibid.*

37. *Ibid.*

38. *Ibid.*

39. "Harry Forbes Won from Abe Attell," *St. Louis Republic*, November 5, 1901, p. 7.

40. Harry Forbes (1897–1922), brother of fellow boxer Clarence Forbes, held the bantamweight crown (1902–03); fought from about 1897 to 1913; and held victories over Casper Leon, Kid Goodman and Tommy Feltz.

41. Some reports had both fighters at the 116-pound mark.

42. "Harry Forbes Won from Abe Attell," *St. Louis Republic*, November 5, 1901, p. 5.

43. *Ibid.*

44. *Ibid.*

45. "Attell's Injuries Serious," *St. Louis Republic*, November 5, 1901, p. 5.

46. *Ibid.* If the number of fights is indeed 38, than a number of battles have fallen through the cracks of many sources and remain unverified.

47. "Sports Big and Small," *Saint Paul Globe*, November 14, 1901, p. 5.

48. "To Stop Prize Fights," *Topeka State Journal*, November 19, 1901, p. 2.

49. *Ibid.*

50. Attell fought Dixon, an elite boxer, in his 28th recorded fight and Forbes in his 34th.

51. Some sources list Newark featherweight Kid Henry as losing by a three-round knockout to Attell on November 30, 1901, in Denver.

52. "Challenge for Terry," *Topeka State Journal*, December 28, 1901, p. 2.

Chapter Two

1. "Regan Now Willing to Meet Abe Attell," *St. Louis Republic*, August 11, 1902, p. 5.

2. The Park Commission authorized the construction of two windmills to pump groundwater for park irrigation rather than purchasing water at exorbitant costs from the Spring Valley Water Company. Also, increased property values made the cost of using land for cemeteries prohibitive.

3. "Make a Draw of It," *Arizona Republican*, March 21, 1902, p. 7.

4. "Attell Wins from Broad," *San Francisco Call*, April 11, 1902, p. 4.

5. *Ibid.*

6. Broad had nothing to be ashamed of as he was one of only three fighters, at that time, who had knocked out Corbett (KO4, March 22, 1901).

7. Benny Yanger (1882–1958), Frank Angone, aka "The Tipton Slasher," fought from about 1899 until 1910, and held victories over Harry Forbes, George Dixon and Austin Rice.

8. Yanger had knocked out Corbett in April of 1900, then drawn him in a ten-rounder in November. He had also defeated Forbes the same year, thus his belief.

9. "General Sporting," *The Jennings Daily Record*, June 5, 1902, p. 6.

10. *Ibid.*

11. *Ibid.*

12. "General Fight Gossip and Pugilistic Talk," *St. Louis Republic*, April 27, 1902, p. 10.

13. *Ibid.*

14. *Ibid.*

15. *Ibid.*

16. The manager of the club insisted that he had the assurance of the police that the fight could take place uninterrupted, however such was not the case.

17. "Youth, Strength and Vitality of the Californian Prove Too Much for the Wonderful Science of Fitzsimmons," *San Francisco Call*, July 26, 1902, p. 2.

18. *Ibid.*

19. "Champion Corbett Is Reported to Be in First-Class Condition," *St. Louis Republic*, August 31, 1902, p. 33.

20. *Ibid.*

21. "Abe Attell Wins," *Washington Times*, September 12, 1902, p. 2.

22. "Regan Now Willing to Meet Abe Attell," *St. Louis Republic*, August 11, 1902, p. 5.

23. *Ibid.*

24. *Ibid.*

25. "Wants to Meet Abe Attell," *Butte Inter Mountain*, September 20, 1902, p. 8.

26. Aurelio Herrera (1876–1927) fought from about 1895 until 1909 and held victories over Kid Goodman, Benny Yanger and Young Corbett II.

27. "Boxer Attell Easily Outpoints Herrera in Fifteen-Round Bout," *San Francisco Call*, October 16, 1902, p. 10.

28. "Sullivan Preparing for His Fight with McClelland," *St. Louis Republic*, November 16, 1902, p. 26.

29. *Ibid.*

30. *Ibid.*

31. "Attell Outpoints Buddy Ryan," *Saint Paul Globe*, December 9, 1902, p. 1.

32. "Lightweight Boxers Will Probably Clash in October," *San Francisco Call*, August 7, 1902, p. 10.

33. "New Training Ideas," *St. Louis Republic*, July 18, 1902, p. 5.

34. Today, the corner of Ellis and Powell, a block from Market Street, is near Hotel Union Square, and across the street from the Passport Office.

35. "Featherweight Boxers Are in Fine Condition," *San Francisco Call,* January 28, 1903, p. 8.

36. "Hanlon and Attell Matched," *Butte Inter Mountain*, January 5, 1903, p. 8.

37. *Ibid.*

38. "Attel [sic] and Hanlon in Twenty-Round Bout," *Butte Inter Mountain*, January 30, 1903, p. 8. This is believed to be one of the first printed references to Abe Attell as "The Little Hebrew."

39. *Ibid.*

40. "General Ring Notes and Boxing Gossip," *St. Louis Republic*, February 2, 1903, p. 4.

41. "Eddie Hanlon Gives Young Corbett a Hard Fight," *Saint Paul Globe*, February 27, 1903, p. 5.

42. "Terry M'govern Regains Health," *San Francisco Call*, March 4, 1903, p. 8. This was likely the first time both brothers fought professionally on same card.

43. Alex Greggains was the manager of the San Francisco Athletic Club.

44. "Attell Defeats Game Eddie Toy," *San Francisco Call*, March 13, 1903, p. 8.

45. The match had been scheduled for St. Louis on July 30, August 6, August 10, and August 16, to only name a few dates.

46. "Attell and Regan Matched at Last," *St. Louis Republic*, July 24, 1903, p. 1.

47. *Ibid.*

48. "Attell Defeats Regan," *Bisbee Daily Review*, September 4, 1903, p. 1.

49. "News of the Fighters," *Indianapolis Journal*, December 6, 1903, p. 7.

50. *Ibid.*

51. "Abe Attell's Bomb," *Butte Inter Mountain*, December 26, 1903, p. 7.

Chapter Three

1. "Won Many Contest by His Cleverness," *Indianapolis Journal*, January 3, 1904, p. 8.

2. *Ibid.*

3. *Ibid.*

4. *Ibid.*

5. "Boxing Exhibitions," *Indianapolis Journal*, January 3, 1904, p. 8.

6. "Attell Draws with Forbes," *San Francisco Call*, January 5, 1904, p. 10.

7. "Abe Attell's Manager Balked Near the End," *Indianapolis Journal*, January 26, 1904, p. 8.

8. Some sources claim 25 rounds.

9. "Discontented with Bout," *St. Louis Republic*, February 3, 1904, p. 7.

10. *Ibid.*

11. "General Fighting Notes," *St. Louis Republic*, February 3, 1904, p. 7.

12. *Ibid.*

13. *Ibid.*

14. Kid Herman (1883–1934), Herman Lanfield, fought from about 1899 until 1913 and held victories over Tommy Sullivan, Austin Rice and Clarence Forbes.

15. "In a Boastful Mood," *Topeka State Journal*, February 19, 1904, p. 2.

16. Patsey Haley (1877–1951), boxer, referee and judge, fought from about 1894 until 1914 and held victories over Maxie Hough, Billy Barrett and Billy Rotchford.

17. Although Haley was a skilled boxer, he would later make his mark as a fair and competent referee. Appointed to the role by the New York State Athletic Commission, he worked during the early days of the Walker Law, or the law that legalized professional boxing in New York State.

18. "Abe Attell Won from Herrera in Six Rounds," *The Evening World*, March 29, 1904, p. 12.

19. *Ibid.*

20. *Ibid.*

21. Jack McClelland (1873–1954), aka "The Pride of Pittsburgh," fought from about 1896 until 1911 and held victories over Solly Smith, Eddie Santry and Tommy Sullivan.

22. "M'clelland Receives Decision Over Attell in Fifteen Rounds," *St. Louis Republic*, June 3, 1904, p. 5.

23. *Ibid.*

24. *Ibid.* The solo case mentioned happened on August 16, 1896, in a battle between Joe Choynski versus Tom Sharkey at San Francisco: Choynski complained that Sharkey had struck him a foul blow, but said that he would not claim foul if allowed to recover from its effects. It was granted.

25. *Ibid.*

26. Jack McKenna was back managing Reagan. The fighter had a fallout with his now former manager Mal Doyle, who was suing the fighter for $82.50 in expenses.

27. "Regan Defeated by Abe Attell," *St. Louis Republic*, June 24, 1904, p. 5.

28. *Ibid.*

29. *Ibid.*

30. "Sullivan Knocks Out Attell in Fifth Round," *St. Louis Republic*, October 14, 1904, p. 8.

31. Tommy Sullivan (1881–1967), Thomas F. Sullivan, aka "Brooklyn Tommy Sullivan," held the featherweight crown from 1904 to 1905); fought from 1897 until 1913; and held victories over Austin Rice, George Dixon, and Clarence Forbes.

32. *Ibid.*

33. *Ibid.*

34. "Furey's Opinion on Bouts Upheld," *St. Louis Republic*, November 21, 1904, p. 9.

35. "Sullivan Escapes Corbett's Notice," *St. Louis Republic*, November 26, 1904, p. 11.

36. "Jews to the Front in Athletics," *Spokane Press*, December 2, 1904, p. 2.

37. Tommy Feltz (1882–1938) fought from about 1899 until 1911 and held victories over Jimmy Devine, Austin Rice and Danny Dougherty.

38. "Feltz Will Arrive To-Morrow Morning," *St. Louis Republic*, December 5, 1904, p. 5.

39. "Attell and Tommy Feltz Battle at the West End Club This Evening," *St. Louis Republic*, December 8, 1904, p. 13.

40. "'Sporting Families' Now Prominent in Games and Athletic Contests," *St. Louis Republic*, December 11, 1904, p. 39.

Chapter Four

1. "Wrestling and Boxing Comment and Gossip," *Washington Times*, February 25, 1905, p. 8.

2. "Attells Are Barred," *Saint Paul Globe*, January 1, 1905, p. 18.

3. *Ibid.*

4. *Ibid.*

5. *Ibid.*

6. "Feather Champion Bouts Proposed," *Washington Times*, January 25, 1905, p. 8.

7. While the tournament Hurtig proposed never took place, the promoter, seeing Cuba as a worthy investment, purchased a theatre and hotel in Havana. Hurtig was stricken with a heart attack and died aboard the steamship *Reliance* on March 9, 1928.

8. "Attell Defeats Tommy Murphy," *Daily Press*, January 29, 1905, p. 3.

9. "Attell and Feltz Battle Tonight," *Washington Times*, February 3, 1905, p. 8.

10. "Wrestling and Boxing Comment and Gossip," *Washington Times*, February 25, 1905, p. 8.

11. *Ibid.*

12. "Hanlon Is Outpointed by Clever Abe Attell," *Evening World*, February 25, 1905, p. 6.

13. Battling Nelson (1882–1954), Oscar Battling Matthew Nelson (Nielsen), held the lightweight crown (1908–10); fought from about 1896 until 1917; held victories over Young Corbett, Jimmy Britt and Joe Gans; and was inducted into the International Boxing Hall of Fame in 1992.

14. "Nelson Meets a Second Defeat," *Minneapolis Journal*, May 23, 1905, p. 8. As Nelson always fought on the square, Attell's decision to take a fight with the lightweight helped remove some his of his ring tarnish.

15. "Battling Nelson No Match for Abe Attell," *Times Dispatch*, May 23, 1905, p. 11.

16. Abe Attell went to England with his manager Billy Day.

17. "Honors for Attell," *Topeka State Journal*, August 30, 1905, p. 2.

18. "Big Talk by Little Pug," *Salt Lake Herald*, October 1, 1905, p. 5.

19. "Attell Outclassed," *Topeka State Journal*, October 5, 1905, p. 6.

20. "Cupid Stays a Fight," *Evening Statesman*, November 7, 1905, p. 8. The two fighters had agreed to meet at the National Sporting Club in London, at 122 pounds, with a side bet of $5,000.

21. "A Drawn Battle," *Evening Star*, November 24, 1905, p. 18.

22. It is the author's opinion, based on his own analysis, that the market was not objective in its observations.

23. This was the earliest instance such a remark was made about Attell's career.

24. "Sporting Brevities," *Spokane Press*, December 1, 1905.

25. "Harry Tenny Knocks Out Monte Attell at Goldfield," *San Francisco Call*, September 16, 1905, p. 11.

Chapter Five

1. "Earthquake in San Francisco," *Evening Star*, April 18, 1906, p. 1.

2. In 1977, seismologists will reduced the magnitude to 7.9.

3. "Flames Are Wiping Out Entire City," *Daily Telegram*, April 18, 1906, p. 7.

4. By 1910 the number of Jews had grown to more than 11,000, nearly one-third of the entire population of the city. By the 1930s, some believed Chelsea had the most Jews per square mile of any city outside of New York City.

5. "Goodwin and Attell Draw," *San Francisco Call*, January 16, 1906, p. 10.

6. "Attell to Meet Bowker," *Palestine Daily Herald*, January 22, 1906, p. 3.

7. Jimmy Walsh (1883–1964) held the bantam crown (1907–07); fought from about 1902 until 1914; and held victories over Tommy Feltz, Danny Dougherty and Bobby Pittsley.

8. "Walsh Released After a Hearing," *St. Louis Republic*, April 1, 1905, p. 5.

9. Record includes newspaper decisions.

10. Most view the division title as being held by Young Corbett II (1901–1904), Jimmy Britt (1904) and Brooklyn Tommy Sullivan (1904–1905).

11. "Knockout Punch Was Lacking," *Barre Daily Times*, February 23, 1906, p. 1.

12. *Ibid.*

13. "Cutting a M'coy Diamond," *Sun*, March 1, 1906, p. 7.

14. "Attell Nearly Knocked Out," *San Francisco Call*, March 8, 1906, p. 10.

15. "Exodus of Broadway Fighters," *Hawaiian Star*, March 15, 1906, p. 7.

16. "Neil's Punch Disastrous Harry Tenny Is Dead," *Evening Statesman*, March 1, 906, p. 1.

17. *Ibid.*

18. "Attell Walloped Logan Fiercely," *Evening World*, March 20, 1906, p. 8.

19. "Attell Prepares for Battle," *Los Angeles Herald*, April 8, 1906, p. 7.

20. The source of that record was not given, and the total was close to what has been verified.

21. "Death and Ruin Follow Earth—Quake Shock in San Francisco," *Lewiston Evening Teller*, April 18, 1906, p. 1.

22. "Wyatt Earp Was Appointed," *San Francisco Call*, December 5, 1896, p. 1.

23. "Lost by a Foul," *Rock Island Argus*, December 3, 1896, p. 1. Wyatt Earp (1848–1929), boxing arbiter, U.S. marshal and frontiersman—full name Wyatt Berry Stapp Earp—was best known for the gunfight at the OK Corral (1881), in which he, his brothers, and his friend Doc Holliday fought the Clanton brothers at Tombstone, Arizona.

24. "Herrera Makes Uncertain Plea," *Los Angeles Herald*, May 30, 1906, p. 5.

25. *Ibid.*

26. "Abe Attell and Herman Matched," *Los Angeles Herald*, April 28, 1906, p. 5.

27. "Little Men in Fine Form," *Los Angeles Herald*, May 9, 1906, p. 5.

28. *Ibid.*

29. "Attell-Herman Fight to Draw," *Los Angeles Herald,* May 12, 1906, p. 8.

30. *Ibid.*

31. *Ibid.*

32. *Ibid.*

33. "Attell Keeps Belt," *Rock Island Argus*, July 5, 1906, p. 7.

34. *Ibid.*

35. *Ibid.*

36. This was Abe Attell's first title defense, and it was successful.

37. Fox was sole owner of the *Police Gazette*, an internationally known sporting publication. The diamond-studded belt, emblematic of the world's boxing championship, was his creation and used to assist the marketing of his publication. It was one of many trophies given out in the world of sports.

38. "Attell Given Decision," *Evening Star*, August 16, 1906, p. 14.

39. "Big Fight to Be Given at Burtis," *Rock Island Argus*, August 23, 1906, p. 7.

40. "Attell May Meet Walsh for $10,000," *Evening Star*, September 17, 1906, p. 10.

41. "Retains the Belt," *Rock Island Argus*, October 31, 1906, p. 3.

42. *Ibid.*

43. "Attell Defeats Aged Decoursey," *Los Angeles Herald*, November 17, 1906, p. 8.

44. "Attell Defends Championship by Defeating Walsh," *Los Angeles Herald*, December 8, 1906, p. 8.

45. *Ibid.*

46. "Abe Attell Returns for Baker Match," *Los Angeles Herald*, December 22, 1906, p. 8.

Chapter Six

1. "A Whole Family of Fighters," *Spokane Press*, January 4, 1907, p. 3.

2. *Ibid.*

3. *Ibid.*

4. See "Casualties in the Prize Ring," *Pacific Commercial Advertiser*, January 14, 1907, p. 7, for a list of individuals.

5. *Ibid.*

6. "Baker Saved by Sponge in Eighth," *Los Angeles Herald*, January 19, 1907, p. 8.

7. *Ibid.*

8. *Ibid.*

9. *Ibid.*

10. *Ibid.*

11. *Ibid.*

12. *Ibid.*

13. Attell refereed a boxing show of the Occidental Club in the Dreamland Pavilion on February 1.

14. "Cupid Does for Abraham Attell," *Los Angeles Herald*, March 15, 1907, p. 8.

15. *Ibid.*

16. "Pugilism," *Evening Times*, April 3, 1907, p. 6.

17. "Attell and Robson," *Evening Times*, April 3, 1907, p. 6.

18. "Robson Fights Draw with Abe Attell," *Labor World*, April 6, 1907, p. 6.

19. "Solomon Backers Not Prominent," *Los Angeles Herald*, May 23, 1907, p. 8.

20. *Ibid.*

21. "Attell Defeats Solomon," *Evening World*, May 25, 1907, p. 4.

22. "I Was Easy Work for Abe Attell,"*Arizona Republican*, May 25, 1907, p. 1.

23. "Fight Situation Shows a Healthy Condition," *San Francisco Call*, May 26, 1907, p. 33.

24. "Kid Solomon Pays Fine for Bird," *Los Angeles Herald*, July 12, 1907, p. 3.

25. "Kid Solomon Calls for Baby Daughter," *Los Angeles Herald*, August 3, 1907, p. 12.

26. "Attell and Walsh Matched," *Topeka State Journal*, September 7, 1907, p. 10.

27. "Not Knocked Out," *Rock Island Argus,* September 13, 1907, p. 3.

28. "Attell Is Willing to Meet Sullivan," *Los Angeles Herald*, September 15, 1907, p. 6.

29. "Keyes in Ring with Baldwin To-Night," *Evening World*, September 23, 1907, p. 8.

30. "Squires Showed Spirit by Taking on Jack Sullivan," *Evening World*, September 27, 1907, p. 14.

31. "Abe Attell Is Convert," *Los Angeles Herald*, October 15, 1907, p. 8.

32. *Ibid.*

33. "Abe Attell Knocks Out Freddie Weeks," *San Francisco Call*, October 30, 1907, p. 10.

34. "Looking for a Fight," *Evening Statesman*, November 30, 1907, p. 3.

35. "Featherweights Settle Terms," *Evening Teller*, December 13, 1907, p. 3.

36. *Ibid.*

Chapter Seven

1. "Attell and Moran Fight to a Draw and Divide Public's 'Easy Money,'" *San Francisco Call*, September 8, 1908, p. 9.

2. Reel 421, Theodore Roosevelt papers, Manuscript Division, Library of Congress, Washington D.C.

3. Owen Moran (1884–1949), aka "The Fearless," fought from about 1900 until 1916; held victories over George Dixon, Monte Attell and Al Delmont; and was inducted into the International Boxing Hall of Fame in 2002.

4. "Feather Weights Struggle Valiantly for Twenty-Five Rounds," *San Francisco Call*, January 2, 1908, p. 8.

5. *Ibid.*

6. *Ibid.*

7. One source quotes not Caesar, but Meyer Attell.

8. "Feather Weights Struggle Valiantly for Twenty-Five Rounds," *San Francisco Call*, January 2, 1908, p. 8.

9. *Ibid.*

10. "Feather Weights Struggle Valiantly for Twenty-Five Rounds," *San Francisco Call*, January 2, 1908, p. 8.

11. "Referee Says the Boxers Were Evenly Matched," *San Francisco Call*, January 2, 1908, p. 8.

12. "Californian Is Eager for Early Return Match," *San Francisco Call*, January 2, 1908, p. 8.

13. "Briton Says He Was Weak from Making Weight," *San Francisco Call*, January 2, 1908, p. 8.

14. From the proper shifting of weight, to positioning (footwork, pivoting, etc.) and execution, punching power, as we know today, comes from numerous elements.

15. "English Champion Finds It Difficult to Make the Required Weight," *San Francisco Call*, January 2, 1908, p. 8.

16. "Abe Attell Is Broke," *Topeka State Journal*, January 28, 1908, p. 2.

17. "Abe Attell Agrees to Meet Neil," *San Francisco Call*, January 18, 1908, p. 8.

18. *Ibid.*

19. "Crack Feather Weight Boxers End Their Heavy Training Work," *San Francisco Call*, February 27, 1908, p. 8.

20. *Ibid.*

21. "Attell Knocks Out Kelly," *Hawaiian Gazette*, March 10, 1908, p. 5.

22. "The Battler Vs. the Jew," *Pacific Commercial Advertiser*, March 25, 1908, p. 3.

23. "Attell Will Match His Cleverness Against Dane's Aggressiveness," *San Francisco Call*, March 17, 1908, p. 8.

24. "Nelson to Meet Attell," *Rock Island Argus*, March 31, 1908, p. 3.

25. "Nelson-Attell Fight Results in a 15-Round Draw," *Evening World*, April 1, 1908, p. 12. Eddie Smith took the fight because Eddie Graney was ill.

26. "Bloody Fight Ends in Draw," *Bemidji Daily Pioneer*, April 2, 1908, p. 2.

27. *Ibid.*

28. "Nelson and Attell Go to a Draw," *Los Angeles Herald*, April 1, 908, p. 8.

29. *Ibid.*

30. *Ibid.*

31. "Bloody Fight Ends in Draw," *Bemidji Daily Pioneer*, April 2, 1908, p. 2.

32. "Fight Fifteen Rounds to Draw," *Salt Lake Herald*, April 1, 1908, p. 8.

33. The *San Francisco Call* reported on April 21, "The fight was witnessed by 4,000 persons." Two special trains from Seattle carried fans to the venue, one went on the excursion steamer Yosemite, the other a locomotive from Everett.

34. "Attell Easily Beats Kelly," *Rock Island Argus*, April 21, 1908, p. 3.

35. "Attell Is Winner," *Seattle Star*, April 21, 1908, p. 2. Billed as for the featherweight championship, the fight was also reviewed as a successful title defense.

36. "Declares That Abe Was Tricky," *Los Angeles Herald*, April 26, 1908, Part IV, p. 1.

37. "Attell Outclassed Tommy Sullivan," *Evening Star*, May 1, 1908, p. 19.

38. "Sullivan Makes No Stand in Bout Which Merits Investigation," *San Francisco Call*, May 1, 1908, p. 8.

39. Matty Baldwin (1885–1918), Matthew M. Baldwin, aka "Bunker Hill Bearcat," fought from about 1902 until 1916 and held victories over Tommy Feltz, Clarence Forbes and Benny Yanger.

40. "Frisco Expects Moran—Attell Fight Will Be a Hot Go," *Albuquerque Citizen*, July 11, 1908, p. 6.

41. "Sporting Sandpoint," *Coeur D'alene Evening Press*, July 25, 1908, p. 2.

42. "Featherweight King Beats Another Dub," *Los Angeles Herald*, July 30, 1908, p. 6.

43. "Marino Sticks with Champion," *Spokane Press*, July 30, 1908, p. 3.

44. "About the Boxers," *Pacific Commercial Advertiser*, August 21, 1908, p. 3.

45. "Attell and Moran Fight to a Draw and Divide Public's 'Easy Money,'" *San Francisco Call*, September 8, 1908, p. 9.

46. "Montanan Loses Middle Weight Title by Knockout Route in Twelfth," *San Francisco Call*, September 8, 1908, p. 9.

47. "Attell and Moran Fight to a Draw and Divide Public's 'Easy Money,'" *San Francisco Call*, September 8, 1908, p. 9.

48. *Ibid.*

49. *Ibid.*

50. "Thinks Decision Unjust," *San Francisco Call,* September 8, 1908, p. 9.

51. "Even Fight Throughout," *San Francisco Call,* September 8, 1908, p. 9.

52. "Briton Claims Victory," *San Francisco Call,* September 8, 1908, p. 9.

53. "Attell and Moran Fight to a Draw and Divide Public's 'Easy Money,'" *San Francisco Call,* September 8, 1908, p. 9.

54. "Jeff Says a Few Things," *Evening Star,* November 1, 1908, p. 3. Attell was also trying to be matched with English feather Jem Driscoll, possibly for Thanksgiving Day afternoon in Colma, California.

55. *Ibid.*

56. Freddie Welsh (1896–1927), Frederick Hall Thomas, aka "The Welsh Wizard," held the lightweight crown (1915–17); fought from about 1905 until 1922; held victories over Willie Ritchie, Ad Wolgast, and Charley White; and was inducted into the International Boxing Hall of Fame in 1997.

57. "Two Greatest Boxers in World Signed Up for Fifteen Rounds," *Los Angeles Herald,* November 3, 1908, p. 6.

58. *Ibid.*

59. "Rialto Gossip" *Los Angeles Herald,* November 12, 1908, p. 6.

60. "Attell Is Resting While His Opponent Is Taking Off Weight," *Los Angeles Herald,* November 24, 1908, p. 6.

61. *Ibid.*

62. "Little Boxing Kings Battle Tonight at Vernon Over Fifteen-Round Route," *Los Angeles Herald,* November 25, 1908, p. 6.

63. *Ibid.*

64. *Ibid.*

65. "Welsh Decisively Defeats Attell in Fifteen Rounds," *Los Angeles Herald,* November 26, 1908, p. 6.

66. *Ibid.*

67. "Abe Attell Pleads That Gambling Debts Are Void," *Evening Bulletin,* December 24, 1908, p. 12.

68. Ad Wolgast (1888–1955), Adolphus Wolgast, aka "The Michigan Wildcat," he held the lightweight crown (1910–12); fought from 1906 until 1920; held victories over Battling Nelson, Owen Moran and Joe Rivers; and was inducted into the International Boxing Hall of Fame in 2000.

69. "Wolgast Finds Many Admirers," *Los Angeles Herald,* December 9, 1908, p. 6.

70. "Attell-Wolgast Fight a Draw," *Daily Arizona Silver Belt,* December 12, 1908, p. 1.

71. Biz Mackey (1883–1962), Frank Mackey, fought from about 1901 until 1916 and held victories over George Dixon, Maurice Rauch and Johnny Kilbane.

72. "Attell Knocks Out Mackey in Eighth," *Los Angeles Herald,* December 30, 1908, p. 7.

Chapter Eight

1. "Weeks Is the Favorite of Tonopah Fans," *Tonopah Daily Bonanza,* January 13, 1909, p. 3.

2. "Abe Attell Signs Up for Battle Thursday," *Ogden Standard,* January 8, 1909, p. 2.

3. "Abe Attell Stopped Weeks in Ten Whirlwind Rounds," *Tonopah Daily Bonanza,* January 15, 1909, p. 1.

4. *Ibid.* That Team Attell didn't complain about the ring size surprises some people.

5. "Abe Attell Stopped Weeks in Ten Whirlwind Rounds," *Tonopah Daily Bonanza,* January 15, 1909, p. 1

6. *Ibid.,* p. 4.

7. *Ibid.*

8. *Ibid.*

9. "Abe Wakes Up," *Hawaiian Star,* January 15, 1909, p. 6.

10. Jim Driscoll (1880–1925), Jem Driscoll, held the British featherweight crown (1912–13); fought from about 1901 until 1919; held victories over George Dixon, Jack Roberts and Pedlar Palmer; and was inducted into the International Boxing Hall of Fame in 1990.

11. "Attell Loses His Money," *Fergus County Democrat,* February 2, 1909, p. 6.

12. "Abe Attell Easily Defeats Eddie Kelly," *San Francisco Call,* February 5, 1909, p. 8.

13. "Driscoll Too Clever for Abe," *Los Angeles Herald,* February 20, 1909, p. 6.

14. Driscoll claimed this to Vincent Treanor of *The Evening World.*

15. "Opinions on the Fight," *Evening World,* February 20, 1909, p. 14.

16. "Attell Outpoints Pierce," *Rock Island Argus,* March 2, 1909, p. 3.

17. *Ibid.*

18. *Ibid.*

19. "Questions," *Evening World,* March 20, 1909, p. 27.

20. Frankie Neil (1883–1970), Francis James Neil, held the bantamweight crown (1903–04); fought from about 1900 until 1910; and held victories over Clarence Forbes, Harry Forbes and Harry Tenny.

21. "Attell Slices Up Frankie Neil," *Norwich Bulletin,* March 24, 1909, p. 3.

22. "Frankie White Knocked Out by Abe Attell," *San Francisco Call,* March 27, 1909, p. 9.

23. Figure quoted from the *Spokane Press,* April 15, 1909.

24. "Attell Breaks Hand and Takes Lay-Off," *Salt Lake Tribune,* April 30, 1909, p. 10.

25. *Ibid.*

26. In the article "Coffroth's Many Bouts," *Topeka State Journal,* April 30, 1909, p. 27, it mentions the deal.

27. "Owen Moran Wants Abe Attell Again," *Ogden Standard,* August 13, 1909, p. 7.

28. "Attell Get the Decision But—," *Tacoma Times*, September 15, 1909, p. 2.

29. "Abe Attell Is Given Decision," *Los Angeles Herald*, September 15, 1909, p. 4. The decision was a surprise to many who felt it should have gone the other way.

30. "Attell Bests Miller," *Salt Lake Tribune*, October 7, 1909, p. 10.

31. "Kline No Match for Abe Attell," *Washington Times*, October 9, 1909, p. 4.

32. "Little Boxers Hold Attention of Fight Fans," *San Francisco Call*, October 28, 1909, p. 11.

33. *Ibid.*

34. "Abe Attell Is Given Decision Over J. Moran," *San Francisco Call*, November 23, 1909, p. 1.

35. Charley White (1891–1959), whose brothers Jack White and Billy Wagner were also boxers, fought from about 1907 until 1930 and held victories over Eddie Murphy, Gilbert Gallant, and Matty Baldwin.

36. "Abe Attell Finds White a Tough One," *Desert Evening News*, December 7, 1909, p. 15.

37. "Abe Attell Willing to Meet Ad Wolgast," *Ogden Standard*, December 4, 1909, p. 2.

38. Mowatt, who had been fighting sporadically over the past few years, took the fight at catchweight.

39. "Ages at Which Pugilists Have Won Championships," *East Oregonian*, April 16, 1909.

Chapter Nine

1. "Attell Retains His Great Speed," *Evening Times*, May 6, 1910, p. 3.

2. "No New Champs in Ring During 1909," *Evening Statesman*, January 7, 1910, p. 3.

3. "Attell Caught at His Old Tricks," *Evening Times*, January 11, 1910, p. 7.

4. "Abe Attell Beats Eddie Kelly in Two Rounds," *San Francisco Call*, January 2, 1910, p. 34.

5. "Personal Stories of Men in the World of Sport," *Spokane Press*, January 31, 1910, p. 8.

6. Frazee was the owner of the Boston Red Sox from 1916 to 1923 and is often recalled for his sale of Babe Ruth to the New York Yankees.

7. "Negroes Afraid of a Frameup," *Evening Times*, July 2, 1910, p. 2.

8. "Mauretania Brings Distinguished List," *Bridgeport Evening Farmer*, February 4, 1910, p. 4.

9. "Easy Bout for Abe Attell," *New York Tribune*, February 25, 1910, p. 9.

10. Neil lost most, if not all, his ring savings on numerous poor investments.

11. "Coffroth Won His Bet with Londoners," *Evening Times*, February 12, 1910, p. 3. The Eccentric club of London was the one made famous by Jules Verne's story "Around the World in Eighty Days."

12. "Shade the Better for Tommy Murphy," *Rock Island Argus*, March 1, 1910, p. 3.

13. "Attell Is Extended by Johnny Marto," *Los Angeles Herald*, March 19, 1910, p. 10.

14. "Attell Beats Owen Moran in New York," *San Francisco Call*, April 2, 1910, p. 18.

15. *Ibid.*

16. "Verbal Scrap Between Attell and Moran," *Spokane Press*, April 12, 1910, p. 1.

17. Harlem Tommy Murphy (1885–1958) fought from about 1903 until 1917 and held victories over Matty Baldwin, Owen Moran and Ad Wolgast. Just as a reminder, that the State of New York forbids decisions.

18. "Tommy Murphy Easy Mark for Abe Attell," *Albuquerque Morning Journal*, May 21, 1910, p. 3.

19. "Attell Retains His Great Speed," *Evening Times*, May 6, 1910, p. 3.

20. *Ibid.*

21. "Nelson at Ranch," *Salt Lake Tribune*, May 29, 1910, p. 50.

22. "M'carey Decision Settles Dispute," *Los Angeles Herald*, June 15, 1910, p. 10.

23. "This Match Not Called a Fight," *Omaha Daily Bee*, June 26, 1910, p. 2.

24. "Jeffries Holds Levee," *Arizona Republican*, July 2, 1910, p. 1.

25. "Black Champion Fails to Best Philadelphia Jack O'Brien," *San Francisco Call*, May 20, 1909, p. 14.

26. "Jeffries Holds Levee," *Arizona Republican*, July 2, 1910, p. 1.

27. "Mill Will Be Wonder of Age, Says Billy Jordan," *San Francisco Call*, July 3, 1910, p. 45.

28. "Attell's Opinion of Gans," *Evening Star*, August 15, 1910, p. 9.

29. *Ibid.*

30. *Ibid.*

31. "Abe Attell Wins," *Salt Lake Herald-Republican*, August 24, 1910, p. 7.

32. "Attell-Marino Scrap a Fast Exhibition," *Tacoma Times*, August 23, 1910, p. 2.

33. "Abe Attell Knocks Out Billy Lauder," *Spokane Press*, September 6, 1910, p. 3.

34. "Attell Beats Charley White," *Evening Standard*, September 17, 1910, p. 2.

35. *Ibid.*

36. *Ibid.*

37. "Abe Attell Matched to Meet Wolgast in Frisco," *Los Angeles Herald*, September 19, 1910, p. 6.

38. "Attell Bests White," *Wenatchee Daily World*, October 8, 1910, p. 6.

39. "Abe Attell and Jack White Box Lively Draw," *Salt Lake Tribune*, October 11, 1910, p. 10.

40. Johnny Kilbane (1889–1957), John Patrick Kilbane, held the featherweight crown (1912–23); fought from about 1907 until 1923; held victories over Monte Attell, George Chaney and Frankie Burns; and was inducted into the International Boxing Hall of Fame in 1995.

41. "Classy Featherweight Boxer Is Good to 'Old Folks,'" *Spokane Press*, November 8, 1910, p. 3.

42. "Vote Mackey to Lemon Club," *Spokane Press*, October 28, 1910, p. 3.

43. "Abe Attell Whips Mackey with Ease," *El Paso Herald*, October 28, 1910, p. 15.

44. "Attell-Moran Draw," *Spokane Press*, November 10, 1910, p. 3.

45. "Sport Spice and Diamond Gossip," *Spokane Press*, November 19, 1910, p. 3.

46. "Feathers Draw in Fast Fight," *Salt Lake Tribune*, November 14, 1910, p. 7.

47. "The Fanning Bee," *Spokane Press*, November 14, 1910, p. 3.

48. Philadelphia Pal Moore (1891–1943), Paul Walter Von Franzke, whose brothers Willie, Reddy, Frankie, and Al were also boxers, fought from about 1907 until 1922 and held victories over Al Delmont, Matty Baldwin and Battling Nelson.

49. "Pal Moore Beaten," *Washington Herald*, December 1, 1910, p. 10. Attell weighed 123½ pounds at ten o'clock and Moore weighed in at 133.

50. "Abe Attell's Fight," *Barre Daily Times*, December 1, 1910, p. 1.

51. "What Attell Thought Before and After," *Evening World*, December 1, 1910, p. 16. Attell always chews gum during his fights.

52. *Ibid.*

53. "Abe Attell One of Wonders of Ring," *Spokane Press*, November 19, 1910, p. 3.

54. "Big Doings in Sport World During Last Twelve Months," *Spokane Press,* December 31, 1910, p. 3.

Chapter Ten

1. "Attell Forced into Ring When Father's Death Left Big Family in Poverty," *Evening World*, February 4, 1911, p. 9.

2. "Boxing," *Omaha Daily Bee*, January 1, 1911, p. 25.

3. "Attell Beaten in Ten Round Go," *Ottumwa-Tri Weekly Courier*, January 12, 1911, p. 2.

4. *Ibid.*

5. Patsy Kline (1892–1950), Pasquale Gengro, fought from about 1907 until 1915 and held victories over Young Britt, Biz Mackey and Young Pierce.

6. "Abe Attell Near to Slumberland," *Evening Star*, January 14, 1911, p. 10.

7. *Ibid.*

8. "Boxing 'Doctors' Disagree," *New York Tribune*, January 15, 1911, p. 10.

9. "Attell's on Points," *Daily Missoulian*, January 24, 1911, p. 7.

10. Some newspapers believed Kilbane was awarded the fight on a technicality.

11. "Atttell-Kilbane Fight Declared No Contest," *El Paso Herald*, February 1, 1911, p. 5.

12. "Attell Not Out of Ring for Good," *Topeka State Journal*, February 1, 1911, p. 2.

13. "Abe Hopes to Meet Driscoll," *Ottumwa Tri-Weekly Courier*, February 4, 1911, p. 5.

14. *Ibid.*

15. "Attell Forced into Ring When Father's Death Left Big Family in Poverty," *Evening World*, February 4, 1911, p. 9.

16. *Ibid.*

17. *Ibid.*

18. *Ibid.*

19. *Ibid.*

20. "Attell Shows Well," *Rock Island Argus*, April 1, 1911, p. 3.

21. *Ibid.*

22. "Magistrates Refuse to Give Warrants for the Arrest of Fighters," *Evening World*, April 1, 1911, p. 6.

23. *Ibid.*

24. "Many Ways to Cheat Scales," *Calmut News*, May 3, 1911, p. 7.

25. *Ibid.*

26. *Ibid.*

27. Figure taken from "Many Good Pugs on Down Path," *Washington Herald*, May 7, 1911, p. 10.

28. "Abe Attell Wants $10,000 Before He'll Box Rivers," *Tacoma Times*, August 14, 1911, p. 2.

29. "I Wouldn't Worry If I Could Sit in Patsy's Corner and Coach Him During His Fights," *Tacoma Times*, September 6, 1911, p. 1.

30. *Ibid.*

31. "Should a Fighter Marry? 'Sure' Says Boxer's Wife," *Tacoma Times*, September 19, 1911, p. 1.

32. *Ibid.*

33. "Robert Edgren's Column," *Evening World*, September 21, 1911, p. 12.

34. *Ibid.*

35. *Ibid.*

36. "Abe Attell Shows Up Young Cohen," *Albuquerque Morning Journal*, November 16, 1911, p. 3.

37. "Easy for Abe Attell," *New York Tribune*, November 21, 1911, p. 8.

38. "Abe Attell Defeats Leo Johnson Easily," *Bridgeport Evening Farmer*, November 24, 1911, p. 7.

39. *Ibid.*

40. "Joe Choynski Is Preparing to Enter Prize Ring Again," *Hawaiian Star*, December 2, 1911, p. 3. In 1901, Choynski knocked out future heavyweight champ Jack Johnson in three rounds.

41. "Fighting Certainly Some Business for Abe Attell," *Evening World*, December 2, 1911, p. 6.

42. "Abe Attell Beats Jones," *New York Tribune*, December 3, 1911, p. 13.

43. "Boxing Bits," *Rock Island Argus*, December 5, 1911, p. 3.

44. "Kilbane Gets Chance to Fight Abe Attell for the Championship," *Evening World*, December 11, 1911, p. 14.

45. Once Attell signed the big deal with Kilbane he was bound to the terms and conditions of that contract which was likely far more comprehensive, including title and health protection, than whatever terms he had with Hogan.

46. "Boxing Game Is Badly Tangled Up," *El Paso Herald*, December 16, 1911, p. 30.

47. *Ibid.*

48. "How to Box," *The Day Book*, December 26, 1911, pp. 10–12; December 27, 1911, Part Two, pp.9–10; December 28, 1911, Part Three, pp. 18–19; December 29, 1911, Part Four, pp. 21–22. The first of a four part series to appear inside *The Day Book* from December 26 until December 29, 1911. The piece was also syndicated to other publications such as the *Tacoma Times*.

Chapter Eleven

1. "Hear Attell's Whine," *Topeka State Journal*, February 1, 1912, p. 7. J. Ed Grillo of the *Evening Star* claimed on January 26 that Attell had been "A Faker for Years" but that he was "not the only one."

2. Knockout Brown (1891–1948), Valentine Braunheim, aka "Kid Brown," fought from about 1908 until 1916 and held victories over Johnny Allen, Kid Goodman and Harlem Tommy Murphy.

3. "Brown Loses Fight," *Topeka State Journal*, January 19, 1912, p. 5. Attell's manager at this time was George Weeden; Attell's services were also being requested to help train Fireman Jim Flynn.

4. *Ibid.*

5. "Attell Swears He Was Doped in Hand," *Bridgeport Evening Farmer*, January 23, 1912, p. 7.

6. *Ibid.*

7. "Deny Drugging in Bout," *New York Tribune*, January 25, 1912, p. 8.

8. *Ibid.*

9. *Ibid.* Haley should have a good understanding, as he fought Attell in 1904.

10. *Ibid.*

11. "Attell Ruled Out of Game," *Tacoma Times*, January 26, 1912, p. 2. Goodman, Attell's second, was also suspended.

12. "Think Attell Decision Will Have Good Effect," *Washington Times*, January 26, 1912, p. 15.

13. On his way West, Attell did see Doctor Reese in Youngstown, Ohio, to treat his badly jammed right thumb.

14. "Hear Attell's Whine," *Topeka State Journal*, February 1, 1912, p. 7. J. Ed Grillo of the *Evening Star*, claimed on January 26, that Attell had been "a faker for years" but that he was "not the only one."

15. "Abe Attell Is in Danger of Losing His Long Worn Crown on February 22," *The Day Book*, January 31, 1912, p. 13. The source also predicted the transfer of title.

16. *Ibid.*

17. "Abe Attell Gives Up Championship," *Evening Times*, February 23, 1912, p. 3.

18. *Ibid.*

19. *Ibid.*

20. *Ibid.*

21. *Ibid.*

22. *Ibid.*

23. "Johnny Kilbane Is the Featherweight Champion," *Tonopah Daily Bonanza*, February 24, 1912, p. 1.

24. "Great Little Fighter Defeated at Last by a Man in His Class, Kilbane," *San Francisco Call*, February 25, 1912, p. 35.

25. *Ibid.*

26. "Abe Attell Denies He Has Hard Feelings," *Daily Missoulian*, February 25, 1912, p. 10.

27. "Jim Jeffries Talks of Fight," *Marion Daily Mirror*, February 24, 1912, p. 6.

28. Advertisement for the Princess Theatre, *Kennewick Courier*, May 24, 1912, p. 6.

29. "Eyton Hits Back," *Tacoma Times*, February 28, 1912, p. 2.

30. "Prepares for Fight," *Topeka State Journal*, February 28, 1912, p. 5.

31. "Did Abe Attell Go Broke When He Lost the Championship," *The Day Book*, March 6, 1912, p. 22.

32. "Fought 3000 Rounds, Made Quarter of a Million, but Gambled It Away; The Passing of Attell," *The Day Book*, March 19, 1912, p. 9.

33. "Ex-Champion Abe Attell Is Whipped by 'Harlem Tommy,'" *Salt Lake Tribune*, March 10, 1912, p. 29.

34. *Ibid.*

35. *Ibid.*

36. *Ibid.*

37. *Ibid.*

38. *Ibid.*

39. "Murphy Gives Abe Attell a Beating," *Tacoma Times*, March 11, 1912, p. 2.

40. It was alleged that Attell contacted Murphy and his manager Buckley three times, but was unable to secure a definitive answer from them regarding their decision.

41. "Abe Attell Sues," *Washington Herald*, March 16, 1912, p. 11.

42. "Fought 3000 Rounds, Made Quarter of a Million but Gambled It All Away," *Seattle Star*, March 19, 1912, p. 2.

43. "Poker Habit Cost Abe Attell Championship," *Salt Lake Tribune*, March 24, 1912, p. 33.

44. *Ibid.*

45. "Attell Preferred Poker Table to Punching Bag," *El Paso Herald*, March 23, 1912, p. 21. Naughton, who was equipped with blinders if needed, failed to discuss Attell's bandaged left shoulder.

46. "Attell Floors Carroll in 7th," *San Francisco Call*, April 24, 1912, p. 12.

47. *Ibid.*

48. "Wells No Match for M'farland," *Evening Star*, May 5, 1912, p. 4.

49. "Abe Attell Goes Back to Nature So He Can Regain Featherweight Championship," *Tacoma Times*, May 25, 1912, p. 2.

50. "Camera Shots of Abe Attell," *Seattle Star*, June 3, 1912, p. 2.

51. "Abe Attell Lives Simple Life Now," *San Francisco Call*, June 1, 1912, p. 14.

52. "Mccarey Denies Wolgast Is Not to Meet Rivers July 4," *Tacoma Times*, June 7, 1912, p. 2.

53. "Attell Comes Back; Gives Marino Ten Round Chase," *Tacoma Times*, July 4, 1912, p. 2.

54. "Attell and Murphy Hammer Each Other to Draw," *San Francisco Call*, August 4, 1912, p. 57.

55. *Ibid.*

56. *Ibid.*

57. "Nolan Puts One Over on Attell," *San Francisco Call*, August 4, 1912, p. 57.

58. *Ibid.*

59. *Ibid.*

60. "Abe Attell Is Shaded by Harry Thomas," *Bridgeport Evening Farmer*, September 14, 1912, p. 7.

61. *Ibid.*

62. "Attell and Walsh Go Twelve Rounds to Draw Decision," *Albuquerque Morning Journal*, October 25, 1912, p. 3. Walsh was believed to be under 124 pounds, Attell was not.

63. "Abe Attell Quits in Midst of a Battle," *San Francisco Call*, November 28, 1912, p. 8.

64. "Attell Departs from Fight Game," *Evening Standard*, December 4, 1912, p. 2.

65. "Now Abe Attell Says 'I'm Still in Game,'" *Arizona Republican*, December 15, 1912, p. 2.

66. "Attell's Confession Verifies the Call," *San Francisco Call*, December 19, 1912, p. 9.

67. *Ibid.*

68. "Kilbane Completes His Destruction of the Attell Family," *Evening World*, December 4, 1912, p. 18.

Chapter Twelve

1. "Attell Wants Just One More Fight," *Evening Public Ledger*, January 27, 1915, p. 12.

2. "Two New Fight Champions Arose During the Past Year," *Evening Times*, January 1, 1913, p. 3.

3. "Attell to Quit Again," *Tacoma Times*, January 1, 1913, p. 2.

4. "Abe Attell Brings Out Tiny Ring Star," *Salt Lake Tribune*, March 14, 1913, p. 8. "Louisiana" would appear on the undercard of Attell's fight with Ollie Kirk.

5. "Attell to Take on Ollie Kirk Wednesday Night," *Bridgeport Evening Farmer*, March 17, 1913, p. 8.

6. "Attell Comes Back; Stops Kirk in Third," *Sun*, March 20, 1913, p. 11.

7. "Murphy Says His Hardest Battle Was Against Abe Attell," *Bridgeport Evening Farmer*, March 10, 1913, p. 7.

8. "Abe Attell Wants to Meet Kilbane in Bout," *Calumet News*, March 24, 1913, p. 7.

9. "Attell Outboxes Walsh in Contest," *Evening Standard*, April 4, 2013, p. 7.

10. "Attell Defeats Walsh in Clever Bout in New York," *Bridgeport Evening Farmer*, April 4, 1913, p. 10.

11. "Attell Punched Hard, but Outfights Walsh," *Sun*, April 4, 1913, p. 11.

12. Both fighters had kept the beam steady at 124 pounds before entering the ring. George Chaney (1892–1958), George Henry Chaney, aka "KO Chaney," fought from about 1910 until 1925 and victories over Charlie Goldman, Young Britt and Philadelphia Pal Moore. Chaney was a southpaw.

13. "Attell Wins Decision," *El Paso Herald*, April 29, 1913, p. 5. The *Baltimore Sun*'s Jack Kincaid supported the accounts.

14. "Rivers Thinks Attell Can Regain Title," *El Paso Herald*, April 18, 1913, p. 10.

15. A Racine featherweight, Matty McCue was being hailed as a rather clever fighter and an interesting match for Attell, if it could be made. A ten-round bout between both fighters was scheduled for Thursday, June 5, in Kenosha, Wisconsin, but never took place.

16. "Kilbane and Abe Attell Off," *Seattle Star*, June 14, 1913, p. 2.

17. "Abe Attell Was Outpointed," *The Day Book*, July 25, 1913, p. 12.

18. *Ibid.*

19. "Attell Is Not in Good Financial Condition," *The Day Book*, December 16, 1913, p. 10.

20. "Attell to Fight Kilbane," *Bridgeport Evening Farmer*, January 7, 1914, p. 14.

21. Shanley's had a reputation for catering to gamblers.

22. "Abe Attell Is Valet to Valuable Library," *Calumet News*, August 10, 1914, p. 7.

23. "$3,000 in Gems Lost by Mrs. Abe Attell," *Sun*, September 2, 1914, p. 12.

24. "Mother of Pugilist Dead," *Evening Times Republican*, September 26, 1914, p. 10.

25. "Attell to Contest Divorce Suit," *Ogden Standard*, December 15, 1914, p. 2.

26. *Ibid.*

27. "Short Bout Should Not Count as a Championship Contest," *El Paso Herald*, December 26, 1914, p. 10. Mrs. Attell believed she lost the bag in New York.

28. "Drop Attell Suit," *Seattle Star*, December 29, 1914, p. 7.

29. "A Tip from a Prize Fighter," *Arizona Republican*, November 25, 1914, p. 4.

30. "Will Age Beat Jack Johnson?," *Ogden Standard*, February 13, 1915, p. 2.

31. "Sporting Once-Overs," *Tacoma Times*, April 8, 1915, p. 2.

32. "Abe Attell Hits Local Portland Boxer at Theater," *Daily Capital Journal*, April 5, 1915, p. 6.

33. "Plaza," *Bridgeport Evening Farmer*, July 17, 1915, p. 12. The *Evening Public Ledger* also reported, on July 24, that "by defeating Charley White in New York the other night Ted Lewis enabled Abe Attell to win $600."

34. "Accuse Chip and Clabby of Faking Fight," *Bridgeport Evening Farmer*, May 15, 1915, p. 8.

35. Located in Fulton County, New York, Glovers-

ville once the hub of America's glove-making industry. Callahan was also identified as Frankie Fleming.

36. "Mrs. Abe Attell Sues for Divorce," *Omaha Daily Bee*, September 23, 1915, p. 5. She also confirmed they had no children or community property.

37. It was noted on October 1 that "Abe Attell, former featherweight champion, was arrested the previous day for contempt of court in failing to appear in court for an examination supplementary to a judgement for $194 due one Mark Bernstein. Attell paid the sheriff the full amount and was released." While this was not in connection to his divorce, it may be an indication of his mindset at the time.

38. "Boxers of Today Afraid of Punch," *Grand Forks Daily Herald*, November 4, 1915, p 8.

39. *Ibid.*

40. *Ibid.*

41. "Abe Counted House; Then Fought Moran," *Southern Herald*, December 10, 1915, p. 1.

42. "Funny Story of Kid Broad," *Tucumcari News and Tucumcari Times*, December 23, 1915, p. 3.

43. *Ibid.*

44. "Abe Attell Former Featherweight," *The Day Book*, January 15, 1916, p. 11.

45. "Champ Kilbane Says He Found Best Left Hand," *Seattle Star*, January 17, 1916, p. 7.

46. *Ibid.*

47. *Ibid.*

48. "Sporting Notes," *El Paso Herald*, April 3, 1916, p. 10.

49. "Abe Attell Opens Store," *Richmond Times-Dispatch*, April 25, 1916, p. 9.

50. "Park," *Bridgeport Evening Farmer*, May 20, 1916, p. 9.

51. "Attell Originator of Bowknot Trick," *Bridgeport Evening Farmer*, April 26, 1916, p. 11.

52. "Huggins Dodges Player Limit Rule," *El Paso Herald*, May 15, 1916, p. 9.

53. "Abe Attell to Try to Stage Come-Back," *Ogden Standard*, October 10, 1916, p. 9.

54. "Sensational Even in Dying," *Tacoma Times*, November 23, 1916, p. 1.

55. *Ibid.*

56. "Plans for Spring Exhibitions Are Being Made by Griffith," *Evening Star*, January 9, 1917, p. 16.

57. "Leonard and Mitchell Throw Shadows Across Freddie Welsh's Trail," *Bismarck Tribune*, January 10, 1917, p. 6.

58. "Pugilistic Ranks Invaded by Hebrews Who Now Hold Four of Seven Championships!" *Fairmont West Virginian*, July 30, 1917, p. 6.

59. *Ibid.*

60. "Abe Attell Is Thirty-Four Today," *Bridgeport Time and Evening Farmer*, February 22, 1918, p. 12.

61. "Tad's Tid-Bits," *Washington Times*, March 16, 1918, p. 12.

62. "Sportography," *Tulsa Daily World*, May 24, 1918, p. 11.

63. "Field Contests Will Mark Yankees' Game," *Washington Times*, May 27, 1918, p. 14.

64. "Help for Monte Attell," *Sun*, July 14, 1918, p. 6.

65. "Attell Wants to Fight," *Seattle Star*, August 23, 1919, p. 17.

66. "Attell to Reenter Ring," *Sun*, August 31, 1919, p. 6. Attell was also working with fighter Fred Fulton.

67. "Throttle Tricky Managers If Boxing Is to Flourish," *Sun*, December 15, 1918, p. 5.

68. "Pacing the Sport World," *Morning Tulsa Daily World*, November 5, 1919, p. 11.

69. The three believed injured detectives went to Roosevelt Hospital, where it was found Frank Oliver was unhurt, McLaughlin was scratched and John Walsh had a possible fracture in his right arm.

70. "Two Detectives Shot in Gambling Raid," *Sun*, January 20, 1919, p. 12.

71. "Millionaire in Crap Game," *Manning Times*, January 22, 1919, p. 1.

72. "Sporting Blood," *Parisian*, July 11, 1919, p. 4.

73. *Ibid.*

74. "Saratoga's Choice: Famous Spa or Gambler's Mecca?" *New York Tribune*, November 9, 1919, Part VII, p. 1.

75. *Ibid.*

76. "Man Accused of Shooting Two Detectives Is Freed," *New York Tribune*, July 25, 1919, p. 18.

77. *Ibid.*

Chapter Thirteen

1. The Reds scored 577 runs, while allowing 401. They played their home games at Redland Field. In 1918, they finished third in the National League.

2. The White Sox scored 667 runs, while allowing 534. They played their home games at Comiskey Park. In 1918 they finished sixth in the American League.

3. "The Sportlight," *Chattanooga News*, September 11, 1919, p. 9.

4. "Big League Chiefs Show Their Loyalty," *Sun*, October 1, 1919, p. 23.

5. *Ibid.*

6. "Cincinnati Rocks in Baseball Frenzy," *Sun*, October 1, 1919, p. 23.

7. "Big League Chiefs Show Their Loyalty," *Sun*, October 1, 1919, p. 23.

8. *Ibid.*

9. "Evers Picks Reds," *Topeka State Journal*, October 1, 1919, p. 12.

10. Eddie Cicotte, believed by most to be the key figure in the "Fix," was so good that even when supposedly not performing during the World's Series managed to keep his ERA below 3.00. Ring Lardner held him in such high regard that Cicotte appeared on his 1915 all-time all-star team. The drop of the odds on the White Sox winning, from 7 to 10 to 5 to

6, prior to Game One, was attributed to a Cicotte sore arm.

11. "Dutch Ruether Joins Ranks of Diamond Stars," *Sun*, October 2, 1919, p. 18.

12. *Ibid.*

13. *Ibid.*

14. Since 1919, no starting pitcher, other than Lefty Williams, has ever lost three World Series games—granted the "Fall Classic" was a bit longer and that a reliever has lost three games (George Frazier, New York Yankees, 1981).

15. "Reds Again Defeat Sox by 4 to 2," *New York Tribune*, October 3, 1919, p. 1.

16. "Moran to Use Eller Today Against Kerr," *New York Tribune*, October 3, 1919, p. 14.

17. "Sox Take Third by Score 3 to 0," *Topeka State Journal*, October 3, 1919, p. 6.

18. "World Series Notes," *Topeka State Journal*, October 3, 1919, p. 6.

19. "Incidents of Game," *New York Tribune*, October 4, 1919, p. 10.

20. "Cicotte Loses His Own Game; Reds Win, 2–0," *New York Tribune*, October 5, 1919, p. 1.

21. "Reds Defeat White Sox in Fourth Game of World Series by a Score of 2 to 0," *New York Tribune*, October 5, 1919, p. 18.

22. *Ibid.*

23. "All Over but Shouting, Declares Manager Moran," *Sun*, October 7, 1919, p. 22.

24. "Felsch's Poor Work Injures Reputation for Being Second Greatest Centre Fielder," *Sun*, October 7, 1919, p. 22.

25. "Extra Day of Rest for Williams Helps White Sox Chances in Game with Reds Today," *Evening Star*, October 6, 1919, p. 21.

26. "60,000 Bet on Reds," *Bismarck Tribune*, October 7, 1919, p. 1.

27. "Cicotte Likely as Sox Pitcher; Sallee for Reds," *Great Falls Daily Tribune*, October 8, 1919, p. 8.

28. "Cicotte Wins; 3 Red Pitchers Beaten by Sox," *New York Tribune*, October 9, 1919, p. 1.

29. "Moran to Try for End with Eller Today," *New York Tribune*, October 9, 1919, p. 14.

30. "Kid Gleason's Sluggers Again Hit Foe Hard," *New York Tribune*, October 9, 1919, p. 14.

31. Fred Lieb, *Baseball as I Have Known It* (New York: Coward, McCann & Geoghegan, 1977), p. 110.

32. "Sun Scattered Early Clouds," *Chattanooga News*, October 9, 1919, p. 9.

33. "National League Champs Win Series; Reds Go Home," *El Paso Herald*, October 10, 1919, p. 14.

34. "Cincinnati Welcomes Home Its Victorious Team; Has Holiday," *El Paso Herald*, October 10, 1919, p. 14.

35. William Simpson "Bill" Farnsworth (1885–1945) was an American sportswriter, editor, and boxing promoter in partnership with Mike Jacobs. Arnold Rothstein (1882–1928), "The Brain," was an American bootlegger, racketeer, businessman, crime

boss, gambler and racketeer who became a kingpin of the Jewish mob in New York. He was publicly exonerated by the State Attorney's Office and White Sox attorney Alfred S. Austrian. Later, he was accused in the theft of grand jury transcripts.

36. "Offered Bribe of $20,000 to Throw World's Series," *Bridgeport Times and Evening Farmer*, October 30, 1919, p. 10.

37. *Ibid.*

38. *Ibid.*

39. *Ibid.*

40. The gambling and shooting incident, which took place on January 19, 1919, had been in the newspapers and Abraham Attell was the only former champion fighter arrested along with Rothstein.

41. "Offered Bribe of $20,000 to Throw World's Series," *Bridgeport Times and Evening Farmer*, October 30, 1919, p. 10.

42. *Ibid.*

43. *Ibid.*

44. Hugh Stuart Fullerton (1873–1945) was an influential American sportswriter and one of the founders of the Baseball Writers' Association of America. His association with the Black Sox scandal will cast him into immortality.

45. "Scandal of World Series in Baseball Will Not Down; Here Is a Way to Settle It," *Evening World*, December 17, 1919, p. 1. Comiskey hired a detective firm after the 1919 World's Series to gather information. Some of these reports are available through the Chicago History Museum.

46. *Ibid.*

47. *Ibid.* Eddie Cicotte admitted that the players came up with the idea of a fix based on rumors they had heard about the 1918 Series. See documents in the Chicago History Museum.

48. *Ibid.*

49. Let the what-if scenarios fly beginning with: Who gave Fullerton the authority to speak for the fans, if he did? And, what if there had been no Fullerton, then what? Comiskey's statement speaks for itself.

50. "Scandal of World Series in Baseball Will Not Down; Here Is a Way to Settle It," *Evening World*, December 17, 1919, p. 1.

51. *Ibid.* Comiskey offered $10,000 for proof that the players did not try to win.

52. Kenesaw Mountain Landis (1866–1944) was an American jurist who served as a federal judge from 1905 to 1922 and as the first Commissioner of Baseball from 1920 until his death.

53. William Thomas "Bill" Burns (1880–1953), "Sleepy Bill," was an American baseball player who debuted as a professional baseball player on April 18, 1908, while playing for the Washington Senators. He played his last game for the Detroit Tigers on May 23, 1912. For one game, in 1910, Burns was a teammate of Chick Gandil's.

54. Joseph Pesch (1873–1923) was a pool hall owner and gambler.

55. *Ibid.* Harry Redmond (1875–1945) was a St. Louis theater owner. Ben Franklin's brother-in-law and Redmond co-owned the St. Louis's Majestic Theater.

56. Mont Tennes (1874–1941), "Jacob," was a Chicago gambler and odds maker. It was Mont Tennes who alerted Comiskey to the fix before Game Two.

57. Sam Pass (1893–1966) was a manufacturer's agent, gambler and friend of many of the Chicago White Sox players and even best man at Ray Schalk's wedding. At a June 1921 extradition hearing, he was unable to identify Abe Attell.

58. *Ibid.*

59. "Commission Must Take Quick Action," *Sun,* December 21, 1919, p. 4.

60. *Ibid.*

61. *Ibid.*

62. *Ibid.*

63. *Ibid.*

64. "Recalling a Few Old Time Featherweights," *South Bend News-Times,* January 5, 1920. p.6.

65. "15 Witnesses Called in Rothstein Inquiry," *New York Tribune,* January 27, 1920, p. 24.

66. "Italian Loses to Champion in Fast Bout," *New York Tribune,* February 10, 1920, p. 13.

67. *Ibid.*

68. "No Title," *Mayesville Public Ledger,* May 13, 1920, p. 2.

69. "Ha! Ha! Another Attell!" *Washington Times,* August 8, 1920, p. 22.

70. "Grand Jury Finds World Series 'Fixer,'" *New York Tribune,* September 25, 1920, p. 1. The cities of Chicago, New York, Cincinnati and St. Louis were singled out by Brigham.

71. *Ibid.* The other well-known sportsmen were player Hal Chase (alleged to have won $40,000 on series), "Nicky" Arnstein, arrested in a Wall Street bond scandal and now in jail after having been at liberty on bonds furnished by Rothstein, and Max Blumenthal, racetrack plunger of New York, alleged to be one of those who contributed to the slush fund.

72. Harold Homer Chase (1883–1947), "Prince Hal," was a first baseman in Major League Baseball and widely viewed as the best fielder at his position. During his career, he played for the New York Highlanders (1905–1913), Chicago White Sox (1913–1914), Buffalo Blues (1914–1915), Cincinnati Reds (1916–1918), and New York Giants (1919). His legacy has been tainted by gambling allegations.

73. "Gambling Plot Finally Bared," *Chattanooga News,* September 25, 1920, p. 9.

74. *Ibid.*

75. *Ibid.*

76. "Gambling Plot Finally Bared," *Chattanooga News,* September 25, 1920, p. 9.

77. "Grand Jury Finds World Series 'Fixer,'" *New York Tribune,* September 25, 1920, p. 1.

78. *Ibid.;* Byron Bancroft "Ban" Johnson (1864–1931), was an executive in professional baseball. As American League founder, he also served as it's first president.

79. "Grand Jury Finds World Series 'Fixer,'" *New York Tribune,* September 25, 1920, p. 1.

80. *Ibid.*

81. "Jury to Grill Ballplayers," *Washington Times,* September 26, 1920, p. 1.

82. "Charges Series 'Fixing' Began in August, 1919," *New York Tribune,* September 26, 1920, p. 23.

83. "Charges Series 'Fixing' Began in August, 1919," *New York Tribune,* September 26, 1920, p. 23.

84. "Eight White Sox Ball Players Indicted," *Washington Times,* September 28, 1920, p. 1.

85. William Joseph Maharg (1881–1953) was former pugilist, auto plant worker and associate of Bill Burns.

86. *Ibid.*

87. *Ibid.*

88. "Will Reinstate Innocent, Drive Guilty from Game, Says Comiskey," *New York Tribune,* September 29, 1920, p. 1.

89. "Attell Angry, Will Expose Series Plot," *New York Tribune,* September 29, 1920, p. 1.

90. *Ibid.*

91. *Ibid.*

92. "Attell Angry, Will Expose Series Plot," *New York Tribune,* September 29, 1920, pgs. 1–3.

93. *Ibid.*

94. "Comiskey Pays Off Men on Spot, Mails Checks to Others Implicated," *South Bend New-Times,* September 29, 1920, p. 1.

95. *Ibid.*

96. Joseph J. "Sport" Sullivan (1870–1949) was an American bookmaker and gambler from Boston, Massachusetts. Rothstein and New York gambler Nat Evans (believed by some to be the fixer that the grand Jury indicted as Rachel Brown) co-owned The Brook, a high-stakes Saratoga casino, not to mention numerous other New York gambling parlors.

97. "Two Gamblers Indicted as Ball Plot "Fixers"; Williams, Felsch Confess," *Sun and New York Herald,* September 30, 1920, p. 1.

98. "Two Gamblers Indicted as Ball Plot "Fixers"; Williams, Felsch Confess," *Sun and New York Herald,* September 30, 1920, p. 2.

99. William J. Fallon (1886?–1927) was a gifted New York City defense attorney and friend of John McGraw.

100. "Bernie Kauff in Fixing Plot, Says Detective," *New York Tribune,* September 30, 1920, p. 2.

101. "Ten N.Y. Gamblers Won $250,000, Says Abe Attell," *Evening World,* September 30, 1920, p. 1.

102. "Seek Man Who Put Up $300,000 Cash to Fix Ball Games," *Evening World,* October 1, 1920, p. 1. The evidence presented thus far to the Chicago Grand Jury has yet to be supported by corroborative testimony according to State Attorney Maclay Hoyne.

103. *Ibid.,* p. 2.

104. "Hoyne Off for Chicago with Proof of Ball

Plt: Jury to Sift All Games," *New-York Tribune*, October 1, 1920, p. 1.

105. *Ibid.*

106. As a reminder: Harry Redmond (1875–1945) was a theater owner—with Ben Franklin's brother-in-law. He would become the prosecution's key witness at the criminal trial.

107. Joseph Pesch (1873–1923) was a pool hall owner, gambler and friend of Harry Redmond.

108. Tom Kearney (1870–1936) was a St. Louis betting commissioner, long-term bookmaker and owner of a cigar store. Is believed to be one of the first to inform Major League Baseball of "the fix."

109. "3 More Indicted in Ball Scandal," *Morning Tulsa Daily World*, October 23, 1920, p. 1.

110. Elmer Joseph "Joe" Gedeon (1893–1941) was a second baseman in Major League Baseball. He played for the Washington Senators, New York Yankees, and St. Louis Browns. According to a brief notation in the 1922 Reach Guide, Commissioner Landis officially and permanently disqualified Joe Gedeon for having guilty knowledge of the conspiracy.

111. "Attell Turns on the Master Mind," *Bridgeport Time and Evening Farmer*, October 30, 1920, p. 4.

112. *Ibid.*

113. *Ibid.*

114. *Ibid.*

115. *Ibid.*

116. *Ibid.*

117. "No Title," *Ogden Standard Examiner*, November 17, 1920, p. 12.

118. "Indicted Sox May Never Be Forced to Face Trial," *New York Herald*, January 24, 1921, p. 11.

119. "Witnesses Have Been Corrupted Court Is Told," *Ogden Standard-Examiner*, March 17, 1921, p. 1.

120. Carl T. Zork (1878–1947) was a garment industry executive and president of the Supreme Waist Company, a St. Louis–based shirtwaist firm. Zork, a boxing enthusiast, promoted Attell's 1912 fight with St. Louis boxer Oliver Kirk.

121. Ben Franklin (1876–1940) was a St. Louis gambler and associate of Carl Zork.

122. Benjamin Levi (1882–1953) and Louis Levi (1886–1961) were gamblers based in the midwest and associates (and it was said brothers-in-law) of David Zelcer, indicted during the second investigation.

123. David Zelcer (1877–1941) was a cigar store owner and Des Moines gambler.

124. "144 Indictments Against 18 Named in Baseball Mess," *Evening Public Ledger*, March 26, 1921, p. 1.

125. "Attell Surrenders on Baseball Fraud; Gives Bond," *New York Tribune*, May 11, 1921, p. 24.

126. "Attell, Freed, Rearrested," *New York Herald*, May 21, 1921, p. 11.

127. Pass, a Chicago businessman and gambler, furnished authorities with information that led to the uncovering of the bribery plot and the confessions of a number of ballplayers that they had thrown games in the interest of gamblers. He testified that he had never met Attell nor had he ever had any transactions with him, and that everything he had testified to before the Grand Jury was on hearsay evidence. Pass was an ardent White Sox fan and friends with many of the ballplayers.

128. "Witness Says He Erred in Accusing Attell," *New York Tribune*, June 7, 1921, p. 20.

129. "Attell Not Man Wanted in Chicago, Says Counsel," *New York Tribune*, May 28, 1921, p. 3.

130. "Abe Attell Freed in Baseball Mix," *Evening World*, June 25, 1921, p. 3.

131. "Baseball Trial May Interrupt Schedule," *Evening Public Ledger*, July 9, 1921, p. 11.

132. The White Sox players cleared in the baseball scandal accidentally met the 12 jurors who found them guilty in a little Italian restaurant on Chicago's west side early on August 3. The jurors and the recent defendants left the restaurant singing together. This according to "Meet Jurors," *Bismarck Tribune*, August 3, 1921, p. 1.

133. "Jury Frees Baseball Conspirators," *Arizona Republican*, August 3, 1921, p. 1.

134. *Ibid.*

135. *Ibid.*

136. "Black Sox Banned from Organized Ball," *Lake County Times*, August 3, 1921, p. 1.

Chapter Fourteen

1. "Abe Attell Barred from Yank's Park," *Free Trader-Journal Ottawa Fair Dealer*, August 9, 1921, p. 4.

2. Kilbane knocked out Frush in the seventh round to retain his title for what would prove to be the final time.

3. "Jewish Gamblers Corrupt American Baseball," *Dearborn Independent*, September 3, 1921, p. 8.

4. *Ibid.*, p. 9.

5. *Ibid.*

6. "Bond Robbery Disclosed by Three Arrests," *Evening Herald*, December 31, 1921, p. 1

7. The trio obtained continuances until January 14. Bail was fixed at $5,000 for Mrs. Attell.

8. "Bond Robbery Disclosed by Three Arrests," *Evening Herald*, December 31, 1921, p. 1. Later, on January 19, 1922, a fourth suspect was arrested Mark von Eschem of the Bronx. Also, William Morris was arrested on January 25, 1922.

9. "Says Damon Runyon," *Washington Times*, April 1, 1922, p. 10.

10. "Attell's Boot Shop Soaked in Gasoline; Police Question Him," *New York Herald*, May 22, 1922, p. 1.

11. *Ibid.*

12. "Attell Swears Foes Laid Fire Plant in His Shop," *New York Tribune*, May 23, 1922, p. 20.

13. "Abe Attell's Brain in Ring Like a Streak," *Great Falls Daily Tribune*, October 9, 1922, p. 6.

14. *Ibid.*

15. Jack Cavanaugh, *Tunney* (New York: Ballantine, 2006), p. 139, mentions Abe Attell's assistance during the fight in obtaining additional adrenalin chloride to restrict the flow of blood from Tunney's broken nose.

16. Attell, along with some of his associates, would often scramble names to pass the time. The surname unscrambled is "Hereon" or "Honker."

17. See "Abe Attell and Truck of Ale Seized by Troopers," *New York Herald Tribune*, July 24, 1924, for additional details.

18. Billy Gibson owned a popular east Bronx restaurant and it was through this venture that he became one of the most "connected" individuals in the city. Gibson also knew Arnold Rothstein. Later, he opened up the Fairmont Athletic Club (Bronx) and even promoted at Madison Square Garden. As business savvy as they come, Gibson was Tunney's final boxing manager.

19. Goldman was the ninth victim in Leonard's comeback.

20. New York resident Marty Goldman died on February 17, 1987 at the age of 76.

21. Max "Boo Boo" Hoff (1892–1941) was a cigar store employee and gambler, before becoming a successful boxing manager and promoter. His stable of Philadelphia fighters became the first to be incorporated, Max Hoff Incorporated (1928). Later, he became one of the most successful Philadelphia gangsters. Hoff had also done some bootlegging with Arnold Rothstein.

22. It was said Hoff provided $20,000 in exchange for 20 percent of Tunney's future championship earnings the day before the fight.

23. Hoff would drop the suit in 1931 without explanation.

24. Tunney signed the contract "Eugene Joseph Tunney," rather than his real name, James Joseph Tunney. One rumor had Gibson inking the deal as a protection mechanism; should the Dempsey camp attempt any monkey business, Tunney's corner could retaliate.

Chapter Fifteen

1. Attell, who had owned numerous establishments over the years, was operating the Abe Attell Bar Restaurant, "specializing in Southern fried chicken," over on 52nd Street & Broadway.

2. "A Newsman's Biggest Story," *Sports Illustrated*, September 17, 1956, pp. 69–71.

3. "The Truth Behind the World Series Fix," *Cavalier*, October 1961, pp. 8–9, 10–13, 89, 96.

4. When the government shut down horse racing for the duration of the war gamblers shifted their attention from the track to the ballpark.

5. Rothstein was capable of financing the fix and a known entity in the gambling world. Preceding the

infamous Al Capone, Rothstein was slowly becoming a larger-than-life personality.

6. "Best odds in" was a "must" for Rothstein, as it would be for any gambler putting up such large stakes. A.R. was aware that Sport Sullivan knew Chick Gandil and could satisfy any money concerns and understood that Gandil could certainly appease his teammates. Sullivan was believed to have had a hand in the 1914 World's Series; the Boston Braves, who were in last place in the NL on July 4, beat the Philadelphia Athletics in a four-game series.

7. Sullivan, whose gambling reputation preceded him, was staying at the Hotel Ansonia, as were the ballplayers.

8. Charlie Weegham, the one-time owner of the Cubs, testified before the 1920 grand jury that he, along with others, had heard the "fix" rumor in Saratoga Springs, New York, back in August.

9. Again, Rothstein mastered the perfect alibi when he met both Burns and Maharg for a very public dinner at the Astor Hotel in Times Square—an action of intent, if you will. Rothstein, whose gambling prowess had become instinctive, may have seen the duo as a trump card, a way to hedge his investment position.

10. Nat Evans could certainly be trusted with A.R.'s stake and Mont Tennes could pacify any local concern amongst the gambling community.

11. As a reminder, Burns testified under oath that he met with Gandil and Cicotte in the lobby of the Hotel Ansonia on Broadway and 73rd street in September of 1919.

12. Gandil, from a majority of accounts, acted as the point man for the players.

13. William Joseph Maharg debuted as a professional baseball player on May 18, 1912, while playing for the Detroit Tigers. He played his last game for the Philadelphia Phillies on October 5, 1916. Maharg was also an amateur boxer. On September 26, 1920, Billy Maharg told his secrets to *Philadelphia North American* sportswriter James Isaminger. Published the following morning, Maharg's interview prompted the confession of four players and multiple indictments. Overnight Maharg became a star prosecution witness. He implicated Attell by stating that the former boxer came to him and Burns once he "fixed" the deal with Rothstein, that he aggressively bet the Series before Game One and that the former fighter only conceded $10,000 of a $100,000 commitment. Bitter over his loses Maharg placed all the blame on Attell. The surface level accusations by Maharg even later absolved Rothstein by calling Attell a liar.

14. In 1924, William J. Fallon, who hung more juries than Judge Issac Parker hung convicts, was tried and acquitted for jury tampering.

15. The issue of the magazine has become a collector's item for conspiracy theorists.

16. In the movie *Eight Men Out*, there is a dramatic scene showing a pensive Arnold Rothstein

awaiting confirmation that the "fix" is on. That signal supposedly came when Eddie Cicotte struck Reds batter Morris Rath in the center of his back. The incident, confirmed via telegraph, was said to have its roots with Abe Attell who corroborated the event to reporter Joe Williams. While the incident certainly doesn't speak to the Rothstein style, we are reminded that Cicotte had hit only two batters in over three hundred innings pitched. In fact, he had hit only 26 batters since 1911.

17. Multiple sources have noted the absence of the complete Cook County Criminal Case Records along with the 1919 and 1920 Chicago White Sox Corporate accounts.

18. A spin on the classic Aldous Huxley line from (Complete Essays 2, 1926–29).

Bibliography

Books

Andre, Sam, and Nat Fleischer. *A Pictorial History of Boxing*. New York: Bonanza Books, 1981.

Asinof, Eliot. *Bleeding Between the Lines*. New York: Pocket Books, 1979.

_____. *Eight Men Out: The Black Sox and the 1919 World Series*. New York: Pocket Books, 1963.

Baker, Mark Allen. *Title Town USA: Boxing in Upstate New York*. Charleston, SC: History Press, 2010.

Cavanaugh, Jack. *Tunney: Boxing's Brainiest Champ and His Upset of the Great Jack Dempsey*. New York: Ballantine, 2006.

Dempsey, Jack, with Barbara Piattelli Dempsey. *Dempsey*. New York: Harper & Row, 1977.

Fitzgerald, F. Scott. *The Great Gatsby*. New York: Collier, 1992.

Fountain, Charles. *The Betrayal: The 1919 World Series and the Birth of Modern Baseball*. New York: Oxford University Press, 2016.

Frommer, Harvey. *Shoeless Joe and Ragtime Baseball*. Dallas: Taylor, 1992.

Goldman, Herbert G., ed. *The Ring Record Book and Boxing Encyclopedia*. New York: The Ring, 1985.

Kahn, Roger. *A Flame of Pure Fire*. New York: Harcourt, 1999.

Heinz, W.C. *The Fireside Book of Boxing*. New York: Simon & Schuster, 1961.

Lamb, William. *Black Sox in the Courtroom: The Grand Jury, Criminal Trial and Civil Litigation*. Jefferson, NC: McFarland, 2013.

Nelson, Oscar Mathæus. *Life, Battles and Career of Battling Nelson, Lightweight Champion of the World*. Hegewisch, IL: self published, 1908.

Pietrusza, David. *Rothstein: The Life, Times, and Murder of the Criminal Genius Who Fixed the 1919 World Series*. New York: Basic Books, 2003.

Oates, Joyce Carol. *On Boxing*. Garden City, NY: Dolphin/Doubleday, 1987.

Roberts, James B., and Alexander G. Skutt. *The Boxing Register*. Ithaca, NY: McBooks, 2002.

Roberts, Randy. *Jack Dempsey: The Manassa Mauler*. Baton Rouge: Louisiana State University Press, 1979.

Sugar, Bert Randolph. *The Ultimate Book of Boxing Lists*. Philadelphia: Running Press, 2010.

_____. *Boxing's Greatest Fighters*. Guilford, CT: Lyons Press, 2006.

Wilbert, Warren N., and William C. Hageman. *The 1917 White Sox: Their World Championship Season*. Jefferson, NC: McFarland, 2003.

Articles/Blog Entries

Attell, Abe. "The World Series Fix." *Cavalier Magazine*, October 1961, 8–11, 13, 89, 96.

Casinberry, James. "A Newsman's Biggest Story." *Sports Illustrated,* September 17, 1956, 69–71.

Gandil, Arnold "Chick," as told to Melvin Durslag. "He Kept Baseball's Blackest Secret for 36 years … This Is My Story of the Black Sox Series." *Sports Illustrated*, September 17, 1956, 62–68.

"Hon. James W. Coffroth," Obituary. *New York Times*, October 18, 1872.

Jones, Jersey. "Controversial Abe Attell Dead at 85; Held Feather Title 12 Years." *The Ring*, May 1970, 26–27, 34.

Nicolaisen, Steve, and the editors of Boxing Illustrated. "Boxing's Centennial: 100 Years of Great Fights and Fighters." *Boxing Illustrated*, November 1992, 22–51, 86–113.

Archival Sources

The Center for Legislative Archives, National Archives
Chicago History Museum
Chicago Historical Society
International Boxing Hall of Fame
The Library of Congress
Society for American Baseball Research

Internet Sources

ancestry.com
BoxRec, boxrec.com

The Cyber Boxing Zone, www.cycberboxingzone.com

ESPN, espn.go.com

ESPN Classic:

"The Chicago Black Sox Banned from Baseball," November 19, 2003, http://espn.go.com/classic/s/black_sox_moments.html.

Eliot Asinof, "The Black Sox Scandal Is Forever," accessed June 14, 2016, http://www.espn.com/classic/s/2001/0726/1231415.html.

Rob Neyer, "Say It Ain't So ... for Joe and the Hall," accessed June 14, 2016, http://www.espn.com/classic/s/2001/0730/1232950.html.

Rico Longoria, "Baseball's Gambling Scandals," accessed June 14, 2016, http://www.espn.com/classic/s/2001/0730/1233060.html.

Find A Grave, www.findagrave.com

geni.com

Heritage Auctions, www.ha.com

International Boxing Hall of Fame, www.ibhof.com

JO Sports, Inc., josportsinc.com/main.php

RootsWeb.com

Wikipedia, en.wikipedia.org

Newsletters

Black Sox Scandal. Newsletter of the SABR Black Sox Committee. Vol. 1, no. 1 (May 2009) through vol. 7, no. 2 (December 2015).

Newspapers

Albuquerque Citizen
Albuquerque Morning Journal
Arizona Republican
Baltimore Sun
Barre Daily Times
Bemidji Daily Pioneer
Bisbee Daily Review
Bismarck Tribune
Bridgeport Evening Farmer
Butte Inter Mountain
Calumet News
Chattanooga News
Chicago Tribune
Coeur d'Alene Evening Press
Colorado Spring Gazette
Daily Arizona Silver Belt
The Daily Capital Journal
The Daily Missoulian
The Daily Press
The Daily Telegram
The Day Book
Dearborn Independent
The Desert Evening News
East Oregonian
El Paso Herald
The Evening Bulletin

The Evening Herald
The Evening Public Ledger
The Evening Standard
The Evening Star
The Evening Statesman
The Evening Teller
The Evening Times
The Evening Times-Republican
The Evening World
Fairmont West Virginian
Fergus County Democrat
Free Trader-Journal Ottawa Fair Dealer
Grand Forks Daily Herald
Great Falls Daily Tribune
Hawaiian Gazette
Hawaiian Star
Indianapolis Journal
The Jennings Daily Record
Kennewick Courier
Labor World
Los Angeles Herald
Manning Times
Marion Daily Mirror
Mayesville Public Ledger
Minneapolis Journal
New York Times
New York Tribune
Norwich Bulletin
Ogden Standard-Examiner
Omaha Daily Bee
Ottumwa-tri Weekly Courier
Pacific Commercial Advertiser
Palestine Daily Herald
Parisian
Pearson's Magazine
Richmond Times-Dispatch
Rock Island Argus
St. Louis Republic
Saint Paul Globe
Salt Lake Herald
Salt Lake Tribune
San Francisco Call
Seattle Star
The Southern Herald
South Bend News-Times
Spokane Press
The Sun
Sun and New York Herald
Tacoma Times
The Times Dispatch
Tonopah Daily Bonanza
Topeka State Journal
Tucumcari News and Tucumcari Times
Tulsa Daily World
Washington Herald
Washington Times
Wenatchee Daily World

Periodicals

Boxing Illustrated
Collyer's Eye

The Journal of San Diego History
The Ring
The Sporting News
Sports Illustrated

Index

Numbers in **bold italics** indicate pages with photographs

Abbott, Mabel 176–177
Abel, Kid 28–29, 32–33, 36, 39, 47
Allen, Billy 131
Andrews, T.A. 170
Anti-Semitism 47, 209, 233
Apostoli, Fred 13
Arnstein, Nick 228, 196*n*71
Attell, Abraham Washington *25, 62, 179*; advice on how to box 141–142, 141*n*48; birth 6; boxing brothers 13 (*see also* Caesar Attell; Attell, Monte); break from McKenna 29; champion's age 113; deception 135; defensive prowess 18–19; defining a champion 106–107; division overview 35–36; divorce from Ethel Egan 173; faith 78; faking fight 4, 51, 146, 148, 162; fixing Murphy fight 159; family life 1911 132–133; first knockout loss 26–27; first loss 19–20; illegal possession 213–214; Jewish fighters 47, 167; losing the featherweight title 148–153; Market Street view *7*; marriage to Elizabeth "Ethel" Egan (Goodwin) 74; marriage to Mae O'Brien 222; moniker 3, 4, 36, 69, 71; mother's death 170; professional debut 11; pulling punches 103, 128, 130, 133, 155; quiting Kirk fight 159; shoe store 175, 211–212; struck by automobile 223; Third Street view *9*; ticket speculating charge 208–209; winning featherweight title 60–61
Attell, Annie Roth (mother) 6, 170
Attell, Caesar (broher) 6, 13, 30, 61, 72, 83, 100, 111, 119, 196, 233; Johnson v. Jeffries offer 111
Attell, Gilbert (nephew) 13, 196
Attell, Monte (brother) 6, 12–13, 22, 31, 34, 36, 45–47, 49–50, 52, 55, 57, 60, 62, 67, 71–72, 78–80, 83, 94, 96, 100, 110, 106, 112, 124, 126, 128, 131, 132, 142, 148, 160, 167–168, 170, 174, 176, 180, 196,

212, 233; accident 6–7; birth 12; blindness 180, 212, 221; losing bantamweight title 124, 126; marriage 71; turning pro 31–32; winning bantamweight title 113
Auerbach, Herman 13
Austrian, Alfred S. 190, 192*n*35

Baker, Harry 69–70, 72–74, 79, 106
Baldwin, Matty 58, 90, *91*
Barnard, J. Augustus 213
Barrow, Ed 186
Barry, Dave 112, 124, 217
Barry, Jim 11
Basilio, Carmen 226
Beecher, Willie 167, 216
Belmont, August 218
Bender, Tony 61, 129–130
Benton, Rube 197
Bezdek, Hugo 185
Bloom, Ike 33, 39, 232
Bloom, Morris 153
Bortz, Sam 214, 223
Bowker, Joe 48, 53–54, 59–60, 63, 68, 75, 112
Bozeman, Jockey 11, 15
Braddock, James J. 219, 226
Brady, William A. 215
Bramble, Tommy 19
Brigham, H.H. 196–197
Britt, Jimmy 9, 34, 40, 47, 53, 57, 60, 62, 64–66, 79, 87, 136, 171, 176, 232
Britton (Briton), Jack 180, 210, 212
Broad, Kid 24–26, 32, 36, 39, 173–174, 224
Bronson, Jimmy 217
Brophy, Thomas 211–212
Brothers, Dr. Joyce 225
Brown, George 11
Brown, Knockout 135–136, 144–*145*, 146, 148
Brown, Rachel 200, 204, 206
Buck, Kid 14–15, 25
Buckley, Jim 154–155, 159
Burke, Jimmy 186
Burns, Frankie 133–*134*, 142, 180

Burns, Tommy 65–66, 70–71, 79, 100, 111, 136
Burns, William "Bill" 193, 193*n*53, 196, 198–204, 206, 226–227, 229

Callahan, Frankie 173–174
Cannon, Ray 212
Canzoneri, Tony 2, 216, 222, 226, 234
Capone, Alphonse "Al" 207–208, 210, 217, 219
Carpentier, Georges 210, 213
Carroll, Jimmy 79, 113, 125, 142, 155–156
Carroll, Peter 11, 31
Carsey, Frank 68–69
Cassidy, Young 14–15
Chaney, George Henry "K.O." 166, 175, 211
Chaplin, Charlie 215
Chase, Hal 196, 196*n*71, 196*n*72, 202–204, 206
Choynski, Joe 12, 47, 120, 139, *140*, 178, 221
Cicotte, Eddie 183, 185, 187*n*10, 187–191, 193, 193*n*47, 195, 197–200, 203–206, 230
Clarke, Joe 140
Clyne, Charles F. 197
Coffroth, James W. 14, 79, 82, 91, 109–110, 112, 115, *116*, 137, 154, 157–159, 165, 167
Cohan, George M. 197, 222, 229
Cohan, Jack 29
Cohen, Harry 210
Cohen, Young Johnny 139
Collins, Dick 11
Collins, Eddie 183, 188–190, 194, 196
Collins, John F. "Shano" 190
Colosimo, Jim "Big Jim" 207–208
Comiskey, Charles A. 188–189, 191, 193–194, 197, *198*–199, 206, 213, 221, 230
Conley, Frankie 113, 124, 126, 141, 143, 148
Conley, Mrs. Frankie 136
Coogan, Danny 14

Corbett, Harry 33
Corbett, James J. "Jim" 9, 12, 23, 33, 35, 37, 47, 64–65, 109, 113, 128, 136, 156, 212, 232, 234; family fame 47
Corbett, Young, II 15, 17, 21–22, 24, 26–28, 32, 33–34, 36–38, 42, 52–53, 54, 59–60, 62, 64, 67, 105, 107, 152, **179**–180, 216, 224
Costello, Buffalo 8
Coster, Joe 128–**129**, 130, 136
Coulon, Johnny 94, 110, 113, 117, 133, 138–139, 142–**143**, 148, 159, 164, 172, 227
Coy, James J. 204
Cravath, Gavvy 185
Cribb, Otto 11
Criqui, Eugene 213, 222, 225
Croll, J.G. "Johnny" 63, 65, 221–222
Cross, Leach 113, **118**, 144, 167, 178
Crowe, Robert E. 203, 206
Cruisenberry, James 194

Dandolis, Nick "The Greek" 222
Daubert, Jake 183, 187
Decker, Kid 15
DeCoursey, Billy 70
Delaney, Jack 219
Delaney, Kid 14
Dell, Frank 11
Dempsey, "Colorado" Jack 15
Dempsey, William H. "Jack" 177, 179, 210, 212–213, 215–217, 221–223, 230, 234
Dever, William E. 203
Dillon, Jack 152, 177
division weights, 1912 160
Dixon, George 1–4, 12, 15–22, 24–25, 29, 33, 35, 38–39, 47, 52, 60, 107, 112–113, 132, 162, 167, 173, 178, 180, 232, 234
Dodson, Kid 8, 11
Dorgan, T.A. "TAD" 179
Dougherty, Danny 15, 22, 42
Doyle, Remy 229
Dozier, Battling 13
Driscoll, Jem 1, 3, 31, 99, 103–**104**, 105–106, 112–113, 115–119, 123, 125–126, 132, 139, 159, 178, 214, 216, 233, 222, 233–234
Dulley, Kid 11
Duncan, Pat 188
Dundee, Johnny 2, 175, 195, 211, 213, 216, 222, 224–225
Dunn, Jimmy 43, 52, 123, **148**, 149, 153, 167
Durslag, Melvin 224
Dwyer, Benny 11

Earp, Wyatt 64
Edgren, Bob 10, 78, 129
Eller, Hod 183, 189, 191
Elmer, Bill 129
Erne, Frank 12, 21, 32, 107, 128, 137
Erne, Young 42–43, 45–46, 53, 75
Evans, Nat 229; see also Brown, Rachel
Evers, Johnny 186

Eyton, Charles 66–67, 78, 97, 151–153, 211

Faber, Urban C. "Red" 183
Fallon, William J. 200, 204–205, 230
Farnsworth, Wilton S. 192, 196
Felsch, Oscar "Happy" 183, 189–190, 196, 198, 200, 204–205
Feltz, Tommy 30, 36, 47, 50–51, 58
Ferns, James "Rube" 22
Finnegan, Jack 12
Firpo, Luis 213
Fisher, Ray 183, 188, 190
Fitzsimmons, Bob 12, 23, 27–28, 36–37, 40, 45, 57, 64–65, 113, 128, 136, 163, 221, 234
Flowers, Tiger 215
Flynn, Doc 11
Flynn, "Fireman" Jim 71, 79, 136, 143
Forbes, Clarence 13, 19, 35, 58
Forbes, Harry 19–23, 26, 30–32, 36–37, 39–41, 47–48, 50, 52, 63, 68, 75, 77, 112, 116, 163, 232
Franklin, Ben 204, 204n121, 206
Frush, Danny 209, 211
Fuchs, Emil 182, 195
Fuller, Edward M. 215
Fullerton, Hugh S. 193–194, 201, 221, 230
Fullmer, Gene 226

gambling 4, 5, 42, 98, 104, 126, 128, 133, 155, 181, 194–197, 200, 202, 207, 209, 212, 218, 228–229
Gandil, Chick 183, 187–188, 196, 198, 200–**201**, 203–206, 224–225
Gans, Joe 32, 36–37, 47–48, 57, 71, 76, 79, 81, 87, 91, 100–101, 121, 128, 136, 163, 180, 211–212, 221, 234
Gardner, Oscar 15, 24
Gate, Charles G. 218
Gedeon, Joe 202, 202n110
Gibson, Billy 134, 215, 215n18, 217, 224
Gleason, Kid 183–**184**, 188, 190–191, 194, 196, 221, 225
Golden Gate Park 23–**24**, 58
Goldman, Marty 216
Goodman, Abraham "Kid" 29, 30, 36, 42, 51
Goodrich, Jimmy 137, 216
Goodwin, Chester 58
Gormon, George E. 205
Gould, Sam 210
Grabiner, Harry 212
Graney, Edward M. 28, 89, 102
Greb, Harry 3, 212–213, 215, 234
Greggains, (Alec) Alex 7–11, 34, 51, 64
Griffith, Clark 186
Griffith, Emile 226
Griffiths, Tuffy 219
Groh, Heinie 183, 188, 190

Hahn, Phillip 197
Haley, Patsy 42, 146, 215

Hanlon, Eddie 10–11, 32–34, 36, 39, 52, 66, 171, 179, 232
Hanlon, James 213
Harris, Harry 21–22, 63, 71, 73, 112
Heeney, Tom 219
Herman, Kid 36, 41, 53, 65–67, 71, 178
Hernandez, Charlie 13
Herrera, Aurelio 22, 30, 36, 39, 42–43, 48, 65–67, 70, 173–174, 216, 224
Herrick, Kid 26
Heydler, John 188, 197
Hill, Joe 11
Hoff, Max "Boo-Boo" 216–217, 216n21
Hogan, "One Round" 140–141
Hoyne, Maclay 201
Hudnall, George M. 212
Huggins, Miller 185
Hurtig, Jules 50

Jackson, Joseph J. "Shoeless" 183, 188–189, 191, 196, 198, 200, 203–206, 212, 230
James, Bill 191
Jeffries, James J. 11–12, 14, 21–23, 27, 32, 37, 57, 65, 79, 81, 84, 114–115, 120, 234
Jennings, Hugh 186
Johnson, Ban 197–**198**, 206
Johnson, Jack 3, 14, 57, 64, 71, 79, 81, **100**, 111–115, 120, 136, 139–140, 159, 174, 205, 234
Johnson, Leo 139, 143, 156
Jones, Kid 11
Jones, Willie 139–140
Jourdan, Ted 196

Kaufman, Benny 130, 166
Kearney, Thomas G. 202, 202n108
Kearns, Jack 224, 232
Kelly, Eddie 86–90, 104, 110, 115, 124
Kelly, Spider 11, 14
Kerr, Dickie 183, 188, 190
Kilbane, Johnny 1–3, 123, 127, 135–137, 140–141, 144, 146–**147**, 148–**149**, 150–153, 155, 157, 159–160, **161**, 163–165, 167–169, 171–172, 175, 177–178, 180, 209, 211, 213, 215, 222, 224–225, 227, 233
Kilbane, Tommy 131–133, 143, 148
King, Buddy 14
Kirk, Oliver 159, **160**, 162, 164–166
Kline, Patsy 107, **108**, 111, 129–131, 135, 140–141, 146, 148, 175
Kline, Mrs. Patsy 136
Kopf, Larry 183, 187–188

Landis, Kenesaw M. 188, 193–**194**, 193n52, 206, 223
Langford, Sam 37, 71, 213, 215, 226, 234
Lardner, Wilmer "Ring" 193, 221
Lauder, Billy 121
Leibold, Nemo 183, 188, 196
Lennett, Kid 7–8, 10–11
Leonard, Benny 3, 167, 176–178,

180, 195, 210–211, 216, 222, 224, 233–234
Levi (Levy), Ben 193, 204, 204*n*122
Levi (Levy), Lou 193, 204, 204*n*122
Lewis, Johnny "Kid" 17
Lewis, Ted "Kid" 178, 210
Lewis, Willie 52, 196
Lieb, Fred 191, 194
Lippe, Al 40, 180, 232
Logan, Phil 63
Lomksi, Leo 218
London, Jack 14, 111, 176–177
Long, Baron 98, 109
Loughran, Tommy 218, 225–226
Lowdermilk, Grover 183, 187
Luque, Dolf 188, 190

Mack, Connie 186, 221
Mackey, Biz 99, 107, 109, 123–124
Madden, Bartley 213
Magee, Sherry 183
Maharg, William 198–201, 198*n*85, 206, 229–230, 230*n*13
Mandell, Sammy 219
Marciano, Rocky 1, 224, 226
Marino, Eddie 91–92, 120–121, 157, 158
Marto, Johnny 117
Masterson, Bat 65, 105, 228
Matthews, William "Matty" 12, 22
Maxim, Joey 224
Mayer, Erskine 189
Maynard, Billy 59
McAleer, Jimmy 195
McAuliffe, Jack 213
McCarey, Tom 68, 70, 73, 75–76, 78–79, 119, 135, 140, 157, 233
McCarey's Carnival 64–66
McCarthy, Cal 16
McClelland, Jack 41, 43–44, 47–48
McConnell, Frank 11, 34
McCormick, Cyrus H. 213
McCoy, Kid 8, 13, 61, 98, 128, 130, 136
McFarland, Packey 87, 89, 109, 126, 128, 137, 153, 164, 216
McGovern, Hughey 50
McGovern, Terry "Terrible" 2, *12*–13, 15–17, 22, 24, 32, 34–37, 45, 47, 57, 59, 60, 65, 87, 107, 112–113, 167, 173, 233, 234
McGraw, John 185, 215
McKenna, Jack 15, 17–23, 27–29, 44–45, 232
McKinley, William 13
McLarnin, Jimmy 219
McMullin, Fred 197–198, 204, 206, 230
Meehan, Jimmy 218
Miller, "Buck" Twin 111
Mitchell, Fred 185
Mitchell, Richie 175, 177, 210
Mohawk 202
Moore, James 221
Moore, "Philadelphia" Pal 119, *125*–126, 177
Moran, Frank 173, 175, 177

Moran, Owen 1, 3, 55, 78–79, 81–86, 91, 92–94, 100, 105–106, 109–112, 116–120, 123–124, 126–127, 143, 168, 174, 178, 233
Moran, Pat 183–184-*185*, 188, 195
Mowatt, Tommy 36, 41, 54, 112
Murphy, "Harlem" Tommy 42, 50–*51*, 57, 63, 75, *99*, 116, 118, 152–155, 157–159, 162, 165, 179, 215

Naughton, W.W. 79, 141, 154–155
Neale, Greasy 183, 187–188, 190
Neil, Frankie 36–37, 48, 50, 62–69, 79, 82, 85–86, 108–109, 112–113, 115–116, 132, 163, 171, 215
Nelson, Battling 1–3, 24, 32, 35, 48, 52–53, *56*–57, 64–67, 71, 75, 81, 83, 86–91, 94, 96, 98, 100–101, 112–113, 115, 121, 126, 128, 136, 141, 156, 163, 170, 173, 175–176, 178–179, 216, 222, 233
Nesbit (Thaw), Florence Evelyn *169*
newspaper decisions 55, 60, 119, 122, 130–131, 133, 138, 142, 214
no decision (no-decision) defined 55
Nolan, Billy 75, 86, 156–158, 162, 232

Oldfield, Barney 73, 215
O'Leary, Joe 11
O'Neil, Kid 11
O'Rourke, Tom 16, 129, 145–146
O'Toole, Tommy 75, 82–83, 110–111

Parker, Kid 14
Pass, Samuel W. 194, 194*n*57, 204–205, 204*n*127, 225
Pep, Willie 2–3, 226
Pesch (Pasch), Joseph 193–194, 194*n*54, 202
Pierce, Young 106, 130
Pieser, Kid 14
Powers, Kid 11

Rariden, Bill 191
Rath, Morrie 183, 187, 188, 190
Rauch, Maurice 30, 33, 39–40, 42, 48, 68
Reagan (Regan), Johnny 29–30, 35–36, 44–45, 47, 49–50, 60, 68, 113
Redmond, Harry 194, 194*n*55, 202
Reilly, Tommy 217
Reisler, John J. 137, 180
Rice, Grantland 184, 193
Rickard, George Lewis "Tex" 101–*102*, 104, 210, 213, 217
Rickey, Branch 185
Ring, Jimmy 183, 188
Ringling, John 213
Risberg, Charles A. "Swede" 183, 187, 189–190, 196, 198, 204–205
Rivers, Jose (Joe) 135, 137, *138*, 141, 148, 151, 157, 162, 166
Robinson, Ray "Sugar" 3, 226

Robinson, Wilbert 184–185, 215
Robson, Spike 74–75
Rosenthal, Herman 218
Ross, Barney 224, 226, 234
Rothstein, Arnold 4, 181–182, 192, 192*n*35, 194–197, 199–200, 202–203, 206, 215, 217–218, 221, 225, 227–230
Roush, Edd 183, 190–191
Ruether, Walter "Dutch" 183, 187, 189, 190–191
Ruhlin, Gus 14, 22, 62
Runyon, Damon 211
Ryan, Buddy 31, 33, 39, 179
Ryan, Tommy 11, 21–22, 32, *46*–47

Sallee, Harry "Slim" 183, 187, 190–191
San Francisco earthquake, 1906 58–*59*, 63–64
Schalk, Ray 183, 187, 191, 194, 196
Schmitz, Eugene 14, 49, 72
Schoenbeim, William 10–11
Shade, Dave 212
Sharkey, Jack 215, 217, 219
Sharkey, Tom 12–13, 40, 64
Sharpe, Harry 29, 43–45
Shor, Bernard "Toots" 211, 224
Siler, George 18, 20–21, 26, 65, 68–69
Silver, Jack 13
Singer, Al 216
Smith, Al 228
Smith, Eddie 30, 87, 89
Smith, Herman 137–138
Smith, Mike 14
Smythe, R.A. 90
Solomon, Benny "Kid" 75–76
Speaker, Tris 185, 189
Sprague, George C. 215
Stallings, George 185
Steele, Freddie 13
Stevens, Ashton 176
Stewart, Joe 21
Stone, Harry *108*, 110
Sullivan, Dave 13, 22, 32, 41, 66, 107
Sullivan, John L. 3, 113, 136, 175, 204, 211
Sullivan, Joseph J. "Sport" 200, 200*n*96, *201*, 206, 225, 229–230
Sullivan, Kid *54*–55
Sullivan, Mike "Twin" 79, 83, 100
Sullivan, Tommy 28, 36, 40–41, 43, 45, 48, 51, 60, 77, 89–90, 129
Susskind, David 227

Tammany Hall 228
Tausend, E.M. 211
Tennes, Mont 194, 194*n*56, 197, 229
Tenny, Harry 55, 62–63, 68
Thaw, Harry K. 169, 214
Thomas, Harry 158–159
Tiger, Dick 224
Torrio, Giovanni "Johnny" 207
Toy, Eddie 14, 34
Tucker, Chick 54
Tunney, Gene 1, 134, 212–213, 215–217, 217*n*24, 219, 222, 234

Turpin, Randy 224
Tyler, Monte (Domenico Santora)
    196

Vanderbilt, Consuelo 213
Vanderbilt, Muriel 213
Vanderbilt, Mrs. William K.
    213
Vanderbilt, William K. 115
Virgets, Phil 177–179

Wagner, Robert F. 228
Walcott, Jersey Joe 226
Walcott, Joe 12, 13, 21, 32, 48,
    64
Walker, James J. 213, 215
Walker, Mickey 212, 222, 234
Wallace, Nunc 16, 112
Walsh, Jimmy 55, 57, 60–61, 63,
    69–71, 75–78, 100, 106, 112–113,
    126, 148, 159, 165, 166, 233

Weaver, Buck 183, 189–190, 196,
    198, 204–205, 230
Weeks, Freddie 71, 78, 101–104
Weighman, Charles 197
Wells, Matt 136–137, 141, *143*
Welsh, Freddie 1, 3, 94–*95*, 96–98,
    100, 109, 126, 136, 143, 169, 171,
    177–180, 216, 233
Welsh, Jack 86, 91, 93, 162
White, Charley 112, 121–*122*, 148,
    171, 178
White, Frankie 109, 121, 123, 175
White, Jack 121, 123, 141, 144
White, Lew 11
White, Tommy 24
Wilkinson, Roy 187, 191
Williams, Christy 32
Williams, Claude P. "Lefty" 183–
    184, 185, 187–189, 191, 196, 200,
    203–206, 227, 230
Williams, Scotty 14, 17

Wills, Harry 213, 215
Winchell, Walter 220
Wingo, Ivey 183, 187, 189
wives of boxers 136
Wolgast, Ad 1, 3, 24, 98–*99*, 100,
    112, 122–123, 126, 136–137, 143,
    148, 153–154, 156, 157, 159, 162,
    165, 175, 178, 222, 233
Wood, Smoky Joe 195
Wray, Ed 194

Yanger, Benny 26–28, 30, 32–33,
    36, 173, 232

Zelcer, David "Bennett" 204–205,
    204n123
Ziegfeld, Florenz 213
Zimmerman, Heinie 197
Zork, Carl 77, 193, 204–205,
    204n120